MARGARET OF ANJOU

Queenship and Power in Late Medieval England

MARGARET OF ANJOU

Queenship and Power in Late Medieval England

Helen E. Maurer

THE BOYDELL PRESS

First published 2003
The Boydell Press, Woodbridge

ISBN 0 85115 927 3

The Boydell Press is an imprint of Boydell Brewer Ltd
PO Box 9, Woodbridge, Suffolk IP12 3DF, UK
and of Boydell Brewer Inc.
PO Box 41026, Rochester, NY 14604–4126, USA
website: www.boydell.co.uk

A catalogue record for this book is available
from the British Library

Library of Congress Cataloging-in-Publication Data
Maurer, Helen E., 1942–
  Margaret of Anjou : queenship and power in late medieval England /
Helen E. Maurer.
    p. cm.
Includes bibliographical references and index.
  ISBN 0–85115–927–3 (Hardback : alk. paper)
1. Margaret, of Anjou, Queen, consort of Henry VI, King of England,
1430–1482. 2. Power (Social sciences) – Great Britain – History – To 1500.
3. Great Britain – History – Henry VI, 1422–1461. 4. Great
Britain – History – Edward IV, 1461–1483. 5. Queens – Great
Britain – Biography. I. Title.
DA247.M3 M38 2003
942.04′3′092 – dc21   2002152495

This publication is printed on acid-free paper

Typeset by Joshua Associates Ltd, Oxford
Printed in Great Britain by
St Edmundsbury Press Ltd, Bury St Edmunds, Suffolk

Contents

For Ed, Eric and Monica

Preface and Acknowledgments

My introduction to Margaret of Anjou came on a warm summer evening in New York City when Shakespeare's Margaret strode across a stage in Central Park in a long, swishing skirt as if she owned the place. I confess that the image was rather appealing. At a time when feminist sentiments were rising and I was personally becoming more aware and critical of the litany of gendered do's and don'ts, the expectations and limitations that I had grown up with but somehow managed to partially ignore, she seemed like someone who could grasp life on her own terms without a second thought. Of course, Shakespeare's Margaret turned out not to be very nice, and she experienced a dreadful comeuppance for her temerity. Although I became hooked on other aspects of the Wars of the Roses, Margaret of Anjou soon drifted into the background, where she remained for some considerable time.

Years later, when I found myself back in school contemplating a doctoral thesis, I came across Rosemary Horrox's call for a study of Margaret's role in the political crisis of the 1450s.[1] It seemed inviting. As a woman with some life experience, I was certain that the project would be interesting. And although I was willing to be surprised, I thought I knew what to expect of Margaret. 'She was a real bitch on wheels,' I prated to at least one colleague.

Happily for me, indeed as any historian may hope, matters turned out to be more complex and more fascinating than my throwaway remark anticipated. Instead of finding clear boundaries defining proper queenly conduct, I found that the lines themselves were porous and subject to considerable manipulation. Instead of a proud harpy flouting accepted notions of her proper role, I found a woman very much concerned with maintaining the image, at least, of conventionality, while dealing with the situation life had given her.

Along the way there were delays, since my own life outside of school had become complicated by a convergence of circumstances, responsibilities and burdens that could not be neatly fixed, but had to be survived. In some sense it would be fair to say that Margaret helped to keep me going. The last stroke, as the thesis neared completion, was a cancer diagnosis. Although I had thought of taking the project farther, for a time it seemed better to tell myself that it had reached an acceptable conclusion, with which I could be content. But life goes on; the mind makes its adjustments and regroups. Eventually, I took a deep breath and sent the typescript out 'as was'. By the time I was offered a contract, it had become possible to plan ahead again, albeit in modest increments, which is just as well, for life is too amazing and too precious to be taken for granted. It

---

[1] Rosemary Horrox, 'The State of Research: Local and National Politics in Fifteenth-century England', *Journal of Medieval History* 18 (1992), p. 399.

is with some sense of wonder that I now find myself putting the finishing touches on a book.

In taking a fresh look at Margaret of Anjou I have incurred enormous debts to others whose work on the male protagonists in the Wars of the Roses has set the standard for debate. In particular, I am indebted to Ralph A. Griffiths, the late Bertram Wolffe, P.A. Johnson, and John Watts. A number of persons offered thoughtful suggestions and criticisms of my work at various stages, many of which I hoarded until it became possible to do a full revision. Others suggested additional sources, helped me to obtain copies of documents or provided individual insights that helped me to envision the book more clearly. I would like to thank Jim Given, who saw the project through with me from start to finish, Lamar Hill, Scott Waugh, Retha Warnicke, John Parsons, Peter Hammond, Harry Schnitker, Tim Tackett, Ann Blair, Sharon Farmer, the participants of the U.C./Huntington Medieval Seminar who read sections of the work-in-progress and Belinda Peters, with whom I've had interesting conversations about pre-modern women. To whatever extent this book succeeds in what it is about, a large portion of the credit must be theirs, though responsibility for any sins and errors is my own. I am grateful to Patrick Sinclair for his help with some of the Latin translations, and assure readers that any remaining infelicities are mine, not his! The staff of the interlibrary loan department at U.C., Irvine, has been unflaggingly helpful, and librarian Deborah Hutchins deserves special thanks for her creativity in getting readable text off an old ultrafiche. Likewise, I am grateful to the staffs of the British Library, the Public Record Office and the Corporation of London Record Office for their past and continuing assistance, and to the Richard III Society for a fellowship that made a research trip to London possible. Without Sharon Michalove's mediation there simply would have been no book, and I must also thank the people at Boydell & Brewer, especially Richard Barber, who remembered the project and was still willing to consider it after a nearly-two-year hiatus, and Caroline Palmer, whose patience and encouragement have seen it to fruition. Paul Whittemore and all my 'sisters' of Healing Odyssey helped me regain enough courage and faith in the future to unpack the thesis and tackle the revisions. My children, Eric and Monica, now grown and with homes and responsibilities of their own, have given me the greatest gift a parent could receive: they have become my friends. And finally, I wish to thank my husband, Ed, with whom I've shared a variety of terrain and weather, and who has always been my dear companion in this great adventure.

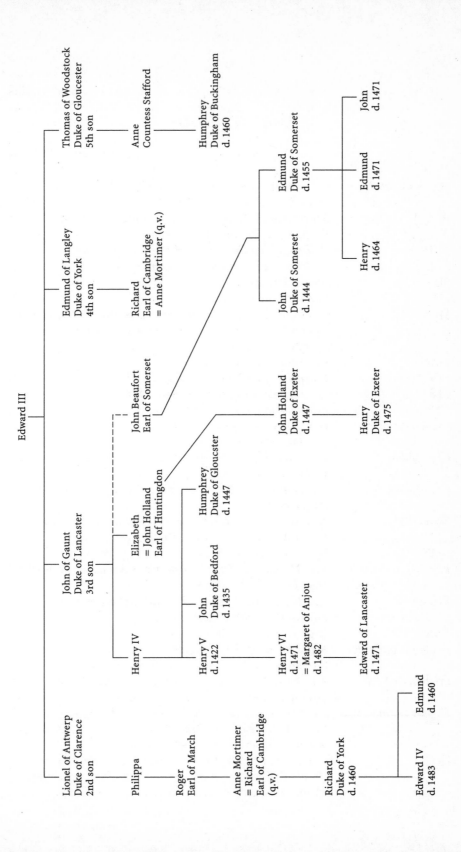

Abbreviations

'Benet's Chron.'	G.L. Harriss and M.A. Harriss, eds, 'John Benet's Chronicle for the Years 1400 to 1462', *Camden Miscellany* 24, Camden Society, fourth series, IX (London, 1972), pp. 151–233
BIHR	*Bulletin of the Institute of Historical Research*
BJRL	*Bulletin of the John Rylands Library*
BL	British Library, London
BN	Bibliothèque Nationale, Paris
Brut	F.W.D. Brie, ed., *The Brut, or the Chronicles of England*, II (unless otherwise noted), EETS, original series 136 (London, 1908)
CCR	*Calendar of the Close Rolls*
CChR	*Calendar of the Charter Rolls*
CLRO	Corporation of London Record Office
CPR	*Calendar of the Patent Rolls*
Croyland Chron.	H.T. Riley, ed., *Ingulph's Chronicle of the Abbey of Croyland* (London, 1854)
CSP, Milan	*Calendar of State Papers . . . in . . . Milan*, I, ed. A.B. Hinds (London, 1912)
CSP, Venice	*Calendar of State Papers . . . in . . . Venice*, I, ed. R. Brown (London, 1864)
Davis, *PL*	N. Davis, ed., *Paston Letters and Papers of the Fifteenth Century*, 2 vols (Oxford, 1971–76)
EETS	Early English Text Society
EHD	A.R. Myers, ed., *English Historical Documents*, IV, 1327–1485 (New York, 1969)
EHL	C.L. Kingsford, *English Historical Literature in the Fifteenth Century* (Oxford, 1913)
EHR	*English Historical Review*
Emden, *Cambridge*	A.B. Emden, *A Biographical Register of the University of Cambridge to A.D. 1500* (Cambridge, 1963)
Emden, *Oxford*	A.B. Emden, *A Biographical Register of the University of Oxford to A.D. 1500*, 3 vols (Oxford, 1957–59)
English Chron.	J.S. Davies, ed., *An English Chronicle of the Reigns of Richard II, Henry IV, Henry V, and Henry VI*, Camden Society, old series 64 (London, 1856)
Flenley	R. Flenley, ed., *Six Town Chronicles of England* (Oxford, 1911). The specific chronicle is indicated in parentheses when not otherwise made clear: e.g., 'Bale's Chron.'

Foedera	T. Rymer, ed., *Foedera, conventions, literae . . .*, V (The Hague, 1741)
Gairdner, *PL*	J. Gairdner, ed., *The Paston Letters*, 6 vols (London, 1904)
GEC	G.E. Cokayne, *The Complete Peerage of England, Scotland, Ireland, Great Britain and the United Kingdom . . .*, 12 vols in 13, ed. V. Gibbs et al. (London, 1910–59)
Giles, *Chronicon*	J.A. Giles, ed., *Incerti Scriptoris Chronicon Angliae de Regnis . . . Henrici IV, Henrici V et Henrici VI* (London, 1848)
Great Chron.	A.H. Thomas and I.D. Thornley, eds, *The Great Chronicle of London* (London, 1938)
'Gregory's Chron.'	J. Gairdner, ed., *Historical Collections of a Citizen of London in the Fifteenth Century*, Camden Society, new series 17 (London, 1876)
Griffiths	R.A. Griffiths, *The Reign of King Henry VI* (Berkeley, 1981). All other works by the same author are cited using short title.
HMC	*Historical Manuscripts Commission*
Johnson	P.A. Johnson, *Duke Richard of York 1411–1460* (Oxford, 1988)
London Chrons.	C.L. Kingsford, ed., *The Chronicles of London* (Oxford, 1905)
Monro	C. Monro, ed., *Letters of Queen Margaret of Anjou and Bishop Bekington and Others*, Camden Society, old series 86 (London, 1863)
PPC	N.H. Nicolas, ed., *Proceedings and Ordinances of the Privy Council of England*, VI, *22 Henry VI 1443 to 39 Henry VI 1461* (London, 1837)
PRO	Public Record Office, London
Reg. Whethamstede	H.T. Riley, ed., *Registrum Abbatiae Johannis Whethamstede*, 2 vols, Rolls Series (London, 1872–73)
RP	*Rotuli Parliamentorum*, V, *1439–1468* (London, 1832)
Stevenson	J. Stevenson, ed., *Letters and Papers Illustrative of the Wars of the English in France during the Reign of Henry VI*, 2 vols in 3, Rolls Series (London, 1861–64)
Storey	R.L. Storey, *The End of the House of Lancaster* (New York, 1967)
Three Chrons.	J. Gairdner, ed., *Three Fifteenth-Century Chronicles*, Camden Society, new series 28 (London 1880)
TRHS	*Transactions of the Royal Historical Society*
VCH	*Victoria County History*
Watts	J. Watts, *Henry VI and the Politics of Kingship* (Cambridge, 1996)
Waurin, *Anchiennes cronicques*	J. de Waurin, *Anchiennes cronicques d'Engleterre*, 3 vols, ed. E. Dupont (Paris, 1858–63)
Waurin, *Croniques*	J. de Waurin, *Recueil des croniques et anchienes istories de*

la *Grant Bretaigne*, ed. W. Hardy and E.C.L.P. Hardy,
5 vols, Rolls Series (London, 1864–91)

Wolffe   B.P. Wolffe, *Henry VI* (London, 1981)

The spelling of passages in Middle English has been retained, except for the replacement of the runic thorn by modern 'th' and occasional shifts of 'u' and 'v' or 'i' and 'j' (often used interchangeably) to make them correspond more closely to modern usage.

Introduction: Starting Points

> She-wolf of France, but worse than wolves of France . . .
> Women are soft, mild, pitiful, and flexible;
> Thou stern, obdurate, flinty, rough, remorseless.[1]

MARGARET OF ANJOU was a vengeful and a violent woman, or so we have been told. In Shakespeare's rendering she literally becomes a bitch, an adulterous she-wolf who mocks her captive enemy, Richard, duke of York, before killing him in cold blood.[2] Though no one nowadays reads Shakespeare for history, his portrayal of Margaret, in the rough dimensions of her character, has proven to be remarkably resilient.

The course of Margaret's queenship lends itself to such an assessment. Married in 1445 at the age of fifteen to the ineffectual Henry VI,[3] Margaret came to England as the symbol of a peace with France that, it was hoped, would allow the English to maintain their embattled French possessions. More prosaically, though no less fervently, it was also hoped that she would soon provide an heir, whose presence would bring a sense of greater stability and normalcy to a reign that had begun in Henry's own infancy. Eight years later, while Margaret was in the latter stages of her only pregnancy, England lost the last of its French territory save for a narrow pale surrounding the port of Calais, and Henry suffered a complete mental collapse that left him catatonic for roughly a year and a half. The king's illness and its aftermath brought Margaret to the political forefront. During the later 1450s she became the effective – and indefatigable – leader of the Lancastrian loyalists in the struggle against their Yorkist opponents that we now know as the Wars of the Roses. The first stage of this civil war ended in a Yorkist victory with Henry's deposition in 1461, his subsequent capture and imprisonment, and Margaret's exile on the continent. Though she remained a queen in name and would later attempt to recover the throne, she would never again reside in England as a queen in fact.

Towards the end of the fifteenth century, the French counselor, diplomat and memoirist, Philippe de Commynes, identified the origin of England's civil wars as a factional dispute and castigated Margaret for encouraging the bloodshed:

> As it turned out that lady [Margaret] would have done much better if she had acted as a judge or mediator between the two parties instead of saying 'I will

---

[1] *Henry VI*, Part III, 1.4.111, 141–2. Shakespeare has the duke of York condemn Queen Margaret with these words just before she stabs him.

[2] Lee, 'Reflections of Power', pp. 215–17, discusses Shakespeare's version of Margaret.

[3] Brooke and Ortenberg, 'Birth of Margaret of Anjou', pp. 357–8, have established the date of her birth as 23 March 1430; it was previously thought to have been 1429.

support this party', for there were many battles as a result and in the end almost everyone on both sides was killed.[4]

Commynes was born around 1447 and thus would have been too young to be much of an observer of English affairs in the 1450s. He probably derived most of his knowledge and assumptions from what he heard from English exiles and diplomats at the courts of Burgundy and France, where he served from the later 1460s.[5] Leaving aside the question of Commynes's accuracy for the moment – and I will later suggest that the reality of Margaret's situation was far more nuanced – he shares the view of a willful, dangerously transgressive Margaret that is to be found in the more vehemently Yorkist sources.[6] His condemnation of Margaret also alludes to the idea of a 'proper' queenly role as mediator and peacemaker that, in fact, had widespread currency. The gendered assumptions underlying Commynes's critique become more evident in its immediate elaboration:

> But princes are told that by means of such questions and disputes they will find out certain information and be able to hold both parties in fear. I would agree if a young king were to do this among the ladies for it will pass the time pleasantly and he might learn something from them, but there is nothing more dangerous than to do it among men such as princes and men of virtue and courage. It is like setting fire to one's house for soon somebody or other will say, 'The king is against us', and then take steps to protect himself.[7]

Although this is written as if it were by way of advice to a male ruler, the subject closest at hand with which comparisons are inevitably to be drawn is Margaret. By encouraging enmity among 'princes . . . men of virtue and courage', she – a mere woman – is understood to have committed a willful act with grievous consequences.

The notion of a willfully partisan, transgressive Margaret, which originated with the queen's opponents and was accepted by Commynes, was creatively embroidered by a succession of English chronicles through the sixteenth century, until it was taken up by William Shakespeare and turned into fine drama.[8] And, although historians have long since rejected Shakespearean excess, it is the view of Margaret that generally still prevails. It is this view that makes it possible for a modern historian to speak of 'the queen's harsh determination' and of her 'unforgiving severity' towards the Yorkists, and for

---

[4] Commynes, *Memoirs*, p. 413. For the date of his writing, see ibid., pp. 34–5.

[5] Ibid., p. 13. His service in Burgundy coincided with Lancaster's brief resurgence, during which Edward IV and other Yorkist refugees found a haven in Burgundian territory from 1470 to 1471. In 1472 Commynes abandoned Burgundy for France, where he entered the service of Louis XI. So long as Margaret's cause afforded Louis no immediate benefit and after it was decisively lost, he appears to have treated her dismissively, if not with contempt.

[6] See, e.g., portions of the *English Chron.*, pp. 79–80, 108–9, that deal with the period 1459–61; the letter of the legate, Francesco Coppini, characterizing Margaret's response to the Yorkists' 1460 'conditions of peace' as too passionate (*CSP, Milan*, I, pp. 37–40); and the wording of Margaret's attainder (*RP*, V, p. 479).

[7] Commynes, *Memoirs*, p. 413.

[8] Lee, 'Reflections of Power', pp. 194–5, notes the role of Yorkist propaganda and the predominantly Yorkist-leaning chronicles in establishing Margaret's image.

this characterization of Margaret to evoke a frisson of recognition from his readers.[9]

A similar fascination surrounds the mid-fifteenth century as a whole. Political studies of the Wars of the Roses have become something of a cottage industry. These years saw the breakdown of medieval personal rule in the absence of any established institutional means of dealing with the breakdown. Contemporary reactions, on all sides, were *ad hoc* and seat-of-the-pants as the situation spun increasingly out of control. Historians have sought the causes of chaos in international policy and the outcome of the Hundred Years War, in dynastic conflict, in the rivalries of overmighty subjects or the ineptitude of an under-mighty king, and in varying combinations of all of these. They have lovingly followed the course of the conflict with emphases reflecting their own interests and convictions and have sought, again variously, to assign meaning to the event as part of a larger continuum of English history.

In the main, all this history of the Wars of the Roses has been male-focused. Although in all of these studies Margaret of Anjou is acknowledged to have been a key political player, the nature of her involvement has received little in the way of fresh analysis. While the characters, activities and possible motives of the male players have received intense scrutiny and ongoing reassessment, very little of that debate has touched Margaret. She remains the vengeful partisan implacably promoting faction, unable to sink the proud power-seeker – or the fearfully protective mother – in the mediatory demands of 'good' queenship.

These patterns have persisted for two reasons. First, men visibly dominated the political scene in fifteenth-century England and left more written evidence of their activities than did women, a situation that once led K.B. McFarlane to lament that '[Margaret of Anjou's] thoughts are less easy to read than those of Margaret Mautby.'[10] Second, however, until quite recently *all* western history was male-centered as a matter of course. The problem that this poses for the inclusion and study of anachronistically prominent women is that they have had to be fitted into male standards and constructs, present as well as past. The result too often has been judgment rather than analysis.

In Margaret's case, efforts to detail her life have tended to be driven by her dramatic appeal as a fierce woman in what was for all intents and purposes a man's world. Thus, Agnes Strickland began her mid-nineteenth-century narrative with the promise that Margaret's history was 'a tissue of the most striking vicissitudes, and replete with events of more powerful interest than are to be found in the imaginary career of any heroine of romance'.[11] Akin in sentiment at least, though improved in documentation, is Mary Ann Hookham's *The Life and Times of Margaret of Anjou*.[12] J.J. Bagley's 1948 biography, *Margaret of Anjou: Queen of England*, while providing better history, is straightforward chronological narrative, written before gender studies and an attention to

---

[9] Griffiths, p. 804.

[10] McFarlane, *England in the Fifteenth Century*, p. 232. The experience and adventures of Margaret Paston, née Mautby, are well known thanks to the survival of numerous family letters.

[11] Strickland, *Lives of the Queens of England*, II, p. 162. Strickland's work was first published in 1840, with a revised edition in 1851.

[12] Published in 1872. There are some very striking similarities between sections of her text and Strickland's.

women's history suggested a more complex view of female experience. His picture of Margaret, however, is entirely familiar: of a woman whose 'fiery determination made compromise impossible and civil war almost inevitable' and whose commitment to a factional interest drove the crown 'into the welter of political intrigue'.[13] Since then, two further biographies of Margaret have maintained both the romantic and narrative traditions.[14] Although several shorter pieces have begun to nibble at the edges of the traditional view of Margaret, the interesting issues surrounding Margaret's overt entry into the political arena in 1453 and her subsequent exercise of power have largely gone unaddressed.[15]

Meanwhile, growing interest in the study of women and power – not merely of the ways in which women have been denied power, but of how women have found ways to exercise power – has directed more attention to the experience of queens.[16] Some recent studies of earlier English queens have adroitly combined biographical history with gendered analysis.[17] In order to move beyond the traditional picture of Margaret's activities, the very real issue of gender must be engaged. Without question, her participation in politics (hence the political scene itself) cannot be understood without examining the ways in which gender dictated her options and the ways she found either to conform to or to circumvent her gendered 'place'. Above all, it must be considered in her relationships to the other political players. It is not enough to say that she was powerful or that she caused certain things to happen; an effort must be made to see how she made her power work. What, in fact, did it mean for Margaret to wield power as a woman and a queen? What opportunities did queenship afford her, and to what limitations was it subject? And, finally, how did these factors impinge on the political situation in which she played a part?

A study of Margaret of Anjou's queenship also has value because she was anomalous: her experience pushed the limits of the gender system that she and her contemporaries accepted and acknowledged.[18] Just as the addition of gender helps to make the political story clearer, so the chaotic political history of the

---

[13] Bagley, *Margaret of Anjou*, p. 77.

[14] Erlanger's *Margaret of Anjou* (1970) is written in the overheated style of a romance novel, while Haswell's *The Ardent Queen* (1976) is comfortable 'popular history' that adds nothing new to the narrative.

[15] Dunn, 'Margaret of Anjou', demonstrates the normality of Margaret's activities as queen prior to the political crisis of 1453. Lee, 'Reflections of Power', examines the role of gender assumptions in the development of Margaret's later reputation, but is too accepting of traditional views of her actual behavior and the reactions it is presumed to have elicited as their basis. Both need to be looked at more closely. Gross, *Dissolution of the Lancastrian Kingship*, chapter 2, concludes that Margaret's power was as nonexistent as Henry's since there is little concrete evidence to show her actually making policy. This view fails to recognize that women from the queen on down tended to exercise power through informal means and that informal power, by its nature, leaves few tracks. Cron, 'Margaret of Anjou and the Lancastrian March on London', and Maurer, 'Margaret of Anjou and the Loveday of 1458', both question traditional views of these events and suggest revisions.

[16] Thus, e.g., Erler and Kowaleski, *Women and Power*, for reassessments of female power; Fradenburg, *Women and Sovereignty*; Vann, *Queens, Regents and Potentates*; Parsons, *Medieval Queenship*; Carpenter and MacLean, *Power of the Weak*; Duggan, *Queens and Queenship in Medieval Europe*.

[17] Chibnall, *The Empress Matilda*; Howell, *Eleanor of Provence*; Parsons, *Eleanor of Castile*.

[18] Cf. (and *pace*) Parsons, *Eleanor of Castile*, p. 249, who has argued that his study of Eleanor of Castile is valuable precisely because she was not one of a handful of 'anomalously prominent' queens such as Margaret of Anjou!

Wars of the Roses casts the gender issues into high relief. Some of Margaret's activities were ordinary; others were extraordinary. Although the material for a study of Margaret of Anjou is fragmented, as it is for other individual medieval women, enough exists to at least glimpse both sides of her life and the efforts that she herself made to present them as a single non-controversial whole. Though we will never know as much of her thoughts as we do of Margaret Mautby's, we need not despair of learning something more about her situation and how she dealt with it than has been handed down.

As a starting point to this discussion it will be helpful to define exactly what I mean by 'power' and how it is to be distinguished from 'authority'. Following M.Z. Rosaldo and L. Lamphere, I understand 'authority' to be the socially recognized right to make certain decisions and to require obedience. 'Power' is the more informal 'ability to gain compliance'. One form of power is influence, amounting to persuasion; another form could obviously be force.[19] At times I will refer to Margaret's 'influential power' to underline the notion that results were obtained through having access and talking to other people, a process that was likely to take time and effort and may not always have had immediate effect or complete success.

The gender system in which Margaret lived theoretically denied that a woman could ever hold political authority. At the same time, however, it permitted and even encouraged women to act in ways that had political consequences; this was most true for the queen. This uneasy duality made transgression possible and even provided Margaret with a loyal following, while it demanded that she continue to present herself as no more than the king's wife and intermediary to his subjects. By invoking the king's authority, or the latent authority of her young son, Prince Edward, Margaret was able to exercise considerable power. It was power, nonetheless, that had to be constantly renegotiated and reaffirmed by further appeals to and displays of male authority. Thus, its exercise involved a pretense, while the need to maintain the pretense automatically limited its reach.

Margaret of Anjou lived in a world of rank and hierarchy, in which inequality was perceived as complementarity, and in which the relationships between the separate parts were necessary for the whole to exist. In this world it was understood that some held authority over others by right. Thus, just as it was assumed that some men held rightful authority over their fellow men, it was also understood to be in the nature of things for men, as husbands and fathers, to have authority over women.

Theoretical justification for female subordination could be found both in 'biological' views of female deficiency going back to Aristotle and in theological doctrines of female inferiority and willfulness that had their roots in the biblical story of Adam and Eve. According to the Aristotelian view, women could best be characterized as 'defective males'. Within this paradigm, woman's 'relative

---

[19] Rosaldo, 'Woman, Culture, and Society', p. 21; Lamphere, 'Strategies, Cooperation, and Conflict Among Women', pp. 99–100. Erler and Kowaleski, *Women and Power*, p. 2, have noted the importance for women's history of separating power from authority via the use of these anthropological definitions.

coldness and formlessness implied a whole set of characteristics that made [her] radically unfit for any activity that was not, in essence, a response to a signal or command from a man'. The conclusion to be drawn was that a proper woman was obedient, while a woman who ruled over men was abusing her own biological nature.[20] Likewise, biblical exegesis might advocate 'equality of association' between the sexes within marriage while still insisting that woman had been created from man's body 'so that she might always look to him as to her beginning'.[21] Moreover, it was understood that when Satan determined to corrupt God's handiwork, he approached woman first, knowing her to be weaker than man. Eve gave in and sinned because she *wanted* to believe what the devil said.[22]

While these two belief systems provided theoretical explanations of why women were as they were assumed to be, the perceived 'facts' regarding woman's nature and her corresponding vices were propagated less abstractly through the popular venues of song, sermon and story. From them a pattern of 'female' character traits emerges that, though not uniformly negative, was inimical to any capacity for leadership.

Faithlessness was one such attribute. In a world that at least paid extravagant lip service to male loyalty in the political realm, where the breaking of one's faith or oath was roundly condemned and where charges of such transgression were self-righteously denied, the belief that inconstancy was an innately female trait was automatically disabling.[23] Songs high and low had a great deal to say about women's faithlessness, not in the high realm of politics, but often as it intersected with another favorite topic: love. In matters of the heart, women simply were not to be trusted, for

> Theyre stedfastnes endureth but a season . . .
> And for they ar chaungeabyll naturally.[24]

Such mistrust of women could also be expressed more generally, as in the warning

> Whan netilles in wynter bere Rosis rede,
> and thornys bere figges naturally,
> and bromes bere appylles in every mede . . .
> Than put in a woman your trust and confidens.[25]

Female changeability came in various guises and often went hand in hand with a

[20] Jordan, *Renaissance Feminism*, pp. 30, 32.
[21] Hugh of St Victor, *On the Sacraments of the Christian Faith*, p. 329 [2.11.4].
[22] Ibid., pp. 121 [1.7.3]; 124–5 [1.7.10]. As a corollary, Eve's sin was considered worse than Adam's.
[23] During the first phase of the Wars of the Roses, ending with Henry VI's deposition, the stated grounds for attainder invariably centered on oath breaking and other willful acts taken contrary to rightful allegiance, regardless of which side was currently ascendant. As political dominance shifted from Lancaster to York, explanations had to be mustered to show that previous condemnations had been based upon false premises, thus invalidating their charges. The underlying assumption, however, was that 'true' men did not betray and that 'false' men who chose to do so were supremely wicked. I discuss this in chapters 11 and 12.
[24] Robbins, *Secular Lyrics*, p. 224.
[25] Ibid., p. 103.

kind of light-headedness. Such 'weakness' might occasion a wink instead of complaint, especially when it involved a woman who, like Eve, could not say no.

> O Lord, so swett ser Iohn dothe kys,
>   at every tyme when he wolde pley;
> off hym-selfe so plesant he ys,
>   I have no powere to say hym nay.[26]

Of course, there was another side to the song-makers' commentary on female nature that also found its way into their verses and gave woman her due, even as it recognized her place.

> A woman ys a worthy wyght,
> she servyth a man both daye and nyght,
> therto she puttyth all her myght,
>   And yet she hathe bot care and woo.[27]

Like the songs, sermons spoke to a belief in female frailty and specifically associated certain vices with women. Foolishness was linked to female sexuality, both as a cause and as an effect. Thus, demons were said to enlist foolish women to entrap and deceive men with their wiles.[28] Women's garrulity was perceived to be a further problem – had not Eve's gabbing with the Serpent led to trouble? – as was her unfortunate tendency to wander, to be out and about for the purpose of seeing and being seen. Along with these things went a love of finery, which was roundly and routinely condemned. Although male excess in dress also came in for scolding, the criticism of men seems to have focused more on status violation than on dress as sexual lure. For women the reverse was true.[29] A woman's worst fault of all was possibly her disobedience to the wishes of her husband. This, of course, assumed a 'normal' state of female subordination and submission, in which obedience constituted the 'proper' female posture. That disobedience occurred was ascribed to woman's contrary nature. Finally, although these complaints added up to a catalogue of female 'weakness', it should still be noted that they did not equate with helplessness. Some female vices were clearly understood to be dangerous, and it was a proverbial commonplace that 'there is no anger . . . greater than a woman's wrath'.[30]

If sermons, then as now, tended to be offered as correctives to behavior, the popular romances provided upscale models of 'good' femininity for those who

---

[26] Ibid., p. 20.

[27] Ibid., p. 31.

[28] Unless otherwise noted, my discussion of the sermons' views of female vice is based on Owst, *Literature and Pulpit*, pp. 385–403. This particular paradigm is drawn from Jeremiah 5:26. Though not all of the sermon discourse on women was misogynistic (see, for example, J. Murray, 'Thinking about Gender', pp. 7–16), such thinking did provide a consistent thread.

[29] Owst, *Literature and Pulpit*, pp. 369, 404–11. While male adornment could be associated with lust, a notion that perhaps becomes more plausible from the mid-fifteenth century as male attire became more revealing, this association does not seem to have been prevalent. But see below, p. 166.

[30] The proverb, 'Non est ira . . . super iram mulieris', was apparently spread wide via sermons (ibid., p. 42, n. 10), and the fifteenth-century *Malleus Maleficarum* held that women were given to inordinate anger and vengeance-seeking (Institoris and Sprenger, *Malleus Maleficarum*, pp. 44–5).

had access to them. It can be no accident that the traits they supported were very often the opposites of those that were criticized or made fun of in sermons and in verse. Thus, the heroines of romance were patient, enduring, submissive, faithful, forgiving, loving, generous and trusting in God.[31] They were the ladies and princesses that the heroes got to marry as reward for their exploits. Though they were often passive figures who lacked the power to act independently, they were nonetheless respected and admired – 'as long as they stayed in their places . . . [as] defined by men'.[32] The one area in which the heroine was allowed an active role was as a mediator or intercessor.[33] This view was congruent with a strand of pastoral thinking that held that a woman might use her persuasive powers to mitigate her husband's harshness towards others.[34]

Even the game of chess had something to say about gender roles. Jacobus de Cessolis, a late thirteenth-century Lombard devotee, used chess to mirror human life in what probably originated as a sermon. His work became immensely popular and was widely copied, eventually becoming one of William Caxton's earliest English publications in 1474.[35] Jacobus observed that when the chess king moved, the queen must follow, since it was in the nature of things for husbands to lead their wives and not the reverse.[36] Above all else, the good queen – and good woman – must be chaste.[37] For Jacobus, a woman's sexuality was her defining characteristic: it provided her with value as a mother, but threatened the social order in her inclination towards temptation.[38] Such emphasis was not peculiar to Jacobus. It was a theme that found expression in all manner of venues so that lust – and resulting promiscuity – became the woman's sin par excellence.[39]

This, then, was the way that gender roles were envisioned and imagined to work – in theory. It was a theory in which female leadership would have been an oxymoron and impossibility. Undoubtedly, some women lived up or down to the best or worst that was either hoped or feared of them. But theory does not necessarily reflect reality, although the two are reciprocally interactive.[40] What passed for public knowledge about women did not always mirror the actual status of real women or the realities of gender relations. Recently, Joel Rosenthal has questioned the 'iron law of [women's] inferiority and subordination' in its application to fifteenth-century England. Although wives were generally perceived to play complementary roles, 'their identities at least in part derivative from their sexual and social union with a man', it was in fact possible for a strong-minded woman to set family policy. What is most interesting about such

---

[31] Marchalonis, 'Above Rubies', p. 92.
[32] Ibid., pp. 89, 93.
[33] Eckhardt, 'Woman as Mediator', p. 97.
[34] J. Murray, 'Thinking about Gender', p. 10.
[35] H.J.R. Murray, *A History of Chess*, pp. 537–9.
[36] Jacobus de Cessolis, *Caxton's Game and Playe of the Chesse*, p. 167.
[37] Ibid., p. 29.
[38] Ibid., pp. 27, 29, 30–35, 170–1, for examples.
[39] A similar concern for female chastity pervades Christine, *Treasure*. See also Karras, 'The Regulation of Brothels', p. 400, for views of prostitution; Fries, 'Feminae Populi', pp. 79–86, for the virgin/whore dichotomy in literature. More generally, see Bullough, Shelton and Slavin, *The Subordinated Sex*, pp. 100–1, on the preoccupation of male Christian clergy with female sexuality.
[40] As recognized by Ortner and Whitehead, *Sexual Meanings*, p. 10.

cases, however, is that even though the wife might set policy, in the eyes of the law and the political-economic framework of the time it was still *her husband's* policy, 'she but a loyal lieutenant or counselor'.[41] Consciously or not, such a stance involved a kind of masking, a pretense that allowed life to conform to the received wisdom regarding what was supposed to be, while it went its own way and did whatever it had to do. It appears that some medieval women writers deliberately adopted and manipulated conventionally self-effacing postures in order to gain a voice.[42]

Women from the higher social orders did, in fact, have occasion to bear responsibility and opportunity to wield considerable power.[43] Moreover, such occasions and opportunities were widespread, the rule rather than the exception. Propertied women 'could expect to exercise a measure of administrative responsibility wherever and whenever the need arose'; what they did with it and how far they took it depended on individual circumstances rather than on theoretical assumptions regarding woman's nature or capabilities.[44] Most often such situations arose during a husband's absence at court, on business or in war, or after his death when his widow gained legal independence. The evidence suggests that individual women – the wives, mothers or great ladies that men knew as individuals – were respected, trusted, sometimes feared. That they could act with wisdom, tenacity and even raw courage in their faithful pursuit or preservation of familial objectives occasioned no surprise; indeed, it was expected of them, whatever their male relations and associates may have thought or spoken of the irresponsibility of 'women' in general.[45] Margaret Paston's defense of the manor of Hellesdon by armed force against the duke of Suffolk's men in July 1465 is a case in point. When she wrote to her husband to report the situation, she asked his advice as to how to proceed. John Paston, who had already heard about the confrontation from his bailiff, commended Margaret for what she had done and, in essence, told her to keep up the good work.[46] Wills provide a further window upon the cooperative relationship between husbands and wives. Trust – and perhaps a canny appraisal that one's wife was the person most likely to uphold the family interest – led many men to name their wives as their executors, though conditions were sometimes attached, such as requiring the widow not to remarry, as a form of control to ensure that she should experience no conflict of interest.[47] Such was the case with William de la Pole, duke of Suffolk, who made his wife his sole executor because 'above all the erthe my singuler trust is moost in her'. He further

[41] Rosenthal, *Patriarchy and Families of Privilege*, pp. 176–7.
[42] Ferrante, 'Public Postures and Private Maneuvers', pp. 213–29. Her examples are Hrotsvit of Gandersheim, Hildegard of Bingen and Christine de Pisan.
[43] This is not to suggest that lesser women had no experience of responsibility or power in their own lives. The experience of high-status women was simply closer, though not equivalent, to that of the queen. See J.M. Bennett, 'Public Power and Authority', for a discussion of peasant women in a somewhat earlier period.
[44] Archer, '"How ladies"', p. 150.
[45] Archer, '"How ladies"', emphasizes the collaborative nature of medieval marriage and covers these points.
[46] Gairdner, *PL*, IV, pp. 160, 162, 164.
[47] Rosenthal, *Patriarchy and Families of Privilege*, pp. 192–3.

advised their son to obey his mother and to believe her counsel and advice, since '[they] shall be best and trewest to you'.[48]

These examples illustrate another important point. Female empowerment depended explicitly or implicitly upon male authorization. Christine de Pisan acknowledged as much when she observed that the husband of a prudent woman possessed of administrative ability would 'be able to give [her] authority to act and govern on [his] behalf', and that only a very foolish man, 'if he sees that he has a good and wise wife, . . . does not give her authority to govern in an emergency'.[49] We should note that in Christine's construction the wife acts as her husband's representative and often on the presumption that he may not be present or may otherwise be unable to act for himself. This is, in fact, what we see happening in real life. In another vein, while warning of the dangers of pride, Christine drives home the point that power and authority are not innate to women, but must be given to them:

> By Almighty God, you who are a simple little woman who has no strength, power or authority unless it is conferred on you by someone else, do you imagine that you are surrounded by luxury and honour so that you can dominate and outdo the whole world at your will?[50]

This admonition, though applicable to women of substance generally, was addressed specifically to the princess.

The queen – or, using Christine's terminology, the princess – was a particular case among women. Subject to the same assumptions and preconceptions as other women, she also had similar opportunities to influence her husband, other members of her family and their close associates, but because her husband was the king, the potential scope of her influence was far greater than that of her lesser sisters. The result was double-edged and contradictory. While the queen's proximity to magisterial authority and her ability to operate within what John Parsons has called 'the interstices' promoted and enhanced her power, her position also left her peculiarly exposed to public scrutiny and reprobation.[51] What this meant was that although some disparity existed between the theory and the reality of 'woman's place' for the queen, as it did for other women, the inconsistencies and contradictions became more noticeable and more problematic when it was the queen who was being observed.

The ramifications of this point can best be appreciated by turning again to what Christine de Pisan had to say about the queen and then by comparing it to her advice to the baroness. In making this comparison it will be well to keep in mind that Christine's *Treasure of the City of Ladies* was written as a practical how-to book rather than as a theoretical abstract: a 'survival manual . . . written for women who had to live from day to day in the world as it was'.[52] This does

---

[48] Archer, '"How ladies"', p. 154; Suffolk's letter to his son is printed in Gairdner, *PL*, II, pp. 142–3.

[49] Christine, *Treasure*, p. 80. The corollary, of course, is that if the wife is not authorized to govern, she has no recourse but to submit and obey.

[50] Ibid., p. 41.

[51] Parsons, 'Family, Sex, and Power', p. 2, notes the conundrum. In *Eleanor of Castile*, pp. 66–7, he illustrates how the situation played out in practice. By 'interstices' he refers to informal and non-institutional avenues of influence, such as intercession, patronage and the education of children.

[52] Christine, *Treasure*, p. 21.

not mean that it is devoid of ideology; rather, Christine's advice is firmly placed within a context of prevalent assumptions regarding female nature and behavior. She tells her reader how to get along in such a context.[53] Thus, while insisting that the princess could and should be capable and responsible, Christine also invests her 'good' princess with the idealized female qualities of humility, patience and charity.[54] Likewise, she places great emphasis upon sexual morality, requiring the princess to ensure the chastity of her female servants, and the older lady companion to chaperon and guide the behavior of the young princess.[55]

The quality of charity, characterized primarily as compassion, took up a theme found in both sermon and story and made the princess a mediator between the prince and his people.[56] This reflected reality, for recent scholarship has demonstrated that intercession was expected of the queen. Not only did it give her a recognized, though informal, means of influence, but it also helped to define and construct 'kingly' behavior. When the king was expected to be strong and wise and stern, the queen's intercession provided a balancing influence that allowed him to bend without appearing weak, to change his mind without seeming foolish and to moderate harshness without forfeiting credibility. Meanwhile, it also confirmed the king's authority through the queen's sub-ordination as appellant.[57]

In Christine's view, however, in addition to her acts of intercession the queen's role as mediator specifically included a broad range of peacemaking activities. If war threatened to break out between her husband and a foreign prince, the good princess should look for a means to peace congruent with the preservation of her husband's honor. In similar fashion, if a powerful subject committed some act against the king's majesty, and it appeared that retribution would lead to greater harm and bloodshed for the kingdom, she should seek to avert conflict by offering her intercession to the wrongdoer in exchange for appropriate atonement.[58] As a practical matter, however, Christine acknow-ledged that resentment and enmities do arise in the course of human interaction. To the princess who found herself so threatened, she advised dissimulation and a show of friendliness, while keeping her eyes and ears open.[59] Thus, much of the princess's activity, according to Christine's dictum, involved conflict management; by these and other means she was to impress people with her worthiness and gain their esteem.

---

[53] Watts, pp. 51–63, discusses the relationship between 'mirror' literature and political ideology and suggests that advice books may have provided 'the chief literary influence on the formation of political views' (p. 56). It appears, however, that influence traveled in both directions and was mutually reinforcing. This is the sense in which Christine's advice must be read: as an elaboration and explication of ideas and assumptions that already had currency and that to some extent reflected existing practice.

[54] Christine, *Treasure*, pp. 47–9.

[55] Ibid., pp. 74–6, 89–105.

[56] Ibid., pp. 47–9.

[57] See Strohm, *Hochon's Arrow*, chapter 5: 'Queens as Intercessors'; Huneycutt, 'Intercession and the High-Medieval Queen'; Parsons, 'The Queen's Intercession'; Parsons, *Eleanor of Castile*, pp. 45–6, 152–3, 219–20, 250–1, for the theory, practice and occasional complications arising from the queen's intercessory role.

[58] Christine, *Treasure*, pp. 50–1.

[59] Ibid., pp. 68–70.

In contrast to her princess, Christine's baroness was far more militant. Since her husband would naturally be away a good deal of the time doing the king's business, she must be able to run things in his absence and protect her people in time of need. For the latter, she must have

> the heart of a man, that is, she ought to know how to use weapons and be familiar with everything that pertains to them, so that she may be ready to command her men if the need arises. She should know how to launch an attack or how to defend against one . . . She should take care that her fortresses are well garrisoned . . . She should consider what manpower she has and can call upon with confidence if the situation warrants it, and for which she will not have to wait in vain nor accept empty promises.[60]

Though there was nothing to prevent Christine's baroness from being a peacemaker if she so chose, the advice to her acknowledged that there might be situations where stronger action was necessary. The point is that she had a wider choice of responses than did the queen. Like Margaret Paston, she could resort to arms to defend the home turf without anyone – except possibly the enemy – batting an eye. She could do this because she was not perceived to the extent that the queen was as an exemplar of female behavior.

This may seem a contestable claim or, worse, one that misses the point. Did not the queen's office, however informally it was constructed, place her in a particular relationship vis-à-vis the realm and all its members, a relationship that was very different from that of the baroness – or of a Margaret Paston – to her competing neighbors? Of course, this is true, and Christine observed that 'any prince ought to avoid as far as he can the spilling of blood, especially that of his own subjects', as a matter of principle. But she also indicated that her hypothetical prince might indeed be preparing to spill the blood of his overmighty subject – as he had some right to do – regardless of potential consequences, because it was his male nature to be 'more courageous and . . . hotheaded' and to do such things. Since 'women [were] by nature more timid and also of a sweeter disposition', it was not only politically wise but entirely natural for the queen to be the peacemaker. Here it is clear that Christine, who acknowledged the needs of office, had grounded her advice on notions of intrinsic gendered nature. As a result, her 'good princess' was a woman who embodied the female ideal and was able to use her female attributes both wisely and advantageously. It was owing to her efforts that the kingdom remained at peace.[61]

In the real world, on the permissive but uneasy ground where practice diverges from theory, women could sometimes do a great many things without anyone worrying overly much about the discrepancies. But the queen was different. Like it or not, she was more visible and hence more vulnerable to judgment than other women. If she came close to the theoretical ideal of queenly – and female – behavior, she was praised. To the extent that she was seen to depart from the ideal, she became an example of female wickedness.

---

[60] Ibid., p. 129.
[61] Ibid., pp. 51–2.

Thus, paradoxically, while the queen's position potentially gave her more power than other women and a wider field for its application, she was also under more pressure to conform to theorized gender roles than they were. And since her misbehavior, particularly in sexual matters, could be construed as an indicator of more widespread disorder in the realm, there was also more incentive for her – or her husband's – enemies to accuse her of transgression.[62]

One of the things that a queen was not supposed to do was to rule. Quite apart from theoretical notions of female subordination that made a woman ruler anachronistic to begin with, the very qualities that 'good' women were supposed to possess – or that 'bad' women were believed to possess – made them unfit to lead. The submissiveness and obedience of the 'good' woman were antithetical to the ability to command and to provide justice that was considered the hallmark of a 'good' king. Likewise, the inconstancy, light-mindedness and unreasonable anger of the 'bad' woman were not qualities associated with good leadership. A century after Margaret, by which time England had faced rule by a queen as a practical issue, John Foxe theorized about the perceived conflict between capacity to rule and female nature and concluded that a 'kingly' woman would not behave in a 'womanly' manner, while 'womanly' behavior was ill-suited to the 'rigors of rule'.[63] Considering queens from the past, he specifically disapproved of Margaret of Anjou, whose 'manly' courage he appears to have equated with female immorality. Accordingly, Foxe judged that 'there [were] more appropriate people than she to help [Henry VI] rule' in his simplicity.[64] Presumably, such persons would all have been male.

With these ideas we return full circle to a consideration of Margaret herself. Although she was subject to many of the same expectations, assumptions and prejudices as other queens (and, indeed, as other women), her experience of queenship was, in fact, unique. It will therefore be helpful to look at the particular hopes and demands that accompanied Margaret's marriage to Henry, that were peculiar to her situation and that later would provide ammunition to her Yorkist opponents, before turning to her exercise of power both in the normal course of queenship and in the extraordinary circumstances of Henry's reign.

[62] Bührer-Thierry, 'La reine adultère', discusses the perceived link between the queen's sexuality and disorder in the realm.
[63] Levin, 'John Foxe and the Responsibilities of Queenship', p. 115.
[64] Ibid., pp. 121–2, citing Foxe, *Acts and Monuments*, III, p. 715, for his characterization of Margaret.

Part I

EXPECTATIONS

1

Arrival

WHEN HENRY VI of England sought a bride in the early 1440s, the war with France had already followed its sporadic course for a little more than one hundred years. The glory days of Agincourt and the treaty of Troyes were long over for the English. Although they hung on, reemerging French power had made significant recoveries of English-held territory while diplomatic efforts to achieve a settlement foundered.[1] It is no wonder that Henry and his councilors turned to France for the marriage hunt, as a potential boon to renewed diplomacy.[2] Yet the decision to seek a French bride was in no way unusual. Nearly all of the queens of England since the Conquest had been French; the protection of English territorial interests in France was a continuing factor in their selection.[3]

Apart from any diplomatic benefits that it might bring, the king's marriage was expected to produce an heir. In Henry's case the need for a clear dynastic succession was particularly pressing. He had succeeded to the throne in 1422 as an infant nine months old. Compounding the uncertainties of a long minority, neither of his paternal uncles (John, duke of Bedford, deceased, and Humphrey, duke of Gloucester, still living) had any legitimate offspring. Thus, any woman who became Henry's queen would be faced with a burden of expectation that in both its specifics and its urgency went somewhat beyond the usual. In the case of the war with France, although her role was perhaps more symbolic than substantive, she would inevitably be linked with the war's immediate outcome. In the case of the succession, she was the vessel through which the continuity of the Lancastrian dynasty was to be assured. On this issue she would be held directly accountable.

Some wiser – or simply more suspicious – heads may have felt misgivings about a marriage to a niece of Charles VII, the French enemy,[4] particularly when

---

[1] France had regained Harfleur and Dieppe in 1435, Paris in 1436.

[2] Giles, *Chronicon*, p. 32, is explicit that the king and his lords pursued the marriage, 'judging [that] the bond of unity and peace between the realms would be fortified by it in various ways' ('aestimantes per eam vinculum unitatis et pacis inter regna multipliciter fortificari').

[3] Crawford, *Letters of the Queens of England*, p. 4. The most recent non-French queens, Philippa of Hainault and Anne of Bohemia in the previous century, had also been selected for political reasons (see Fryde, *Tyranny and Fall of Edward II*, pp. 181–2; Mathew, *Court of Richard II*, p. 16).

[4] Griffiths, pp. 482–3. Parsons, 'Intercessionary Patronage', p. 151, for earlier distrust of Margaret of France, second wife to Edward I. Such feeling was not limited to French queens, but included any foreign-born; see Parsons, *Eleanor of Castile*, pp. 63, 67.

she came virtually dowerless and England's only concrete gain from the arrangement was a 23-month truce. Evidence suggests, however, that many more regarded – or could be persuaded to view – the marriage as the answer to their genuine desire for a peace settlement. That such feelings were shared by French and English alike, who could not possibly have hoped for peace on the same terms, reveals to us the tenuous nature of Margaret's position as a political game-piece. For the moment, though, her contemporaries gave themselves up to celebration. Upon Margaret's formal betrothal to Henry by proxy at Tours on 24 May 1444, the French shouted out 'Peas [peace], peas, peas be to us!'[5] Further festivities took place at English-held Rouen, and the earl of Suffolk, who had negotiated the marriage, was welcomed back to London by a joyful citizenry.[6] Probably soon after arrangements for the truce were settled and the proxy betrothal made, commissioners were appointed to obtain loans to cover the expense of bringing Margaret to England 'with all haste goodely possible . . . and . . . to purveye for the solempnitee of hir coronacion in maniere and fourme accustumed'. The commissioners were instructed to cast the whole matter in a positive light by assuring their listeners that '[the king] standeth in right good truste and hope of a pees finalle to be concluded and had betwix him and his uncle of F[rance]' and by informing them that a truce had been established 'undre the whiche the saide pees shal mowe behovefully be treated t[o] good conclusion and an ende'.[7] A letter of 19 July 1444 from Henry to the abbot of Bury St Edmunds requesting just such a loan plays upon the hope for peace by linking it explicitly to the opportunity for further negotiation provided by the truce.[8] We see here the intermingling of several things: an official line to be propagated, which no doubt expressed the genuine hopes of its perpetrators; the equally real hopes of its intended listeners, to whom it was expected to appeal, and a considerable potential for over-simplification and wishful self-delusion on both sides.

The preparations by the London common council for Margaret's ceremonial entry into the city must be viewed within this context, where official propaganda and widespread public sentiment went hand in hand and reinforced each other. In the Journal entries, comprising a rough minutes of the council's meetings, we see its members haggling over what should be worn to greet Margaret when she arrived. The debate began on 6 August 1444 with a decision in council that the mayor and aldermen would ride to meet her wearing saffron gowns.[9] Over the next couple of weeks the matter of dress continued to be debated, until on 26 August the recorder noted with evident relief that it was finally resolved: the City livery would consist of azure gowns with red hoods.[10]

[5] *Brut*, p. 486.
[6] Bagley, *Margaret of Anjou*, p. 38; Griffiths, p. 486. For Suffolk's welcome, see *RP*, V, p. 73.
[7] *PPC*, VI, pp. 322–5. The quotations are from p. 323. Although the undated instructions are editorially ascribed to late 1444, they were surely issued somewhat earlier since they appear to involve the first announcements of the truce to the commissioners themselves as well as to the more general public. They also refer to Suffolk's embassy sent to France to conclude these arrangements 'but late agoo' (p. 322).
[8] T. Arnold, *Memorials of St Edmund's Abbey*, p. 245.
[9] CLRO, Journal IV, fol. 37b.
[10] Ibid., fol. 39b: 'finaliter concordatum est'.

On the next day the council granted £1,000 towards the king's marriage and 500 marks to outfit the city, and appointed John Chichele, with whatever citizens seemed suitable to him, to arrange and oversee the latter.[11] Through autumn and winter the council went forward with measures to collect and receive the monies towards the king's gift and the queen's reception. On 8 April 1445, as Margaret's arrival drew near, it ordered the inspection of roofs and window lattices to be sure that they were strong enough to hold the people who were bound to stand on them to catch a glimpse of her. Tavern signs and poles were to be secured from falling lest they injure someone, and a general warning was issued to keep people out of the gutters and off the walls of houses where loose tiles or stones might fall.[12]

Margaret landed in England on 9 April. On the twelfth the council suddenly realized that some of the aldermen would not be able to ride horseback because of their infirmities, and all previous sheriffs were co-opted to turn out in scarlet to bring the number of the party up to twenty-four.[13] On 22 April it was agreed that minstrels would precede the mayor and the mercers' company when they went to meet Margaret, but that none of the other companies were to have them.[14] With an eye to the future, the mayor issued a mandate on 21 May to repair the city gates after the coronation, and the next day Suffolk and others appeared before the council on Henry's behalf to thank them in advance for the reception they had mounted and the expenses they had incurred for Margaret's arrival and coronation.[15]

The overall picture thus presented by the Journal entries is of a council occasionally mired in detail but determined to make a good impression and to put on a grand show. When Margaret arrived at Blackheath on Friday 28 May, after a slow, month-long journey from the vicinity of Southampton during which she was accompanied and entertained by a variety of lords already vying for her approval and future goodwill, she was met by the mayor and aldermen and the companies – all in their blue and scarlet – and welcomed to the city.[16] It appears that the whole town turned out to participate in the celebration.

The centerpiece of Margaret's London reception was a triumphal progress that took her past eight pageants designed for the occasion. Besides providing

[11] Ibid., fol. 40. 'Johannes Chichele camerarius assignatur cum civilibus quales sibi videbitur oport[unos] ad superindend[um] et ordinand[um] pro apparatu civitat[is].' The grant may have been, in part, a response to Henry's search for money.

[12] Ibid., fols 44, 49b, 73b.

[13] Ibid., fol. 74b.

[14] Ibid., fol. 76. The mercers were the leading London livery company, and the mayor, Henry Frowick, was a mercer (W. Davis, *Ancestry of Mary Isaac*, pp. 233–4).

[15] Ibid., fols 78b, 79. Although the activities described seem more appropriately to have followed the coronation, the days and dates given are correct for 1445. The visit by Suffolk may also have served to update the council on Margaret's progress and to finalize the schedule for her arrival.

[16] 'Gregory's Chron.', p. 186; *Brut*, p. 489; 'Robert Bale's Chronicle', in Flenley, pp. 119–120; BL, Cotton Vitellius A. XVI, in *London Chrons.*, p. 156; and the *Great Chron.*, pp. 177–8, are the best sources for her reception and coronation. The pertinent sections of the first two are more or less contemporaneous; William Gregory, a skinner, was an alderman at the time and would have been an eyewitness (see Gransden, *Historical Writing*, II, pp. 230–1; and *EHL*, pp. 91–2). 'Bale's Chronicle' dates from around 1461 (Flenley, pp. 70–1). Cotton Vitellius A. XVI and the *Great Chronicle* were written in the late fifteenth and early sixteenth centuries respectively (see *Great Chron.*, pp. lxxii–lxxiii, for the relationship between the two texts and their common derivation).

entertainment and edification, such large-scale civic displays served a number of overlapping social functions involving affirmations of identity, solidarity, and order. In what was at the time an innovation, all but one of the pageants were accompanied by spoken text.[17] That the speeches were in English underlines the communal aspect of the ceremony. It also suggests that Margaret had acquired at least some proficiency in the language – which could always be helped along by an interpreter – prior to her arrival. These speeches addressed her directly, as well as the attendant public, regarding the benefits to accrue from the marriage, her role as queen and the standard of conduct to which she should aspire. In short, though very much idealized, they spoke of expectations.[18]

Peace played a central thematic role in Margaret's reception. At the South-wark approach to London bridge she encountered the first pageant, where the figures of Plenty and Peace greeted her, along with a written biblical injunction to be fruitful and multiply.[19] With this conventional reminder of the queen's primary role and Plenty's opening words of welcome, Peace got right to the heart of the matter:

> So trusteth youre poeple, with affiaunce,
> Through youre grace and highe benignite,
> Twixt the reawmes two, Englande and Fraunce,
> Pees shal approche, rest and unite,
> Mars sette aside, with alle hys cruelte,
> Whiche to longe hath troubled the reawmes tweyne,
> Bydynge youre coumfort in this adversite,
> Moost Cristen Princesse, oure lady sovereyne.[20]

Thus, the very first pageant established an explicit link between Margaret's marriage and the hoped-for peace.

This theme was elaborated through the next three pageants. The second one, upon the bridge, likened Margaret to the dove 'that brought the braunche of pees' to Noah as a sign that the Flood would end. This speech closed with a reaffirmation of her welcome that suggests a pause in the dramatic proceedings. Following custom, Margaret would spend the night in the Tower before continuing on to Westminster for her coronation.[21] While she must have seen the first two pageants on the day of her entry into the city, the others lay along her next-day's route. The opening lines of the third pageant support this assumption:

> Oure benigne Princesse and lady sovereyne,
> Grace *conveie you forthe* and be youre gide
> In good life longe, prosperously to reyne. [my italics]

---

[17] Kipling, 'London Pageants', p. 6.
[18] In comparison, the welcoming pageants for Katherine of Aragon in 1501, though much more elaborate, did not lay the same burden of expectation upon her as Margaret's did. See Kipling, *Receyt of the Ladie Kateryne.*
[19] Kipling, 'London Pageants', p. 19; Kipling, ' "Grace in this Lyf"', p. 78.
[20] Kipling, 'London Pageants', pp. 19–23, for the texts and locations of the pageants.
[21] 'Gregory's Chron.', p. 186; Flenley, p. 119; 'Benet's Chron.', p. 191; *Brut*, p. 489.

Again, it took up the peace theme. In this pageant, however, Margaret appears as its agent rather than just the token of its approach,[22] for as 'Madame Grace, Chauncelere de Dieu' tells her:

> . . . pees schall floure and fructifie.
> By you, Pryncesse and lady sovereyne.

The fourth pageant elaborates upon her agency. In it Margaret is compared to St Margaret, whose name she bears. Both appear as virgin intercessors, types of the Virgin Mary, whose mediations bring peace to both heaven and earth.

> 'Aungeles of pees shall have dominacioun,'
> . . .
> Werre [war] proscribed, pees shal have hys place;
> Blesside be Margarete makyng this purchace.
>
> Conveie of Grace, Virgyne moost benigne,
> Oo blessid Martir, holy Margarete,
> Maugre the myght of spirites maligne
> To God above hire praier pure and swete
> Maketh now for rest, pees, and quiete,
> Shewed here pleynly in this storie,
> Oure Queene Margarete to signifie.

The closing lines of its text refocus attention on the specific issue of peace that was introduced in the first pageant:

> Desired pees bitwixt Englande and Fraunce,
> This tyme of Grace by mene of Margarete,
> We triste to God to lyven in quiete.

The three remaining pageants with spoken text take up a different theme: the queen's spiritual quest for eternal glory. Margaret, a bringer of grace through her role as peacemaker between realms, must herself seek grace and the eternal peace of the afterlife through her pursuit of goodness in this life. The last two verses remind the queen and other onlookers that each one must 'make acompte and rekenynge' at the final Judgment, and that 'ioie, . . . blis . . . [and] greet ffelicite' await the saved.[23]

At this point we may revisit an issue already raised: to what extent was Margaret's image as bringer of peace an official construct as opposed to a genuine reflection of popular sentiment? The answer appears to be that it was both, and where one left off and the other began is difficult to sort out. Naturally, the crown had an interest in presenting the king's marriage in the most hopeful light possible. This does not mean, however, that the pageants were no more than 'a gigantic display of propaganda to stir the citizenry'.[24] We

---

[22] Cf. Kipling, '"Grace in this Lyf"', pp. 78–80, for an analysis of Margaret's representation as agent of peace. He finds her agency more consistently set out in the first four pageants than I do. I discuss the problem of her actual agency in the next chapter.

[23] Ibid., pp. 80–2, for an analysis of these three pageants.

[24] Griffiths, p. 488.

must not downplay the role of public feeling in eliciting and encouraging such a display. At one time, when the poet John Lydgate was generally assumed to have written the pageants at the behest of the crown, it was easier to view them solely as an instrument of official policy.[25] Lydgate had produced celebratory verses for the Lancastrian regime in the 1420s and early '30s, including some that were associated with civic pageants.[26] More recently, however, it has been convincingly demonstrated that Lydgate did not write them and that they more likely represented 'the journeyman work of one or more civic pageant devisers'.[27] Although revised notions of authorship do not negate the presence of propaganda, they do suggest that it may have had more than one source. If the assignment of John Chichele to organize the activities for Margaret's London reception included the devising of the pageants,[28] it seems most likely that the verses' author was a person – or persons – hired by Chichele and his committee specifically for that purpose. This puts the pageants' propaganda component squarely in the hands of the common council and increases the likelihood that they combine genuine public sentiment along with political acceptability.

At the end of this volume of the Journal, on one of several folios that were used – and reused – for trying out quills, practising letters, random scribbling and the occasional odd comment, is an intriguing entry:

> Right grac[ious] lady as welcome be ye to this citie of London as our quene or princesse be [. . .][29] these days/
>
> Right glor[ious] princesse & good ['lady' – crossed out] & most benigne lady[30]

It appears that the writer was trying out greetings. The words are faintly reminiscent of the 'welcome as evere princesse was' in the first verse of the first pageant and of 'Oure benigne Princesse and lady sovereyne' that introduces the verses of the third pageant. These lines are followed by a date – 'Saturday, 10 July' – that is too late to link them to Margaret's welcoming ceremonies, although the combination is accurate for 1445.[31] Whatever the specific occasion that provoked them, they may reflect a kind of discussion and testing that went on in council when such matters arose.

And what of Margaret herself in all of this? We can only guess at her feelings upon her welcome into London and at her reactions to the pageants intended both to glorify and to instruct; we cannot know her inmost thoughts. The individuality that she certainly possessed is encompassed by the image. To the people who witnessed the ceremony of her triumph, she was presented as the

---

[25] See, for example, Griffiths, pp. 488–9 and n. 47, p. 536, citing C. Brown, 'Lydgate's verses on Queen Margaret's entry into London', *Modern Language Review* 7 (1912), pp. 225–34.

[26] McCulloch and Jones, 'Lancastrian Politics', p. 107; Griffiths, pp. 219–21; Emden, *Oxford*, II, p. 1186. But Kipling, 'London Pageants', pp. 25–6, n. 13, points out that Lydgate 'merely versified an account of the pageantry' for Henry VI's 1432 triumph; he did not create the pageants for it.

[27] Ibid., pp. 9–13, for the full argument against Lydgate's authorship; the quote is from p. 13.

[28] The word *apparatus* could mean both 'preparation' and 'decoration'; by the late fourteenth century the concept had expanded to include stage property.

[29] Undecipherable word.

[30] CLRO, Journal IV, fol. 229. This volume of the Journal contains entries for 1443–47.

[31] Other years in which the tenth fell on a Saturday were 1451, when her whereabouts are uncertain, and 1456, when she was in the midlands.

emblem and the promise of a hopeful future. Though some may have viewed the display with skepticism, it is likely that many more simply drank it all in. Thus, on her passage through the city to Westminster for her coronation, she – and the litter that she rode in and the two horses that drew it – were dressed and trapped in white to signify virginity. Likewise, she wore her hair loose about her shoulders beneath a crown of gold decorated with pearls and precious stones.[32] We do not know its color. The book that John Talbot, earl of Shrewsbury, presented to Margaret as a wedding gift depicts her as what we might call a 'honey blonde'.[33] Fair hair, however, was yet another attribute associated with virginity. The Virgin Mary was frequently painted with blonde hair, and by the later fifteenth century it had become customary to portray all English queens as blondes.[34] A letter written more than a decade later by Raffaelo de Negra to Bianca Maria Visconti, the duchess of Milan, hints at a different reality with its secondhand information that Margaret was 'a most handsome woman, though somewhat dark and not so beautiful as your Serenity'.[35] In her procession through London she was accompanied by lords on horseback and ladies in 'chairs', with the mayor and aldermen and the crafts – and everyone else it seems – all marching and milling and helping themselves to wine from the conduits (which ran, according to the *Brut*, 'bothe white and rede'). On Sunday 30 May, Margaret was crowned at Westminster. Feasting and three days of jousting and other celebration followed her coronation while everyone made merry. It had all been a very good show, from anyone's point of view, and on 18 June the mayor, aldermen, and commonalty praised and congratulated each other for their part in it.[36] England had a queen.

Margaret of Anjou was only fifteen years old, yet she came from a line of strong women, accustomed to wielding power when necessity dictated. It is important to emphasize the word *necessity*. These were not women who sought power for its own sake, but who, when the need arose, had the ability and the self-confidence to step forward and take charge. Margaret's paternal grand-mother, Yolande of Aragon, with whom she had spent eight years of her childhood, had been regent in Anjou for her eldest son, ruling the duchy and resisting English military pressure, supporting the Dauphin through the days of his disinheritance and even marrying him to her daughter Marie. Margaret's mother, Isabelle of Lorraine, had continued to claim her husband's rights and fight his wars while he was a captive awaiting ransom. Indeed, as J.J. Bagley once observed, 'politics, war, and administration seemed to be the natural vocations of women in [Margaret's] family'.[37]

Yet at the time of Margaret's marriage to Henry, it is doubtful whether the English valued these attributes at all or even considered them. It is even less likely that they sought them, for their politically active queens sometimes found

---

[32] Chamberlayne, 'Crowns and Virgins', pp. 54–7, for ongoing associations of queenship with virginity; p. 56, for visual representation of the queen as a virgin.
[33] BL, Royal MS 15 E. VI, fol. 2b.
[34] Chamberlayne, 'Crowns and Virgins', pp. 61–2.
[35] *CSP, Milan*, p. 19.
[36] CLRO, Journal IV, fol. 81b.
[37] Bagley, *Margaret of Anjou*, pp. 25–7. The quote is from p. 26.

themselves in trouble and were then regarded as meddlesome. Isabella, wife of Edward II, elicited sympathy as long as she was perceived to be acting against her husband's 'evil counsellors' the Despensers, whom others also hated. Once she and her lover, Roger Mortimer, began to rule, this changed. When her son, Edward III, seized power in a coup, he punished her for her share in 'Mortimer's rule' by stripping her of her lands and sending her into genteel retirement. Since it was awkward to hold Isabella publicly accountable for her actions, Mortimer was made to bear the blame for all that had been done, while she was portrayed as the foolish victim of his subtlety.[38] Alice Perrers – no queen, but Edward III's mistress during his later years – was criticized for exercising improper influence, for, as the bishop of Rochester put it, 'it is not fitting or safe that all the keys should hang from the belt of one woman'.[39] And Henry VI's own mother, Katherine of Valois, who had never been a meddler, was accorded no political voice during his minority, though she was closely involved in his early upbringing.[40] When the English discovered 'meddlesome' traits in Margaret, some at least were not pleased.

But it must be understood in any study of Margaret's activities as queen that the operative word remains *necessity*. Although she had been born and bred to power, she was also a child of her time who knew and understood her proper place. The tenacity with which she clung to it is remarkable, even when she had in actuality stepped far outside it. For the moment, however, necessity lay far in the future. In the eyes of the people who greeted her she was a symbol: of dynastic continuity and of a peace with France favorable to England. So high were the expectations raised by the marriage that John Capgrave was still able to claim, rather blindly, in late 1446 or early 1447 that peace was imminent.[41] More telling, and more pathetically hopeful, is the entry at the end of a continuation of the *Brut* ending in 1445/6: 'And in this yere [1445] . . . come the ambassatours of Fraunce to London, forto trete for peas betwene England and Fraunce . . . by the grace of God for a fynal peas.'[42]

---

[38] *Brut*, I, pp. 257–61, demonstrates this pattern of shifting attitudes towards Isabella. See Crawford, *Letters of the Queens of England*, pp. 81–92, for a succinct summary of her activities and subsequent treatment.

[39] Given-Wilson, *Royal Household*, pp. 147–8.

[40] Griffiths, pp. 56, 60–1.

[41] Capgrave, *Liber de Illustribus Henricis*, p. 135: 'Which marriage all people deem would be pleasing to God and the realm because peace and an abundance of benefits come with it.' ('Quas nuptias reputat omnis populus fore Deo gratas et regno, pro eo quod pax et abundantia frugum cum ipsis adventarent.')

[42] *Brut*, p. 490. This portion was written no later than early 1446 (*EHL*, pp. 91–2).

2

France

ENGLAND's high hopes, symbolized by the marriage, were to be doubly disappointed: temporarily in the matter of the dynastic succession, permanently in the case of the French settlement. Coincidentally, but unfortunately for the Lancastrian regime and for Margaret personally, both issues worked themselves out over the same eight-year period so that the effects of one on the public psyche were complicated and exacerbated by the effects of the other. In the case of the Hundred Years War, its ignominious end left bitter memories and an undercurrent of resentment that later could be mined in support of more recent grievances.

In early 1444, when negotiations began for the marriage of Henry VI of England to Margaret of Anjou, niece to Charles VII of France, the war had again reached an impasse. Its next stage, much less its final outcome, remained uncertain. While we may assume that everyone hoped to gain something from the negotiations, what each hoped for over the long term would scarcely have been the same. Considering the disparity of long-range interests, it is no wonder that the resulting marriage agreement only provided for a 23-month truce while further discussions continued.

Though no one at the time could have predicted the exact course events would take, the end result for the English amounted to utter defeat and disaster. The truce, which they had hoped would either lead to a more permanent, favorable settlement or buy them time to extricate themselves by other means from a bad situation, did neither. Instead it led to continued haggling and, when hostilities resumed, to the eventual loss within eight years of all English-held territory on the continent except for Calais and its immediate surroundings. Significantly, the first agreed-upon surrender was of the occupied county of Maine and of the English claim to Anjou. Within six months of Margaret's coronation, her father, René of Anjou, was offering Henry a lifetime alliance and a twenty-year truce through Charles VII's ambassadors and with Charles's blessing, in return for the cession of Maine.[1] As the agreement proved difficult to implement, as negotiations foundered, frictions increased, and the French again took up the offensive, one thing led to another.

---

[1] For the particulars of England's losses over these eight years see Griffiths, ch. 18; Wolffe, ch. 11; for differing views of the agreement to surrender Maine see Griffiths, pp. 494–5; Wolffe, pp. 171–4; Cron, 'Duke of Suffolk', pp. 77–99; Watts, pp. 221–36.

The piecemeal loss of so much territory within such a short time came as a bitter shock to the English so that, even before the final debacle, James Gresham could complain to John Paston in a letter of 19 August 1450 that 'we have not now a foote of londe in Normandie'.[2] Gresham's use of the word *we* reveals the emotional stake of the community in what it had come to identify as communal interests.[3] Accustomed to more than a century of pronouncements regarding 'their kings' rights in France', the English in England perceived the loss of territory and the collapse of the royal claim as their own loss and disgrace, even though many had already abandoned full-blown financial support for the war in view of diminishing personal returns. [4] For the English in France – the soldiers and the men holding property there who had settled with their families – the denouement also brought a sense of betrayal, a sense that they had been sold out. As they made their way back to England, it was soon possible to see in London 'diverse long cartes with stuff of armor and bedding and houshold as well of English as of norman goodes and men women and children in right pouer array pitewus to see dryven out of normandy'.[5] When alms did not suffice or when anger and frustration surfaced, returning soldiers turned to 'theft and misrule', causing outbreaks of disorder.[6] Although other factors also lay behind domestic strife,[7] the impact of these returnees should not be disregarded. The chronicler – and surely others as well – perceived them as a problem. So long as this perception existed to feed resentment over the ending of the war, the actual contribution of such persons to lawlessness was immaterial. In addition, failure in France linked up with and exacerbated other issues as foci of discontent: the impoverishment of the crown, the rivalries between magnates, and the sense that royal justice and favor were themselves partisan.[8]

In a growing atmosphere of disillusionment, anger and frustration over the course of the war, it is not surprising that people sought to assess blame for the disaster, nor that they turned against William de la Pole, by that time duke of Suffolk, who had been Henry's chief negotiator for the marriage settlement and a principal in subsequent discussions with France. When the commons prepared a bill of impeachment against him following his arrest in early 1450, the animus behind their specific charges seems in large part to have been the 'grete rumour and fame, how that this Roialme of Englond shuld be sold to the Kynges Adversarie of Fraunce . . . which shuld be doone and ymagined by the labour of the seid Duke'.[9] The pro-Yorkist *English Chronicle* complains that

---

[2] Gairdner, *PL*, II, p. 162.
[3] Keen, 'End of the Hundred Years War', p. 297.
[4] Keen, *England in the Later Middle Ages*, p. 407; in 'End of the Hundred Years War' he explores in more detail the psychological dilemma of an England divided in its mind over the French territories. Cf. Wolffe, pp. 264–6.
[5] Flenley ('Bale's Chron.'), p. 134.
[6] Ibid., pp. 128, 136, 137.
[7] Storey, p. 17, whose work amply demonstrates its pre-existence. Griffiths, ch. 20, also discusses the various causes of lawlessness.
[8] See, e.g., Scattergood, *Politics and Poetry*, p. 98. It is not my purpose here to explore these matters separately or to argue that any one was the most important precursor of civil war. All became interlinked as they fed off each other in a mutually supporting framework of discontent.
[9] *RP*, V, p. 177. Griffiths, pp. 676–84, for a detailed account of the proceedings against Suffolk and his subsequent murder.

'treson grew under tho trewes . . . be alienacion of Anges and Mayne, and wilful lesying of al Normandy', and reports

> the comune vois and fame [in 1450] . . . that the duke of Suffolk . . . hadde maad delyveraunce of Aunge and Mayn withoute assent of this lond unto the kyng of Cicile the quenes fader; and hadde also aliened and sold the duchie of Normandie to the king of Fraunce.[10]

By the time the chronicle was written, soon after Henry's deposition,[11] this charge had become an article of faith against his government.[12]

Inevitably, the marriage itself began to be tainted by association as hopes of what it would accomplish proved more and more illusory. The pageants that had greeted Margaret upon her arrival set out the tension between expectation and actuality. Although they appeared to give her agency, reality allowed her only the most marginal role in peacemaking.[13] She had taken no part, of course, in the discussions leading up to the marriage settlement, nor would she have a voice in the negotiations that followed. Meanwhile, the pageants had insisted that both her presence and her mediation would bring peace. The problem for Margaret in this construction was that when peace failed, she incurred blame. And even before the marriage was blamed for the failure of policy, people had begun to note with disapproval that she had come without a respectable dowry and that the extravagant cost of the marriage – reckoned at more than £5,500 – had been borne by England.[14] Raffaelo de Negra's letter of 1458, in which he recounts that the first thing his English informant told him about Margaret was that 'the king of England took her without any dowry, and he even restored some lands which he held to her father', reflects the currency of such talk in the 1450s, as does Dr Thomas Gascoigne's oft-repeated description of Margaret: 'with whom England received nothing of goods, but the loss of Maine and Anjou, which lands her husband, Henry VI, gave in perpetuity . . . to the queen's father'.[15]

Nevertheless, the chronicles are somewhat slow to make the explicit connection between the marriage and the loss of France. Although the continuation of the *Brut* ending in 1461 calls it

> a dere mariage for the reame of Englond; ffor it is knowen verely that, for to have [Margaret], was delyvered the Duchie of Angeo & the Erldome of Maign, which was the key of Normandie, for the Frensh men tentre[16]

[10] *English Chron.*, pp. 61, 68. 'Gregory's Chron.', p. 189; Wright, *Political Poems*, II, p. 230, also blame Suffolk for 'selling' Normandy.
[11] *EHL*, p. 129.
[12] Harriss, 'Struggle for Calais', p. 45, n. 1.
[13] See below, pp. 52ff.
[14] Escouchy, *Chronique*, III, p. 277, reports the dowry at 20,000 francs and her mother's unrealized claims to Majorca and Minorca. Wolffe, p. 180, and Griffiths, pp. 315–16, for the cost of bringing Margaret to England: 'the single most expensive enterprise embarked upon by Henry's government after his return from France in 1432' according to the latter. Stevenson, I, pp. 443–60, for individual expenses.
[15] *CSP, Milan*, p. 18; Gascoigne, *Loci e Libro*, p. 204: 'cum qua nihil bonorum Anglia recepit, sed perdicionem Cenomanniae et Andagaviae, quas terras maritus suus, Henricus Sextus, dedit in perpetuum . . . patri reginae', cf. pp. 205, 221. For further discussion of Gascoigne, see below, pp. 29–30.
[16] *Brut*, p. 511.

its writer then takes a different tack and concludes that the *real* cause of England's ill fortune was the breaking off of earlier marriage negotiations with the count of Armagnac, thus shifting blame for subsequent troubles to the king's broken promises.[17] This portion of the *Brut* was written between 1464 and 1471, after Henry's deposition.[18] The Yorkists had used his alleged oath breaking in 1460–61 to justify seizing the throne, and this may have encouraged the writer to seek a similar pattern in Henry's earlier behavior as the cause of all his troubles. Another chronicler writing at about the same time merely notes how few French attendants accompanied Margaret to England.[19] Only at the very end of the fifteenth century and the beginning of the sixteenth does the account found in both BL, Cotton Vitellius A. XVI and the *Great Chronicle* blame the marriage directly – though not Margaret personally – for the loss of France.[20] Their contention that the English agreement to give up Maine and Anjou was part of the marriage settlement may derive from angry charges made in an atmosphere of suspicion and frustration following the losses of territory.

In the less formal world of rash statement and deliberate slander, extremities of feeling become more apparent. A peculiar document that can be identified as an effort to ridicule Margaret's father, René of Anjou, satirizes his extravagant pretensions and mocks the supposed benefits to be gained by marrying his daughter.[21] In what purports to be a proclamation, René is made to introduce himself as the 'kyng of alle kynges, Lord of alle lordes, Souden of alle Surry [Sultan of all Syria], Emperour of Babilon, steward of Helle, Porter of Paradise, Constable of Ierusalem, Lord of Certossis' and, more outrageously, 'Cosyn to youre crist that was nailed on the rode'. While René might be identified by the explicit reference to Jerusalem – one of his empty titles was King of Jerusalem – the writer's real purpose seems to have been to overload the description in a way that the reader would immediately perceive as ridiculous. This sorts well with René's numerous paper claims, which he was never able to realize in practice.[22] The proclamation's subsequent offer to 'Henry kynge of England, the frenshe womman sone', reveals a bitter cynicism:

> And so be that he wol wed my doughter, I wel becom cristen, & alle my meyne, And wol gef hym iij Milions of gold, And delyvere hym the holy cros, with al the Reliques in my kepyng; And I shal make hym Emperour of xxxvij kynges cristen . . . And to stonde with hym agaynst alle Cristen kynges.[23]

All these promises of wealth and support to follow the marriage are just as extravagant and empty as the initial claims of René's power. No wealth comes

[17] Ibid., p. 512.
[18] *EHL*, p. 119.
[19] 'Benet's Chron.', p. 190. This chronicle was written 'some years before 1471', but, it would seem, in the 1460s (ibid., p. 157).
[20] *London Chrons.*, p. 155; *Great Chron.*, pp. 176–7.
[21] Printed in Furnivall, *Political . . . Poems*, pp. 12–14; its source is BL, Cotton Vespasian B. XVI, fol. 5. See Appendix I for its association with René and comparison with other documents in a similar vein.
[22] In addition to the dukedoms of Anjou, Lorraine and Bar, René claimed the titular kingships of Naples, Sicily and Jerusalem.
[23] Furnivall, *Political . . . Poems*, p. 13.

with the marriage; in the same breath the writer dismisses all hope of alliance and loyal support.

The description of Henry as 'the Frenchwoman's son' must also be considered. Though accurate enough, it seems to echo the sentiment of earlier verses written shortly after the death of Henry V, which express concern that Queen Katherine will raise her son to favor France.[24] If the phrase is emotionally loaded, as I suspect, it reflects newly reawakened but perennial suspicions regarding foreign-born consorts and underlines the writer's jaundiced view of Henry's marriage to René's daughter.[25] In this sort of discourse we see a part of the dilemma facing Margaret: by making her the symbol of English hopes-to-be-gained, she was also set up to be their stand-in when they failed. Her own inescapable Frenchness became part of the explanation of failure.

Her father's activities helped to fuel the fire. When war broke out again in 1449, René participated in the French actions in Normandy. In 1450 he was one of the commanders at the siege of Caen.[26] A London chronicler, convinced of René's role, would later observe:

> The dolfyn and the kyng of Cecile the quenes ffader laboured in such wyse that they gate all normandy withoute ony greet resistence and the erledome of Angeou demayn which hadde be the olde enheritaunce and right evermore and tyme out of mynde of the kynges of Engeland. And then wer all the Englisshmen dryven and sent oute from ffraunce Normandy and Angeoy and cam into this land in greet mysery and poverte.[27]

In the expanding process of popular blame laying, Margaret began to come under personal attack. In November 1447, Thomas Hunt, yeoman keeper of Gloucester castle, and John Cosgrove, keeper of the prison of Guildford castle, were indicted for words against the king and queen. Hunt had accused Henry of killing his uncle, the duke of Gloucester, and said he wished that the duke had killed the king and queen since Gloucester would have made a better king. Some months later Cosgrove said that he wished that the king had been hanged and the queen drowned because things had never gone right since she arrived in England.[28] Although the immediate impulse behind these comments was the suspicious, but probably natural, death of the duke of Gloucester, who had favored a hard line towards France, Cosgrove's remarks may reflect a deeper disillusionment.

Still more explicit in their hostility to Margaret are a series of notes written around 1457 by Dr Thomas Gascoigne, twice chancellor of Oxford.[29] It must be

---

[24] Wright, *Political Poems*, pp. xxxi–xxxii, 130: 'Regina fallit habens patrem, sequitur sua proles,/Fallit item dictum, dat ramus semper eundem/Fructem quem stipes, interdum sunt variantes.' ('Having a father the queen deceives; her offspring follows suit; in the same way the saying that the branch always gives the same fruit as the tree misleads; sometimes there are variations.')

[25] E.g., Gascoigne, *Loci e Libro*, pp. 219–20, inveighs against foreign-born queens. Parsons, *Eleanor of Castile*, pp. 63–4, 67, for perceptions of Eleanor as a 'foreigner'.

[26] Griffiths, pp. 255, 251.

[27] Flenley ('Bale's Chron.'), p. 128.

[28] PRO, KB9/256/13: 'Et quod nunquam fuit amendum [lit. 'never had (anything) been corrected'] in Anglia ex quo ipsa veniebat in terram Angliae.'

[29] Gascoigne, *Loci e Libro*, p. vi, for their dating. The last dated entry was for December 1457, and an earlier passage regarding Margaret (p. 205) wonders: 'And what will follow from the queen's actions in

emphasized that these notes are not pieces of consecutive history, but a string of repetitive diatribes on more or less the same subject. Gascoigne has been described by two historians as 'a bitter partisan, who indulged freely in scandalous gossip' and, more bluntly, as 'the arch-rumour-monger of late-Lancastrian England'.[30] Yet, uncannily and uncomfortably, he occasionally hits close to the mark. For this reason it is necessary to consider him carefully.

Gascoigne's complaint regarding Margaret is twofold: first, he claims that the marriage – and Margaret herself – were directly responsible for the losses in France, and second, he states that Margaret took over the government to detrimental effect after Henry's illness in the mid-1450s. The first claim is what concerns us here.[31] Gascoigne starts out with the assertion that Suffolk had agreed to give up Maine and Anjou, with Henry's consent, as a bargaining chip in obtaining a safe conduct for Margaret to journey to England. Without the surrender of territory there would be no Margaret and no marriage.[32] This story of blackmail is patently false.[33] Nevertheless, it is probable that France – and certainly Anjou – hoped for such a concession, and possible that the matter was informally raised at the time of the marriage negotiations. As early as 1442 it had been acknowledged in writing that Maine could be handed over at some future time as part of a peace agreement.[34] It seems likely, then, that Gascoigne's angry accusation represents a strand of popular belief that arose after the peace process failed and that would later be picked up and presented in even simpler terms by Cotton Vitellius A. XVI and the *Great Chronicle*.

But Gascoigne himself did not leave the story as he started it. He repeated it three times more, each time with more detail and greater elaboration. His final version requires a closer look, for it adds the following specific indictment of Margaret:

> And thus the king of England, Henry VI, granted and gave [away] Maine and Anjou at the request of his queen Margaret, daughter of the duke of Lorraine who called himself king of Sicily . . . and that aforesaid queen of ours begged the King of England that [they] so be given to her father at the urging of William Pole, duke of Suffolk, and his wife, who earlier had promised to request it.[35]

It is most unlikely that Suffolk unilaterally engineered the surrender of territory.[36] In June 1445, perhaps with a real appreciation of how difficult

---

1457, God knows.' ('Et qualia sequentur ex reginae actibus, anno Domini 1457, Deus scit.') Gascoigne died in March 1458.

[30] *EHL*, p. 166; Griffiths, p. 487. But cf. Pronger, 'Thomas Gascoigne', for his career and a more positive view of his scholarship.

[31] See p. 139 below, for his second claim.

[32] Gascoigne, *Loci e Libro*, p. 190, for the story's first appearance.

[33] Griffiths, p. 487; Wolffe, p. 181.

[34] Jones, 'Somerset, York and the Wars of the Roses', p. 292 and n. 4, citing BN, N.A. Fr., 3642/804, which granted land rights to the county to Edmund Beaufort, duke of Somerset, with this reservation.

[35] Gascoigne, *Loci et Libro*, p. 221: 'et sic concessit et dedit rex Angliae, Henricus vj^tus, Cenomanniam et Andegaviam ad peticionem reginae suae Margaretae, filiae ducis Lotringae, qui vocavit seipsum regem Ceciliae . . . et regina ista praedicta peciit a rege Angliae sic dari patri suo, per instanciam Willelmi Pulle, ducis Suthfolchiae, et uxoris suae, qui antea sic peti promiserant.' The earlier versions of the story are on pp. 190, 204–5 and 219.

[36] Griffiths, p. 487.

further negotiations were going to be and an accurate sense that anyone engaged in them would be venturing the thin ice of public opinion, he requested and was granted that an account of his efforts be enrolled in the records of parliament. At that time he specifically denied having discussed any details of the peace treaty still to be negotiated, asserting that he had referred all matters to the king and had at no time exceeded his instructions. Moreover, perhaps suspecting that talks would stick on such emotion-laden matters as territorial rights and hoping to strengthen the English bargaining position as much as possible, he voiced a strong warning to provision and refortify the English-held lands in case the negotiations failed.[37] He was praised in parliament for his 'diligent labours ... notable wysdam, proidence and discrecion'.[38] Two years later in May 1447, by which time he had begun to be blamed for the surrender of Maine, he was allowed to declare officially, in Henry's presence and before witnesses, that he had done nothing disloyal or contrary to crown interests, a statement that was apparently endorsed by all present including the dukes of York and Buckingham.[39] Whatever had transpired, and whoever had been privy to it, Suffolk clearly intended for it to be understood that he had never acted alone.

But there may still be reason to believe that Margaret played a personal role in the decision to surrender territory. And superficially it would appear to involve exactly the sort of pleading that Gascoigne describes.

At the heart of the matter is a pair of letters written to Charles VII by Henry and Margaret in December 1445, forming part of a three-way personal correspondence.[40] Henry's letter of 22 December agreed to give up the town and castle of Le Mans and all other occupied territory within the county of Maine for a number of reasons, including favor towards 'our dear and well-beloved companion the queen, who has requested us to do this many times'.[41] A quick reading of Margaret's letter, written a few days earlier, appears to corroborate what Henry wrote. In it she offers to 'stretch forth the hand, and ... employ ourselves herein effectually to our power' to achieve a final peace. Moreover, specifically regarding Maine she says that she 'will do for [Charles's] pleasure the best that we can do, as we have always done'.[42] Indeed, the conclusion that Margaret actively lobbied her husband on Charles's behalf has several points to recommend it apart from Henry's own assertion of the queen's influence: she was Charles's niece; her father was to be the recipient, and she was, after all, French! Most historians who have considered Margaret's role at all have tended towards this view, though with occasional reservation.[43] As an

---

[37] *RP*, V, p. 74: 'which ordinaunce and provision so made knowen and notified, he supposed verely shall be grete mene to the better conclusion of peas'.

[38] Ibid., p. 73.

[39] *Foedera*, V, i, pp. 176–7.

[40] Five of Margaret's letters to Charles survive. Stevenson published two of them; three more exist in manuscript in the Bibliothèque Nationale.

[41] Stevenson, II, ii, p. 640. The letter begins on p. 638.

[42] Stevenson, I, p. 165.

[43] See, e.g., Bagley, *Margaret of Anjou*, p. 49; Wolffe, pp. 183, 184–5, who refers to Margaret as Charles's 'advocate' and 'protégée'; Keen, *England in the Later Middle Ages*, p. 400; Jacob, *The Fifteenth Century*, p. 479; Lander, *Wars of the Roses*, p. 47 note, who sees her as an 'unwitting tool' because of her inexperience. Cf. Gillingham, *Wars of the Roses*, pp. 57–9, and Griffiths, p. 495, who both believe that

example, it has been argued that she would have considered it 'axiomatic that Maine should be returned to her family [since] it belonged to them'. Moreover, having been raised by her grandmother Yolande of Aragon, ever a fierce supporter of France, the 'politically inexperienced' Margaret would have followed her example.[44] These are not unreasonable suppositions, as far as they go. If left unqualified, however, such an argument fails to consider that, as queen of England, Margaret would have acquired interests and goals that differed from those of the family she was born into.[45] This was a fact of marital life that the strong women behind her – and most certainly the redoubtable Yolande – would have understood. Had she wished to advance her father's interests, she would not have done so in disregard of her husband's.

A more careful reading of the correspondence suggests a different analysis. The representation of Margaret in the pageants as a mediator for peace was not entirely wishful thinking. Recent work on queenship has shown that one of the queen's accepted roles was that of mediator and intercessor between the king and others.[46] Christine de Pisan endorsed it as a means of obtaining or preserving peace.[47] With this in mind, Margaret's words make better sense if considered as mediation in support of diplomatic gamesmanship than as unwarranted meddling. To see them in this light, they must be placed in context.

Peace negotiations resumed in London in the summer of 1445 following Margaret's arrival. Despite the exchange of many words and pleasantries, no agreement could be reached on anything of substance beyond a seven-month extension of the truce and a proposal that the two kings meet personally to discuss a final peace.[48] The three-way correspondence appears to have begun as a result of the impasse and as a first response to the suggestion of a meeting. When a second French delegation arrived in November to continue talks, it also brought personal messages from Charles VII to Henry VI and Margaret, suggesting that the 'best and aptest means' of achieving peace would be for Henry to surrender the county of Maine to his father-in-law, René of Anjou.[49] There is no record of any discussion of Maine over the summer, although the more contentious issues of Normandy, Gascony and the French crown had been on the table.[50] The first written reference to it as an actual bargaining counter occurs in René's instructions of 17 October 1445 to Charles's envoys. In return

Margaret actively lobbied Henry but doubt her real influence because of her youth. Griffiths, p. 255, concludes that her role was of 'minor consequence'.

[44] Cron, 'Duke of Suffolk', pp. 94–5. She does not believe, however, that the idea to cede Maine originated with Margaret. Instead, she suggests Bertrand de Beauvau, seigneur de Precigny, who had long known her family and had come to England with the French embassy.

[45] The book that John Talbot, earl of Shrewsbury, gave to Margaret emphasized her 'new' interests (Reynolds, 'Shrewsbury Book', p. 113, though our conclusions regarding Margaret's response differ).

[46] See, e.g., Huneycutt, 'Intercession and the High-Medieval Queen'; Parsons, 'The Queen's Intercession in Thirteenth-Century England'; Howell, Eleanor of Provence, pp. 20, 257–9, 298–9. For positive views of female persuasion more generally, see Farmer, 'Persuasive Voices'.

[47] Christine, Treasure, pp. 50–1.

[48] Griffiths, pp. 490–3, discusses them in some detail, drawing largely upon a journal kept by one of the French ambassadors (cited in n. 50, below).

[49] Stevenson, II, ii, pp. 639–40; Escouchy, Chronique, III, p. 149. Charles's letters are no longer extant, but are referred to in Henry's and Margaret's replies.

[50] Stevenson, I, pp. 87–148.

for Maine, they were to offer Henry a lifetime alliance with René and a twenty-year truce, as Charles had recently authorized in letters patent to René.[51] Apart from René's undoubted pleasure at the prospect, the acknowledgment of Maine's likely cession some three years before may have made it seem a relatively safe issue to pursue.[52]

On 17 December, Margaret was the first to respond to Charles. Her letter combines formality with cordiality; although it might appear to promise much, it adroitly sidesteps unequivocal commitment in a way that ends up promising nothing. To make this point, it will be necessary to quote the letter at length. Acknowledging receipt of Charles's letters, she writes:

> In as much as we perceive the good love and the entire will that you have towards my lord and myself, the great desire which you have to see us, and also the fruitful disposition and liberal inclination which we know to be in you in regard to peace and good concord between both of you, we herein praise our Creator, and thank you thereof with a good heart and as kindly as ever we may; for no greater pleasure can we have in this world than to see an arrangement for a final peace between him and you, as well for the nearness of lineage in which you stand the one to the other, as also for the relief and repose of the Christian people which has been so long disturbed by war. And herein, to the pleasure of our Lord, we will, upon our part, stretch forth the hand, and will employ ourselves herein effectually to our power in such wise that reason would that you, *and all others*, ought herein to be gratified.
>
> And as to the deliverance which you desire to have of . . . Maine, . . . *we understand that my said lord has written to you at considerable length about this*; and yet herein we will do for your pleasure the best that we can do, as we have always done, as you may be certified of this by [Charles's ambassadors] Cousinot and Havart, whom may it graciously please you to hear, and give credence to what shall be related to you by them upon our part at this time; making us frequently acquainted with your news and of your good prosperity and health; and therein we will take very great pleasure and will have singular consolation.[53]

Her letter can be analyzed in stages. Much of it is designed to promote good feeling: the flattery, the allusions to shared interests and Margaret's offer to mediate. But we should note that she does not present herself as Charles's agent or as the representative simply of his point of view; the result should gratify not only Charles, but *all others* as well. More concretely, in regard to Maine, although Margaret offers to do her best for him, whatever that means, she specifically notes that her husband has already dealt with it in a letter that – she says – he has already written. The logical conclusion to be drawn is that although she is willing to play the intermediary, there may be limitations to what she can do. The request to give credence to the bearers is very common. Though it may indicate that they were entrusted with further information of a

---

[51] Lecoy de la Marche, *Le roi René*, I, pp. 258–9; Griffiths, p. 495 and n. 80. Although the French would later claim that the concession was based initially on an oral promise (Beaucourt, *Histoire de Charles VII*, IV, pp. 284–5, citing BN, MS Fr. 18442, fol. 173; Escouchy, *Chronique*, III, p. 194), the alleged agreement, if genuine, has left no other traces.
[52] Jones, 'Somerset, York and the Wars of the Roses', p. 292.
[53] Stevenson, I, pp. 165–6, emphasis added.

politically sensitive nature, that is not necessarily so, and the letter's last section seems to have more to do with health and personal news than it does with politics.

Since the possibility of Maine's surrender was already public knowledge – at least within governmental circles – Henry's agreement of December could hardly have been made in secret.[54] It seems likely that the negotiators and other councilors knew of the plan, approved it, and perhaps even advised Henry on how to pursue it, though only he could authorize it.[55] This demands that we take a closer look at what Henry said to Charles.

Whoever was responsible for its content, Henry's letter of December 22 to Charles was not a weak-willed capitulation, but a piece of bargaining strategy. Following the usual introductory formalities, it reads:

> Knowing that you would be very glad that we should make deliverance of . . . Maine, to . . . our very dear father and uncle, the king of Sicily [René] and Charles of Anjou, his brother . . . and . . . that it appeared to you that this was one of the best and aptest means to arrive at the blessing of a peace between us and you; wishing effectually to prove the great desire and affection which we have to attain . . . peace, . . . out of the love and affection which we have towards your most noble person, whom we would desire to please from the bottom of our heart *in every way which is honourable, possible, and lawful*; favouring also our most dear and well-beloved companion the queen, who has requested us to do this many times, and out of regard to our said father and uncle, for whom it is most reasonable that we should do more than for others who are not so nearly connected with us, . . . we signify and promise in good faith and on our kingly word to give and deliver . . . Maine, by the last day of April next coming, . . . *upon the surrender to us of the original letters* whereby you granted to our said father and uncle . . . to make alliances during their lives, and to make truces with us for the said country of Anjou and Maine during twenty years.[56]

First, Margaret's requests seem less important in the overall scheme than Henry's understanding that Charles considered this the best way to make progress towards peace and his own expressed wish to prove himself no less desiring of the same. In other words, the cession of Maine should be seen as an earnest of his good intentions in the pursuit of other goals. Moreover, the promise is conditional upon the receipt of Charles's original letters authorizing the alliance and truce. Thus, it seems that Henry and his councilors believed they stood to gain more in the long term by having René's (possibly more active) assistance as an ally than they stood to lose in the short term by the surrender of Maine.[57] Obtaining Charles's original authorization would seem to qualify as his earnest of good intentions and would perhaps provide the English with some assurance that the deal could not be altered after they had done their

---

[54] Cf. Wolffe, p. 189.
[55] Watts, pp. 222–9, 232–4, argues that many of the lords, including York, would have understood what concessions were likely to be necessary and were supportive of the peace policy. He notes, however, that only Henry could take responsibility for concessions, since everyone else wished to avoid charges of 'stirring' him (p. 223).
[56] Stevenson II, ii, pp. 639–41, emphasis added.
[57] Watts, p. 226.

part. We should also note the qualifiers attached to Henry's expressed desire to please Charles: that anything done should be 'honorable, possible, and lawful'. They suggest that although Henry is willing to make concession, he does not offer to concede everything merely at Charles's bidding.

Margaret's role in Henry's letter is a part of this bargaining strategy. As Paul Strohm has shown, the queen's intercession could be used to soften the king's position in a matter where he might otherwise be inclined to take a hard line. Because the queen speaks from a marginalized position, outside the systems that produce male power – in this case, Margaret having nothing to do with the actual peace negotiations – her entreaties pose no threat to male authority. In fact, the queen 'as *femina ex machina* . . . serves a welcome facilitating role exempted . . . from any longer-term impact on the male conduct of affairs'. The king may reconsider and revise his actions in this one instance without further commitment, in ways that it is assumed will ultimately prove to have been wise. Meanwhile, the juxtaposition of the pleading queen reinforces notions of the king's innate masculine strength.[58] If the idea of a strong Henry seems startling, we must remember that this letter is part of a diplomatic correspondence. It would make no sense to portray him as anything less. Margaret's placement between other family members may also have served to increase the sense of familial good will and obligation that provides the basis for Henry's concession, which Charles might be expected to reciprocate. Thus, Margaret's role in this letter remains a distinctly supporting one – of proposals that she neither initiated nor had any direct say in negotiating.

More letters followed as the two kings tried to schedule a personal meeting and as the cession of Maine was delayed.[59] Margaret wrote to Charles again on 20 May 1446, acknowledging a letter that he had written to her in March. After expressing her own pleasure upon learning that he was well and assuring him of Henry's and her own health, she noted Charles's desire to see her at the kings' proposed meeting and his

> hope that we would help to the best of our power to direct and rectify the matters which shall be treated between you two in it, and herein you desire that we would render our assistance.
>
> Truly we hope, most high and powerful prince, our very dear uncle, *that it will be the pleasure of my said lord that we be with him at the said convention*, and that in it, *by the mediation of the grace of the Holy Ghost*, we may see . . . a fruitful conclusion in the matter of a general peace, which we desire with cordial affection above all earthly things . . . and upon our part we will busy ourselves herein, and will assist in *all that shall be possible for us to do* in the matter. Praying you with a hearty desire that you would be pleased to continue and persevere in the good disposition and inclination which we know you have for the good of this peace, *and conduct yourself herein with every desire of good concord, which we hope you will do as a good Catholic prince is wont and ought to do*. And, very high and powerful prince, our very dear uncle, be pleased always to signify to us all matters agreeable

[58] Strohm, *Hochon's Arrow*, pp. 102–4. The quotation is from p. 104.
[59] On 22 December, Henry wrote a further letter to Charles that dealt with their intended meeting (printed in Escouchy, *Chronique*, III, pp. 151–3).

to you, with a view to their accomplishment, by us to the best of our ability, joyfully and with a right good heart.[60]

This second letter is more circumspect than the first. True, Margaret still presents herself as eager to please: to be present at the meeting, to see a 'fruitful conclusion' (through the mediation of the Holy Ghost!), and to do what she can towards that end. Yet the language is highly political: smoothly reassuring while skirting actual commitment. 'All that shall be possible for us to do' leaves open the question of what can actually be done, which may not turn out to be much; the offer of future assistance is similarly open-ended. Finally, the admonition to Charles to conduct himself as a good son of the Church ought is quite remarkable, coming as it does from the sixteen-year-old queen to her forty-plus uncle. At this point, the surrender of Maine, which was supposed to have taken place by the end of April, had not occurred,[61] nor does it appear that Charles's letters of authorization to René – the English condition for the transaction – had been delivered. While we cannot say with certainty that Margaret intended this as a gentle warning against double-dealing, the passage itself permits such an interpretation.[62]

By 10 December 1446, when Margaret's third letter was written, the planned meeting of kings had been postponed, while the business of Maine dragged on. More than half of this longish letter is taken up with inquiries and good wishes regarding Charles's well-being, along with reassurances that she herself was well. It then briefly segues to matters that Charles evidently had brought up in his correspondence of September:

> In as much . . . as you ask and urge us perseveringly to extend the hand to my dread lord that on his part he be always inclined to the good of the peace, may it please you to know in truth that we are employing and will employ ourselves with a good heart so far as will be possible for us. And we know certainly that my dread lord has a very good and perfect will.[63]

Here, Margaret simply asserts Henry's good will while assuring Charles that she will be helpful insofar as she can. The letter closes with a request to let her know if there is anything that she may do for him and more wishes for a good, long life. Though its overall content seems more personally 'friendly' than her previous letter, it is also more vague in what it offers. Nowhere does it mention possible meetings or desired conclusions, and its defense of Henry's good intentions undermines the notion that he might need prodding.

---

[60] Stevenson, I, pp. 183–6, emphasis added; the section quoted begins on 184.

[61] For one thing, Somerset, who completely controlled the county, was stalling (Jones, 'Somerset, York and the Wars of the Roses', pp. 292–3). See below, p. 89 and n. 51.

[62] These phrases do not appear in Margaret's other extant letters to Charles or in her letters to other persons. Since their use in this letter appears to be selective rather than habitual, and since the circumstances of the negotiations at this time are compatible with hypothetical intent, it should be considered.

[63] BN, MS Fr. 4054, fol. 94. My translation. ('En tant . . . que nous priez et exhortez a perseveramment tenir la main pardevers mon tresredoubte Seigneur que de sa part il soit tousiours enclin au bien de la paix, vous plaise savoir pour verite que adez nous ysommes emploiee et emploirons du bon cuer si avant quil nous sera possible. Et savons certainement que mond tresredoubte Seigneur y a tresbon et parfait vouloir.')

Margaret wrote two more letters to Charles of which we have knowledge. The first, of 20 December 1446, is a letter of credence for Adam Moleyns, bishop of Chichester and keeper of the privy seal, and John Sutton, lord Dudley, who were going back and forth as ambassadors during the negotiations. Like her letter of 10 December, it ends with an offer to do something to please Charles. Henry's own letter of credence was written three days later. Margaret's last letter, of 28 July 1447, simply recommends one Jehan Cambray, the brother of one of her squires, who was seeking help in obtaining justice in some matter.[64]

As a final exercise to put Margaret's apparent eagerness to do all she might for Charles into perspective, it may be helpful to compare her offers with short passages in letters written to him by two other persons about entirely different matters. The first is from a letter of Richard, duke of York, written on 21 September 1445 when he was trying to arrange a marriage between his eldest son (then aged three!) and one of Charles's daughters. In closing, he asks Charles 'to send me your most gracious and good pleasure, that I may do and accomplish it with all my power, and with a right good will'.[65] York was not involved directly in the peace negotiations, nor was he yet at odds with Henry's court. It would appear, in fact, that Suffolk had suggested the match.[66] York's 'offer' was an exercise in polite good manners: a testimonial to his own sincerity in pursuing the marriage.

The second example is from a letter of Edmund Beaufort, duke of Somerset, of 28 February 1449. Most of his letter is devoted to complaint, for at this time both he and Charles were accusing each other – or their representatives – of breaking the truce. Nevertheless, the duke wrote: 'If there be any matter which you desire, I will perform it most cordially, if it be possible.'[67] In a further letter of 9 March he again urged Charles to '[let] me know if there is anything agreeable to you which I can do, so that I may perform it with all my heart'.[68] These are all standard phrases, neither to be taken too literally, nor devoid of meaning. Their purpose was to keep channels open and to allow for further discussion.

And that is precisely the sense in which the 'offering' phrases in Margaret's letters must be understood. This analysis does not negate the idea of Margaret as an 'activist' queen, but it underscores the need to understand her 'activism' in the terms of her own time. As the letters themselves demonstrate, they are less the work of a committed advocate than an effort to fulfill the queen's accepted role as mediator and peacemaker, with an eye 'always [to] preserving the honour of her husband' as prescribed by Christine de Pisan, while striving to foster an atmosphere of cooperation and trust.[69] Despite the enthusiasm of her first letter, she was still careful to indicate that decisions concerning Maine were really Henry's business and that hers was a supporting role. Measuring her age and inexperience against the political acumen displayed in the letters, it seems

[64] Ibid., fols 79, 80, 76.
[65] Stevenson, I, p. 163.
[66] Johnson, pp. 48–50, for the marriage proposal.
[67] Stevenson, I, pp. 231–2.
[68] Ibid., p. 234.
[69] Christine, *Treasure*, p. 50.

likely that Margaret received some advice on how to frame her replies to Charles.[70] It is also likely that her letters were deliberately written to complement Henry's as part of the bargaining strategy, rather than on the sly.[71] This sorts well with the view that the cession of Maine in return for an Angevin alliance and twenty-year truce had conciliar backing.[72] Indeed, the queen's letters make the best sense if seen as part of this larger picture.

These observations do not change the fact that her involvement in the dialogue of negotiation could be viewed with later suspicion. Clearly it was so viewed by Gascoigne, and, as any polltaker understands, the opinion of one must be considered to represent the opinions of at least some others. We do not know where he got his information – it may represent a strand of current gossip that had some basis in leaks regarding the three-way royal correspondence – but in assessing it we should note that he wrote out his complaints in the mid-1450s, by which time Margaret's actual intervention into politics had taken a non-traditional turn. If he felt that there was much to complain about at that time, it would have been both easy and natural to extrapolate backwards and to blame Margaret personally for a disaster still keenly felt.[73]

While it is likely that Margaret's popularity diminished as a result of the French losses, this outcome had much less to do with her own activities than it had with the disappointment of expectations raised by her marriage to Henry. In her dealings with Charles, she was bound by kinship – and perhaps by real familial affection as well[74] – to care for his 'estate and prosperity', both public and private. Yet her marriage to Henry had made her, by extension, Charles's potential enemy. When she wrote to him as her 'very dear uncle of France' and styled herself 'queen of France and England', both of them would have been aware of the disparity of interest embodied in these descriptions. As she began to see just how difficult peacemaking really was, she became increasingly circumspect. When the agreement to surrender Maine foundered, Margaret's mediations no longer had a place. Increasingly irrelevant to the situation on the ground, they ceased.

---

[70] Griffiths, p. 495, suggests this in passing.

[71] Parsons, 'Intercessionary Patronage of Queens', pp. 146, 151, for intercession as partnership between king and queen.

[72] Watts, pp. 225–6 and n. 86, which observes that Margaret's chamberlain, James Fiennes, must have known about her letters.

[73] We must not underestimate the staying power of the Hundred Years War as a 'live' issue. In 1475, twenty-two years after the final English defeat, Edward IV was able to mount a force of at least 11,451 fighting men, the largest English invading army sent to France during the fifteenth century. See Lander, 'Hundred Years' War', pp. 237, 321, for the numbers; Ross, *Edward IV*, pp. 209, 211, 223–5, for the seriousness of Edward's original intentions, and pp. 234–6, for popular resentment when anticipated military action did not materialize.

[74] A later addition to Berry Herald's chronicle describes in dramatic detail how both Charles and Margaret wept so at their parting that they could not speak (Bouvier, *Chroniques*, pp. 270, n. b, 440). It may or may not be reliable (Cron, 'Duke of Suffolk', p. 91).

3

Motherhood

MOTHERHOOD was the defining moment for a queen consort – or for any wife – in a system based on lineal inheritance. The queen who bore an heir fulfilled her basic duty as a queen; the other things that she might do or that might be expected of her would be either gravy or gall. It was unfortunate for the dynasty, and a personal misfortune for Margaret, that she did not bear a child until eight-and-a-half years after her arrival in England, and that the birth closely followed the final debacle in France and her husband's descent into physical and mental stupor. This issue, like the loss of France, involved the undermining of heightened hopes and expectations. This goes a long way to explain the rancor that could be directed towards Margaret on its account and the use that could later be made of it as a specifically gendered charge in the propaganda battery of her Yorkist enemies.

In 1445, at the time of the marriage, there was no reason to expect that it might not prove immediately fruitful. Both partners appear to have been healthy, normally intelligent, and reasonably attractive.[1] It is important to distinguish Henry's poor kingship – which is beyond question – from the absence of any apparent physical or mental deficits prior to 1453. His image as a model of saintly otherworldliness emerged full-blown only after his death and received its chief impetus during the reign of the first Tudor, Henry VII, who was concerned to propagate such a view to further his own claims as legitimate king. Though Henry VI was regarded as a pious man during his lifetime, his piety does not seem to have been abnormally pronounced or fixated.[2] This was an ostentatious age in which a great many people expressed themselves according to their means, and all fifteenth-century English kings were ecclesiastical benefactors.[3] Following Richard II's deposition, when it was often difficult for subsequent kings to feel entirely sure of their tenure, the 'creative use of benefaction as spectacle' could be a valuable propaganda device to enhance the king's standing.[4] Although Henry's ecclesiastical patronage 'is

---

[1] For Henry, see Griffiths, pp. 231, 241; Wolfe, pp. 10, 13, 70, but cf. pp. 16–18, for negative contemporary comments. For Margaret, see Wolfe, p. 171; Bagley, *Margaret of Anjou*, pp. 29, 36.

[2] For differing views of Henry's piety and later reputation, see Griffiths, pp. 248–50; Wolfe, pp. 3–12; Lovatt, 'Collector of Apocryphal Anecdotes', pp. 182–8.

[3] Rosenthal, 'Kings, Continuity and Ecclesiastical Benefaction', p. 161. Cf. Wolffe, pp. 141, 145, whose contention that Henry's piety was notably ostentatious I find unconvincing.

[4] Rosenthal, 'Kings, Continuity and Ecclesiastical Benefaction', p. 171.

probably a good indication of his priorities', Joel Rosenthal suggests that the relationship between Henry's weakness as king and the extent of his patronage was not accidental.[5] Nor ought we to assume uncritically that Henry was pathologically fearful of sex. His outspoken rejection of lust (when he was barely sixteen) and vow to abstain from intercourse outside of marriage may have reflected both the officious posturing and pained sincerity of youth.[6] Neither one precludes an interest in sex within matrimony. If, as seems likely, Henry became more pious in his later years, it is not to be wondered.[7] In some sense he could only have understood his catastrophic illness and the struggle it precipitated as an inexplicable act of God; likewise, it may have been easier for him to deal with his deposition and subsequent imprisonment through an ever-increasing reliance on faith.

When the marriage hunt was set in motion, the twenty-year-old Henry showed a normal interest in his potential brides. In 1442, as negotiations opened with the count of Armagnac for a marriage with one of his three daughters, Henry sent hurried messages after his ambassadors, 'signed . . . of our own hand, which as you well know we are not accustomed to do in other cases', instructing them to have portraits made of the three girls 'in their kirtles simple, and their faces, like as you see their stature and their beauty and colour of skin and their countenances, with all manner of features' so that he might select the one that he preferred.[8] Although the tale of how Henry later requested a portrait of Margaret is a later concoction,[9] it seems unlikely that he would have been indifferent to her appearance. Upon her arrival in England, Henry adopted a chivalric tradition in her family by paying her a visit in disguise, dressing up as a squire to deliver a letter to her that he had written. While Margaret was busy with the letter, she paid him no attention and apparently dismissed him afterward, none the wiser. Upon learning somewhat later of her letter-bearer's actual identity, Margaret was said to be mortified that she had kept him on his knees.[10] Whether she really had no idea who he was may be open to question. If, as seems likely, she did suspect he was the king, the visit and her overt response involved a kind of play-acting that emulated the characters and conventions of chivalric romance.[11]

While it is impossible at this remove to assess the private quality of Henry's and Margaret's marriage or each partner's feelings for the other, they do appear to have gotten on rather well. During the early years of their marriage, prior to 1453, they spent considerable time together.[12] Henry's attitude towards his marriage appears to have combined sober commitment with attentiveness to his

[5] Ibid., p. 164.

[6] Griffiths, p. 235, for the first suggestion. The incident was reported by Piero da Monte, the papal tax collector for England, in a letter to the archbishop of Florence (published in Schofield, 'England and the Council of Basel', pp. 93–4).

[7] Wolffe, p. 305, observes that from mid-August 1456 until 10 July 1460, when he was captured by the Yorkists at Northampton, Henry spent a third of his time in abbeys and priories.

[8] *EHD*, IV, pp. 256–7.

[9] As demonstrated by Cron, 'The "Champchevrier Portrait"'.

[10] Warnicke, 'Henry VIII's Greeting', pp. 578–81, for the development of the ritual in Margaret's family; *CSP, Milan*, I, pp. 18–19, for the anecdote.

[11] Warnicke, 'Henry VIII's Greeting', pp. 575–6; idem, *Anne of Cleves*, pp. 48–9, 131–2.

[12] Griffiths, p. 257 and n. 133, p. 271.

wife's interests. In January 1445, as preparations for Margaret's arrival went forward, Henry sent the 'ryng of gold, garnished with a fayr rubie' that had been used for his sacring at his coronation in Paris to be broken up and remade as Margaret's wedding ring.[13] In March, while she was being feted at Rouen prior to her departure for England, she was presented with a hackney, 'splendidly equipped, with an empty saddle', as a gift from her husband-to-be.[14] A year later, in March 1446, Henry was instructing John Spryngwell of Norfolk to obtain horses for the queen – coursers, palfreys, hackneys, sumpter horses and others – for riding and other uses.[15] Margaret's interest in good horseflesh is attested by her own letter to John Godwyn, asking that he obtain and bring her a certain mare and colt, which had apparently caught her eye.[16] The king and queen may also have shared some interests. On 30 March 1448 Henry granted Margaret a license to found Queen's College at Cambridge, in response to her petition.[17]

In other circumstances the length of time it took Henry and Margaret to produce a child would not necessarily have been so catastrophic. The man who eventually challenged Henry's throne, Richard, duke of York, and his duchess had been married for about ten years before they had children. They wed sometime before October 1429, when he would have been eighteen and she, fourteen years of age.[18] Their first child, a daughter named Anne, was born on 10 August 1439 when the Duchess Cecily was twenty-four, a little older than Margaret when her son was born.[19] By the end of 1455 the couple had produced a dozen children.

Nevertheless, the circumstances of Henry's lengthy minority and an heir presumptive – Humphrey, duke of Gloucester, Henry's uncle – without legitimate offspring heightened public sensitivity to this aspect of Margaret's role as queen. Upon Gloucester's death in February 1447 with no sign of a direct heir to Henry VI on the horizon, the dynastic succession became an even greater question mark. Possible candidates to be regarded as the next heir presumptive included John Holland, duke of Exeter (who died the following August and whose claim then passed to his son Henry), Richard, duke of York, and Edmund Beaufort, earl (soon to be duke) of Somerset.[20] Of the three, York alone could claim descent from Edward III through a legitimate male line; Exeter and Somerset inherited through either a female or a bastard line.[21] If inheritance

---

[13] Foedera, V, I, p. 139.

[14] Joubert, 'Le mariage de Henry VI et de Marguerite d'Anjou', p. 322.

[15] Foedera, V, i, pp. 139, 158.

[16] Monro, p. 131.

[17] Discussed below, p. 66. CPR, 1446–52, pp. 143–4; Searle, History of Queen's College, pp. 15–26, for Margaret's foundation of Queen's College, with copies of all the relevant documents.

[18] Johnson, pp. 1–2. The duke was born on 22 September 1411; the duchess, on 3 May 1415.

[19] GEC, V, p. 213, note g. Margaret was born on 23 March 1430; her son on 13 October 1453.

[20] For a discussion of this vexed issue and of the contemporary importance of lineage, see Griffiths, 'Sense of Dynasty'. Cf. Johnson, pp. 99–100, for a different view of the choices posed by Gloucester's death.

[21] Although the Beaufort children of John of Gaunt had been legitimated in 1397, they had been excluded from the royal succession in 1407 (CPR, 1396–99, p. 86; CPR, 1405–08, p. 284). Theoretically at least, this exclusion could have been reversed. Jones and Underwood, King's Mother, pp. 23–4, discuss this issue and conclude that the alteration to the patent made in 1407 was not binding on Henry IV's successors.

through a female was permitted, then York had an additional claim that was better than Henry's own – a claim that he ultimately made. Margaret's failure to produce the anticipated heir as promptly as many must have hoped exacerbated the insecurities and rivalries inherent in this situation.[22] As a result she incurred public wrath and ridicule that eventually made possible later charges that her son was a changeling or a bastard.

Rumors about the couple's failure to produce a child began to surface as early as October 1446. At first, blame was cast upon Bishop Aiscough of Salisbury, the earl of Suffolk and others for keeping Henry from having 'his sport' with the queen.[23] While there is no particular reason to suspect Aiscough of such advice,[24] the hazards of early childbearing were well known, and it is possible that the couple initially delayed conjugal relations until Margaret was older.[25] Nevertheless, the fact that René of Anjou sent representatives to England with his daughter to witness and report her coronation before he signed off on the treaty of Tours suggests that they would also have been able to assure him that the marriage had been consummated.[26] In 1448 a disgruntled felon being held in Canterbury gaol accused his neighbor in the isle of Thanet of complaining that

> oure quene was non abyl to be Quene of Inglond, but and he were a pere of or a lord of this ream he woulde be on of thaym that shuld helpe to putte her a doun, for because that sche bereth no child, and because that we have no pryns in this land.[27]

For the record, we should note that the felon also accused his neighbor of coin clipping and of taking woolsacks by night into the marsh to sell to smugglers ('Frensshmen of Depe'). Thus it appears that his primary concern was to implicate his neighbor in *something*, most likely to mitigate his own sentence. Nevertheless, the accusation of treasonable language constitutes a credible charge; like the coins and the wool it seems to represent a kind of thing known to have been going on, whether the neighbor was actually guilty or not.

The imprisonment in 1451 of Thomas Young, one of the duke of York's councilors, illustrates the aggravation of political tensions at the center as a result of the queen's continued failure to produce a child. Young had proposed in parliament that York be formally recognized as heir presumptive. This would have intensified existing rivalry between the dukes of York and Somerset. If it also implied that the queen was barren, it would have insulted Margaret as well.[28]

In this atmosphere Margaret must have felt increasingly pressured to produce an heir. Later in life she would complain of poor health having interfered with the rigorous fasting that she undertook during times of 'many

---

[22] Griffiths, p. 675, discusses the problem of the succession as it impinged on York.

[23] Wolffe, p. 17, citing PRO, KB9/260/85.

[24] Griffiths, p. 256, notes that since 'Aiscough . . . had married the royal couple . . . he, more than most, would have longed to see the dynasty secure'.

[25] Parsons, 'Mothers, Daughters', pp. 63, 65–68.

[26] Devon, *Issues*, p. 452; Cron, 'Duke of Suffolk', pp. 82–3, suggests that they witnessed the marriage.

[27] *HMC, Fifth Report*, p. 455a, citing M. 238, 1448 in the dean and chapter of Canterbury Archives.

[28] Jones, 'Somerset, York and the Wars of the Roses', p. 289 and n. 2.

sufferings and tribulations', surely a reference to the years after 1453.[29] If she resorted to similar fasting in the earlier years of her marriage, it likely would have exacerbated the couple's fertility problems, whatever their other causes. Early in her marriage Margaret made at least two visits to Becket's shrine at Christ Church, Canterbury, which had some associations with fertility.[30] Since this would have been too soon to posit extraordinary concern upon her part, the visits probably also reflected conventional piety and perhaps a sharing of her husband's interest in a particular and popular site.[31] The same cannot be said, however, of her visit to the shrine of Our Lady of Walsingham in the spring of 1453.[32] Walsingham had particular appeal to women for its reputed efficacy in supplications involving pregnancy and childbirth.[33] It seems that Walsingham – and possibly a journey there – had been on Margaret's mind for several months. On 1 January 1453 the queen's 'year's gifts' included an offering for Walsingham of a gold tablet with the image of an angel holding a cross, embellished with pearls, sapphires and rubies, her costliest gift that year apart from her gift to the king.[34] Although Margaret could not have been certain of her pregnancy so early, she may have been hopeful.[35] Thus, the gift to Walsingham has rather the look of a pledge-in-advance, and Margaret's visit would have fit a typical pattern of giving personal thanks at the appropriate shrine after the miracle or cure had taken place.[36]

The news of Margaret's condition was received with signs of genuine joy and, no doubt, relief. Henry expressed his own pleasure in a lifetime annuity of £40 awarded to Richard Tunstall, the esquire of the body who informed him of it.[37] He also obtained a 'demy ceynt' – identified in the warrant as a jewel of some sort – for Margaret during her pregnancy.[38] Though he would not learn of the

---

[29] Morrison, *Women Pilgrims*, pp. 164–5, from *Calendar of . . . Papal Registers, 1458–1471*, pp. 273–4.

[30] Searle, *Chronicle of John Stone*, pp. 39–40, 42; Morrison, *Women Pilgrims*, p. 18. Margaret's visits were in September 1446 and September 1447.

[31] Searle, *Chronicle of John Stone*, pp. 40, 42, 43, 45, 50–1, 52, 56, reports visits by Henry VI in November 1446, December 1447, March and December 1448, February 1450, August 1451 and April 1453. Wolffe's itinerary verifies all of these visits except for the ones of February 1450, which it places in 1451 (p. 368), and April 1453, but indicates that Henry also was at Canterbury in September 1447 at the same time as Margaret (p. 366). It is impossible to know whether Margaret accompanied her husband without being mentioned on his other recorded visits.

[32] A letter from the duchess of York to Margaret somewhat later in the year mentions their meeting after the queen left the shrine (published by Rawcliffe, 'Richard, Duke of York', pp. 232–9, who misdates their meeting to 1452). Davis, *PL*, I, pp. 248–9, has demonstrated that the queen visited East Anglia in the spring of 1453 rather than in 1452. Johnson, p. 122, n. 110, citing BL, Egerton Roll 8364, conclusively establishes the timing of her visit by a night she spent in Hitchin with the duchess of York in April 1453.

[33] Morrison, *Women Pilgrims*, pp. 3, 17–18, 23–9, 32. Hall, *English Medieval Pilgrimage*, p. 122, attributes the later interest in Walsingham of Henry VIII and Catherine of Aragon to their 'longing for a male heir'. Henry visited the shrine immediately after the birth of his son in 1511 and sent it more offerings after the child died. Two years later Catherine wrote of her plans to go on pilgrimage there, as she had long since promised.

[34] Myers, 'Jewels', pp. 115, 124.

[35] If the birth was a week overdue, it is 'just possible' that Margaret suspected something at the beginning of January, though hopefulness has never had to depend upon suspicion! I am grateful to Claire W. Culver, C.N.P., for her calculations in this matter.

[36] Noted by Finucane, *Miracles and Pilgrims*, p. 92.

[37] *RP*, V, p. 318, reports the annuity in Tunstall's exemption from the act of resumption of 1455. I have found no evidence of it in the patent rolls.

[38] Stevenson, II, ii, pp. 507–8. Payment of £200 for it was ordered on 20 October 1456.

child's birth until the end of 1454 upon his recovery from illness, he was clearly happy then to find that he had a son.[39]

Positive feelings extended well beyond the immediate circle of Henry and the court. The City of London provided the king with monetary gifts on 2 May, 1 August and 8 August 1453.[40] Although the situation in France would have increased financial pressures on the crown in that year, these dates – the last two in particular – may also reflect knowledge of Margaret's pregnancy. When Cecily, duchess of York, wrote to the queen in the latter half of 1453, she described the child whom Margaret was carrying as 'the most precious, most ioyfull, and most confortable erthely tresor that myght come unto this land and to the people therof' and wished that God might send the queen further offspring 'for the greete trust and most confortable suerty and wele of this realme and of the kynge's true leige people of the same'. There is no reason to suspect insincerity.[41] From Duchess Cecily's point of view, the presence of a direct heir or heirs to the king would eliminate the question of whether or not the duke was heir presumptive, which had been a source of suspicion and a focus of rivalry. Her husband's claim to be the king's 'obeisant liegeman' despite his pointed criticism of the government would become more credible as it became more difficult to charge that he was driven by personal ambition.[42] A letter of 19 August from John Tanner to the prior of Christ Church, Canterbury, shows how word of the queen's pregnancy spread. Tanner had on that day learned of Margaret's condition from a master Jakys Hawte, who had come looking for the prior, having just received the news from his wife.[43]

More striking and significant, however, were parliament's protection and continuation of Margaret's existing privileges and the grant to her by charter of new ones on 21 July 1453: full royal judicial rights on her estates and a life-right to all moveables forfeited to the king.[44] R.A. Griffiths has noted the extra-ordinary nature of the latter grant, but his attribution of it to Margaret's 'good relations with the king and her good accord with this parliament' somewhat understates the case.[45] Certainly by the end of July the queen's pregnancy would have been known, and it seems likely that in some sense the grant was her reward.

Despite the sudden onset of Henry's illness in August 1453 – or perhaps to preserve a sense that all was well[46] – plans for the much-anticipated birth went forward. On 10 September the mayor and aldermen of London turned out in

---

[39] Gairdner, *PL*, III, p. 13.
[40] Barron, 'London and the Crown', pp. 93 and 106, n. 34. The grouping of three gifts so close together also seems somewhat unusual.
[41] Rawcliffe, 'Richard, Duke of York', p. 234. For the letter, see pp. 237–8.
[42] For a more detailed discussion of York's situation, see below, pp. 151ff. By this time he had become an outspoken critic of the duke of Somerset over the latter's role in Normandy. Their rivalry was exacerbated by the succession question.
[43] *HMC, Various*, I, p. 223, from the dean and chapter of Canterbury Archives, Christ Church Letters, vol. I, no. 63. Though several persons named James or Jakys Haute can be found around this time, a positive identification of any one of them as this particular man has not been possible. See W. Davis, *Ancestry of Mary Isaac*, pp. 156, 170–2.
[44] *RP*, V, pp. 229, 258–263; *CCR, 1447–54*, pp. 390–2; *CPR, 1452–61*, pp. 114–16.
[45] Griffiths, p. 261; see also Johnson, p. 123, n. 114.
[46] Griffiths, p. 721, suggests an initial attempt at a cover-up.

scarlet to convey Margaret ceremoniously by water to Westminster for her lying-in. The dukes of Somerset and Buckingham also accompanied her.[47] There on 13 October, the feast of the translation of Edward the Confessor, Margaret gave birth to a son who was promptly named Edward in honor of the saint. Bells were rung, and the *Te Deum* was sung.[48] Giles St Lo, Margaret's butler and usher of her chamber, brought the news to London and received a purse from the common council containing ten marks sterling as a reward.[49] Messengers carried the news to Canterbury and, we may presume, to other parts of the kingdom as well.[50] On the fourteenth, Bishop Waynflete of Winchester, who was also Henry's confessor, baptized the prince, while Cardinal Kemp, archbishop of Canterbury and chancellor of England, the duke of Somerset and the duchess of Buckingham stood as his godparents.[51] There was no stinting on the ceremony. Ten pounds were spent on wax candles, and a total of £554 16s. 8d. was paid for the infant's embroidered chrisom-cloth, along with 20 yards of russet cloth of gold and 540 brown sable-backs, probably for the queen's churching.[52]

Nevertheless, despite the joy that undoubtedly accompanied the birth of an heir, it seems that there was talk. 'Bale's Chronicle', which provides the most elaborate account of the prince's birth, also reports that 'peple spake stranngely' about it.[53] The strange talk alluded to could have involved a number of things: the length of time that it had taken the king and queen to produce an heir, the recent loss of France and its implications for the infant's future, or uncertainties regarding the king's health being the more obvious. Although the gossip may have involved questions regarding the child's legitimacy, there is no particular reason to believe that it did, and it is clear from the passage as a whole that the chronicler assumed the child to be the rightful prince and heir. Indeed, this is the only chronicle that even hints that the prince's birth might have been regarded with skepticism. All others report it in matter-of-fact terms that preclude such doubt: 'the Quene was delyvered of a fair Prynce', 'the furst sone of kyng Harry (was born)'.[54]

Several years later, however, explicit allegations about the prince and his mother began to appear. On 23 February 1456 one John Helton was drawn, hanged and quartered for making bills charging that Prince Edward was not the *queen's* son.[55] Not surprisingly under the circumstances, Helton recanted before dying. This incident did not occur within a contextual vacuum: two days later the duke of York was forced to resign his second protectorate. Helton's execution is indicative of rising tensions amid the political jockeying for position that accompanied the king's resumption of authority. Margaret was

[47] CLRO, Journal V, fol. 120.
[48] Flenley ('Bale's Chron.'), p. 140.
[49] CLRO, Journal V, fol. 125b; for his career see Griffiths, p. 782, and Myers, 'Household of Queen Margaret', p. 405.
[50] Searle, *Chronicle of John Stone*, p. 87.
[51] Ibid.; *English Chron.*, p. 70.
[52] Myers, 'Household of Queen Margaret', p. 425 and nn. 4 and 5. The issue roll entry is published in Devon, *Issues*, p. 478; Hookham, *Life and Times*, I, p. 435.
[53] Flenley ('Bale's Chron.'), p. 141. The author was a Londoner (*EHL*, pp. 95–6).
[54] *London Chrons.*, p. 169; *English Chron.*, p. 70; cf. 'Benet's Chron.', p. 210, *Three Chrons.*, pp. 69, 149; *Great Chron.*, p. 186.
[55] 'Benet's Chron.', p. 216: 'Edwardus princeps non fuit filius regine.'

undoubtedly one of the persons, if not the chief person, lobbying for York's ouster. The events of the past year, from the battle of St Albans to the establishment of the second protectorate, had given her ample reason to regard him with suspicion.[56] While York still clung to the protectorate, a newsletter of 9 February reported that his discharge had been expected that day, but that the duke's appearance at parliament together with the earl of Warwick and 300 armed men left matters unresolved. Though some said that King Henry was amenable to keeping York as his 'chief and principall counceller' during pleasure, the Yorkists' appearance in arms had given others second thoughts. Opinion divided on whether York would manage to keep his protectorate on its original terms or not. The writer concluded this portion of his letter with the pithy observation: 'The Quene is a grete and strong labourid woman, for she spareth noo peyne to sue hire thinges to an intent and conclusion to hir power.'[57] Though I have found no direct link between York and Helton, the latter's charges seem very much a part of this ongoing dynamic.

Rumors of some sort continued to circulate through 1457. In late March the London common council warned the City companies not to meddle in affairs touching the king, queen or prince, but to curb their tongues and utter any unseemly, scandalous or disgraceful words at their peril.[58] The warning followed a Coventry meeting of the king's council in which York was berated for 'inquieting' the realm.[59] In October a royal commission went to Norfolk to inquire into 'any treasons, misprisions, insolences or slanders committed by [a] John Wode . . . against the king's person or majesty or royalty and against the persons and honour of queen Margaret and prince Edward'.[60] Although the exact nature of the gossip is unspecified, it is difficult to imagine anything other than allegations concerning lineage and legitimacy that would impinge upon the honor of a three-year-old prince and his mother.

At the end of the decade, probably following the Yorkists' attainders in autumn 1459, such allegations can be identified as an active part of their propaganda.[61] Instead of questioning Margaret's motherhood, however, they denied her chastity. The *English Chronicle* reports that 'the quene was defamed and desclaundered, that he that was called Prince, was nat hire sone, but a bastard goten in avoutry'.[62] Despite the ambiguous 'hire', the context makes it clear that Henry's fatherhood – and Margaret's chastity – were being questioned. Shortly before the Yorkists' invasion in June 1460 an anti-Lancastrian ballad was affixed to the gates of Canterbury, in which the reference to 'fals heryres fostred' alludes in more circuitous fashion to the prince's alleged bastardy.[63]

How, then, did one rumor turn into another? Why the shift in view,

---

[56] See pp. 119–23, below.

[57] Gairdner, *PL*, III, pp. 74–5.

[58] CLRO, Journal VI, fol. 117b.

[59] *RP*, V, p. 347.

[60] *CPR, 1452–61*, p. 404.

[61] I discuss them more fully within that context on pp. 176–8, below.

[62] *English Chron.*, p. 79. For all his Yorkist bias, the chronicler seems not to credit the bastardy charges (ibid., p. 70).

[63] Ibid., pp. 91–2.

regarding both the nature of the prince's 'disability' and the nature of the queen's 'transgression'?

It seems likely that the earlier rumor had its inception in some offhand remark about how long it had taken Margaret to conceive. Since women generally bore the blame for infertility,[64] some contemporaries may have thought that if it had taken her so long to become pregnant, the child could not possibly be hers. In 1456, as Margaret began to move against York and to 'interfere' in public policy, any such doubts would have been ready at hand. The actual allegation that the prince was a changeling could serve a dual purpose. First, it attacked Margaret directly as a woman: she could not do what a proper woman would do, which was to have a baby. But also, obliquely, it drew attention to the impropriety of what she was doing instead.[65]

As politics polarized between a Yorkist faction and a more amorphous group of Lancastrian loyalists with Margaret as their shadow leader, and as the stakes in the conflict escalated, the rumor was co-opted by the Yorkists to serve a particular political agenda. Along the way, the approach shifted away from questioning Margaret's ability to questioning her morality. This is certainly the gist of certain remarks attributed to Richard Neville, earl of Warwick, in 1460: that 'royal power [was then] in the hands of [Margaret] and those who defile the King's chamber'.[66] On 15 March 1461, Prospero di Camulio, the Milanese ambassador to the court of France, skeptically reported that Margaret was said to have poisoned King Henry after getting him to abdicate in favor of his son, and that she planned to marry the duke of Somerset.[67] These allusions to infidelity and sexual promiscuity constitute charges that were particularly and uniquely damaging to a woman's reputation. Their understood effect would have been to discredit her in all other areas as well, through a process of association.[68] Moreover, by insinuating that disorder existed within the royal family, they bolstered perceptions of disorder within the wider realm.[69]

More important, as it became clear that York would claim the throne, it was necessary to cast doubt on Henry's paternity in order to undermine Prince Edward's claim to present and future loyalty. Thus, very shortly after the Yorkist victory at Northampton there was an upsurge of rumors that the prince was not King Henry's son.[70] The need to foster such rumors became even more acute after Henry's deposition. On 27 March 1461, Camulio reported to Francesco

---

[64] Cadden, *Meanings of Sex Difference*, pp. 251–3.

[65] Parsons, *Eleanor of Castile*, p. 66, observes that 'when [the queen] was seen to intrude herself into the political sphere, critics dwelled on the corruption of her idealized domestic roles as wife and mother'.

[66] Pius II, *Commentaries*, II, p. 269. Head, 'Pius II and the Wars of the Roses', p. 145, n.18, suggests that this section of the *Commentaries* was written after Henry's deposition in 1461.

[67] *CSP, Milan*, I, p. 58. The Somerset in question would have been Henry Beaufort, son of Edmund, who had been killed in the first battle of St Albans in 1455. He had become the Lancastrians' military commander.

[68] Levin and Sullivan, *Political Rhetoric*, p. 6; Howell, *Eleanor of Provence*, pp. 149–50, for the use of personal slander to discredit an earlier queen; Macdougall, *James III*, pp. 54–6, for rumors of promiscuity regarding Margaret's contemporary, Mary of Guelders; Levin, 'Power, Politics, and Sexuality', pp. 101–2, for similar criticism of Elizabeth I. Christine, *Treasure*, pp. 56, 74–6, 86–7, 89–105, 115–17, 150–2, 171–5, returns again and again to the value of chastity in her advice to women.

[69] See below, p. 178; Maurer, 'Delegitimizing Lancaster'.

[70] *English Chron.*, p. 98; 'Benet's Chron.', p. 226; *CSP, Milan*, I, p. 27.

Sforza, duke of Milan, that the English were saying that 'his Majesty [Henry VI] remarked at another time, that [Prince Edward] must be the son of the Holy Spirit, etc.' Camulio dismissively labeled such talk as no more than 'the words of common fanatics, such as they have at present in that island'.[71] Nevertheless, it was vital to the Yorkists, while their ability to hold the throne remained uncertain, to do what they could to deny the possibility of any Lancastrian lineal claim beyond Henry.

Though it is not implausible that a queen in Margaret's situation might have had an extramarital affair, there is no concrete evidence that she did.[72] Nor is there any reason to believe that Prince Edward was not both Henry's and Margaret's child. Contrary to rumor, Henry appears to have behaved in all respects as if he thought the child were his.[73] Yet it is easy to see how such charges would find a use in Yorkist propaganda at the point when it was beginning to promote the superiority of York's lineage to Henry's. They also provided a gendered criticism of the Yorkists' leading opponent, a 'grete and strong labourid woman' who was perceived to have transgressed the boundaries of her proper place. In western society women have tended to be held accountable, first and foremost, for their sexuality. To charge that the prince was a changeling or the product of adultery was to attack Margaret directly as a woman, making her sexuality the stand-in for all the other things that some people were beginning to find objectionable about her.

---

[71] Ibid., p. 58.

[72] It must be conceded, however, that such an affair could not have been allowed to leave traces; it would have been covered up.

[73] See above, pp. 43–4; also Scofield, *Life and Reign of Edward IV*, II, p. 463, for a message from Henry expressing concern for his wife and son in 1464, while he was at Bamburgh and they were in France.

Part II

MEDIATIONS

4

Business-as-Usual

WHILE the political and dynastic circumstances attending Margaret's marriage to Henry VI led to heightened expectations of what their union would accomplish, the marriage also brought with it a whole series of less far-reaching and more immediately concrete assumptions on the part of her new people. Individually and collectively, they expected Margaret to do certain things for *them*: in short, to exercise the 'good ladyship' that was the prerogative of social standing, and to do so on a queenly scale.

In its most basic terms, good lordship/ladyship can be defined as favoring, protecting, or otherwise nurturing the interests and well-being of certain lesser persons. The practice created its own returns by encouraging loyal service and by providing the dispenser with supporters, friends and future influence. But it also had a moral dimension: benefaction was regarded as a duty of the greater towards the lesser, an expression of right order within a correctly ordered and ranked society, that was promoted in the 'mirrors' and other literature of the time.[1] On our part as latter-day observers there is a tendency, implicit in the definition itself, to view the corresponding activity from the point of view of the dispensing lord or lady. We see that he or she attempted to provide in various ways for a variety of people, and we note the extent to which these efforts were successful. Even the observation that a particular man gained office through the influence of another becomes a commentary on that other's ability to provide. What this ignores is the extent to which the dispensing of good lordship/ladyship actually involved a kind of symbiotic interaction between the dispenser and the intended recipient.[2] It is clear, however, that the recipient could not have been indifferent to the benefits that he or she stood to receive; they did not simply materialize unlooked-for out of the blue. In fact, the designated benifactee or his/her friends often took the first step in seeking them out.[3] This does not involve a difference in kind in the activities involved, but requires a shift in perspective on our part. In the case of Margaret of Anjou, it demonstrates the expected and accepted nature

---

[1] E.g., Jacobus de Cessolis, *Caxton's Game and Playe of the Chesse*, pp. 50–1, 53–4; Christine de Pisan, *Treasure*, pp. 77–9; Gower, *Mirour de l'Omme*, lines 12937–72, 13057–152, 15349–16080; Hoccleve, *Regiment of Princes*, lines 4643–746.

[2] Mertes, 'Aristocracy', pp. 48–51, 54, 56; Horrox, 'Service', pp. 63–70, provide a good sense of this symbiosis.

[3] Mertes, 'Aristocracy', p. 48.

of her activities as good lady and patron, even when some of her specific efforts were rejected or resented.

As a further point, which also has broader implications for an understanding of women's role in the social and political fabric of late medieval England, good lordship/ladyship frequently involved acts of mediation or even outright intervention. Indeed, personal mediation was an integral part of social and political interaction on all levels; it should not be thought of as something originating outside of and occasionally impinging on the system, but as part of the system itself and an aspect of business-as-usual.[4] As such, it was not a specifically gendered activity: both men and women appear in mediating or intermediary roles. In the case of women, however, who were by their gender systematically denied access to formal office and the institutional channels of power that went with it, the role of mediator/intermediary provided a means to exert influence via informal channels embedded in the system.

This observation may call into question the separation of public and private spheres, dear to the hearts of feminist theorizing and much of women's historiography. Although it is true that women's activities have often been limited to the private sphere of hearth and family, leaving the public, political realm for men to bustle in,[5] the boundary between the two seems, in fact, to have been somewhat porous at this time.[6] This situation was especially true of queenship. Although gender placed limitations upon the queen, as it did upon other women, she 'hardly ever occupied a purely domestic arena . . . the marriage that entailed her submission to [the king's] authority guaranteed her exaltation at his side'.[7] So positioned, the queen was peculiarly able to use the 'interstices' of power: as an intercessor with the king, as the educator of her children and as patron. As John Parsons notes, these 'informal, relational areas allowed queens [and other wives] to traverse the cloudy limits between unofficial and official, margin and center, "private" and "public"'.[8] The point I wish to make here is somewhat different: that although these 'interstitial areas' could be of particular use to women, whose access to power was otherwise limited, some of them, at least, were as likely to be inhabited by

---

[4] A simple definition of this might be 'whatever informal processes or interactions occur in a particular society to make things happen or to get things done'. Although much of the discussion involves patronage, I prefer this homegrown term, both for its evocation of a broad range of ordinary activities and for its emphasis on process over outcome.

[5] There is little agreement on when such relegation first took place or when it increased. Anthropologists have tended to view the phenomenon as something that 'is'; historians have tended to place the (increasing) separation of the two spheres either within or adjacent to their own periods of expertise. For the anthropological view see Rosaldo, 'Woman, Culture, and Society', and Reiter, 'Men and Women in the South of France'. Rosaldo later expressed caution regarding the use of the public/private model in 'The Use and Abuse of Anthropology'. For some historians who have placed the separation anywhere from the ninth to the sixteenth century, see Schulenburg, 'Female Sanctity'; Facinger, 'A Study of Medieval Queenship'; McNamara and Wemple, 'The Power of Women through the Family'; Howell, 'Citizenship and Gender'; and Kelly-Gadol, 'Did Women have a Renaissance?' Such differing results do not necessarily invalidate each other; rather they attest to the complicated nature of the problem and the inescapability of individual perspective in dealing with it.

[6] Orlin, *Private Matters and Public Culture*, and Schwoerer, *Lady Rachel Russell*, have observed the intermingling of private and public affairs and the lack of a clear distinction between them in early modern England.

[7] Parsons, *Eleanor of Castile*, p. 66.

[8] Ibid., pp. 249–50.

men.[9] A man's ability to play the intermediary in the course of business-as-usual was a source of esteem and a necessary component in contemporary assessments of his power.[10] This suggests two things. First, that in a society where politics operated on a personal level and where political participation depended in large part upon one's connections, we would be wrong to assume that an unofficial, private act (such as playing matchmaker or recommending a person to minor office) was necessarily devoid of political implications.[11] But secondly, although only men were openly acknowledged to have political lives, my study of Margaret suggests that women were also expected and called upon to do things within the intermediary system that were known to have directly political consequences. To explicate this I will consider among other things the phenomenon of female networking.[12]

While the permeability of the boundary between public and private spheres could be used to empower the queen, it also left her at permanent risk of being perceived as a transgressor. Through a series of circumlocutions, she might succeed in obtaining unusual power while maintaining an appearance of propriety, but the need to maintain the enabling mask ultimately hindered her effectiveness. This was the trap in which Margaret later found herself.

Margaret's extant letters provide a window upon her efforts to act as 'good lady'. To the extent that they have been studied or used as evidence, their treatment is as revealing of the assumptions and milieu of the persons citing them as it is of Margaret herself. Writing in the early 1870s, Mary Ann Hookham found in them 'agreeable [evidence of a] new and charming phase in [Margaret's] character', in which she, apparently full of good Victorian sentiment, sought time and again to forward the course of 'true love' and to secure preferment for her clean-living clerks. Although Hookham was dismayed to note that many of Margaret's efforts were ignored (and seems to have assumed by extension, but without proof, that most or all came to naught), she describes Margaret's letters as non-political as if this were an accolade.[13] In the postwar 1940s, J.J. Bagley made a similar observation that 'there is not a single letter of political importance' among them and dismissed them as revealing no more than Margaret's 'active and officious part in that social life which was a by-product of the political world', along with her ill-considered – and I am tempted to add 'female' – impetuosity.[14] Since then, studies of patronage and women's history have taken the field. Regarded as an example of patronage, Margaret's letters show her 'care . . . to offer preferment to those who served her' as well as her own resourcefulness and

---

[9] Watts, pp. 87–90, discusses the quasi-public, quasi-private nature of the royal household and observes (p. 88) that within it 'every private place, *man* or function had the potential to acquire public significance' (emphasis added).

[10] Present-day references to an 'old boys' network' attest to the longevity of such notions.

[11] I consider those matters 'political' that have some direct impact on official policy or institutions or that affect the public relationships between people.

[12] For a later example of a woman whose informal influence was sought in political matters by men and women alike, see Schwoerer, *Lady Rachel Russell*, pp. 190–7. Many of her activities involved female networking.

[13] Hookham, *Life and Times*, I, pp. 380–7; the quotation is from p. 381. These observations and those that follow all apply to the collection published by Monro.

[14] Bagley, *Margaret of Anjou*, pp. 56–7.

persistence as a patron.[15] Appreciation of the customary nature of Margaret's activities in this area has added to the picture.[16] But this ongoing analysis can be taken further. The letters can, in fact, elucidate some of the issues suggested above. It will be clear from my earlier comments that I am inclined to view the practice of good lordship/ladyship more as a process than as a result, and that I see it as a process in which the specific favor or benefit is usually actively sought. It should also be clear that I am less certain than Hookham or Bagley that all these letters are apolitical. Although some of them assuredly are, by anybody's definition, others are not. Instead, it seems that many of the letters inhabit positions on a continuum of human interaction where both personal mediation and personal intervention are necessary components of business-as-usual. One end of the continuum phases into what we recognize as politics, but it does so with no clear sense of a boundary having been crossed.

Before proceeding to the argument, a few words are in order about the letters themselves and the kind of sample that they provide. My sample consists of eighty-two letters written between 1445 and 1461, all but one of which come from a late fifteenth-century commonplace book.[17] Seventy-four of them were edited and published by Cecil Monro in 1863; I have included the seven that he missed,[18] plus one additional letter that fits into the general pattern of business-as-usual.[19] I have omitted a remaining handful of extant letters that do not fit this pattern: Margaret's part in the three-way correspondence over Maine, already discussed;[20] a letter requesting holy water from Canterbury that almost certainly had to do with Henry's illness; one written shortly before Henry's deposition, when Margaret and her army were threatening London, and another written during her exile.[21]

Eighty-two letters are not many, as samples go, and they can only represent a portion – we cannot be sure what portion – of the total number of letters that Margaret wrote in the ordinary course of what would eventually prove to be an extraordinary queenship. Nevertheless, I would argue that they can in some sense be considered representative since they cover a variety of different interests and actions taken by Margaret either on her own behalf or on behalf of her servants and other supplicants. To aid my own analysis of the letters I used a simple statistical analysis. The numbers it produced should be regarded as suggestive rather than sacred.[22]

Only fourteen of these letters represented efforts made purely in Margaret's own interest.[23] All of the others were written on behalf of or in the interest of

[15] Griffiths, p. 258.

[16] Dunn, 'Margaret of Anjou', pp. 117–21.

[17] BL, Add. MS 46,846.

[18] Two more letters that he published as 'Margaret's' actually belong to Henry VI. See Otway-Ruthven, *The King's Secretary and the Signet Office*, pp. 119–20, for a somewhat more recent assessment of the manuscript.

[19] *EHD*, IV, p. 280; from Exeter Cathedral, MS 3498/23.

[20] See above, pp. 31–7.

[21] Discussed below, pp. 115–16, 190, and 207.

[22] The diagram on the next page will assist in following the numbers.

[23] Eight involved the preservation of game for her hunting pleasure or other sport-related requests (Monro, pp. 91, 100–1, 106, 131, 137, 141, 143); three concerned the payment of her dower from the

MARGARET OF ANJOU'S LETTERS

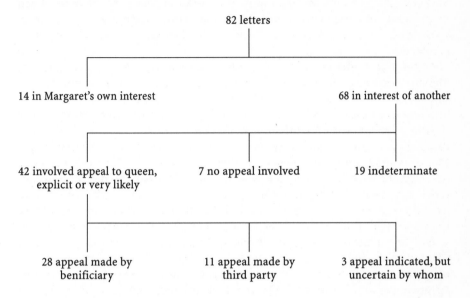

another person.[24] Of this group, forty-two – well over half – involved an appeal for intervention or mediation to Margaret, either by the letter's beneficiary or by a third party on the beneficiary's behalf.[25] Only seven of the sixty-eight letters did not seem to involve an appeal, and the nineteen remaining were of indeterminate status in that I could see no way to decide whether an appeal had been made. In short, within this sample a relatively large number of persons were asking Margaret for favor, aid or intervention, either for themselves or for others. That they asked or otherwise planted their ideas in Margaret's head further indicates their assumption that she did these sorts of things in the course of business-as-usual; moreover, that there was some likelihood that her efforts would be successful (a different matter from our knowledge after the fact that some of them failed).

So what were these things that people expected Margaret to do? They looked for her help in obtaining an office or position, a marital partner, charitable aid,

customs of Southampton (ibid., pp. 112–13, 148); two had to do with construction or repair (ibid., pp. 140–1; BL, Add. MS 46,846, fol. 43b–44), and one was a circular letter demanding immediate attendance (ibid., fol. 33).

[24] In three of these, Margaret also had a specific interest of her own. In the first she asked that John Lory, a cordwainer, be excused from attending inquests in London during the time that he was working for her; in the second she requested exemption from customs duties for Antony Hewet of Rome, who was bringing valuables into the country for her personal use; and in the third she requested more general favor from the port officers for her mother's chaplain, who was about to journey back to her – as the bearer of messages, we may presume (Monro, pp. 111, 123, 136–7). Though it may be argued that Margaret had a residual interest in all of her efforts to dispense favor, these were the only letters where her private interest was so clear.

[25] In thirty-one an appeal was explicitly indicated; in twelve more it seemed highly likely, based upon the letters' context, content and wording.

or more general favor or favored treatment from someone else. They sought her protection from harassment and the pressure she could exert to bring about a settlement or redress of grievances. All of these activities involved some form of mediation or intervention; in a number of instances Margaret either requested or pressured another person to perform the actual mediating act. A look at some specific examples from her letters will help to put these matters in perspective.

All but one of the third party appeals were made by persons identifiable as Margaret's servants, and most of their requests were for help in obtaining a secular position for someone else.[26] Thus, the 'instance and supplication of certein our servants attendinge right negh aboute oure personne' prompted her to write to the mayor of Southampton and his brethren to request that Robert Bedale be admitted to the office of water bailiff.[27] When Edmond Clere ('our squire') sought Margaret's help in getting 'his cousin T. S.' made sergeant of Norwich, she wrote to the bishop, Walter Lyhert, who was also her confessor, to enlist his good lordship towards T. S. since 'the Mair, Aldermen, and Commonaltie of . . . Norwich . . . wol be gretly reuled and demened by you in this partie'.[28] But Margaret's servants also sought other favors and interventions. They spoke up in support of one T. Bugdon, whose marriage, said to be lawfully contracted, was being resisted mightily by the girl's father; and on behalf of Ralph Josselyn, a draper of London said to have been wrongfully disseised of some property.[29] In the first instance she sent a strong but diplomatic letter to the recalcitrant father, requiring him to cease all further obstruction 'otherwise thanne right lawe and good conscience asken and requiren in this partie'; in the second, she wrote somewhat more circumspectly to the duke of Exeter, who had been enfeoffed in the disputed manor by Josselyn's opponents, appealing to his 'good and naturale disposicion towards the faver and tendernesse of trouth and justice' (as opposed, presumably, to his disposition towards his own self interest) to stay out of the squabble and let the draper have his manor back. As a last example of the range of requests from third parties, Piers Preston, a yeoman of the crown, appealed to her for help in obtaining alms for a poor couple who wished to wed; Margaret responded with a letter to the executors of Cardinal Beaufort, who had left the residue of his goods for just such charitable purposes.[30]

---

[26] Seven out of eleven letters, written on behalf of five different persons, sought secular positions. The exception involved a formal request from the king that she see to the delivery of some oaks for timber that he had granted as a gift from her 'outwoods' of Kenilworth, a part of her duchy of Lancaster endowment (ibid., p. 156). Margaret relayed the message to her chancellor William Booth, requesting him to issue the proper warrant to her keeper. This seems much more of a direct business deal than the requests from her servants, who ultimately relied upon her personal favor; nevertheless, it represents a 'third party request' by Henry on behalf of his grantee.

[27] Ibid., p. 113.

[28] Ibid., pp. 119–20. It appears that she intended that his mediation support her own letter to the city in favor of T. S. For other letters of this type, see ibid., pp. 140, 158–9.

[29] Ibid., pp. 125, 107–8. In the latter case the appellant was acknowledged to be heir to the property 'by negh possibilite'.

[30] Ibid., p. 102. Two more of Margaret's letters seek charitable aid in the form of care and shelter (ibid., p. 95, and BL, Add. MS 46,846, fol. 56b). Although their wording suggests the presence of an appeal ('we be enformed that . . .'; 'for asmoche as we understand that . . .'), it cannot be determined whether

Already, in these few letters, we can see Margaret performing as good lady in several different ways in response to various appeals. The letters show her, her appellants and occasionally the recipients of her letters all playing the role of intermediary in order to get things done. The things that she is asked to do are not gender specific; fostering marriage, for example, was not merely a 'female' activity. As an important socio-economic strategy that affected the wealth and status of the families and individuals involved, it was of interest to males from the king on down.[31] The fact that these appeals were made by third parties underlines the notion that they were accompanied by some expectation of success. Part of the appeal of being a servant lay in the opportunities it provided to distribute aid or favor to someone else within the system and to accrue esteem as a result.[32] There would be no point in approaching Margaret for any of these matters if it were not thought likely to succeed.

Though we may also assume that these 'third party' appellants regarded their various appeals and Margaret's resulting actions as normal and proper, the same cannot automatically be said of all the recipients of her letters. Good ladyship from one perspective could be perceived as unwonted interference from another. A clear instance of resentment and rejection is presented by the case of Alexander Manning and the sheriffs of London. Manning was the keeper of Newgate gaol in 1450. It appears that he got wind of a plan to replace him at Michaelmas; in retaliation he turned the prisoners loose on Michaelmas eve and they immediately created havoc.[33] On 7 October 1450 the mayor and aldermen declared that his custody of the prisoners had been negligent, 'to the great disturbance of the city', and determined that he should lose his office and be imprisoned himself 'until it be otherwise advised'.[34] At some point during this imbroglio, most likely before his actual removal and before he resorted to drastic action, Manning's situation came to the attention of 'certein [of Margaret's] servants right negh attending about [her] personne', who appealed to her for help. The result was two letters, written to the 'sheriffs that next shall be' of the City of London and to the mayor. These letters are undated; I have used their tone and content to place them in the chronology of events.[35] In the first, written to the sheriffs, who held the office of Newgate in their gift, she recommended Manning to the office of keeper,

> to the which, as we understand, he is right hable and suffisant, both in his trouth and discrecion and also in his governance, like as, for the tyme that he

such appeals would have been made by third parties or by the beneficiaries themselves. My own inclination is to think that these situations were brought to Margaret's attention by third parties.

[31] Waugh, *The Lordship of England*, pp. 32–52, and 190–3, for the king's interest in marriage as a means of strengthening the bonds of lordship between himself and his subjects and between his subjects themselves.

[32] Horrox, 'Service', pp. 66, and 68, for the pleasure taken by John Paston III in recommending John Stratton as a potential servant to his own master, William, Lord Hastings.

[33] Griffiths, p. 646. 'Benet's Chron.', pp. 202–3, specifically blames the keeper ('custos') for the incident; 'Bale's Chronicle' (Flenley, p. 135) simply reports the prison revolt on Michaelmas eve.

[34] CLRO, Journal V, fol. 48. The translation is Monro's, p. 161n. Michaelmas term began on 6 October.

[35] Monro, pp. 162–3, nos. 132 and 133. My reconstruction of events reverses the order in which Monro believed these and the next letter to have been written.

occupied it herbifore, he was founden of good bering and of sad disposicion, as
it is said,

and asked that he be admitted to it at Michaelmas. The letter to the mayor
requested that he excite and stir 'the shirefs that shalbe for the nexte yere, to
admitte [Manning] to the said office at Michelmasse nexte commyng, after
th'entencion of oure writying unto theym in that bihalf'. In tenor these are
much like other letters that Margaret wrote in support of office-seekers. Though
perhaps not impossible, it does seem unlikely that she would have given such a
positive recommendation to someone known to have misbehaved badly while
in office; to have done so would only have courted ill will. Whatever the case
may have been, Margaret's recommendation was ignored; Manning was
removed from office as planned and apparently punished.

Margaret wrote a further letter to the sheriffs on Manning's behalf – it would
seem to the new ones, now ensconced in office. This letter was indeed
peremptory and heavy-handed:

> Trusty and welbeloved, we suppose verreily that it is clerely in yor remembrance
> howe that, now late, for certein consideracions and grete instance, we wrote unto
> you for the recommendacion of Alexandre Mannyng unto th'office of keper of
> Newgate, longyng unto yor disposicion, as it is said, wherin as yet oure said
> writing hath take noon effecte ne expedicion, unto oure greet merveil; wherfore
> we desire and praye eftesones, right affectuously, that, at reverence of us, ye wil
> accepte and restore the said Mannynge ageine unto the said office, withe suche
> tendernesse and faver, that he may perceive thise oure lettres unto him avvailable,
> to th'accomplissement of oure entencion in this partie.[36]

The letter bears only a partial date of 'the xxiii day'. I assume that the month
would have been October, for on 5 November 1450 the mayor and aldermen
concluded that because of his negligence 'Alexander Mannyng, late Keeper of
the gaol of Newgate . . . shall not hereafter be readmitted, by any future sheriffs
of the City, to occupy or exercise the office aforesaid, in any manner
howsoever'.[37] This measure seems to have been taken in response to Margaret's
pressure. Since the office was in the sheriffs' disposition, as she herself
acknowledged, it appears that the objection was not to her recommendation
of a person per se, but to her perceived encroachment on their territory,
particularly after her blatantly demanding final letter. It was a bad bit of
business on Margaret's part, for it won her no friends in the City.

The stipulation that these 'third party' requests involved secular positions
automatically raises the question of how clerical positions were handled. The
evidence of Margaret's letters indicates that the search for benefices followed a
different course. For one thing, it appears to have been understood that she
would be on the lookout for positions for her unbeneficed clerks. In a letter to
Master Gilbert Kymer, chancellor of Oxford and dean of Wymbourne Minster,
she indicated that she had 'certein right good and notable clerks, of grete fame
and vertueux disposicion, attending in our service, as yet by us unpromoted,

[36] Ibid., p. 162, no. 131.
[37] CLRO, Journal V, fol. 51. The translation is Monro's, p. 161n.

and destitute of benefices' in the hope that he would keep this in mind when a prebend at Wymbourne next fell vacant.[38] In only one instance, involving a disputed position, does the phrase 'we be enformed' in her letter indicate that someone had specifically gone to her for intervention. Her other letters, recommending a person to a specific position or asking that the next available benefice in a particular place be reserved for someone, show no evidence of any appeals having been made to her, though it does seem likely that someone would have notified her of existing or impending vacancies.[39]

In a majority of the cases where an appeal to Margaret was either explicitly indicated or seemed highly likely, it was made directly to her by the person(s) concerned rather than through a third party intermediary. Most of these came from persons with a prior connection to Margaret, where good ladyship might be expected as a matter of course, but there are some where a previous connection is less clear or perhaps nonexistent. Typical of the direct appeals of persons connected to Margaret are requests by her tenants for protection from harassment. When she learned that the threats of Edmund Pyrcan, squire, had caused William Southwode, her bailiff of the lordship of Hertingfordbury, to go in fear of his life, she sent a strongly worded letter to Pyrcan advising him to leave Southwode and her other tenants in peace or risk her displeasure, 'at yor peril'. She did allow, however, that 'in case ye finde yow agreved ayeinst any of oure seid tenants there, yf ye will compleyne yow unto us, or oure counceil, ye shul be remedied, as the case justly requireth'.[40]

It made good sense, of course, to acknowledge that complaints against her own people were possible and to hold out the promise of a just response to legitimate grievances. Although we don't know just how far Margaret would have gone towards accommodation, some evidence that she meant what she said may be found in her letter of 17 August 1448 on behalf of the abbess and convent of Stratford le Bowe. In it she directed her masters of horse, aveners, purveyors and other officers of her stable to

> take no goodes of thaires ne logge in any of theyre houses in the same towne. But suffre theim peicibly tenioye theire livelode to theire most availe and proufitte withoute attempting interupcion or empechement to the contrarie of this present graunt and proteccion at yor peril for thus it pleaseth us to be doon.[41]

Although the letter does not explicitly indicate that the abbess had appealed to Margaret, the specificity of her orders – particularly the part about lodging – leads me to believe that a complaint had been made and that this was Margaret's response.

[38] Monro, p. 136.

[39] Ibid., pp. 91–3, 129, 138, 139, 157, 164.

[40] Ibid., p. 126. Other letters involving the protection of her tenants may be found on pp. 99, 122–3, 127–8, 146–7, 154, and BL, Add. MS 46,846, fol. 57. For a somewhat similar group of letters involving protection or some form of legal intervention on behalf of various individuals who were not Margaret's tenants, but who seem to have been associated with her as servants or employees, see Monro, pp. 100, 111, 124, 149–50, 150–1. Almost half of all of these letters were written to persons who were expected to act as further intermediaries, either by putting a stop to certain actions of their own servants or by acting as arbiters in the resolution of disputes.

[41] BL, Add. MS 46,846, fol. 44.

It was also possible for appeals to be made to the queen by persons who had
no prior association with her and whose business did not directly concern her.
This was the case with 'oon William Dorset', who sought Margaret's aid
regarding 'divers injuries and disheritances doon unto hym and his wyf'.
Margaret forwarded Dorset's petition along with her own letter on his behalf
to the archbishop of Canterbury, who, as Monro observed, was likely to have
been chancellor at the time. Her letter asked that a remedy be found so that
Dorset might have whatever was rightfully his.[42] In this instance, it appears that
Dorset's motivation in petitioning the queen was simply to go to the top. His
letter demonstrates the range of persons who could appeal to the queen for
intercession.

Another matter, of which the letters offer tantalizing hints, is the possibility of
female networking within the system of intermediaries. The clearest example of
this, taken from outside my sample, may be seen in the letter written to
Margaret by the duchess of York in the late summer or early autumn of 1453.
This letter was occasioned by the duke's estrangement from the king's favor,
which understandably was causing him 'infinite sorrow, unrest of hert and of
worldly comfort'. The duchess wrote to assure Margaret that her husband was
in fact 'as true, and as humble, and as obeisant liegeman . . . as any creatur on
lyve' and to plead with her 'to be a tendre and gracious meane un to the highnes
of our said soverayn lord for the favour and the benewillence of his hand to be
showid unto my said lord and husbond'.[43] It is not clear whether the duke had
asked his wife to approach the queen in his behalf[44] – a possibility that is not at
all unlikely – or whether the duchess, perceiving the problem, had decided for
herself to try to mend things. In any case, the basic structure of the situation
remains the same: here was a woman appealing to another woman to try to
patch things up between their men. The letter also makes clear that a similar
supplication (or perhaps the initial stages of this one) had been made by the
duchess in a previous face-to-face meeting with the queen in spring. It scarcely
needs to be pointed out that the matter being negotiated by these women was
highly political in its implications.[45]

With this as introduction to the subject, two of Margaret's letters that seek
female favor and mediation take on added interest. In the first, addressed to the
duchess of Somerset, Margaret noted that the king had granted her squire,
Robert Edmunde, the sum of 360 francs and was presently writing to the duke
in his behalf, apparently to ensure that the money should be paid. That was, in
fact, the heart and nub of Margaret's own concern, for she wrote:

> We desire and hertly pray yow, that, atte reverence of us, ye will, by yor good
> and tendre mediacion, shew herin such diligence to th'accomplissement of my
> lord's entencion, that oure said squier may rejoisse [enjoy] my said lord's

[42] Monro, p. 116. The archbishop in question could have been John Stafford, John Kemp or Thomas
Bourgchier, each of whom served for a time as chancellor between 1445 and 1455.
[43] Rawcliffe, 'Richard, Duke of York', pp. 237–8.
[44] As claimed by Rawcliffe, 'Richard, Duke of York', p. 233.
[45] See below, pp. 90–1, 96, for a discussion of this letter within the context of Henry's breakdown in 1453
and the factional crisis precipitated by his illness.

graunt, and the rather by contemplacion of this oure prayer; as oure full trust is in yow.[46]

Monro regarded this letter with a certain huffiness: 'that such a letter, requesting the "mediation" of the wife of the minister with her husband, that effect might be given to a royal grant, should have been deemed requisite or fitting' was quite beyond him, and could only be regarded as yet another proof of Henry's weakness.[47] In reality, it looks like yet another aspect of business-as-usual, which recognized that in order to make something happen, certain things had to be done, often in various ways and more than once. If we are to read some special significance into this letter, apart from the queen's obvious interest in seeing that the grant be paid (and since Edmunde was 'her squire', she may have lobbied for it in the first place), it may be that Margaret had a more objective view of Somerset's failings[48] – and how to get around them – than she is generally credited with having. On another occasion she wrote directly to him on behalf of John, Viscount Beaumont, who had letters from the king requesting that he be 'recompensed and seen unto after his estate, and after the quantite of lyvelod that he hath lefte in the counte of Manor [Maine]', and asked Somerset to see to it.[49] In 1448 Charles VII had granted compensation to the English who had lost their lands in Maine. Somerset (who had himself lost property) was lieutenant and commander-in-chief in France and Normandy at the time and was expected to divide this money among its intended recipients. Unfortunately, he was also perennially short of funds needed to maintain the English presence, and York would later charge that he had embezzled the money.[50] Beaumont appears to have been the only landowner in his predicament – apart from Somerset himself – to have actually received recompense, perhaps a testimony to the efficacy of the queen's mediation.[51]

The second of Margaret's letters involving female networking was written to an unnamed woman whom Monro could only identify as either the duchess of Suffolk or the duchess of Somerset. In it, Margaret first thanked the recipient for the favor she had already shown towards her clerk of the signet, George Asheby, 'as mene to yor husbande . . . towards expedicion of payment of his wages deue unto him by the [late] Duc of Glouc[ester]', then asked that she continue her efforts in this matter.[52] Taken together, these two letters, along with the duchess

---

[46] Monro, p. 118.

[47] Ibid., p. 117.

[48] Thomas Basin's contemporary character description makes much of his 'insatiable avarice' and desire to add other's goods to his own (Basin, Histoire de Charles VII, ed. Samaran, II, p. 66).

[49] Monro, p. 119. Beaumont, described as 'Henry VI's confidant' (Griffiths, p. 262), had been created count of Boulogne in 1436 and granted the feudal viscountcy of Beaumont in France in 1441 (GEC, II, p. 62). Meanwhile, he had become steward of the honor of Leicester in 1437, whence he drifted into Margaret's service as did many others of Henry's officers and servants, becoming her chief steward in 1452. In 1459 he was made chief steward for the northern parts of the duchy of Lancaster (Somerville, History of the Duchy of Lancaster, p. 421).

[50] Jones, 'Somerset, York and the Wars of the Roses', pp. 297–9; Gairdner, PL, I, p. 107.

[51] Jones, 'Somerset, York and the Wars of the Roses', p. 298 and n. 5. Beaumont had been appointed constable of England in 1445; Somerset replaced him in 1450. Both men belonged to Henry's inner circle, but it is difficult to know just what they thought of each other.

[52] Monro, p. 114. The similarity in subject matter to the first letter may suggest that the recipient was again the duchess of Somerset; however, the greeting of that letter was addressed to Margaret's

of York's letter, provide evidence of the informal, yet accepted role that women played as intermediaries. Nor should the importance of such female participation be underestimated.[53] While letters, petitions and warrants could always be set aside at least temporarily, even when they came from the king, the attentions of one's wife might have been harder to ignore.

A third letter hints at a wider scope of possibility in its suggestion that women could and did take part in 'delegations' – at least before the queen. In it, Margaret reproached Sir John Forester, knight, for his harassment of her tenants of Hertingfordbury, informing him that 'this same day, ther have be bifore us a greete multitude, *both of men and women* . . . compleyning them that ye have, and yet be, dayly, about to destroie and undo them for ever'.[54] None of the other letters regarding her tenants' complaints specify the exact makeup of the complaining parties. Yet it seems likely that women were present, since on a comparable occasion shortly before Henry's – and Margaret's – deposition the petitioning body clearly included women. When Margaret's Lancastrian army had routed the Yorkists at the second battle of St Albans and recaptured the king, the City of London, fearful of the queen's intentions and the likelihood of her vengeance upon them, sent a delegation to negotiate composed of the duchess of Bedford, the duchess of Buckingham and Lady Scales, along with a selection of unidentified clerks and curates.[55] Clearly, women were expected to play an official, public and political role in certain circumstances.

Nevertheless, it would be a mistake to argue that women were not, as a group, politically disabled or that their ability to function as independent participants in public life was not severely limited. The women's delegation just noted bears this out. They were called upon in a specific instance to perform a specific task. It was a task, moreover, that they undertook on behalf of men: the mayor and aldermen of London, whose own ability to negotiate their way out of a difficult and threatening situation had been compromised by their previous support of the Yorkists. The women were to act as representatives and intermediaries until the situation cleared. They had not been invited to become full and continuing participants in the political life of either the City or the realm.

Twelve of Margaret's letters involve a kind of 'follow-up' to acts already taken or concurrently being taken by Henry. I have discussed three of them already. One was her letter to the duchess of Somerset asking that she lobby her husband to see that Henry's monetary grant to Robert Edmunde be paid.[56] I rejected Monro's view that Margaret's appeal to the duchess should be regarded as an

---

'cousine', as the greeting of this was not. The duke of Gloucester died in early 1447, and the duke of Suffolk was murdered in 1450. Greater proximity to Gloucester's death may make Suffolk seem the more likely candidate, but there is really no reason to assume that the arrears of Asheby's wages would not have dragged on much longer.

[53] Mendelson and Crawford, *Women in Early Modern England*, p. 231, suggest that such cooperation among women gave them a kind of 'collective power'.

[54] Ibid., p. 127, emphasis added.

[55] CLRO, Journal VI, fol. 10 [Binder 4, photopage 454]. The churchmen are mentioned in *London Chrons.*, p. 173.

[56] See pp. 60–1, above. The other letters involved Henry's grant of timber from one of her estates and the recompense of Viscount Beaumont for lands lost in Maine (p. 61, above).

impropriety that would not have occurred but for Henry's weakness. Nevertheless, the question that he raised is in some sense a fair one, even though the way in which he raised it may be more revealing of his own nineteenth-century assumptions regarding 'woman's place' than it is of the reality of Henry's power as king. Henry was, undeniably, a weak king. It will be useful to examine Margaret's other follow-up letters to ascertain her interest in these cases and the need, if any, for her intervention.

In some of these letters the accomplishment of whatever it was that Henry had done or granted would not seem to have been in any doubt. Instead, it appears that Margaret wished to associate her own favor with his, perhaps to provide a demonstration of her own good ladyship, and to apply pressure to nudge some grants more swiftly through the bureaucratic pipes than may have been usual. All of these factors are clearly present in a letter to the archbishop of Canterbury, in his position as chancellor, regarding a pardon granted to Alice Marwarth, 'a poore widowe'. The letter indicates that Margaret herself had requested the pardon – the bill, signed by Henry, was being conveyed to the chancellor by one of her servants 'sealed under oure signet' – and that she was anxious to have the letters patent expedited.[57] In a less detailed, but similar, vein a pair of letters asked that prompt attention be given to the formalization of two grants of office. Though Margaret was probably instrumental in obtaining the first, for someone identified as 'our welbeloved Maister J.C., late clerke and familiar servant of oures', the second is less certain.[58] A further two letters seem simply to associate Margaret with the king's favor.[59] In all of these instances, it appears that the queen had taken a special interest in the beneficiaries for one reason or another; whether she played the role of instigator in obtaining Henry's favor towards them or not, she wished to be associated with it. At the same time, the ultimate success of these grants would not seem to have been dependent upon her involvement.

A very different situation may obtain in the case of Margaret's Enfield tenants who were troubled by officers of the City of London. To the mayor, aldermen and sheriffs she wrote:

> Albeit that it hath pleased my lord's highnesse to take oure tenants of Enfeld into his proteccion . . . as it appereth by his grant therof under his signet; yet, nevertheles, summe of yor officers, havyng no rewarde [regarde] thereto, unadvisely toke fro day to day the horses of our said tenants, into [unto] greet contempte of my lord's proteccion, and to oure displeasir. Wherfore, we pray you that at reverence of us ye will geve in comandement unto all yor officers t'obeie my said lord's proteccion, suffring our said tenants to leve in quiet and rest in that bihalf. So that we have no cause to pourvei other remedie in yor defaulte, as we trust you.[60]

---

[57] Monro, p. 160.

[58] Ibid., pp. 132 and 128, the latter simply on behalf of 'W'.

[59] Ibid., pp. 142, 147. The first was written to the customers of the port of Boston in support of an annuity granted to John Wenham and his wife upon their marriage; the second supported letters of safe conduct granted to Guille Alany, the master of the Breton ship the *Jenet*.

[60] Ibid., p. 99.

One naturally wonders what 'other remedie' Margaret may have had in mind if the king's protection of her tenants – which she had probably requested – continued to be disregarded; it was not apt to have been pleasant. Indeed, what she seems to be saying here is that if the City officers persisted in disobeying the king, they would have to answer to her, with a strong warning not to press their luck. It would be helpful to know when this letter was written and under what circumstances; unfortunately, it is undated, and the recipients are not identified by name.

A somewhat similar letter on an entirely different subject – the promotion of the queen's chaplain John Hals – may help to elucidate the power relationship between king and queen, which can only be perceived and understood as it impinged upon their subjects. This situation illustrates both the possibilities and the limitations of the queen's position, and it also shows how Margaret had to represent herself in order to take advantage of the one while having to overcome the other.

John Hals became one of Margaret's chaplains soon after her arrival in England, and in due course she set out to procure his advancement, as she had done for others.[61] In 1453 she enlisted the help of the duke of Somerset and the earl of Wiltshire to secure for him the archdeaconry of Norwich.[62] In September 1455 he received papal provision to the bishopric of Exeter at Henry VI's request, but was unable to assume office. Early on in the duke of York's first protectorate, the position had been promised to George Neville, the earl of Warwick's younger brother, and the establishment of York's second protectorate in November assured that such promises would be kept. Hals bowed out. He became the queen's chancellor in 1457, and in that same year both she and Henry recommended him to the deanery of Exeter. There must have been resistance, or at least foot-dragging, for on 31 October the king wrote to the chapter to remind them of his recommendation, 'wherein we trust for certain that you have done and will do your part and diligence to the accomplishment of our desire in this matter', and to assure them that his will was 'immutable'. It was, on the whole, a mild letter.[63] Margaret's own letter to the chapter, written a week later, was not. Remembering 'how that both my lord and we have now lately written unto you at various times our several letters of especial recommendation [for John Hals]', she proceeded directly to the business at hand:

> Whereupon since our said writing we understand by various reports made to us that some persons of you, having no regard that my lord is your founder, whose request you owe in duty to obey before all other, labour the contrary of my said lord's intention and ours, to our great marvel and displeasure if it be so. Wherefore we desire and heartily pray you forthwith that . . . you will . . . be inclined and yield to the accomplishment of my lord's invariable intention and ours in this matter, giving my lord's highness and us no other cause than to have

[61] See Emden, *Oxford*, II, pp. 856–7, for Hals's career.
[62] Myers, 'Jewels', pp. 115 n. 2, and 129. She gave them a pair of inexpensive gold rings worth 4s. 6d., apparently to authenticate whatever communication she had with them.
[63] *EHD*, IV, p. 281, from Exeter Cathedral, MS 3498/22.

everyone of you according to your desert in such things as you may have to do towards us both, for your preservation and also otherwise in tender remembrance of our good grace for this in time to come.[64]

Edward Ellesmere, Margaret's master of the jewels, conveyed both letters to Exeter. Hals was admitted to the deanery in 1457 and held it until his promotion to the see of Coventry and Lichfield in 1459.[65]

If we dissect these letters in order to reconstruct what was happening, several points emerge. First, Henry referred to Hals only as 'our trusty and well beloved clerk'. As Margaret's chancellor, he was more closely associated with her; the idea to recommend him to the deanery was likely to have been hers. Second, Henry did not once mention Margaret in his letter, nor did he indicate that they had jointly recommended Hals. One might ask: why should he? After all, he was the king. And that is precisely the point. In contrast, Margaret referred to Henry repeatedly, being careful to associate her wishes with his and to present her case in a manner that made her indignation and stern words no more than the supporters of his rights and intentions. In 1457 when this letter was written, Margaret's power was in the ascendant; as the author of the *Brut* observed, 'the gouernance of the Reame stode moste by the Quene & hir Counsell'. Yet, for all the steel in her words – so notably absent from Henry's letter – she could only allude to her own power through indirection. Possessed of real power but lacking authority of her own either as woman or as queen, she could only give voice to her power in support of her husband's, the king's, authority. My contention is that Margaret had power, but no legitimately recognized – or recognizable – authority. As Henry's wife, her only means of 'legitimating' her public exercise of political power, which amounted in some sense to her rule, was to continue to appeal to Henry's authority as king and to continue to claim an intermediary status for her own actions as representations or manifestations of his authority.

It must be emphasized that the only thing unusual about Margaret's representing herself in such a manner was the use to which she ultimately put it. As noted above, she associated her favor with Henry's in various instances where his action or grant was the definitive factor and the outcome would not seem to have been in any doubt. She also appealed to his authority, as in the case of her tenants of Enfield, or enlisted his support for a candidate whom she had already recommended to become the next prioress of Nuneaton.[66] When both king and queen wrote to William Gastrik on behalf of a yeoman of the crown who wished to marry Gastrik's daughter, it may have been a matter of shared interest in support of their servant and a sense that two letters

[64] Ibid., p. 280, from Exeter Cathedral, MS 3498/23. This letter is also printed in *HMC, Various*, IV, pp. 85–6.
[65] Emden, *Oxford*, II, p. 857, considers him to have been something of a reformer on the grounds that he was reputed to have appointed 'learned and discreet men' to the see's prebends. He remained loyal to Margaret; on 20 January 1461 he was among the lords who took an oath at York to persuade Henry VI to uphold the agreement recently made between Margaret and Mary of Guelders, queen regent of Scotland, for aid against the Yorkists, perhaps in return for the marriage of Prince Edward to a sister of James III. For more on the Lincluden agreement, see pp. 191–2, below.
[66] Monro, p. 164. This letter is undated but must have been written before 2 November 1451, by which date Maud Everingham was prioress (*CPR, 1446–52*, p. 500).

were more persuasive than one.[67] If Monro's dating of the letter to Gastrik is correct, both it and the previous one were written some time before Margaret's ascendancy. In other words, they show her associating her wishes with Henry's in the more normal course of business-as-usual, where questions of relative power – or whether either of them was really in control – intrude upon simpler matters of mutual reinforcement, and where Margaret automatically and perhaps unthinkingly placed herself in a supporting role, even when, as in the case of Nuneaton, the idea to promote a particular candidate had originally been hers.

A somewhat similar situation may be observed outside the context of the letters in connection with the founding of Queen's College. In later 1447, perhaps in emulation of Henry's own foundations, Margaret formally petitioned the king to grant her license to found a college at Cambridge, as no English queen had ever done before, 'to conservacion of oure feith and augmentacion of pure clergie . . . and to laud and honneure of sexe femenine'.[68] On 30 March 1448 Henry granted her a license and the lands on which to found her college; she issued her own letters patent on 15 April. In the main, her charter simply repeats the provisions set forth by Henry on 30 March, though in her own name; however, the text makes clear that she is acting together with him in establishing the college.[69] Although Margaret seems to have had a clear sense of her value and worth as a woman – a value and worth she was willing to proclaim and intended to commemorate – she understood her role and her place in the terms of her own time, which made her, by definition, a subordinate and supporting figure. Later, when she became an acknowledged political actor, the need to maintain an image of subordination worked to undermine her efforts.

[67] Monro, pp. 153–4. Monro believes the letter was written within a few years of 1445.
[68] Searle, *History of Queen's College*, pp. 15–16.
[69] Ibid., pp. 18–26; the king's grant of 30 March is also printed in *CPR, 1446–52*, pp. 143–4.

5

Cade's Rebellion

THE UPRISING known as Jack Cade's Rebellion provides a further instance when Margaret's influence was associated with an action ostensibly taken by Henry. In this case, however, much more was at stake than individual benefaction. The granting of pardon to hundreds of persons at a crucial moment in the course of the rebellion helped to restore a measure of control in a situation where control had largely been lost. If we return to the idea that business-as-usual encompasses a variety of human negotiations and mediations, often conducted on a private level but sometimes having political implications, the strategic pardoning of rebels is a clearly political act. It also represents an extension and magnification of Margaret's accepted role as good lady: if Henry in pardoning the rebels was playing the role of godly king, was not Margaret in her role as intercessor taking the part of the ultimate Good Lady?[1]

Cade's Rebellion ran for more than a month, from late May into early July 1450. Though primarily a Kentish uprising, it also involved significant numbers of men from neighboring Essex, Sussex and Surrey. The rebels' complaints ranged from a list of purely local abuses to national issues involving the king's ministers, the impoverishment of the crown and the loss of Normandy. They drew support from a variety of social strata and at one point occupied London. Long after the rebellion itself had collapsed, popular discontent and its attendant violence continued.[2] At the time that the pardons were offered, the rebels had been driven out of London, but Henry, who had withdrawn to the midlands in the midst of the troubles, was hardly operating from a position of strength. Nevertheless, the situation provided an opportunity for the government to regain the upper hand. Whoever suggested it, the offer of pardon made practical sense: by appealing to persons who may have been having second thoughts, it undermined whatever rebel unity existed. Even the numbers of persons appealing for pardon – whatever their reasons – could be used to weaken rebel resolve.[3]

Be that as it may, the preamble to the pardon expressed something rather

---

[1] Parsons, 'Intercessionary Patronage', p. 148.

[2] Harvey, *Jack Cade's Rebellion*, provides the most detailed treatment of the rebellion and its context. Chapter 6 is especially useful for its discussion of subsequent popular disturbances and continuing disaffection, in particular pp. 131–59, which deal with the immediate aftermath of the rebellion through 1451.

[3] Ibid., pp. 96–7, stresses the importance to the government of seizing this opportunity.

different in its assertion that clemency was the virtue most befitting a king and that he should be to his subjects the kind of ruler that he would wish God to be to him. Having obliquely compared the king's role to God's, the preamble next pointed out the intercessory role played by Margaret's 'most humble and persistent supplications, prayers and requests' in persuading the king to show mercy.[4] It is a little difficult to separate real conviction from conventional rhetoric and to sort out genuine responsibility from window dressing. The connection made between royal clemency and subjects' shame may be sufficient to suggest a practical, as well as a pious, side to the reasoning that went into it, and it may not be amiss to suggest that these motivations coexisted easily. Margaret's intervention, though presented in a formulaic manner, comes across as somewhat more concrete, a view that is supported by the chronology of events and the known or suspected whereabouts of both king and queen.

Matters first came to a head between king and rebels in mid-June 1450, when both sides camped in force at Blackheath outside London. Initially, it appears that Henry was in no mood to bargain and was ready to meet the rebels in arms; his uncharacteristically martial stance may have been a response to the outbreaks of violence and threatening talk that had erupted since the beginning of the year. These, in turn, had been triggered by the losses in Normandy and the growing unpopularity of the duke of Suffolk and others of his circle. In early January, Adam Moleyns, the bishop of Chichester, who had been a co-negotiator with the French and keeper of the privy seal, was murdered. Suffolk himself was accused of treason at the end of the month and placed in the Tower. During this time, as the commons pressed for Suffolk's impeachment, scattered disturbances and brief risings occurred in the southeast.[5] In mid-March, in an effort to 'save' Suffolk from condemnation, Henry ordered him banished. He was murdered on 2 May while attempting to leave England under safe conduct. Meanwhile, the spiral of vituperation directed against Henry's ministers had widened to include the king himself. At the end of March, John Ramsey, a London vintner's servant, was executed for saying that the king would be 'put from his crown'.[6] Around the same time, a commission in Ipswich accused two

---

[4] The full text of the preamble can only be found in PRO, C66/471, m. 13. The section I refer to reads: 'Nos tamen ad nostre mentis intuitum & consideracionem reducentes quod inter illas quas animo fastigioque regio convenit & oportet inesse virtutes nulla magis eum deceat quam clemencia que peccandi pudorem subiectarum plebum mentibus ingerere solet & afferre ac praeter hoc attendentes quod talem exhibere se convenit principem suis subditis qualem sibi esse vult & desiderat supremum & excelsum principem deum hiis & aliis multis persuasi promotique piis consideracionibus & inter alia humilimis ac instantissimis supplicacionibus precibus atque rogatibus serenissime ac amantissime conthoralis atque consortis nostre Regine . . . perdonavimus . . .' ('Nevertheless, recalling to the reflection and consideration of our mind that among those virtues fitting and proper to the royal person and dignity, none befits him more than clemency, which is apt to bring about and put the shame of sinning in the minds of his subject people, and considering as well that it is fitting to show himself such a prince to his subjects as he wishes and desires God to be supreme and high Lord to him, persuaded and moved by these and many other pious considerations, among others by the most humble and persistent supplications, prayers and requests of our most serene and beloved wife and consort the queen . . . we have pardoned . . .') The abstract printed in CPR, 1446–52, p. 338, only attributes the pardon to 'the request of the queen'.
[5] Harvey, Jack Cade's Rebellion, pp. 64–7.
[6] Flenley ('Bale's Chron.'), p. 129; PPC, VI, p. 108; cf. CPR, 1446–52, p. 320, where he is referred to as 'John Frammesley, vynter', and Kingsford, 'Historical Collection', p. 515, which describes him as 'an olde poure man'.

beggars of plotting Henry's overthrow and his replacement by the duke of York. Their 'secret' plot was alleged to have the support of men from Wales, Scotland, and Ireland.[7] Nonsensical as this charge may seem, it may yet be regarded as a barometer of the unease and outright paranoia that had taken hold. Meanwhile, a poem that must have been circulating in the spring complained in remarkably direct language of the crown's impoverishment, which it blamed on persons close to Henry. The poem went on to warn the king: 'Be ware . . . how thou doos; Let no lenger thy traitours go loos', and, as if to ensure that the message was perfectly clear, closed with the lines

> O rex, si rex es, rege te, vel eris sine re rex;
> Nomen habes sine re, nisi te recte regas.[8]

When the rebels at Blackheath refused to disperse, insisting instead that they had come only in support of the king's right, and when a reconnaissance party reported the rebels' strength, the king's council advised Henry to find out what they wanted. Accordingly, an embassy made up of the archbishops of York and Canterbury, the bishop of Winchester, the duke of Buckingham and Viscount Beaumont were sent to talk to them. It may be that the embassy urged the rebels to seek pardon.[9] What is clearer is that after having listened to the rebels' grievances and having promised that the king would consider and respond to them within a specified time, nothing of the sort happened. Instead, Henry proceeded to Blackheath with his army, and the rebels melted away into the night, pursued by companies of the king's men. Up till this point it would seem that clemency was the virtue farthest from the king's mind.

During the next few days, several things happened. One of the king's companies was ambushed and routed, its leaders slain. Other companies apparently turned to indiscriminate destruction throughout the Kentish countryside.[10] Some of the retainers who had been gathering to increase the king's strength, perhaps influenced in part by the behavior of the royal forces, began to take up the rebels' demands and to call for the removal of certain 'traitours aboute the king', an act that could be regarded as mutiny.[11] To quell opposition, Henry permitted the arrest of his treasurer, the hated Lord Say, and Say's son-in-law, William Crowmer, a sheriff of Kent, but had them placed in the Tower where presumably they would be safe. The king was then at the queen's manor of Greenwich. It seems likely that Margaret was with him, and, if she was, it is possible that she spoke to him of pardon. No pardons were offered, however, and Henry moved to Westminster on the other side of the Thames, on the other side of London, and farther from the troubles.

---

[7] Harvey, *Jack Cade's Rebellion*, p. 116; Johnson, p. 79. In June three more men were indicted for complicity in Suffolk's death and for plotting to bring in someone from 'outside the kingdom' to make king, surely a reference to York (Virgoe, 'Death of William de la Pole', pp. 498–502).

[8] Wright, *Political Poems*, II, pp. 229–31: 'O king, if king you are, rule yourself or you will be a king without substance;/You have a title without substance unless you rule rightly.' Lord Say, the treasurer, and Thomas Daniel, an esquire of the body and one of Suffolk's men, were named specifically; the rebels would later execute Say. The poem also charges Suffolk, then still alive, with 'selling' Normandy.

[9] As suggested by Griffiths, pp. 611, 628.

[10] These depredations are described by Harvey, *Jack Cade's Rebellion*, pp. 84–5.

[11] Flenley ('Bale's Chron.'), p. 132; Wolffe, p. 236.

This, apparently, was not far enough. Soon thereafter, despite the pleas of the mayor and commons of London not to abandon the city, that they were prepared to 'lyve and dye with him' in its defense, Henry removed to Kenilworth in the safer midlands.[12] Bagley believed that it was Margaret who persuaded the king to withdraw from London for his own safety, but I have found no evidence to support this contention, and later writers do not suggest her influence.[13]

Once the coast was relatively clear, the rebels gathered again at Blackheath and occupied Southwark on 2 July.[14] The following day, after a brief siege, they entered London, and for the remainder of that and the next two days they proceeded to pillage and wreak havoc. Say, Crowmer and several others were executed. By the evening of 5 July the Londoners had had enough and determined to take a stand to prevent the rebels from reentering the city from their base in Southwark. Fighting broke out on London bridge and continued through the night with heavy losses on both sides, but the rebels could not regain the city. This was the point at which the general pardon was offered, whereupon the rebels either fled or dispersed.[15]

The pardon, issued to Cade (under his alias of 'John Mortymer') and a handful of his followers on 6 July, was granted as a matter of course to several thousand others on the seventh.[16] While it would be unwise to rely on the pardon lists to determine exactly who participated in the rebellion since others may have availed themselves of pardon as a form of insurance against future reprisals,[17] the sheer numbers involved suggest that many felt themselves affected. In issuing the pardons, someone seized the opportune moment, when the tide appeared to be turning, but the rebels had not actually been defeated. Some of the chronicles say that Cardinal John Kemp, archbishop of York and, more pertinently, chancellor of England, was responsible.[18] He would have been the logical chief negotiator; he was himself a Kentishman, and he appears to have been the brains behind some of the king's political moves in the rebellion's aftermath.[19] The decision to act at this point may well have been his. What is certain is that Henry, roughly ninety miles away at Kenilworth, was not in the best position to act upon the rapidly changing situation, even though he remained in communication with London.[20] While it may be that a pardon had been discussed and had even been prepared in the early days of the rebellion, and while it must have been certain from the outset that a pardon would have to be offered to some people at some time, Henry's own behavior

[12] *Three Chrons.*, p. 67. Griffiths, pp. 613–14, suggests that he left London on 25 June and was at Kenilworth by 1 July; Wolffe, pp. 237, 368, puts him at Kenilworth by 7 July.

[13] Bagley, *Margaret of Anjou*, p. 69.

[14] 'Benet's Chron.', p. 200, and 'Bale's Chron.' (Flenley, p. 132) agree on the Southwark date, but put the return to Blackheath on either 29 or 30 June respectively.

[15] 'Gregory's Chron.', p. 193; Flenley (Gough), p. 156; *Brut*, p. 519; *London Chrons.*, p. 161; *Great Chron.*, p. 185; 'Benet's Chron.', p. 201.

[16] Wolffe, p. 238, says that some 3,000 persons received pardon. *CPR, 1446–52*, pp. 338–74, for the pardons issued.

[17] Griffiths, pp. 619–22. The pardon covered all offenses prior to 8 July 1450.

[18] *Three Chrons.*, p. 68; *Brut*, p. 519; *London Chrons.*, p. 161.

[19] Storey, pp. 81–2; Griffiths, 'Duke Richard of York's Intentions', p. 279.

[20] Devon, *Issues*, p. 476.

at Blackheath and after does not support the view that he was particularly eager to grant it. Moreover, Cade's 'hasty departure' after having been granted pardon may reveal his own sense that the negotiators were 'more inclined to clemency than their royal master'.[21] Still, the wording of the preamble, which may have been composed after the pardons were negotiated, probably would have pleased the king, and the fact that it served to defuse the main thrust of the rebellion, even though disturbances continued, would have pleased him more.

How important, then, was Margaret's role? Griffiths considers it 'possible' that she had remained in London, and Wolffe flatly states that she was 'still at Greenwich'.[22] If she had remained near London, it seems likely that her involvement went beyond whatever conversations she may have had with Henry prior to his departure. It is probable that she would have remained in contact with the chancellor. A well-established tradition of the queen's intercession for pardon existed in both literary narrative and ceremonial practice.[23] Yet the act involved more than ritualized performance. Through intercessory appeals the queen asserted her own influence and acquired acceptable power to affect the course of events.[24] Although intercession assumed a limited sphere of action for the queen, it actually operated as an enabling device in the public, political world by bringing mercy and justice into balance through the queen's agency. As in the case of the correspondence over Maine, Margaret's intercessory role helped to construct kingship by allowing the king to temper manly, uncompromising justice without appearing weak.[25] By doing this, it helped to legitimate the act of pardon itself.

If Margaret's role, as presented in the pardon's preamble, seems faintly to echo the intercessory role of the Virgin, it would not have been an unfamiliar echo to the people of her time. In the fourteenth century an English Franciscan had advised:

> When a man seeks to turn aside a king's anger . . . he [first] goes secretly to the queen and promises a present . . . So when we have offended Christ, we should first go to the Queen of heaven and offer her . . . prayers, fasting, vigils, and alms . . . and she will throw the cloak of mercy between the rod of punishment and us, and soften the king's anger against us.[26]

By comparing Mary to an earthly queen, the writer was doing no more than acknowledging the intercessory role that the latter was already presumed to

[21] Harvey, *Jack Cade's Rebellion*, p. 97.

[22] Griffiths, p. 662, n. 215; Wolffe, p. 238. The latter provides no source for his assertion.

[23] Strohm, *Hochon's Arrow*, pp. 99–102, for a discussion of Jean le Bel's highly stylized account of Queen Philippa's intercession with Edward III on behalf of the burghers of Calais; pp. 107–11, for Anne of Bohemia's efforts to effect a reconciliation between Richard II and London in 1392; Parsons, 'Ritual and Symbol', pp. 64–5, for the use of pardon as spectacle at the queen's coronation. Although French queens could grant pardon on their own authority, English queens could only obtain it through intercession with the king. I have found no evidence of pardons being granted as a part of Margaret's coronation ritual.

[24] Parsons, 'The Queen's Intercession', p. 161.

[25] Strohm, *Hochon's Arrow*, pp. 102–5.

[26] Little, *Studies in English Franciscan History*, p. 149, citing Eton MS 34, fol. 10r. The Franciscan, who fl. c. 1320, may have been either John Spiser or Robert Silke (Little, pp. 141, 146).

have.[27] This does not necessarily suggest that any of the rebels approached Margaret to intercede for them, as we know she was approached for all kinds of other, more mundane mediations. Nevertheless, by lobbying for pardon, she automatically placed herself in an intercessory position between the persons to be pardoned and the only authority that could grant it. Thus the pardon in its formal, rather formulaic fashion presented Margaret's role in a way that fitted contemporary assumptions about queenship, political authority and, more generally, the way that society worked.

It should not be thought, however, that Margaret's role in the pardon was merely an effort at peacemaking. As I have argued above, the pardon had the practical purpose of drawing support away from the rebellion. The decision to offer pardon at that particular moment was a bit of hard-nosed politics. That Margaret was capable of a rougher kind of justice is demonstrated by a curious letter, written some fifteen years after Cade's Rebellion and five years after Henry's deposition. In it, a J. Payn gave John Paston a minutely detailed account of his misadventures and mistreatment during and after Cade's Rebellion.

It seems that Payn, who had been a servant of Sir John Fastolf, had been sent by his master to the rebels' second encampment at Blackheath to find out what they wanted and what they were up to. There he was kidnapped by the rebels, who threatened him and eventually 'forced' him to join them in their pillage of London. (At that point in the story, Payn dwelt in loving detail on the various goods and articles of clothing that he claimed the rebels had taken from him.) Adding injury to insult, he was then 'put . . . oute into the batayle atte Brygge' by Cade himself; there he was wounded 'and hurt nere hand to deth' during the six hours that he spent fighting – he does not specify which side he fought upon. At this point the story becomes somewhat hazy, but, pressing on, he picks it up back home in Kent, where 'they' (who are not clearly identified) took all his family's moveables and came close to hanging his wife and five of his children. After that trouble Payn himself was 'apechyed' by the bishop of Rochester to Queen Margaret, who had him arrested and thrown into the Marshalsea, where he lay 'in rygt grete durasse, and fere of [his] lyf, and was thretenyd to have ben hongyd, drawen, and quarteryd' if he did not accuse his master, Fastolf, of treason. Payn refused, was hauled off to Westminster, and would have been sent to Windsor had not a pair of cousins, who were yeomen of the crown, intervened and obtained the king's pardon.[28] This, at least, was Payn's story.

Several observations and connections can be made. A number of persons named John Payn (or Payne) are mentioned in the patent rolls, and two of them received pardons. The first, a John Payne, gentleman, of Merworth, Kent, was among the many who received a general pardon on 7 July 1450.[29] The battle on the bridge ended on the morning of the sixth, and J. Payn's story of what happened to him thereafter cannot be made to fit; therefore, the gentleman from Merworth is not our man.

[27] For further discussion of the Marian associations with queenly intercession, see Parsons, 'The Queen's Intercession', pp. 153–62.
[28] Gairdner, PL, II, pp. 153–6.
[29] CPR, 1446–52, p. 369.

A likelier candidate might be John Payn, a yeoman and a smith of Pecham, Kent, who '[had] submitted to the king's grace' and was pardoned on 2 November 1451 'for all treasons, felonies, murders and trespasses from 7 July [1450] until 10 June last, and of any consequent outlawries and forfeitures; provided that this pardon extend not to misdeeds done on the sea and waters'.[30] Payn was named in three indictments of June 1451, accusing him and others of gathering to assault and kill the king's men and of otherwise disturbing the peace – and in the last indictment, of plotting to depose and kill the king.[31] It is difficult to say how seriously one should take these charges. A scan of the surrounding indictments reveals that a large number of persons were indicted for theft, assault and rape – what might be considered more general mayhem, having little or nothing to do with the politics of either victims or perpetrators, and which likely was encouraged by the continuing presence of political unrest. Since Payn received pardon, the most serious charges were probably exaggerated. In any case, his tribulations better fit the sort of timeline required by J. Payn's account, and they may help to explain the latter's confusing references to loss of goods.

If Payn from Pecham was indeed 'our' Payn, his story needs to be looked at more carefully. For one thing, there is the matter of Sir John Fastolf. It is difficult to imagine why the queen would have wished to accuse him of treason. Instead, he appears to have been highly trusted: he was named to commissions to investigate treasons and other matters in Surrey on 11 April 1450, in Norfolk and Suffolk on 1 August 1450, in Kent and Sussex on 14 December 1450, while on 13 January 1451 he was appointed to a special commission to look into the activities of William Parmynter (or Parmenter) and other specifically designated troublemakers.[32] That leads us to a second matter. Parmynter had become the self-proclaimed leader of a group of die-hard rebels after Cade's death in July 1450. A number of his supporters eventually submitted to the king, 'naked to the waist and with ropes round their necks'. One of these was John Claydych, pardoned on 16 October 1451. His pardon is only a few entries away from Payn's, and although it is more detailed, it also includes the rather unusual exemption of 'misdeeds done on the sea and waters'.[33] Parmynter is not mentioned in Payn's pardon, nor is the business about halters, but a note in the calendar abstract links it to a preceding pardon, which can only be Claydych's. It therefore appears that Payn was suspected – rightly or wrongly – of rather more than his story lets on. Perhaps Fastolf would have known the truth of it, but in 1465 he was dead.

If this identification of Payn is correct, we may conclude that he was in later life an avid storyteller, who was perhaps not averse to creative modification to

[30] Ibid., p. 497. Virgoe, 'Death of William de la Pole', p. 498, associates the exclusion with Suffolk's murder.

[31] Virgoe, 'Some Ancient Indictments', pp. 250, 251, 252. Just to confuse matters, another 'John Payn' served as a juror for at least some of the indictments (ibid., pp. 247, 253).

[32] *CPR, 1446–52*, pp. 381, 388, 435, and 437. Fastolf became more active as Suffolk's influence came under fire. He had previously lost lands to Suffolk in East Anglia (Harvey, *Jack Cade's Rebellion*, p. 71).

[33] *CPR, 1446–52*, p. 497. Harvey, *Jack Cade's Rebellion*, p. 152, notes that a large number of 'unpunished misdoers', including some who had been Parmynter's men, submitted to Henry in such a fashion at Blackheath in February 1451.

suit his own purposes. His purpose in 1465 is suggested by his plea to John Paston 'tendyrly to consedir the grete losses and hurts that your por peticioner heath, and heath jhad [sic] evyr seth [Cade's Rebellion]' and the fact that Paston was Fastolf's executor.[34] In 1465 there was nothing good to be said of Margaret. The story of Payn's harsh treatment at her hands, almost ending in his execution, would have gone down well and perhaps secured him some benefit. But if we 'replace' his story in 1450/51 along with the indictments of John Payn, it seems that in the turmoil that continued long after the rebellion proper had ended, Margaret would have been justified – by her lights – in acting decisively to arrest someone suspected and accused of consorting with known enemies. So much lies in the eye of the beholder: that was true in 1465, as it had been in 1451 and as it would be again in 1453, when the country was plunged into the unprecedented crisis of Henry's madness and perceptions, misperceptions, suspicions and conflicting points of view became the common coin of faction and, ultimately, of civil war.

[34] Gairdner, *PL*, II, p. 153 and n. 3.

Part III

THE CRISIS OF KINGSHIP

6

Context

IN AUGUST 1453 the political landscape of England underwent a dramatic shift when Henry VI fell ill. While there can be no question that he had already shown himself to be a weak king, it is only when the whole of Henry's reign is considered that he emerges as perhaps the greatest disaster ever to occupy the English throne. The crisis of his illness and its aftermath make such a judgment possible.

Thus, Henry's character and the exact nature of his personal inadequacy remain open to question and reinterpretation. He has been depicted as a saintly simpleton and as a willful, if frequently wrong-headed, policy maker.[1] More recently, John Watts has observed the difficulty in distinguishing the king's private personality from his publicly constituted persona, since 'the institutional and conceptual conditions of kingship conspired to make [him] formally responsible for everything done in his name . . . [so that] we cannot know whether the stuff of policy comes from without or within'.[2] Moreover, we must distinguish Henry's behavior after his illness from his behavior before.[3] This is not necessarily to suggest that Henry did not fully recover from his malady, but to observe that his increased passivity in the later 1450s may have owed something to the psychological aftereffects of the experience itself and to the deteriorating political situation that soon followed his recovery.

With hindsight it is easy to say that the resulting situation had been brewing for a long time and that it had many separate components. Henry's competence and kingship had been criticized from the 1440s into the '50s,[4] and there had been scattered outbursts of violence ever since Cade's Rebellion; it is possible that civil war would have come about through a combination of rivalries and disaffections without the trigger of the king's illness. But Henry's breakdown and its attendant uncertainties brought an added urgency to accumulated grievances. Overarching and transforming all of them was the question of what to do about Henry himself. What was to be done when an adult king with no mature heir was completely incapacitated? Who was to rule for him, and

---

[1] Lander, *Conflict and Stability*, p. 68; Wolffe, pp. 132–3.
[2] Watts, p. 106. I am less convinced that the conclusion to be drawn is that policy throughout the reign was consistently the creation of persons other than Henry himself.
[3] Cf. Watts, p. 104, where he cites examples from various points in the reign to argue that Henry's ineptitude was consistent throughout.
[4] Storey, pp. 34–5; Wolffe, pp. 16–18. In May 1448 the London common council admonished the guild wardens to guard their tongues in matters touching the royal person (CLRO, Journal IV, fol. 217b).

under what conditions? These questions brought Margaret to the political forefront even as they made possible an overt power struggle that eventually challenged Henry's throne.

There has been a tendency among historians to acknowledge Margaret's emergence as a political actor but then to shy away from looking at it too closely. A part of the problem lies in the traditional habit of regarding the Wars of the Roses from the perspectives of its male protagonists. There is nothing particularly wrong with that, so far as it goes – men visibly dominated the fifteenth-century English political scene – but it relegates a Margaret of Anjou to the role of adjunct, even when it acknowledges that she became a protagonist herself at some point. On a more concrete level, in Margaret's case it has led to certain assumptions about her activities and her allegiances that have colored our overall perceptions of her role and public personality as queen. Some of them must now be questioned.

A second problem in dealing with Margaret as yet another, albeit more shadowy, protagonist in the struggle – to be assessed as one of the boys, as it were – is that it avoids engagement with the very real issue of her gender.[5] Margaret was not, nor ever could be, simply 'one of the boys'. Although gender did not prevent Margaret from acquiring power, it dictated the terms on which she could obtain and exercise it and, by extension, affected the entire course of political events. With this in mind, the traditional, male-oriented perspective on the Wars of the Roses needs to be rethought and somewhat reconfigured.

To address these issues it will be necessary to jettison or at least to question some of the traditional assumptions about Margaret's position and sympathies in 1453, when the crisis began. Then, in reconstructing and reassessing the developing situation with Margaret as a central figure, several questions will need to be considered. When and why did she become the duke of York's dire enemy? Why did she unexpectedly put herself forward as a political contender? How, specifically, did her gender impinge upon the temporary 'resolution' to the crisis by the establishment of York's protectorate in 1454, a matter that prefigures its continuing influence upon subsequent events? While we may lament the opacity of Margaret's role and thinking at the precise moment when she made her bid for recognized authority,[6] sufficient evidence exists in scattered places to resolve some matters beyond question. By correlating what we have it may be possible to suggest a general outline to the problematic rest.

In discussing the crisis of Henry's illness it makes sense to begin with the event itself and the nature of the problem it posed. Stripped of our hindsight knowledge of the denouement, it is the context in which Margaret's actions – and those of all the other protagonists – have to be understood. Henry was staying at the manor of Clarendon, near Salisbury, when according to 'Bale's Chronicle' he 'sodenly was take and smyten with a ffransy and his wit and reson

---

[5] Thus, Griffiths, p. 723, does not doubt Margaret's power, but has not investigated the role of gender in determining the means by which she exercised it, beyond observing that a queen's regency was unacceptable to England on account of its astonishing novelty. Likewise, Watts, p. 326, acknowledges the constraint that gender placed on Margaret's freedom of action, then loses sight of it as he goes on to discuss her rise to power and does not explore its effect on political ideology (pp. 335–50). These are legitimate choices, yet they leave undone the work of reassessing Margaret's role.

[6] As has Griffiths, p. 722.

withdrawen', a description echoed by the contemporary 'Giles's Chronicle', which also notes that his incapacity lasted for a year and a half.[7] His collapse was as unexpected as it was total. Prior to his illness the state of his health appears to have been unremarkable; there was no reason to anticipate that such a thing might happen. His lack of judgment, bad enough in a king, could not have been seen to presage anything worse. Efforts in our own time to diagnose Henry's malady can only be speculative and are really relevant only to us.[8] In his time, for all practical purposes, it made as good sense to ascribe his illness to the will of God or to blame it on sorcery.[9]

Whatever the cause, Henry's symptoms could scarcely have been more alarming: he was oblivious and unresponsive; efforts to communicate with him and to get him to speak met with no recognition.[10] Moreover, it appears that his condition was also accompanied by physical weakness. On at least one occasion he required the support of two men in order to walk, unless that aspect of his illness can be attributed to the potions, laxatives, enemas, poultices and 'cuppings with or without scarification' to which he was subjected in an effort to cure him.[11] A petition for payment of wages to the grooms and pages of Henry's chamber duly notes the 'dailly attendaunces and nyghtly waching' that he required at this time.[12] There was no knowing whether he would recover or not, or when such a recovery might occur. In mid-October he was moved from Clarendon to Windsor, where he remained for the next fourteen months.[13]

Although it is possible that his condition fluctuated and that he began to have some 'better days',[14] it seems rather more probable that he showed no real improvement until the latter part of December 1454 and that his 'recovery' was in some ways as abrupt and unexpected as the onset of his illness had been. Significantly, on 30 December, Margaret presented their infant son to Henry for his recognition and apparently also filled him in on at least some of the events that had transpired during his illness.[15] Had his improvement occurred gradually, over an extended period of time, and had he been sufficiently cognizant to recognize his son or to carry on a lucid conversation at a much earlier date, such important matters would have begun to happen sooner. On balance, then, it seems that his improvement came about suddenly, but that at the time of Margaret's visit it had lasted through enough days to provide

[7] Flenley, p. 140; Giles, *Chronicon*, p. 44. The latter was composed in or soon after 1460 (*EHL*, p. 156). Griffiths, p. 715, puts the onset of his illness at the beginning of August; Wolffe, p. 270, favors a date towards its middle.

[8] See, e.g., Green, *Madness of Kings*, p. 68.

[9] Storey, p. 136, noted examples of the latter, citing PRO, KB9/273, nos 2 and 7. After the first battle of St Albans some people foisted blame on the late duke of Somerset for having taken Henry to Clarendon where he fell ill ('Gregory's Chron.', pp. 198–9).

[10] Gairdner, *PL*, II, pp. 295–6; *RP*, V, p. 241.

[11] Ibid.: 'he was ledde betwene II men'; *Reg. Whethamstede*, I, p. 163, for a more comprehensive picture of physical weakness, which may be no more than a creative gloss on the former (as suggested by Wolffe, p. 272); *Foedera*, V, ii, p. 55, for the doctors' permission to treat Henry as they saw fit (also printed in *PPC*, VI, pp. 166–7).

[12] PRO, E28/84/20.

[13] Wolffe, p. 370.

[14] Ibid., p. 273; Griffiths, pp. 758–9, n. 12.

[15] Gairdner, *PL*, III, p. 13.

reasonable assurance that it would not be reversed.[16] For the moment, however, we must relegate Henry's recovery to an uncertain future and attempt to reconstruct the situation at the onset of his illness, as it impinged on Margaret.

In August 1453, despite the disastrous course of events in France, culminating the previous month in the destruction of the English army at Castillon and the loss of Gascony, there is reason to believe that Margaret's popularity was at its highest since her arrival in England. Though she could not affect the outcome of the war, she had at last resolved the matter of a Lancastrian heir. At this time she was approaching, if not into, her eighth month of pregnancy, for which she had already been more than generously rewarded.[17] In addition, she had shown herself to be an attentive 'good lady' and, in the case of the pardons to the Cade rebels, had presented herself – or had been presented – in an appropriately and acceptably supporting role.

With Henry's collapse, the future governance of England and the future of the dynasty itself were cast into the profoundest doubt. Margaret's pregnancy, heretofore seen as a happy resolution to one set of problems, became a potential contributor to others. Assuming that she carried the child to healthy term and assuming that it turned out to be male, it still had to survive to competent adulthood before it could rule. In the absence of a lineal heir or a designated heir presumptive, existing rivalries between Henry's likely guardians and possible successors might come to a rapid head and resolve themselves through violence, as indeed they did. The prospect of a long minority, the second in the century, did not eliminate the potential for violence and usurpation, but extended the likelihood of an ongoing power struggle over influence, if nothing more, far into the uncertain future. As the days passed and Henry showed no signs of imminent recovery, the dangers inherent in the situation would not have been lost upon Margaret, nor upon the rival lords who perceived their own futures and future prospects to be at stake.

Some evidence of the dangers in the situation as seen by an outside, though by no means impartial, observer may be found in a contemporary poem by Charles of Orléans.[18] Having rejoiced at the English military defeat, he turns in the third stanza to their deteriorating domestic situation:

> N'ont pas Anglois souvent leurs rois trays?
> Certes ouyl, tous en ont congnoissance.
> Et encore le roy de leur pays
> Est maintenant en doubteuse balance;
> D'en parler mal chascun Anglois s'avance;
> Assez monstrent, par leur mauvais langaige,
> Que voulentiers lui feroient oultraige.
> Qui sera Roy entr'eux est grant desbat;
> Pour ce, France, que veulx tu que te dye?

---

[16] This is corroborated by the reactions of the bishop of Winchester and the prior of St John's, who saw Henry on 7 January and found that he spoke to them 'as well as ever he did'. Upon leaving his presence they wept for joy (ibid.).

[17] See p. 44, above.

[18] The first and third stanzas (out of four) are published by McLeod, *Charles of Orleans*, pp. 326–7, who dates the poem to 1453. The full text is printed in Bruneau, *Charles d'Orléans*, pp. 26–7.

De sa verge dieu les pugnist et bat
Et t'a rendu Guyenne et Normandie.[19]

One must, of course, approach this verse with caution. It is impossible to know just how much Orléans actually knew of the English situation or from whom he learned it. He had been taken prisoner at the battle of Agincourt in 1415 and had spent the next twenty-five years in gentle captivity while awaiting ransom. For a part of this time he was in the keeping of the earl (later duke) of Suffolk, whose wife was a granddaughter of Geoffrey Chaucer and who was himself a dabbler at writing poetry. They became close friends. When Suffolk was arrested on charges of treason in 1450, it was alleged, among other things, that he had persuaded Henry to release Orléans so that the two villains then might help Charles VII to deprive Henry of his realm of France, and that Suffolk had even siphoned money from the treasury to pay Orléans' ransom. It is likely that Orleans had become acquainted with a number of people during his English sojourn and that he maintained contact with some of them after his return to France. The last line of the verse, which appears at the end of each stanza as a recurring refrain, clearly indicates that the poem was written after the English defeat.

That being the case, unless it was written within days of the war's denouement, it was almost certainly written after Henry's collapse. We may wonder whether the king's 'doubteuse balance' refers solely to the existence of popular disaffection or to the uncertain condition of the king himself. There had been occasional remarks over a number of years regarding his unfitness as a king; some had gone so far as to suggest that he ought to be replaced by someone fitter, but there appears to have been no noticeable increase in such observations at this time. Nor is there any indication that there was any serious plan to supplant Henry after he fell ill. The 'grant desbat', then, over 'who [would] be king' seems to reflect the anxieties and outright squabbling that soon arose over who would rule for him, in his place. In any case, the poem, though likely exaggerated to suit the writer's intentions and mood, conveys a sense of the pressures, uncertainties and fears that were rampant within the English government at that time.

Because of the bitter enmity that came to exist between Queen Margaret and Richard, duke of York, and because of York's death at the hands of Margaret's troops at the end of 1460 and Henry VI's forcible deposition two months later by York's son, there has been a tendency among historians to take this enmity somewhat for granted, without looking too closely for its origins. Within the

---

[19]   Haven't the English often betrayed their kings?
         Yes, certainly, everyone has knowledge of it.
         And again the king of their country
         Is now in a doubtful balance.
         Each Englishman puts himself forward by speaking ill of him;
         So they show by their bad words
         That they would willingly do him insult.
         Who will be the king among them is the great debate.
         For this, France, what do you want me to tell you?
         With his rod God punishes and beats them
         And has returned to you Gascony and Normandy.

framework of a male-centered political history that views Margaret largely as adjunct or heir to male rivalries this elision does not seem overly significant. A further aspect of the male-centered framework, its focus on the intentions of the male protagonists – in this case, York's – has also obscured Margaret's place in the overall picture. As a result, although York's intentions and his role in the mid-century conflict have been reassessed and reevaluated, the assessment of Margaret has not kept pace. We are still stuck with a view that takes her hatred largely as a given or that seeks to explain it in the simplest terms.[20]

Among the more recent explanations of Margaret's enmity towards York, one requires further consideration at this point because it posits her 'early' hostility, prior to the crisis of 1453, based upon two pieces of evidence that, if correct, might provide both cause and proof. The first of these involves York's adoption of the surname 'Plantagenet', alleged to have occurred around 1448 based on its appearance in 'Gregory's Chronicle' under a heading of that date. Since it formerly had been used by Geoffrey of Anjou, the father of Henry II, its allusions to a superior royal descent 'must have been particularly offensive to Margaret of Anjou'.[21] In fact, I am aware of only one occasion on which it is certain that Richard, duke of York, used this name: in October 1460, when he explicitly laid out his claim to the throne.[22] Its appearance in 'Gregory's Chronicle' must also be regarded with skepticism. Although the text, which breaks off in 1470, is in a single hand, the writer appears to have copied previously written material before continuing with his own account of the years from 1454.[23] It is possible that the surname was added in the course of this later copying, when its use had become current. In any case, Margaret's presumed offense in 1448 can only be suppositional in the absence of any real proof of its existence.

The second piece of evidence is more serious, consisting principally of a letter purportedly written in 1454 by Richard Southwell to John Paston, complaining that the king and queen had warned the duke and duchess of Norfolk, in whose household Southwell had an appointment, to have nothing more to do with him since he owed his good will and service to York. In particular, Southwell asserted that Margaret had been at pains during the two previous years to insist to Norfolk that 'the King and she coude nor myght in no wyse be assured of hym and my Lady as long as we wer aboute hym'. The letter bears the date of 6 October only; Gairdner ascribed it to 1454. If this date is accepted, the letter appears to confirm York's own complaint made before the king's council in late 1453 of previous efforts to ostracize him.[24] The letter names the duke of

[20] E.g., Hookham, *Life and Times*, I, p. 318, asserted that by 1450 'the Duke [of York had become] an object of serious mistrust to the Queen' because he already aimed for the throne; Bagley, *Margaret of Anjou*, pp. 70, 71, believed that 'Margaret unhesitatingly threw her . . . influence on to Somerset's side' as claimant to be heir presumptive, causing York to resort to force and to regard her as an enemy; Griffiths, pp. 722–3, 823, also assumes Margaret's support for Somerset in opposition to York, though he attributes her real enmity to the fact that York's rule was preferred to her own during Henry's illness.

[21] Wolffe, pp. 35, n. 26, and 323, n. 48; 'Gregory's Chron.', p. 189.

[22] *RP*, V, pp. 375, 377, 378.

[23] *EHL*, p. 96.

[24] Wolffe, p. 276; Gairdner, *PL*, III, pp. 3–4; *CPR, 1452–61*, pp. 143–4. Watts, p. 294, n. 145, accepts a date of 1452–54 for the letter. Though he does not explicitly posit the queen's hostility towards York at

Somerset as a go-between in these machinations; based on everything that is known of the enmity between York and Somerset at this time or of the later enmity between York and Margaret, it all makes sinister good sense. Nevertheless, the connections collapse under scrutiny.

In the first place, York's complaint, addressed to the king's great council on 21 November, names no perpetrators but simply states that his own erstwhile council members have been told not to attend upon him, 'by what meanes he watte never'. The complaint does not indicate how long this situation had lasted, but its principal focus seems to be upon the present and the very recent past, in other words the circumstances of York's initial exclusion from the king's council that had been called to deal with Henry's incapacity. It should be noted that on this same date the duke of Norfolk accused the duke of Somerset of treason for his alleged culpability in the loss of France; Somerset was arrested on the twenty-third and placed in the Tower.[25] This is the context in which York's charges must be understood.

While we might safely assume York's intent to implicate Somerset in whatever had been going on, Margaret's involvement is far less certain without corroboration. Southwell's letter, in fact, does not provide it. A more recent editor of the Paston letters has argued on the basis of internal evidence that the letter was more likely to have been written in 1458.[26] This would place it at a time when Margaret was politically active and had greater reason to be suspicious of York. In this case, the 'Somerset' mentioned in the letter would not have been York's arch-rival, but his son Henry Beaufort, then aged twenty-two and eager to carry on the family vendetta. In 1458, Norfolk and his wife were serving the queen, which may lend more substance and credibility to Margaret's pressures upon them, reported by Southwell, to avoid association with 'friends' of York.[27]

If there is no concrete evidence of hostility between Margaret and York prior to the crisis of 1453–54, there is some indication that they were on reasonably good terms.[28] York's recent biographer, P.A. Johnson, goes so far as to characterize Margaret as 'a politically neutral figure', whose attitude prior to January 1454 was 'if anything sympathetic to York'.[29] Since his interest is in elucidating York's activities rather than Margaret's, he does not ponder what political neutrality might have meant to Margaret in her role as queen and whether neutrality itself might have been a role-specific means of mediating politics.

Leaving that question aside for the moment, there is no reason to believe

this point, considering the letter's content it is hard to see how such hostility could not be implicitly assumed. Overall, he seems chary of attempting to map its development, though it appears here and on p. 325 that he attributes it to the queen's support of Somerset.
[25] Gairdner, *PL*, II, pp. 290–2; Giles, *Chronicon*, p. 44; 'Benet's Chron.', p. 210.
[26] Davis, *PL*, II, p. 176. Davis notes that John Paston's brother William, referred to in the letter, would have been only eighteen in 1454 and not likely at that time to have had the sort of influence alluded to by Southwell.
[27] GEC, IX, pp. 607–8; *CSP, Milan*, I, p. 19.
[28] For the argument that York had, in fact, received considerable favor from Henry VI through the 1440s see Jones, 'Somerset, York and the Wars of the Roses', pp. 289–90, 295; Pugh, 'Richard Plantagenet', p. 127.
[29] Johnson, pp. 128–9.

that York in any way opposed Margaret's marriage to Henry, and he may even have regarded it with relief for its lowering of tensions connected with the dynastic issue.[30] More certain than speculative, he also saw the situation as a grand opportunity for personal gain. On 18 April 1445, having conducted Margaret from Pontoise to Honfleur whence she sailed for England, he eagerly wrote to Charles VII in pursuit of a proposed marriage between his eldest surviving son, Edward, then not quite three, and one of Charles's daughters.[31] Whoever originated the idea, the letter indicates that Suffolk had been playing the part of matchmaker and go-between with York's full approval. There is no evidence to suggest that Margaret either supported or opposed these negotiations.[32] Undoubtedly, she would have heard of them during the course of her progress to the coast, but what she thought cannot be known with any certainty. Considering the ages of the children involved – the daughter that Charles was willing to offer was only one-and-a-half – she scarcely can have viewed the project as a threat to Henry's and her dynastic prospects. York continued to pursue the marriage up until the end of 1445 when Charles apparently broke off negotiations.[33] There is nothing to link Margaret to the failure of York's hopes.

In 1448, Margaret and York were somehow allied in a dispute over the manor of Clements in the hundred of Rochford, Essex.[34] John and Agnes Ingowe had been 'forcibly dispossessed' of the manor in April by persons who promptly enfeoffed it on the dukes of York and Somerset. The Ingowes must have got it back, for they were evicted a second time in July by a different party 'led by' Alice Arnold of Moulton, Lincs., who again enfeoffed it on both York and Somerset. At that point the Ingowes retaliated by enfeoffing Clements on the duke of Suffolk. In August 'a large force . . . of [York's] Essex tenants' again drove the Ingowes out. Although the eventual outcome of this incident cannot be determined, Johnson concludes that 'York, despite the queen's support, probably lost'.[35]

The evidence adduced in support of Margaret's involvement is an undated letter that she wrote to York's officers and tenants in the hundred of Rochford, thanking them for their 'good faver, frendship, and supportacion' shown towards '[her] servant and squier John Stoughton, and Alice Arnold, his cousine, touching theire possession in the manoir of Clements' and requesting that such favor and support be continued.[36] It turns out that Stoughton, *alias* Stokton, of Hacconby, Lincs., had been a sergeant of the catery in the royal household, a position he appears to have left by the latter part of 1447 and in

[30] Griffiths, p. 675.

[31] Stevenson, I, pp. 79–82. York's first-born son named Henry – presumably to honor the king – seems to have died in infancy (Johnson, p. 36, n. 50).

[32] In September 1444, York in his capacity as lieutenant-general sent letters to the queen of France, Margaret, the duke of Orléans and the bastard of Orléans regarding the peace, as well as 'other matters, business, and secret affairs touching the good of the king [Henry VI]', but the specific nature of these matters is not stated (Stevenson, II, ii, pp. 468–9).

[33] Griffiths, p. 505; Stevenson, I, pp. 83–6, 160–3, 168–70. York's last letter was of 21 December.

[34] This account is based upon Johnson, p. 72.

[35] Jones, 'Somerset, York and the Wars of the Roses', p. 294, n. 8, sees their joint enfeoffment as evidence that York and Somerset had not yet become enemies.

[36] Monro, pp. 145–6.

which he was succeeded by his brother William. He was subsequently to have gone to Calais to attend to its victualling under the duke of Somerset, but seems not to have left England until the middle of 1452.[37] In 1454 during York's protectorate he was pardoned for various outlawries in London and Essex, including 'certain trespasses and contempts in entering with Alice Arnold . . . widow, a manor of James, earl of Wiltshire, [and others]'.[38] The Ingowes are not mentioned, and the manor in question may not have been Clements, but Stoughton's association with Alice Arnold in shady dealings involving property is confirmed. Regarding the relationship between York and Margaret in this matter, it is less clear to me just who was supporting whom, and it may be that all of the persons involved in the Clements affair would have seen themselves as upholding their own separate interests. Nonetheless, it also seems that in this case the interests of York and Margaret coincided. They probably coincided again in 1449, soon after York's arrival in Ireland, when he obtained the election of Michael Tregurry to the recently vacated archbishopric of Dublin. Tregurry had been one of Margaret's chaplains, and she had previously been active in his behalf.[39]

More telling are the New Year's gifts that Margaret made to the duke of York and his – or his wife's – servants. All five of her surviving jewel accounts record such gifts. On 1 January 1453, the last year for which an account is extant, Margaret gave 66s. 8d. to the servants of the duke, precisely the same amount that she gave to the servants of the duke of Somerset and of Cardinal Kemp.[40] It is my belief that this equivalence was deliberate and that it was designed to send a clear message of Margaret's political neutrality to both rival dukes. Since this contention goes against the grain of most understandings of her sympathies, it requires careful explanation. Some general observations about the practice of New Year's gift giving and Margaret's habits in particular will help to provide a context for her gifts of 1453.

To a certain extent, such gifts were routinely given. As Diana Dunn has recently cautioned, they ought not to be taken as 'evidence . . . of any direct political involvement by the queen'.[41] Although I agree that it would be unwise to assume Margaret's overt political favor from the presence of a particular person's name on her gift list, we still must not overlook the potential embedded in the practice for it to serve as a kind of symbolic language, whose meaning, depending on the circumstances, could be deliberately and actively political.[42]

---

[37] A series of entries in the Patent and Close Rolls supports this identification of Stoughton. See *CPR, 1446–52*, pp. 104, 250, 512, 549–50, 572; *CCR, 1441–47*, pp. 416–17; *CCR, 1447–54*, pp. 268, 363.

[38] *CPR, 1452–61*, p. 150.

[39] Johnson, pp. 74–5; Monro, pp. 91–3.

[40] Myers, 'Jewels', p. 119. The accounting period ran from Michaelmas 1452 to Michaelmas 1453. The other surviving accounts are for 1445–46, 1446–47, 1448–49, and 1451–52. Thus, we have five accounts for an eight-year period before the onset of Henry's illness and the subsequent polarization of political positions.

[41] Dunn, 'Margaret of Anjou, Queen Consort', p. 125.

[42] Howell, *Eleanor of Provence*, pp. 69, 191, 225, for that queen's New Year's gifts as political strategy, though she also recognizes gift giving as part of 'normal social intercourse' (p. 79). See pp. 168, 169–70, 171, 181, 182, for Eleanor's gifts of rings at other times to obtain support.

Certainly, the notion of gift giving as a symbolic activity is commonplace.[43] On the most obvious level, in a society devoted to ostentation and attention to the pecking order such as fifteenth-century England, gift giving made an important statement about the giver's status, wealth and generosity. Likewise, it involved recognition of the recipient's status. In Margaret's New Year's gifts, we see a correlation between the value of the gifts and 'the precise rank and importance of the recipient', as A.R. Myers observed. But Myers also noted that Margaret's choice of recipients was prompted by the desire 'to placate, reward, or protect' certain individuals.[44] This suggests that there was more to gift giving than simple status recognition and that it must be regarded as an interactive process expressing a relationship between giver and recipient.

We must also remember that a person's importance may depend on circumstance as well as titular rank, while circumstance can also determine the need to send a person a particular message. Dunn indeed acknowledges that something of the sort could be going on when she suggests that Margaret's gift to the duke of Gloucester in 1447 may indicate a lack of 'personal antagonism towards this opponent of the peace policy [towards France]' and a distancing of herself from 'any plot by Suffolk and his faction' against the duke.[45] Although it may seem a semantic quibble, I would put the matter a little differently: rather than reflecting an absence of feeling or alignment, the gift makes a positive statement about the queen's political neutrality. Regardless of Margaret's personal feelings towards Gloucester, her gift makes more sense as an intentional signal, a message from her as it were that 'I am not your enemy'. This fits much better with the queen's expected and accepted role as intermediary and peacemaker. It also suggests that we should consider such overt signs of the queen's neutrality as an explicit form of political mediation.

The records of Margaret's gifts to the servants of prominent persons reveal something of the careful balancing act that such gift giving involved.[46] First, a clear pattern can be seen regarding the value of the gifts. Typically, the highest sum received by anyone's servants was 66s. 8d; a cluster of recipients appears for this figure in every year for which we have a record, and in only one year (1447) was it exceeded. A little lower on the scale a second grouping of gifts occurs in all but one year (1449) at 53s. 4d. Though lesser sums in varying amounts were also given, they seem to form no further groupings. A second feature of these lists is the prominence of women on them: the wives of peers whose own servants received gifts from the queen. This calls to mind the likelihood of female networking that I have previously remarked upon, though it may also suggest that Margaret simply liked these women and wished to show her

---

[43] See, for example, recent work by Enright, *Lady with a Mead Cup*, pp. 1–22, 34–5, for the queen's role in a drink-offering ritual that served to establish hierarchy and maintain cohesion within the Germanic warband of the early Middle Ages; Meneley, *Tournaments of Value*, for women's maintenance of male value systems through behind-the-scenes socializing and gift giving in present-day Yemen. The classic work on gift giving is Mauss, *The Gift*.

[44] Myers, 'Jewels', p. 114.

[45] Dunn, 'Margaret of Anjou, Queen Consort', p. 125.

[46] Myers, 'Jewels', p. 119 and n. 6, from which the following information is drawn.

affection for them in this fashion.[47] Without denying either of these possibilities – particularly the latter – there seems to be something else afoot. Where clusters of high-ranking persons are represented through their servants, only one of them is typically a male secular peer; the others are either prelates or women. If this may be taken as a further recurring pattern, the appearance of York's and Somerset's servants as the recipients of identical sums in 1453 is anomalous. A final matter deserving notice is the mutuality of these particular gifts. In each case they were given to the servants of persons who had themselves sent gifts to the queen.[48] What this means is that if gift giving can be regarded at times as a kind of symbolic language, the records of these gifts to people's servants represent the last traces of what was once a dialogue.

By looking again at how the duke of York fits into these patterns it may be possible to discern the outline of the 'messages' that Margaret was sending him up to 1453 and even occasional snatches of the 'dialogue' itself. On 1 January 1446, when Margaret had been in England for less than a year, her gift to York's servants of 53s. 4d. – which placed him in the second category of recipients – was matched by her gifts to the servants of the duchesses of Bedford, Buckingham and Exeter. In that year only the servants of the duke of Gloucester, who after all was Henry's uncle and heir presumptive, and those of the archbishop of Canterbury received more (66s. 8d.). At that time York's negotiations for a marriage between his son and a daughter of Charles VII may not yet have fallen through, and it seems likely that he expected to be reappointed lieutenant of France.[49] This initial gift, then, was very likely to have amounted to little more than a formal recognition of York's rank and status, and perhaps an acknowledgement of his role in escorting Margaret across France.

By the following year, however, York's situation had changed appreciably. The marriage plans had definitely foundered. In the course of trying to resolve payment of the £38,666 13s. 4d. he claimed were owed him in arrears by the government for his expenses and service in France, he had been charged with mismanagement and favoritism in the payment of his soldiers by Adam Moleyns, bishop of Chichester.[50] Finally, in December the lieutenancy of France had been given to Somerset.[51] York would not be appointed to the lieutenancy of Ireland until the following July. Although the notion that York's Irish appointment amounted to an exile can be rejected, it is still true that it removed him from the center of action.[52] Margaret's New Year's gift to York's

---

[47] The duchesses of Bedford, Buckingham and Exeter, whose servants regularly received gifts from Margaret, were also the frequent recipients of personal gifts (Myers, 'Jewels', p. 124 and n. 6).

[48] This is explicitly stated in the account for 1452–53, which was printed in full by Myers, and his accompanying note indicates that this was the general rule where gifts to other persons' servants were concerned.

[49] Johnson, pp. 49–50. His term of office had expired during the previous year.

[50] Ibid., pp. 52–7, finds the bishop's charges to be partially true. Moleyns was a councilor, closely associated with the duke of Suffolk and the king. York ended up agreeing to waive £12,666 13s. 4d. Pugh, 'Richard Plantagenet', pp. 125–6, also discusses York's finances and regards the duke's initial claim as a position from which to bargain.

[51] Apparently as an incentive towards obtaining his cooperation in the surrender of Maine, not as a punishment of York (see Watts, p. 228; Jones, 'Somerset, York and the Wars of the Roses', pp. 291–3).

[52] Griffiths, pp. 419–20, 508; Pugh, 'Richard Plantagenet', pp. 127–8; Watts, pp. 237–8. Cf. Johnson, pp. 69–70, who acknowledges that the appointment did offer benefits, opportunity and honor. While I dispute Johnson's contention that York opposed the surrender of Maine – at least before it was

'servant' in 1447 was an uncharacteristically high 100s., substantially more than the standard 66s. 8d. that she gave to servants of the duke of Gloucester, who outranked him, the archbishop of Canterbury and the duchesses of Bedford and Buckingham. It is not unreasonable to see in this a form of reassurance and pacification, a message that the queen was aware of York's concerns.

In 1449, the next year for which we have record, the servants of the *duchess* of York received a gift of 66s. 8d. from Margaret, along with servants of the archbishop of Canterbury, Cardinal (and archbishop of York) Kemp, and the duchesses of Bedford, Buckingham and Exeter. No secular lord's servants received a gift that year, although the duke of Suffolk received a personal gift. Since the available evidence indicates that Margaret was not in the habit of making gifts to either the duchess of York or her servants, there may have been a particular reason for this switch, and it is tempting to wonder whether she appears on this list as a neutrally female stand-in for her husband or whether she had been doing a bit of intermediation with Margaret on his behalf around this time. What we do know is that York had been dragging his feet about leaving for Ireland and that he may have been in some difficulty because of disorders that his men had been causing in Wales.[53] The accounts are missing for the next two years, which makes any attempted interpretation of this apparent anomaly even murkier than it would be with a continuous record.

When the evidence resumes in 1452, the duke's servants (along with those of the cardinal, the archbishop of Canterbury and the duchesses of Bedford and Somerset) received the high amount of 66s. 8d., while the duke himself as well as the duchesses of Bedford, Exeter and Somerset were the recipients of personal gifts. There would have been good political reasons for such recognition by the queen. York had returned to England from Ireland unbidden in the autumn of 1450, in the aftermath of the Cade affair, and had been welcomed – at least by his own supporters – as the champion of needed governmental reform. By contrast, Henry had regarded York's arrival with the deepest suspicion, a feeling that echoed York's growing attitude towards the court.[54] Such mutual misgivings were not unreasonable. Although York did not create the troubles of 1450, his mere existence provided a potential focal point for the disaffected. Most blatantly, Cade had used the alias of 'Mortimer', a name reflecting York's own lineage, in order to gain support, and a rumor had spread – which the rebels denied – that they had called for Henry's deposition and replacement by the duke.[55] For his own part, York protested the allegations that were made about his loyalty and increasingly directed his hostility towards the duke of Somerset,

politically expedient to do so – the balance of evidence he and others have produced leads me to believe that the duke was opportunistic, self-righteous and easily affronted.

[53] Johnson, pp. 71–2. Griffiths, pp. 673–6, finds that York had little influence at court around this time and was largely cold-shouldered, a view that Watts, pp. 237–9, disputes.

[54] The most recent discussion of the trajectory of their mutual suspicions, as revealed in their correspondence of 1450, is Hicks, 'From Megaphone to Microscope'. See also Griffiths, 'Duke Richard of York's Intentions'; Johnson, pp. 81, 104–5.

[55] Harvey, *Jack Cade's Rebellion*, p. 78 and n. 29. For varying versions of the rebels' complaints and demands, see pp. 186–91. It must be noted, however, that such a rumor could work to the advantage of either the rebels or York's enemies, albeit in different ways.

whom he came to see as the author of all his difficulties.[56] Over the next several months, the pressures created by domestic discontents and the loss of Normandy increasingly converged, and nothing that either occurred by happenstance or was done by deliberation served to allay the fears and suspicions of either king or duke.

Matters came to a temporary head in May 1451 when Thomas Young, one of York's attorneys and councilors, petitioned parliament for York's formal recognition as Henry's heir presumptive, presumably under the assumption that he would have the commons' full support. Henry's options came down either to acceptance of the petition or to its substitution by 'a parliamentary declaration in favour of Somerset as heir presumptive'. Each option presented distinct difficulties, and Henry's response was to avoid both by dissolving parliament and having Young clapped into the Tower. These actions made York's future cooperation with any government that included Somerset even less likely, while 'his consequent exclusion from the [king's] council-table brought a decade of instability to Lancastrian England'.[57] At year's end the relationship between king and duke was marked by mutual unease, as each regarded the other with anxiety and waited to see what he would do next.

Although Margaret may have perceived Young's petition as an insult,[58] her gifts show that she was still publicly following a neutral course. In this context, her New Year's sign of queenly recognition could be seen as an astute and appropriate political move. By providing a personal gift to York and a substantial monetary gift to his servants she acknowledged his importance and signalled that she was not his enemy. In essence, by invoking the queen's neutrality and placing herself outside the overt political fray, she performed the accepted queenly role of mediator to diminish the adversarial relationship between the king's court and the kingdom's highest magnate. It must be remembered, moreover, that the gift giving was not one-sided. By approaching the queen with gifts, it was possible for the magnate to signal his loyalty and to appeal his situation.[59]

Margaret's gifts to the duchess of Somerset and her servants are an interesting sidebar to the whole affair. The duchess was a daughter of Richard Beauchamp, earl of Warwick, an important person in her own right,[60] but she was also her husband's wife, who could in some sense represent his interests on Margaret's gift list, while her gender kept her from being a direct threat to York's interests or status. It is also worth remembering that she appears to have been involved in some networking with Margaret.[61] If Margaret relied at times upon the

---

[56] For the development of York's public enmity towards Somerset around this time, see Jones, 'Somerset, York and the Wars of the Roses'. He argues that it was not Somerset's appointment as lieutenant of France *per se* that aroused York's ire, but his subsequent handling of the war, in particular his ignominious abandonment of Rouen in 1449, in which York saw a personal affront to his own honor. But cf. Hicks, 'From Megaphone to Microscope', pp. 255–6.

[57] Johnson, pp. 98–100, who considers that York stood behind Young's petition.

[58] As suggested by Jones, 'Somerset, York and the Wars of the Roses', p. 289 and n. 2.

[59] See above, p. 71.

[60] She was coheiress to her mother's Berkeley estates and, along with her sisters, contested the devolution of the Beauchamp lands upon their half-sister and her husband, Richard Neville, the present earl of Warwick. Storey, pp. 231–6, discusses these matters; see also Johnson, p. 93, n. 87.

[61] See above, pp. 60–1.

duchess's influence on her husband, the personal gift may be more apt to reflect the relationship between the two women and only peripherally – and ambivalently – refer to the duke of Somerset.

In any event, if Margaret's gifts to York and his servants in 1452 represented a pacification effort, it must also be admitted that it was not successful. In February, in what came to be known as the Dartford incident, York openly accused Somerset of treason for the English losses in France and their domestic consequences, as well as of seeking his own undoing with the king 'through . . . envy, malice, and untruth . . . to corrupt my blood, and to disinherit me and my heirs, and such persons as be about me'. Despite his declaration of loyalty to the king, York also indicated that he was willing to take matters into his own hands to remove Somerset from the king's presence, using force if necessary.[62] The outcome of the confrontation went against York: he did not have the lordly support he had anticipated, and the king rejected his arguments. He was forced to take a humiliating public oath of loyalty, and Somerset emerged with more influence over Henry than he had before.[63]

Margaret's gifts of 66s. 8d. each to the servants of York and Somerset in 1453 (matched only by her gift to the servants of Cardinal Kemp) reflect these changes in status and power. Although Somerset had acquired absolute preeminence in the king's court, York remained the highest-ranking magnate in England. Both had to be recognized, but the situation required tact. Margaret's solution was to honor both equally and so to preserve at least the appearance of the queen's neutrality. Her gift of a jewelled saltcellar worth £28 to the duchess of Somerset may or may not have had political significance.[64] As far as York was concerned, however, the queen's message was still clearly 'I am not your enemy'.

The appeals by York's wife to Margaret in 1453 prove that this was the case. Duchess Cecily's letter, most probably written in the late summer or early autumn of 1453, and the personal meeting that preceded it would scarcely have occurred had there been no reason to believe that the queen could still be approached as a neutral – and possibly favorable – intermediary on the duke's behalf. Calling York's situation an '[estrangement] from the grace and benevolent favour of . . . the king' put a rather mild face on his problems.[65] The persecution of his followers after Dartford had continued into 1453, while Somerset's influence at court had reached its apogee.[66] York's complaint to the

[62] Gairdner, PL, I, pp. 97–8; printed in more modernized English in Myers, EHD, IV, pp. 269–70; cf. MS Rawlinson B. 355 in Flenley, p. 107. For York's formal articles against Somerset, see Gairdner, PL, I, pp. 103–8.

[63] Johnson, pp. 107–20, who emphasizes the use of propaganda by both sides. Cf. Griffiths, pp. 983–700; Wolffe, pp. 253–6.

[64] Myers, 'Jewels', pp. 114–15, and 126, n. 6, finds that Margaret gave fewer and less expensive gifts in 1453 than she had in the years immediately following her arrival in England. In 1453 the duchess of Somerset was the only person of her rank to receive an individual gift. Myers attributes this pattern to Margaret's increasingly straitened financial circumstances.

[65] Rawcliffe, 'Richard, Duke of York', p. 237.

[66] For the case of Sir William Oldhall, York's chamberlain, see Johnson, p. 119. Harvey, Jack Cade's Rebellion, pp. 116–18, considers the indictments against him and others, charging them with a plot to overthrow the king in 1450, to have been largely fabricated. But cf. Griffiths, pp. 618, 685–6, 699. For Somerset, see Johnson, pp. 121, 125.

king's council of his ostracism, though not without its own ulterior motive, must still be regarded as evidence of his anxieties regarding the court. Yet, clearly, he saw Margaret as a potential source of help.[67]

If it now seems evident that Margaret's presumed enmity towards York must be reevaluated, what of her support of Somerset? While he had undeniably become one of her chief advisors by 1453,[68] there does not seem to have been any longstanding connection between them, and it appears that his rise in Margaret's favor followed upon his growing influence over Henry, which itself occurred in the aftermath of Suffolk's death and Cade's Rebellion and may have been due in part to the mutual suspicion existing between the king and York.[69] On 16 November 1451 she granted him a 100-mark annuity. Its payment on Michaelmas 1453 is recorded in the only surviving account book of her receiver-general.[70] While it is impossible to say what specifically prompted the original grant, it is worth recalling that the incident involving York's attorney Thomas Young had occurred in the summer of 1451 and that York received a personal gift from Margaret in addition to the gift to his servants on the following New Year's. Although a direct connection between these matters cannot be posited, it may be reasonable to suggest that the queen's gifts or grants to important personages – and rivals at that – would not have been made without due regard for both. In any case, the grant of an annuity would have provided a recognition of Somerset's status at court and would have established a formal relationship between the queen and the duke.[71]

We can approach the nature of their relationship in different ways. The entry for 1453 states that the annuity had been granted to the queen's 'very dear cousin . . . for the good counsel and praiseworthy service that [he] has given and will give [her] in the future, as well as for the great good will and kindness that he will show [her] in her urgent affairs'.[72] To a modern reader, 'very dear cousin' seems to express genuine warmth – and this may be what Margaret intended – but in the fifteenth century such phrases often constituted a polite

---

[67] The duchess of York was subsequently invited to attend Margaret's churching, along with all the other ladies of the higher nobility (Hunter, *Three Catalogues*, pp. 227–8). While this may have been done *pro forma*, it demonstrates the queen's continuing pursuit of a publicly inclusionary stance.

[68] Griffiths, p. 262.

[69] Jones, 'Somerset, York and the Wars of the Roses', p. 286, for the timing; pp. 292–3, for his difficulties with the crown over the surrender of Maine. Griffiths, p. 305, points out that 'Somerset's emergence as the royal favourite *par excellence* was no foregone conclusion'. As Somerset increasingly became the focus of York's hostility, his status with the king would have risen.

[70] Myers, 'Household of Queen Margaret', p. 418.

[71] Cf. Watts, p. 294 and n. 144, who considers Margaret 'a valuable ally to Somerset', providing him one 'route to influence over both king and household'. He cites Jehan de Waurin's belief that the queen's favor lay behind Somerset's ascendancy (Waurin, *Croniques*, V, pp. 264–6), but concedes that this may have been hindsight. Waurin's chronicle from 1444 on was written and then revised after the decisive defeat of the Lancastrian cause in 1471, and 'a particularly fine copy' of the whole was made for Edward IV (Gransden, *Historical Writing*, pp. 289, 291).

[72] Myers, 'Household of Queen Margaret', p. 418: 'carissimo consanguineo suo Edmundo Duci Somerset' pro bono consilio suo et laudabili servicio quod . . . eidem Regine impendit et impendet infuturum aceciam propter magnam affeccionem et benevolenciam quam . . . Regine eidem in urgentibus negocijs suis ostendet.' Wolffe, p. 276, translated 'ostendet' – which is a future tense – as 'had shown'. Obviously, the difference in tense makes a great deal of difference to our understanding of what Margaret's 'urgent affairs' might have been. See p. 93 and n. 83, below, for my discussion of this matter.

boilerplate having more to do with status recognition than with affection. For example, *carissimus* appears in the greetings of letters in Latin from both James II of Scotland and the king of Aragon to Charles VII of France.[73] In French, Henry VI referred to both the duke of York and the earl of Dorset (later duke of Somerset) as *tres chier et tres ame cousin*.[74] The greetings of contemporary letters in English run the gamut from 'trusty and well-beloved' (to the relatively lowly) to 'right trusty and right entirely beloved' and the like to the more exalted; the rule of thumb seems to be that the higher the status of the person written or referred to, the more superlative the phrase.[75] The reference to services given and to be performed may also follow a kind of formula. Somewhat similar phrases appear in the household accounts of Queen Elizabeth Woodville for 1466–67, where they also involve annuities.[76] What emerges from this comparison is the expectation of both queens that past behavior rewarded will be continued into the future. In this respect, the annuities appear to establish a contractual relationship between donor and recipient.

The fact that the annuity involved a monetary grant as well as a service relationship is significant. Rosemary Horrox has pointed out that monetary payment was associated with subordination.[77] Although her discussion involves fees and gifts, it may be argued that an annuity given in the expectation of continued service occupied a middle ground between the two. Service, of course, was considered honorable by all, and service to one's superior enhanced one's own importance. The king – and his wife by extension – stood at the top of the social ladder. In theory, at least, it was impossible for anyone save the king to be Margaret's social superior. We may safely assume that Somerset was pleased and honored by the annuity as a symbol of the queen's regard.[78]

At the same time, from Margaret's point of view, Somerset's growing practical influence over the king would have made it prudent for her to establish and in some way formalize her own links with him. We need not regard such action as an effort at this stage to have a hand in governance. Nevertheless, we have seen Margaret's active engagement in the interventions and mediations of what I have called business-as-usual, which cannot be viewed in isolation from the realm of politics, and it should come as no surprise that she should choose to cultivate her husband's new chief counselor. Even so, with these things understood, we need not regard the annuity as an act of cynicism.

---

[73] Stevenson, I, pp. 194, 221, 310. Richard II similarly addressed the duke of Bavaria (ibid., p. lxxv).
[74] Stevenson, II, i, pp. 313, 329, 341.
[75] Margaret's letters illustrate this principle. She also addressed or referred to the duke of Exeter, earl of Northumberland, duke of Somerset, duchess of Somerset, Viscount Beaumont, Lord Bourgchier, duke of York and duke of Norfolk as *cousin* (Monro, pp. 107, 110, 115, 118, 119, 122, 146, 155). The term was used flexibly to cover any sort of blood relationship.
[76] Myers, 'Household of Queen Elizabeth Woodville', p. 465, for an annuity to the physician, Domenico di Sirego, 'pro bono, laudabili et gratuito servicio, ante hec tempora impenso et in futuro impendendo' ('for the good, praiseworthy and agreeable service given before these times and to be given in the future'). See also pp. 466–7, annuities to John Rede, Sir Richard Roos and Sir Lawrence Raynford.
[77] Horrox, 'Service', pp. 66–7. Margaret's New Year's gifts are illustrative: she gave sums of money to others' servants, but gave 'real' gifts to individuals she wished to honor.
[78] Basin's view of Somerset's avarice (see p. 61, n. 48, above) suggests that the annuity may also have been a particularly shrewd means of obtaining his support.

There is no reason why genuine gratitude and genuine self-interest could not coexist.

Further evidence of Margaret's favor towards Somerset might be seen in the fact that he, together with the duke of Buckingham, escorted her to Westminster for her lying-in.[79] At the same time, they seem to have been the premier magnates on hand.[80] Somerset, the duchess of Buckingham and Cardinal Kemp stood as godparents to the infant prince.[81] But how likely was it that Margaret would have chosen lesser persons for this honor? The duke of York was not in London, and his estrangement from the king would have made him an unlikely choice in any event.

Thus, the relationship between Margaret and Somerset may have been more complex – and less transparent – than the fact of an annuity might initially seem to suggest. What is clear is that it set up a relationship that was defined primarily by Margaret's needs and expectations, not the other way around. Moreover, we have records of four specific situations in which Margaret needed his cooperation or aid: her letter requesting his favor towards Marguerite Stanlowe, one of her gentlewomen; her letter to the duchess of Somerset asking that she apply pressure on her husband to see to the payment of a grant to Margaret's squire, Robert Edmunde; her letter requesting recompense for her steward, Viscount Beaumont, for his lands in Maine; and the entry in her jewel account of 1452–53 indicating his involvement in the advancement of her chaplain, John Hals.[82] If the text of the 1453 entry rehearses, word for word, the language of the original grant, we may wonder whether any of these matters qualify as the 'urgent affairs' to which it refers. On balance, I am inclined to think not. This 'extra' reference to future good will and kindness required in connection with the queen's urgent business goes well beyond the expectation that good counsel and service already rendered would be continued and therefore seems unusual.[83] This may suggest – although we cannot know for certain – that the sentence was added in 1453 to reflect the dilemma presented by Henry's illness. Within this context it seems particularly apt. In the autumn of 1453, Margaret surely would have needed and counted upon the future cooperation and good will, not only of Somerset, but of York and all the other lords. This point needs to be emphasized, for it holds the key to Margaret's behavior during the crisis and to her eventual emergence as the leader of a 'Lancastrian' party.

[79] CLRO, Journal V, fol. 120.
[80] In 1447 Buckingham had been granted special precedence over all dukes that might thenceforth be created, except for descendants of the king's body (GEC, II, p. 388).
[81] Searle, *Chronicle of John Stone*, p. 87; *English Chron.*, p. 70.
[82] Monro, pp. 115, 118–19; Myers, 'Jewels', p. 129. The letters are undated but must have been written after Somerset's return to England in 1450 and most probably before his imprisonment in 1453.
[83] See pp. 91–2 and nn. 72 and 76, above. I see no reason to assume that the future tense 'ostendet' in the record of Somerset's grant was a scribal error. Only two of the eight records of annuity payments that follow Somerset's indicate a reason for the grants: one is for 'good service'; the other is in recompense of expenses.

7

Debate

WHEN HENRY VI fell ill, the inclusive cooperation among the lords that Margaret would have needed did not take place. Private differences were not set aside in the interest of a higher public good.[1] Mutual mistrust spawned fear in these unsettling circumstances; together with the unparalleled opportunity the situation offered for self-aggrandizement, such feelings conspired to undermine cooperation. Both Somerset and York reacted to the crisis as if the primary demand it placed on them was for self-preservation, seen to be possible only with the political neutralization, if not destruction, of the other. Initially, there appears to have been a cover-up. While much of this may be attributed to the uncertainty of Henry's prognosis and the all-too-human inclination to do nothing in the hope that the problem would somehow resolve itself or miraculously go away, it also seems likely that Somerset promoted the cover-up as a means to his own political salvation.[2] As news of the summer's French disasters, amounting to near-total defeat for the English, spread through England, his position had become vulnerable.[3] He had presided over the loss of Normandy as lieutenant of France and York's replacement. In the public eye the recent loss of Gascony had followed in direct descent, and there was little question of whom to blame.

Meanwhile, on the domestic scene, a feud between the junior members of the Neville and Percy families had come to blows in late August after brewing all summer and threatened to cast the north into regional war.[4] Ongoing efforts to bring the situation under control had met with little success, and Somerset's government appears to have been incapable of imposing order. Between 7 June and 10 August a series of letters were sent by the king (or at least in his name) to the rivals and their adherents, demanding appearance before the council and their keeping of the peace.[5] They had little effect, unless it was to delay the outbreak of serious violence until the king's collapse became known.[6]

---

[1] Rosenthal, *Purchase of Paradise*, pp. 125–6, observes a competitive individualism among the fifteenth-century nobility that frequently made cooperation difficult in other matters.

[2] Griffiths, p. 721; Johnson, pp. 122–4; Wolffe, pp. 273, 275. Its success seems doubtful; the author of 'Bale's Chronicle', a Londoner, certainly knew of the king's illness (Flenley, p. 140).

[3] Griffiths, p. 720; Somerset's alleged misdeeds in France figured prominently in the charges Norfolk brought against him later in the year (Gairdner, *PL*, p. 291), an indicator of their public resonance.

[4] Pollard, *North-Eastern England*, pp. 255–7.

[5] *PPC*, VI, pp. 140–55.

[6] As suggested by Watts, p. 301.

Communications then ceased until 8 October when a handful of letters were sent in Henry's name to the earl of Westmorland, the bishop of Durham and the archbishop of York, thanking them for their efforts towards peacekeeping, and to the earls of Salisbury and Northumberland and their recalcitrant sons, demanding that they enforce or keep the peace and threatening severe consequences if they did not.[7]

As Henry's illness showed no signs of resolution, it became clear that the crisis would have to be faced squarely and that a solution would have to be found for the realm's governance. Accordingly, a great council was summoned, to which, tellingly, York was not invited. His exclusion may have precipitated his wife's letter to Margaret.[8] Duchess Cecily's letter indicates that some time had elapsed since the personal meeting of the two women in April, and it had to have been written after Margaret's pregnancy was openly acknowledged in the summer. Quite possibly, it was written after the onset of Henry's illness, and the duchess's appeal to Margaret to mediate *with the king* may raise the question of what York actually knew about the situation at that time. Although the effectiveness of the duchess's letter and, consequently, of Margaret's role in obtaining York's invitation to the council remains uncertain, it may be noted that when a summons was belatedly sent to York on 23 October, one of its signatories was Walter Lyhert, the bishop of Norwich and Margaret's confessor. Another was William Waynflete, bishop of Winchester, whose servants had received gifts from Margaret in 1452 and '53. A third, John Sutton, lord Dudley, was recommended to Charles VII in a letter of Margaret's dated 20 December 1446 as *n[ot]re feal et bon ame*,[9] a description that need not be taken literally to be understood as an indication of intended favor. Of the six remaining signatories, only one, Richard Beauchamp, bishop of Salisbury, might be considered to have been sympathetic towards York; most of the others were king's men.[10] Neither Somerset nor the chancellor, Cardinal Kemp, signed the invitation, and it is possible that they were absent.[11] Nevertheless, as there is no reason to believe that the signers as a group were predisposed towards York, there is likewise no reason to suspect that they were out to get Somerset. The admonition to York contained in the summons must be taken literally: that a prime reason for assembling a great council was 'to sette rest and union betwixt the lordes of this lande'. Although some of this effort was surely to be directed towards resolution of the Neville/Percy feud, the York/Somerset dispute would also have to be addressed if 'a new [and] more sufficient authority' was to be created.[12] York was to be given a hearing, but the hoped-for outcome was to be a setting-aside of grievances and a unity of

---

[7] *PPC*, VI, pp. 158–63. While it may be that the hiatus is apparent only, due to a loss of documentation, I am inclined to believe that it was genuine and resulted from the uncertainty and confusion attendant upon the king's condition.

[8] Griffiths, p. 720, who is skeptical of its influence.

[9] BN, MS Fr. 4054, fol. 79: 'our faithful and good friend'.

[10] *PPC*, VI, pp. 163–4. Johnson, p. 125, notes that the lords Dudley and Sudeley had done quite well during the years of Somerset's ascendancy and emphasizes that 'such a group could [not have agreed] to summon York other than on grounds of legitimate right'.

[11] Ibid., p. 124.

[12] Cf. Watts, pp. 301–3, especially n. 188; p. 302 for the quotation. The sense that all would have to pull together in order to do this seems to be implicit in the message that was sent to York.

purpose that were perceived to be needed in the extraordinary circumstances of Henry's incapacity.[13] Margaret would have had every reason to support such a goal, and it is fully consistent with her behavior towards York up to this point.

We must also remember that during roughly the same period as York's concerns were being negotiated and addressed, Margaret was reaffirming her favor towards Somerset through his involvement in her child's christening. His annuity must likewise be seen as a part of this larger picture. Although the date of its current settlement was predetermined and only coincidentally connected with the events of the autumn, the reiteration – or new elaboration – of its terms makes a kind of poignant sense under the circumstances. He, like York, was being charged with responsibility for his future behavior, in his case directly to Margaret. An unanswerable question that might help to resolve exactly what was going on concerns Somerset's apparent absence on the day that York was finally invited to join the council. Was the invitation issued behind his back? Or, since he was a chief party to the 'variance betwixt . . . lordes' that was to be resolved, was it deemed advisable for him not to sign the invitation? Had he been a signatory, the problem could not have been referred to in such deliberately neutral terms without obvious disingenuousness.

Of course, it is fruitless to ponder what might have been or to wonder what outcome would have resulted had things gone differently. They did not. When York arrived in London on 12 November, he was bent on vendetta. The gathering of a larger number of lords also meant that there were persons on hand with less prior commitment to a goal of 'rest and union'. Although it is too early at this stage to speak of factions, the council meetings immediately took on an air of partisan politics. John Mowbray, duke of Norfolk, who may have arrived with York, spoke in his behalf and openly denounced Somerset for treason, blaming him specifically for the loss of Normandy and Gascony and, more generally, for having acquired 'over grete autoritee in thys royaume'.[14] Norfolk's involvement made any accommodation between the two rivals 'more difficult to organize, [while it] gave York the political advantage of the public support of another great lord'.[15] Soon enough, York was applying pressure of his own by charging that his own councilors had been hindered from attending him and by obtaining a guarantee that this situation would be remedied.[16] That matters came to a head quickly and that people were aware of the extreme delicacy of the situation is shown by the actions of the London common council. On 14 November, two days after York's arrival, it warned the guilds to mind their tongues and to show no favor towards any particular lord; on the same day it issued a proclamation by the king's council in Henry's name commanding that no one, of any condition, was to 'go iakked saletted [i.e. wearing jacks and sallets] nor in

---

[13] Johnson, p. 125, considers these efforts to have been genuine, but 'sadly over-optimistic'.

[14] 'Benet's Chron.', p. 210, for the date of York's arrival and Norfolk's denunciation of Somerset. The writer implies that the two things occurred in quick succession. The gist of the latter may be found in Gairdner, PL, II, pp. 290–1. This document is not Norfolk's original bill against Somerset, but a follow-up to his rebuttal of Somerset's response.

[15] Johnson, p. 126.

[16] CPR, 1452–61, pp. 143–4. This was on 21 November.

any other wise armed or wepened be nyght ne be day' on pain of forfeiture of his weapons and imprisonment.[17]

Meanwhile, despite pressure from York and Norfolk, it is clear that the council or a significant number of its members were reluctant to throw their weight behind York and were doggedly trying to obtain a peaceful resolution of differences. At this juncture it is also important to note that the London common council was still adhering to its policy of strict neutrality. On 20 November its members agreed to 'delay' calling upon the duke of York on the grounds that they would neither concern themselves with nor show favor to anyone unless required to do so by the king and his council.[18] Norfolk's subsequent 'petition' indicates that a debate of sorts took place.[19] According to the petition, Somerset had defended himself against Norfolk's initial charges, and Norfolk had countered with a rebuttal 'yn such wyse that y trowe to be sure ynough that there shall no vayllable thyng be seyd to the contrarie of my seyd replicacion'. But then nothing had happened, as the council took no action, leading Norfolk to complain:

> whereuppon y have requyred to have ouverture of justice by yow, whych ye have not yhyt doon to me, whereoff y am so hevy that y may no lenger beere it, speciallie seth the mater by me pursued ys so worshipfull for all the royaume, and for you, and so greable to God, and to alle the subgettys of thys royaume, that it may be no gretter.

Having made its bid for sympathy while claiming the support of God and the populace, the petition next accuses Somerset of bribery – the only thing that could 'have turned [the] hertys [of the council] from the wey of trouth and of justice' – but slips in the admission that 'othyr [have taken] a colour to make an universell peas'. Norfolk skates past this matter, thus belittling it and diminishing its significance, by turning quickly to the loss of France, upon which he spends much time. The petition ends with a request that it be exemplified under the great seal and a warning that 'in case ye make not to me ouverture of justice upon the seyd caas, y shall for my discharge do my peyn that my seyd devoirs and the seyd lak of justice shall be knowen through all the royaume'. Given the level of bitterness then spreading through the country over the most recent disasters in France, this would not have been perceived as an idle threat.

Norfolk's petition can only be understood as a piece of tough politics. Apparently, it had its effect, for the opposition – including stubborn holdouts for reconciliation – caved. On 23 November, Somerset was arrested and sent to the Tower. He would never be formally charged or brought to trial, thus

---

[17] CLRO, Journal V, fol. 131.

[18] Ibid., fol. 132b.

[19] Gairdner, *PL*, II, pp. 290–2, from which all quotes are taken. I concur with him in ascribing it to late 1453, though its precise dating remains tenuous. Here, I have placed it before Somerset's arrest on 23 November, though its request that he be tried may argue that it was written after he was in custody. Three points support my view: Somerset was not likely to have waited until after his arrest to respond to Norfolk's charges, nor Norfolk to strike back; the allusion to peacemaking efforts links the petition to the council's initial agenda that autumn, and the vigor of Norfolk's efforts would help to explain the growing animosity between him and Cardinal Kemp (see below, p. 103 and n. 42). Cf. Johnson, pp. 131–2; Hicks, *Warwick*, pp. 109–10.

demonstrating 'the essentially political and personal nature of the campaign against him'.[20] That same day, perhaps fearing outbreaks of violence, the common council ordered the aldermen to see to the lighting in their wards and to ensure that the citizenry had sufficient arms in their homes to keep peace in the city.[21] Sometime after his arrest, in a letter to James II of Scotland, Somerset claimed that he had only been sent to the Tower for his own protection. The council appended a memorandum denying any responsibility for the duke's communication and stating that he had been arrested on suspicion of treason.[22] Whatever the council members' actual sentiments, their desire to cover themselves is clear.

With Somerset out of the way, it might have seemed that York's ascendancy had been assured. But there remained the matter of Henry and what was to be done about the realm's governance if he remained incompetent. Parliament, originally summoned to meet in November, had been put off until February. Meanwhile, the council attempted to provide for the 'pollytyque rule and governance of this [Henry's] land', but waffled insofar as its members decided on 5 December that they as a body would only do whatever needed to be done to maintain the law and keep things under control 'as of veary nesestye must be entended unto untill the tyeme there poure be more ample by awtoryty suffycently declared'.[23] By this time, council attendance had dropped: a smaller group was gathered on this day than had been present at a previous meeting on 30 November. Of the lay peers attending, all but one who subscribed to the council's decision had close connections to York.[24] If this represented a move by York to consolidate his power, it was only partially successful.

Margaret would have viewed these developments with anxiety, if not alarm. As long as the king remained incompetent, formal arrangements would have to be made to govern the realm in his name. She would not have quibbled at that. Yet the long-term security of the dynasty and the preservation of the crown for her son demanded a reasonable unity of purpose among its lords. Whatever Somerset's intentions may have been – and there is no need to assume that they were any more high-minded – York's actions since his arrival in London guaranteed that personal antagonism and vendetta would not be set aside. Instead, they raised the stakes in the conflict. Margaret would not have had to believe that York aimed for the throne to understand that he had effectively sabotaged any hope of voluntary cooperation in support of a royal 'center'. Although Somerset's removal worked to York's advantage for the moment, it resolved nothing, but left a burning fuse. It may well have seemed that the only thing that could prevent the fuse from burning to its end was the king's recovery.

Accordingly, sometime around the Christmas holidays or shortly thereafter an attempt was made to rouse Henry, then at Windsor, from his stupor. Both

[20] 'Benet's Chron.', pp. 210–11; Griffiths, p. 721.
[21] CLRO, Journal V, fol. 133b.
[22] Kekewich et al., *The Politics of Fifteenth-Century England*, pp. 183–4.
[23] Griffiths, 'King's Council', p. 317.
[24] Ibid., pp. 72–3. The single exception was the duke of Buckingham.

Margaret and the duke of Buckingham presented Henry's infant son to him for his blessing, perhaps believing that this of all things would bring him to his senses. Their continued efforts elicited no response, save that 'ones [Henry] loked on the Prince and caste doune his eyene ayen, without any more'.[25] After this disheartening result, events appear to have taken on a life of their own, moving inexorably towards an as yet uncertain conclusion. Parliament was scheduled to meet in February. The governance of the realm remained unresolved; a number of lords were arming themselves and their men as if in anticipation of a showdown, and no one was truly in control.

This was the atmosphere in which Margaret acted. She presented a bill of five articles that, if accepted, would have established her as regent. Our sole source of knowledge regarding Margaret's proposal is a detailed newsletter of 19 January written by John Stodeley to advise the duke of Norfolk, who had been deeply embroiled with York in the power machinations of the autumn.[26] It would have been intended to provide him with practical, concrete information to guide his own actions, not simply as retailed gossip. According to Stodeley, the bill's first four articles would have given Margaret the 'hole reule of this land', the right to appoint all state officers and sheriffs, the patronage of bishoprics and all other benefices belonging to the king and 'suffisant lyvelode assigned hir for the Kyng and the Prince and hir self'. He did not know the content of the fifth article. As a guess, it may have involved the custody of her son.

Although Margaret's proposal has been described as a 'course of breathtaking novelty' for England,[27] it was not, in fact, without precedent. In 1253 Henry III named his queen, Eleanor of Provence, as regent during his absence on the continent and provided her with real authority in governance second only to his own. For a period of ten months, assisted by a council chosen by the king, she ruled.[28] While Eleanor may have been somewhat anomalous in a society in which the queen's direct power was already diminishing to indirect intercession in response to the increasing bureaucratization and institutionalization of government,[29] the experience of her successful regency might still have supplied a useful model.

To better understand how this could be, we must explore with new eyes the situation in which Margaret – and England – found themselves. In the first place, although her proposal certainly had the effect of contributing to uncertainty and to the increasing polarization of interests among the nobility, it must first be seen as a response to tension rather than its cause. The devolution of the crisis precipitated by Henry's illness into a personal war between York and Somerset, with its concomitant openings for the pursuit of vendettas between other lords, posed a danger to the dynasty that a queen's regency could rise above, at least in theory, as the leadership of any one of the

[25] Gairdner, *PL*, II, pp. 295–6.
[26] Ibid., pp. 295–9. Margaret's proposal is on p. 297.
[27] Griffiths, p. 723.
[28] Howell, *Eleanor of Provence*, pp. 112–24; for earlier queens as temporary regents see Parsons, *Eleanor of Castile*, pp. 71–2.
[29] Huneycutt, 'Intercession and the Queen', esp. pp. 131, 138; Parsons, 'The Queen's Intercession', pp. 149–50; cf. Howell, *Eleanor of Provence*, p. 261.

affected lords could not.[30] Thus, I believe that Margaret's proposal constituted an effort to protect her son's interests by maintaining or re-creating a real royal 'center' that stood above private enmities and could command – and demand – the loyalty of all.[31]

Stodeley's letter, in fact, supports this analysis, though its structure is misleading. It begins with an account of Margaret's and Buckingham's failed efforts to rouse the king and then proceeds to a list of who was raising men or otherwise preparing for conflict. Because it places Margaret's bill between the names of those who would be identified eventually as 'Lancastrians' and those who presently supported York, it creates the impression of two cohesive camps preparing for a showdown. This oversimplifies the picture and underestimates the chaotic nature of all these preparations. To illustrate this point it will be necessary to go over the letter in detail.

In order, Stodeley reported that Cardinal Kemp was arming his servants to act as his bodyguards; that the earl of Wiltshire and Lord Bonville were raising men in Somerset; that the duke of Exeter and Lord Egremont had sworn themselves to an alliance; that the earl of Wiltshire and the Lords Beaumont, Poynings, Clifford and Egremont were raising men to come to London in force; that Thomas Thorp, a baron of the exchequer and speaker of parliament, was composing articles against the duke of York; that Thomas Tresham, William Joseph, Thomas Daniel and John Trevilian, four of the king's household men, had proposed that a garrison be established at Windsor to protect the king and the prince; that the duke of Buckingham was having badges made, 'to what entent men may construe as their wittes wole yeve theym'; and that the duke of Somerset's men had taken up all the lodgings in the vicinity of the Tower, where he was being held. Next comes the description of Margaret's bill. This is followed by a report of the duke of York's activities and of those currently associated with him and advice to Norfolk as to how he should himself proceed.

Stodeley said that York was expected to arrive in London with his son the earl of March (then not yet eleven!) and an escort on the twenty-fifth. Richard Neville, earl of Warwick (York's nephew), and the earls of Richmond and Pembroke (the king's half-brothers) were to accompany him, 'everych of theym with a godely feliship'. Both York and Warwick had arranged for additional and apparently substantial forces to travel separately and to be in London ahead of them – in Warwick's case, a thousand men. In addition, the earl of Salisbury (York's brother-in-law and Warwick's father) was expected to arrive on the twenty-first or twenty-second with his troops. Stodeley's advice to Norfolk was to come with a proper escort, but also to have 'a nother gode feliship' arrive either ahead of him, as the others had planned, or else soon after. Moreover, he warned Norfolk to avoid writing letters to raise men lest they fall into the hands

---

[30] Storey accords these feuds and rivalries an overall importance that I have not. Although noble rivalries preceding the crisis and Henry's inability to control them were a large part of his failure as king, the foregrounding of the York/Somerset feud in autumn 1453 and York's 'resolution' of it by having his enemy imprisoned signalled a potentially open season for everybody else. In such a situation a queen's regency might have proved a counterweight against these centrifugal forces.

[31] Cf. Howell, *Eleanor of Provence*, pp. 32–3, 111–12, for Henry III's recognition of Eleanor as protector of their son's interests should he die.

of the cardinal and the lords as a previous letter had done, causing 'moche harme and no gode'. Norfolk was also to guard against Somerset's ambushes and spies, believed to be everywhere – although Stodely proudly described himself and some eight others as spies – and to tell the cardinal or any other who might question his arrival in force that he was only providing for his own security since Somerset and those 'holdyng his [i.e. Somerset's] opynyon ayenst the wele of the Kyng and of the land, [had] made grete assemblees and gaderyngs of people, to mayntene th'opinion of the seid Duke of Somerset and to distrusse my Lord [i.e. Norfolk]'.

While we must place some faith in this letter since it is all we have, skepticism is also due. Although its organization gives the impression that York's actions followed and were prompted by potentially hostile activities taken by others, this clearly cannot be the case. If anything, the arrival dates for York and the Nevilles suggest that they had been raising men at the same time as everyone else, if not earlier. The impression that it gives of two opposing camps clearly allied with either York or Somerset also breaks down under scrutiny. At this stage, individual feuds and grievances were still paramount, though they had begun, coincidentally, to intersect.

Bonville, supported by Wiltshire, had been carrying on a family feud with the earl of Devon that went back more than a decade. Devon, who had been associated with York during the Dartford incident of 1452 and later imprisoned, had been due to come up on charges of treason at the next session of parliament, but was freed from detention after York joined the council in autumn. The possibility of renewed quarrel and likely vendetta would have been in the air.[32] Likewise, Egremont and Poynings, both scions of the Percy family, were principals in its feud with the Nevilles. Clifford seems to have been drawn into the quarrel on the Percy side when his son rode with Egremont to ambush a Neville wedding party in August 1453. What Exeter was up to at this point was anybody's guess.[33] Beaumont had a long-standing association with Henry and his court, and he had become Margaret's chief steward. But he also had ties to York.[34] His relationship with Somerset is not clear. Based upon his own expression of commitment to the queen a couple of months later, he may have been acting at this time in her support.[35] What is not clear from Stodeley's letter – and should not be taken for granted – is whether Wiltshire, Beaumont, the Percy lords and Bonville, whom he mentions in one breath, were all raising men as part of a concerted, joint effort, or whether he mentions them together because they all happened to be raising men at the same time to support their various projects.

In contrast to most of the others, Buckingham had not been involved in the quarrels of the day, but he was undoubtedly the king's man, as well as his own.

---

[32] Storey, pp. 84–92, 99–101, 138; Wolffe, pp. 251–2; Griffiths, pp. 574–7.

[33] Thomas, Lord Egremont, was a younger son; Henry, Lord Poynings, was heir to the earldom of Northumberland. The origins of the Neville/Percy feud and the Neville/York alliance have been discussed recently by Pollard, *North-Eastern England*, pp. 245–59; cf. Hicks, *Warwick*, pp. 86–91. See also Storey, pp. 124–32, 134–6, pp. 142–9, for Exeter; Griffiths, 'Local Rivalries'.

[34] Johnson, p. 228, considers him to have been one of York's councilors during the 1440s.

[35] See above, p. 61, for Margaret's intervention with Somerset on Beaumont's behalf.

It appears that his preparations were meant as a precaution against any and all contingencies. Since he and Margaret together had tried to rouse Henry, it seems likely that he understood and possibly sanctioned her intentions. Thorp was an adherent of Somerset's; however, he was also privately engaged in a legal battle with York. He seems to have written his articles from Fleet prison whence he had been committed after losing a judgment to York during the previous Michaelmas term.[36] Tresham, Trevilian, Daniel and Joseph were all household men; the first three, at least, had been associated with the court before Somerset's ascendancy and had long benefitted from their association.[37] Joseph seems more of a cipher. Although he together with Thorpe were later made scapegoats after the first battle of St Albans, he may indeed have been as 'insignificant' as B.P. Wolffe characterizes him.[38] If their bill to protect the king was not prompted by Margaret or by a genuine concern for Henry, it seems most likely to have been motivated by self interest with an eye to preserving their own positions and benefits.

Cardinal Kemp presents a peculiar problem. 'Benet's Chronicle', which is decidedly Yorkist in sympathy, describes him as Somerset's chief friend at this time.[39] Somerset may have been instrumental in Kemp's elevation to the archbishopric of Canterbury in 1452. Henry recommended him to the prior and chapter after consultation with his council 'and especial with suche as ben of our blode' – surely at that time a reference to Somerset.[40] A second chronicle indicates that Kemp tried to prevent the duke's imprisonment, thereby earning Norfolk's enmity.[41] Years later, in 1478, William Worcester claimed to have come upon evidence that Norfolk had been conspiring to have Kemp dismissed from office just prior to the latter's death in March 1454.[42] How Kemp's dismissal might have been legally accomplished is by no means clear. Stodeley's letter, on the other hand, seems to depict a more physical basis for Kemp's fear. Apart from the business of bodyguards, it closes with an addendum reporting

[36] Johnson, pp. 130–1, outlines the case, which involved the alleged confiscation of property belonging to York from the bishop of Durham's London house. He suggests (n. 22) that the similarity of these charges to previous charges made by Somerset against one of York's men raises 'suspicions of a quid pro quo'. For Thorpe's career, see Roskell, *Parliament and Politics*, II, pp. 201–27.
[37] For Trevilian, see Wolffe, pp. 109–110, 116; Griffiths, pp. 362, 613. For Daniel, see Wolffe, pp. 109, 122, 237; Griffiths, pp. 309, 329, 336–8, 363, 365, 428, 585, 612–13. For Tresham, see Griffiths, p. 341; for his career, Roskell, *Parliament and Politics*, II, pp. 267–77. Both Trevilian and Daniel were indicted by Cade, and Daniel was particularly hated.
[38] Wolffe, p. 297. I have found only one reference to him in the Patent Rolls prior to this time. On 10 January 1453, Joseph, styled the 'king's serjeant', received a grant of goods and chattels worth £100 that had been taken from Robert Gooldes and William Gloutesham, both Somerset gentlemen, who had been indicted for treason (*CPR, 1452–61*, p. 93).
[39] 'Benet's Chron.', p. 211.
[40] Sheppard, *Christ Church Letters*, p. 18. A little less than a year later Somerset made an indenture with the prior of Christ Church to lease a messuage within the abbey precincts (Sheppard, *Literae Cantuarienses*, III, pp. 214–15).
[41] Giles, *Chronicon*, pp. 44–5: 'Kempe . . . sic ab aliquibus dominis, et specialiter a duce Norfolchiae minatur, quod citius elegit mori quam vitam ducere mortis' ('Kemp . . .was so threatened by some lords and especially by the duke of Norfolk that he chose to die rather than to lead a life that was death.')
[42] Worcestre, *Itineraries*, p. 153. Johnson, p. 132, accepts this report, but attributes Norfolk's actions to his frustrated efforts to bring Somerset to trial. Watts, p. 304, n. 189, suggests that Kemp may have been responsible for Norfolk's binding over on 11 December 1453 in the sum of £12,000 (*CCR, 1447–54*, p. 476). If so, this may also help to explain Norfolk's enmity.

that an encounter with the mayor and merchants of London had left Kemp badly frightened. Whatever the nature of the threat, it appears to have been genuine and genuinely feared – and one wishes that we knew the contents of Norfolk's letter that Stodeley says fell into Kemp's hands, causing such 'harm'. The Yorkist-leaning chronicler nevertheless presents the chancellor's opposition to Somerset's arrest as an act of integrity rather than of partisan loyalty and ends with an encomium of him as a man whose like would not be seen again.[43]

In sum, then, although interests had begun to merge, we cannot yet speak of real factions. It is not at all certain that Kemp or anyone else – with the exception of Somerset's own men who were gathering about the Tower – were genuinely 'holding Somerset's opinion' or acting in his behalf. Nevertheless, the situation was extremely volatile. The minutes of the common council for 1 February underline the unease attendant on these circumstances. As it had done in the autumn, the council issued orders to see that the streets were well lit at night and that the peace was kept. In addition, appealing to the soothing effects of music, the waytes were to go about with their minstrels to entertain the people. Most importantly, no one was to attend on any lord of any party, and the council emphasized that neither the mayor nor the aldermen would call on any lord.[44]

Meanwhile, the problem of governance continued unresolved. Parliament, originally scheduled to meet on 11 February at Reading, was prorogued to meet at Westminster on the fourteenth. Cardinal Kemp appears to have been using delaying tactics to keep full power out of York's hands, though his ultimate purpose is not clear. It is possible that he still hoped for Henry's recovery, or he may have been attempting to retain power in the hands of the council or to prevent its further polarization.[45] If he and Margaret shared an interest in maintaining a governmental 'center', he may have been foot-dragging to allow more time for the consideration of a queen's regency.

On 13 February, virtually at the eleventh hour, Kemp finally raised the question of who should exercise the king's power to hold parliament in his absence. A substantial number of lords subscribed to the duke of York's appointment.[46] He appears to have been given full power in this regard, including the power to dissolve parliament.[47] When parliament opened, York

[43] Giles, *Chronicon*, p. 45: 'cui similem priorem puto nec habere sequentem' ('whom I consider to have no previous or subsequent likeness'). Both Storey, p. 82, and Griffiths, p. 724, characterize him as a man of principle and moderation.

[44] CLRO, Journal V, fol. 145b. Orders to keep the peace against the lords' arrival had already been given on 22 January (ibid., fol. 143).

[45] Johnson, pp. 129–30; Griffiths, p. 726.

[46] PRO, C81/1546/76: the archbishop of York; the bishops of London, Winchester, Ely, Norwich, Hereford, Salisbury, Lincoln and Durham; the earls of Warwick, Salisbury, Devon, Worcester (the treasurer), Oxford and Shrewsbury; Lords Cromwell, Greystoke, Grey of Ruthyn, FitzHugh, Dudley, Clinton, FitzWarin, Stourton, Scrope and Berners. It is impossible to say whether this amounted to unanimous consent by all those present when the matter came up.

[47] *RP*, V, p. 239, and *Foedera*, V, ii, p. 54 (the latter taken directly from the patent rolls), provide identical versions of the Latin text: 'Eidem Consanguineo nostro [York] ad Parliamentum ... Tenendum, & in eodem Procedendum, & ad Faciendum omnia & singula ... necnon ad Parliamentum illud Finiendum & Dissolvendum, de assensu Concilii nostri, plenam ... committimus Patestatem.' Grammatically and logically, the phrase 'with our council's assent' qualifies the verb 'committimus' and its object that concludes the sentence ('we entrust full power') and thus pertains to all of the functions regarding the

circumvented the commons' request for Thomas Thorp's release from prison to resume his position as speaker, and a new speaker, Sir Thomas Charlton, was elected.[48] The continued detention of Thorp might be construed as a victory for York, yet the real question of how government should be constituted for the duration of Henry's incapacity still remained unresolved. Though no record remains of the discussions, they dragged on for more than a month. This fact alone suggests that Margaret's bid for regency was not lightly dismissed. Since the commons at this time 'had the highest proportion of household members in it of the reign',[49] some of them may have supported her.

The twin welcomes given to both queen and duke by the mayor and aldermen of London soon after parliament opened reveals the atmosphere of ongoing uncertainty as matters balanced between Margaret and York. On Wednesday 20 February, the common council agreed to turn out in scarlet to meet the queen upon her arrival and to meet the duke in similar fashion on Friday.[50] Absenteeism among the lords provides a second indicator of the situation. In order to resolve the question of governance, a full attendance was necessary. It appears, however, that many lords tried to avoid participation and thus evade responsibility for any decision that might be taken, to the point that on 28 February fines were imposed on absentee peers in order to compel attendance.[51]

The creation of the king's son as prince of Wales and earl of Chester by charter on 15 March was a significant step, though its value may have been more symbolic than practical.[52] In more ordinary circumstances, there would have been no pressing need to grant the child these titles so early in his life. Thus, Edward the Black Prince, the eldest son of Edward III, had been made earl of Chester at the age of three and prince of Wales when he was thirteen.[53] Even the unanticipated death of Henry V, which made Henry VI king at the age of nine months, had created no succession crisis, for the principle of dynastic inheritance of the crown went unquestioned in England.[54] The situation in 1454, however, was unique. Although Henry VI might still suddenly die, given the serious nature of his illness, his death does not seem to have been considered imminent, and the six months of his illness already elapsed could have provided

---

conduct of parliament being granted to York. In short, the commission simply acknowledges the council's actual role in providing York with these powers while preserving the still-necessary fiction that the king was both cognizant and in charge. Cf. *CPR, 1452–61*, p. 153, where the abstract indicating that the council's separate assent was required to dissolve parliament appears to be a misreading of the text.

[48] *RP*, V, pp. 239–40.

[49] Johnson, p. 130.

[50] CLRO, Journal V, fol. 150.

[51] Griffiths, p. 724; *RP*, V, p. 248. Johnson, p. 132, connects problems of attendance with the lack of a decision on Margaret's bill. See also Roskell, 'Problem of Attendance of the Lords', p. 189, who also finds that the lords were 'loth to overlook the queen's claim to a regency' and that absenteeism signalled 'their reluctance to commit'.

[52] *CChR, 1427–1516*, p. 127. No further action was taken until 13 April, when a commission was named to invest him with the insignia of office (*CPR, 1452–61*, pp. 171–2). The ceremony actually took place upon 9 June. See below, p. 116.

[53] GEC, III, pp. 172–4.

[54] Griffiths, p. 12, who also considers the parliamentary statute of 1406 validating the Lancastrian succession an affirmation of this principle.

some inkling that he was apt to linger.[55] During such an indefinite and potentially extended period, much could happen, particularly in an atmosphere of rivalry and tension when it was no secret that one of the contenders for power (York) had a couple of years earlier tried to get himself named heir apparent.[56] In these circumstances, the titles may have been intended to reassure the realm and, more particularly, Margaret.

There was, however, a further way in which this development could have worked in Margaret's favor. One of the points of her bill had requested the assignment of sufficient livelihood for the king, the prince and herself. The creation of her son as prince of Wales would place authority over the principality – including its revenues – in the hands of the prince's council regardless of who held the government of the realm.[57] Thus it may have represented a step towards the financial security that Margaret desired. In addition, although it is hazardous to extrapolate from hindsight, the prince's council would later emerge as an instrument of her own power.[58] While we do not know who instigated the creation, it may have been brought about by pressure from the queen herself.[59]

The hints of deal making embodied in the situation make one wonder about the nature of the deal in progress.[60] A letter written by the earl of Salisbury, dated only to '7 March', but which also seems to allude to bargains made, might add something to the existing mix – if it could be attributed conclusively to 1454.[61] In it the earl seeks the queen's good ladyship through an intermediary and refers to letters recently written by Margaret to the council, which appear to involve the resolution of some troublous matter. But the letter also indicates that the queen's favor depends upon getting something in return, and Salisbury insists – three times – that a promise he has made will be kept. It is all very mysterious and tantalizing, though incapable of definitive solution. As a speculation then, if the letter could be firmly linked to 1454, it might suggest a bargain in which Margaret agreed to give up her bid for a regency in exchange for sufficient assurances regarding her son's rights.[62]

Be that as it may, it appears that discussions bogged down again, with no sign of a resolution to the real question on the horizon. On 19 March, while refusing to sanction further grants for the defense of Calais, the commons recalled the

---

[55] Suggested by the provision in York's appointment as protector that Prince Edward should succeed him in office when the latter came of age (*RP*, V, p. 243).

[56] Griffiths, p. 692; Johnson, p. 98; Watts, p. 278, all accept that York stood behind the affair of Thomas Young.

[57] Johnson, p. 133. In the event, a council was not established until the beginning of 1457.

[58] Griffiths, p. 781. See pp. 133–6, below.

[59] The formal origin of the charter appears in a council warrant of 15 March (PRO, C81/1546/79), which was signed by twenty-two lords, including York, who appear to represent a cross-section of interests and allegiances.

[60] Watts, pp. 307–8, suggests that some sort of *quid pro quo* was involved; he envisions it as the acquittal of the earl of Devon – a supporter of York in 1452 – on treason charges in return for the formal recognition of the prince of Wales.

[61] BL, Cotton Vespasian F xiii (i), art. 64. It has been published in Flemming, *England under the Lancastrians*, pp. 128–9, and recently discussed by Hicks, *Warwick*, pp. 155–6. I consider the problems posed by its content and dating at greater length in Appendix II, below.

[62] Since this is speculative, the rest of the discussion in this chapter does not depend on this particular interpretation of the letter or on the suggestion that Margaret willingly withdrew her claim.

chancellor's testimony at the opening of the parliament at Reading one year past that a 'sadde and a wyse' council would be established to oversee the equitable ministration of justice, and coupled the reminder with a plea for peace. Although these requests were likely to have reflected the commons' greater concern for 'the restoration of peace and order in the realm' than the issue of who was to be entrusted with the king's power,[63] the presence of such a council along the lines of that provided Eleanor of Provence might also have made a queen's regency seem less threatening to established order. Kemp promised the commons a 'good and comfortable aunswere; without eny grete delay or tariyng'.[64] What his answer to the conundrum might have been cannot be known, for three days later he was dead. He was an elderly man, approaching his eightieth year. Nevertheless, his death appears to have been unanticipated and unexpected.[65]

The loss of the chancellor made action imperative. Accordingly, on 23 March the lords spiritual and temporal 'thoroughly agreed' to send a deputation to the king at Windsor to inform him of this development and, not incidentally, to ascertain whether he was capable of 'herying and understondyng therof'. The deputation consisted of the bishops of Winchester, Ely and Coventry and Lichfield; the earls of Warwick, Oxford and Shrewsbury; Viscounts Beaumont and Bourgchier; the prior of St John's and the Lords Fauconberg, Dudley and Stourton. They were to inquire into Henry's wishes regarding the archbishopric of Canterbury and the chancellorship and also remind him of his intent to establish a council, wherefore a list of 'certaine Lordes and persones' had been established who should 'take upon theym the seid charge' unless the king chose to change or set aside any of them. Finally, the delegation was warned to speak of all these matters 'to noo persone but onely unto the Kyng'.[66] Margaret's whereabouts are not certain at this time, and her inclusion in this restriction cannot be determined. Since Beaumont was her servant and remained loyal to her, she probably knew what was afoot whether she was supposed to or not. On the twenty-fifth the deputation reported back that their efforts had been to no avail; on three separate occasions they had tried to get Henry's attention and to elicit some response 'by all the means and weyes that they coude thynk . . . but they cowede have no aunswere, worde ne signe'. Two days later, on 27 March, York was named protector and defensor of the realm. He was at pains to obtain an act stating that he had not sought the office himself, but that the lords, 'in whom by th'occasion of th'enfirmite of [the king] restethe th'exercice of his auctoritee', had freely chosen him. The lords agreed that it would also suit them to have it recorded that they had acted purely of necessity.[67] York appears to have 'won' the contest with Margaret as much by default as by choice. J.J. Bagley

[63] *RP*, V, p. 240; Griffiths, p. 724.
[64] *RP*, V, p. 240.
[65] Kemp was born c. 1375. Emden, *Oxford*, II, p. 1032, suggests that he had suffered poor health from 1452 and attributes to it his inability to halt the drift towards civil war. Quite to the contrary, the picture that we have of his activities during his last months does not suggest frailty. If his handling of the situation was ineffective, it is difficult to imagine how anyone could have done better under the circumstances.
[66] *RP*, V, pp. 240–1.
[67] Ibid., pp. 241–2.

inadvertently, but neatly, encapsulated the situation when he wrote that in the circumstances 'sober minds thought that to appoint a woman as regent would make still more unobtainable the strong government that all *men* [then] felt was essential'.[68] For that, they needed a man.

Although fifteenth-century England was likely to have been startled and amazed by the queen's bid for regency, and although her French origins would have provided an additional deterrent to her acceptance at this time, to say that her effort failed simply because of its novelty misses the nuances of the situation in early 1454 and ignores past precedent, however distant. There was, in fact, good reason to take Margaret's bill seriously, and it was the same reason that would have impelled her to submit it in the first place: the need for a 'center' that could stand above magnate rivalry and command the loyalty of all. Without such a center, there could be no long-term security for either the dynasty or the realm. It would have been evident by the time parliament met, if not sooner, that York was not going to provide it.[69] Consequently, there was no tide of support for him from any direction, despite the fact that he was the only clear male choice for the governance in terms of rank and lineage.

There were two possible alternatives to York: governance by a council or governance by the queen. Although the commons had already expressed their wish, in a different context, for a sad and wise council, government by council would have had its drawbacks, not the least of which would have been the potential for a continuation of partisanship and divisions among its members that would have hindered efforts at concerted and effective action.

Whether Margaret *could* have provided a center had she been given the opportunity is moot. In theory, however, her position as queen with its attendant connotations of mediation and intercession gave her the only credible claim to supply one. That being said, the fact remains that there was no tide of support for her either. It appears, therefore, that no one was overly enthusiastic about any of the three alternatives and that the matter dragged on because there was no such support. In short, it came to a choice between unsatisfactory solutions that could neither be dismissed outright nor wholeheartedly accepted. Kemp's death added yet another level of urgency to the ongoing crisis; under this additional pressure the fallback resolution, dictated by a complex of assumptions, was York.

What, then, went wrong for Margaret, if there was more to it than simple consensus that a woman could not even be considered? It may be that the very thing that provided her with a centrist claim also prevented her from grasping it: she was the king's wife, and Henry, though alive, remained catatonic. Although the queen enjoyed a 'right of distinct property' that permitted her a degree of legal independence not accorded to other wives,[70] she remained in all

---

[68] Bagley, *Margaret of Anjou*, p. 75, emphasis added.

[69] It may be doubted that Somerset would have behaved any differently; he was simply not at large.

[70] Chambers, *Course of Lectures on English Law*, I, p. 177. Specifically, she was regarded as *feme sole* in her capacity to acquire or alienate lands or goods in her own name, to sue or be sued, to receive grants of lands or goods from her husband and to bequeath her separate possessions by will. Chambers claimed that this right had existed 'for many centuries', citing Anglo-Saxon examples. See also Fisher, 'The Queenes Courte', p. 316, who notes that the queen's status as *feme sole* allowed the king to avoid responsibility for her debts.

other respects her husband's subordinate. This is most evident in her accepted public role as intercessor. Though she could plead, in some sense acting as her husband's conscience, it was still his will that authorized effective action in response to her pleas.

The theoretical unity of person created by marriage, despite the queen's practical exemptions from it, affected her options in other ways. Although the king could grant her property, to do with subsequently as she pleased and free from his control, it does not appear that he could grant away any aspect of his decision-making capacity or public authority to her as an independent person. Like other wives, she could act as agent for and representative of her husband insofar as her actions could be construed, in theory, as the expressions of his authority and will.[71] These were the grounds on which Eleanor's regency had operated.[72] This is also the kind of thinking that Margaret explicitly invoked in some of her letters when she associated her wishes with Henry's or presented her own wishes as embodiments of the king's will.[73] It is, moreover, the form of self-representation to which she generally resorted during her later political ascendancy, with a certain degree of success.

In the circumstances of early 1454, however, there was one insurmountable obstacle to this approach. The theoretical possibility of wifely agency seems to depend upon the presumption that the husband is cognizant and capable of the authority and will that are to be represented, and Henry was neither. In contrast, a male who was authorized to act in the king's behalf and in his interest would not be in the same theoretical position as the wife; as a male he automatically possessed some kind of authority and was presumed to have a separate will.[74] The possibility that Henry might die, leaving his wife as regent during a lengthy minority and raising the specter of a power grab by her new husband should she remarry, would also have argued against a queen's regency.[75]

This all becomes clearer when the formalities of York's appointment are considered. His designation as protector was made in Henry's name, as if Henry himself made the grant and the decision.[76] Obviously, Henry's involvement was fictitious, but it was a necessary fiction in that it reflected the contemporary

---

[71] Blackstone, *Commentaries*, I, p. 430: 'A man cannot grant any thing to his wife, or enter into covenant with her: for the grant would be to suppose her separate existence; and to covenant with her, would be only to covenant with himself . . . [but] a woman indeed may be attorney for her husband; for that implies no separation from, but is rather a representation of, her lord.' Although Blackstone's observations pertain to marriage in general, rather than to the specific case of king and queen, if allowances are made for the queen's exceptional privileges, the basic rules still seem to apply.

[72] Howell, *Eleanor of Provence*, pp. 114–15, 117, 118–20, 121, 124, 271.

[73] As in her promotion of John Hals, discussed above, pp. 64–5.

[74] Blok, 'Female Rulers', observes that women typically have acquired authority in the absence – actual or voluntary – of a male presence to whom they might 'normally' be deemed subordinate (i.e. a husband or father). In Margaret's case, however, Henry's 'absence' did not work to her advantage for the reasons outlined here. Instead, her power appears to have been greatest when she was able to associate it with the king's authority, an approach that would prove to be self-limiting. I deal with these issues in Part IV, below.

[75] Parsons, *Eleanor of Castile*, p. 45.

[76] *Foedera*, V, ii, p. 55; *CPR, 1452–61*, p. 159; but cf. *RP*, V, p. 242, where his position rests solely on the authority of the lords assembled in parliament. Until the letters patent could be issued in Henry's name, the duke continued to be styled as the king's lieutenant in parliament.

understanding of how such things were done and how they had to be. Given that the recipient of the protectorate was a male, to whom the king could grant office and with whom he could covenant, and who could then be understood to act of his own will and volition, albeit at all times presumably in the king's interest and behalf, the fiction worked. If an attempt is made to replace York with Margaret, the understood structure becomes ridiculous and insupportable. Here we have the wife, to whom the king cannot grant away his power in the first place, and who can only be assumed to act as the instrument of his (presently nonexistent) will in the second!

We all recognize that in the normal course of things people do not live and behave precisely according to theory. But when one is the king or queen, theoretical (as opposed to practical) reality takes on greater importance, and the natural discrepancies between theory and practice become more visible and more keenly felt.[77] Some evidence of the ramifications that this had for the queen's activities and behavior may be found in the advice of Christine de Pisan. Her 'princess' embodies all of the idealized female virtues of charity, chastity, patience, humility and obedience, along with the practical virtue of being able to manage her household sensibly; whereas her 'baroness' is a more active figure who must be prepared to take her husband's place during his frequent absences, both as administrator and, if necessary, as military leader.[78] It thus appears that at the top of the female social ladder, although opportunities for influence through contact with one's husband (the prince) became greater, the repertoire of 'appropriate' female responses had by the fifteenth century became more circumscribed.

As a final, further matter, the position York was given, essentially identical to the protectorate of 1422 established during Henry's infancy, was one that because of its military connotations could only be held by a man. Specifically, his duty was to defend the kingdom from enemies, external or internal. Beyond that, his authority was much more limited than a regent's would have been, making him only the first man in the council, a little more equal than others. So it may also be that England's own traditions had left it ill-disposed toward a long-term regency of any kind, a view supported by the lords' explicit rejection of the titles of 'tutor, lieutenant, governor, and regent' in defining the limits of York's power and authority,[79] whereas the lesser position of protector was gender-exclusive in conception. If his role was envisioned as 'first man in the council', that in itself would have been gender-limiting as the council was assumed to be, by definition, an all-male institution.

---

[77] Rosenthal, *Kings and Kingship*, p. v, notes that kings were vulnerable on account of their public visibility; thus they 'worked to polish the kingly image because, in the full light of public discussion and speculation, it could so quickly tarnish'. Clearly, Henry VI was one king whose image did not match the public's idea of what 'kingly' should be.

[78] Christine, *Treasure*, pp. 47–50, 56–9, 62–5, 75, 76–7, 128–9. She does specify that the baroness should seek the advice of 'wise old men' (i.e. her husband's counselors) lest she be perceived to rely too much on her own initiative (p. 129).

[79] *RP*, V, p. 242. Griffiths, 'King's Council', p. 312, considers the instructions to the delegation that visited Henry as evidence that a regency had at that point been rejected. Although this may be so, it still does not explain how one gets from a council – the topic of inquiry – to a protectorate. One may argue whether the need for a protector was self-evident or not; the delegation was not similarly instructed to discuss the need for this office with the king.

On the surface, at least, it appears that Margaret accepted the council's resolution of the crisis of government and the appointment of York as protector without overt protest. It was not the result she had initially desired, but she may have been resigned to live with it. She may have received reassurance in the form of her son's creation as prince of Wales and in the conditions accompanying York's formal appointment. For the time being, although she had been recognized as a political player, she would spend most of the next two-and-a-half years in the political shadows, perhaps to wait and watch. Nevertheless, despite her relative invisibility, these years were crucial, for they provided the context for her subsequent actions.

8

Enmities

TO ALL OUTWARD appearances, Margaret seems to have accepted York's protectorate quietly. No one expressed either surprise or dismay at her acceptance. We cannot even be sure of the extent to which it rankled her; it was, after all, what she as a woman was supposed to do. Nevertheless, she appears to have been treated with a certain care and caution. In part, this was simply due to her status as queen, but it also reflects her unexpected foray into high politics and the realization that she had suddenly become a largely unknown quantity.

The patent formalizing York's appointment was issued on 3 April. According to its conditions he was to serve as protector during the king's pleasure or until the king's son came of age and might assume the office if he so chose.[1] Besides the provision for Prince Edward contained within York's appointment, a similar patent of the same date granted him the office when he reached the age of discretion if he would take it.[2] These terms provided constitutional reassurance that matters regarding the succession should stay on the straight and narrow and may have been intended to placate Margaret, whose own hopes had just been rebuffed, if, indeed, they were not added at her own insistence.[3] When the new protector received limited rights to royal patronage and a salary of 2,000 marks per year via parliamentary act, the queen's rights and possessions were specifically safeguarded.[4]

On the day before York's appointment, Richard Neville, earl of Salisbury, had been named chancellor, undoubtedly on York's wishes. Although Salisbury was York's brother-in-law, he had been conspicuously part of Henry's entourage at Dartford in 1452.[5] Their recently discovered common interest was politically driven, having much to do with the ongoing feud between the Nevilles and the Percies in the north, as well as the conflict between Salisbury's son Warwick and the earl of Somerset on the one hand, and York's need for powerful support on the other. It was an arrangement from which both stood to benefit, but which did nothing to ameliorate the drift towards faction.[6]

---

[1] *CPR, 1452–61*, p. 159; *Foedera*, V, ii, p. 55.
[2] Ibid., see also *RP*, V, p. 243.
[3] Griffiths, p. 726, suggests the latter.
[4] *RP*, V, pp. 243–4.
[5] Wolffe, p. 252. He was paid £333 6s. 8d. for his attendance on the king (Devon, *Issues*, pp. 475–6).
[6] Griffiths, pp. 726–7; Johnson, p. 135.

Nevertheless, York's protectorate should not be viewed as the triumph of a Yorkist 'party'. There were, as yet, no recognizable 'parties'. Instead, individual rivalries still remained paramount in the absence of solid factional positions.[7] This picture is strengthened by the minutes of three great council meetings that occurred between November 1453 and April 1454. Although the minutes indicate that factional allegiances had begun to play a role by December, it was still possible in April for nearly everyone – even the 'Yorkists' – to hedge their support after the establishment of York's protectorate. At the council meeting of 3 April, the day that York's position was formalized by patent, the new chancellor called upon the lords who had been named as councilors to express their willingness to serve. With near-unanimity they initially demurred, their responses mingling pronouncements of high-minded intentions with blatant excuses. Four lay peers, led off by Norfolk, pleaded chronic ill health. Five bishops and the prior of the Hospital of St John's found themselves suddenly conscience-smitten about their duties elsewhere.[8]

Various reasons may explain this general reluctance to commit. Some protests were undoubtedly made for effect, to assure onlookers that the protestor was not unbecomingly eager for power.[9] But another reason was likely to have been loyalty – or duty – to the queen. This appears to have been the case with Viscount Beaumont, who at first excused himself from serving on York's council because 'he was with the quene for the wiche he would not departe in takynge uppone hym this charge', a statement that easily invokes a double meaning of physical attendance and political support.[10] In a pertinent commentary on the council's formation, Beaumont also reminded those present that

> it was conteyned in thartycles of the counsell that every man shuld have full freedom to saye what he thowght in matters as of counsales, without any displeasure, indignacyon or wrothe of any other person for his sayinge the wyche he wold shuld be kept and observed.[11]

It appears that, to him at least, the freedom of all council members to express themselves without fear of recrimination was a matter of concern. These observations have some bearing on Margaret's political emergence as an acknowledged power in her own right. It must be emphasized that she did not appear as the representative of one or another lord's interest. Her bid for regency had embodied a claim to represent the dynasty itself, above the interests of particular lords. Available evidence indicates that it had not been casually

[7] Storey, pp. 137–41.

[8] Griffiths, 'King's Council', pp. 313–15, discusses the meeting; pp. 317–19, for the minutes, from Harvard University, fMS Eng. 751, fols 213r–214v. Besides Norfolk, the 'sickly' peers were the duke of Buckingham, the earl of Oxford and Lord Cromwell; only the latter was elderly and perhaps in poor health, though he fought at St Albans the following year. The bishops held the sees of Winchester, Worcester, Norwich, Lincoln and Coventry and Lichfield. Other excuses included lack of experience and poverty.

[9] Hicks, *Warwick*, p. 99.

[10] Griffiths, 'King's Council', pp. 314, 319, who accepts Beaumont's loyalty as unequivocal and uncompromising. In the end he agreed to serve, but his attendance is only twice attested (*PPC*, VI, pp. 209, 233).

[11] Ibid., p. 81.

dismissed whatever consternation it most likely caused. In the difficult situation of Henry's incapacity, in which everyone from York on down was anxious to have his commitment to 'the honour, prosperite and welfare, of th'estate and dignite of [the king]' set down in writing,[12] Margaret's rival claim would continue to be an uneasy reminder that much lay in the eye of the beholder, and that the 'true' representation of dynastic interest remained open to question.

Moreover, all of the evidence that private interests had not been – and would not be – set aside provided further cause for the lords' evasiveness. To contemporary sensibilities, the wheel of fortune provided a familiar motif. The wheel had recently turned, raising York's position and his prospects, but it could turn again, and what went up inevitably came down. Thus a combination of concerns fed the general reluctance to participate without demur in a council under York's leadership. At the least, those who ended up participating over their initial objections could later say that they had done so of necessity and under pressure.

The council that emerged did in principle represent a balance of interests. Four of its two dozen members had direct connections with Margaret: William Booth, archbishop of York, her former chancellor; Walter Lyhert, bishop of Norwich, her confessor; Viscount Beaumont and Lord Scales, who were her servants. The king's household was also strongly represented.[13] In practice, however, the council was plagued by absenteeism. Many of its members attended sporadically, and after the initial formative session of 3 April some did not attend at all.[14] It is likely that these patterns to some extent reflected continuing uneasiness about being associated with the protectorate. Such misgivings are demonstrated by the lords' failure to take further action against Somerset. In July there was some movement to resolve his case, but the great council at which the matter arose was poorly attended, and York was able to wriggle out of releasing him on bail. Instead, a trial date was set for the end of October, but it never took place.[15]

Although Margaret appears to have accepted the protectorate, she did not immediately drop out of sight. At the end of April and the beginning of May, the London common council received letters from York, Salisbury and the queen.[16] Unfortunately, their substance was not recorded, nor is it even certain – though it may be suspected – that they all dealt with the same matters, whatever they may have been.

It may be also that the queen still retained some hope that the situation could be remedied in a manner more to her liking. In short, she may have sought a miracle. A curious letter exists, written by Margaret to the prior of Christ Church, Canterbury, and bearing only the date of 30 April. In it Margaret asked the prior 'tacerteine us of suche holy water and relik as ye have . . . for the grete

[12] *RP*, V, p. 242.

[13] Griffiths, pp. 726–8; Johnson, pp. 135–7, for its composition and allegiances. But cf. Hicks, *Warwick*, p. 111, who points out the absence of any direct rivals of York or the Nevilles.

[14] Johnson, p. 139, for particulars. Booth and Lyhert were regular attendees; Beaumont showed up twice, in July and November (see n. 10, above).

[15] Johnson, pp. 143–4, 146, 152; Wolffe p. 284.

[16] CLRO, Journal V, fols 162 and 162v. There is no record of them in the published Letter Books (i.e. Sharpe, *Cal. of Letter-Books: Letter-Book K*).

zele, love and affeccion that ye have towards my lords helth and welefare'. The letter was entrusted to the king's almoner, Henry Sever, who was to return with the water. Though the year in which it was written cannot be established beyond all possible doubt, it can be attributed with a very high degree of probability to 1454.[17] The letter was likely to have been written in Henry's presence, in response to his observed condition. Moreover, it was written at Windsor, where Henry had been moved from Clarendon after he fell ill and where he would remain until his recovery. Sever's role fits this interpretation. He had long associations with Henry, having become one of his chaplains in 1437 and having been chosen by the king as the first provost of Eton. He had become Henry's almoner by 1448 and was still holding that office in July 1454, when the protector with the council's advice allotted him certain horses and a carriage.[18] With his background, he was a man who would have been trusted to handle such a sensitive matter as this. This letter, then, can best be understood as a last-ditch effort by Margaret to work a miracle. If Henry recovered, York would have to give up his protectorate, and all bets would be off.

No miracle occurred, and on 9 June, Margaret was present at her son's investiture as prince of Wales. Although Buckingham, Salisbury and 'manye othyre Lordys off astate' were also in attendance, York was then in the north, dealing with problems caused by the Percies and the duke of Exeter.[19] She appears thereafter to have quietly bided her time, with no further attempts to put herself forward. Yet she continued to be treated with both care and caution. In November, when substantial reductions were ordered in the size of the king's household, her establishment experienced very little change from its size in 1452–53.[20]

York's first tenure as protector lasted for about ten months. Towards the end of December, Henry recovered his faculties and found that he had a son, whereupon 'he hild up his hands and thankid God therof'. The report of what he said at this time, sketchy as it is, leaves the impression that he had no knowledge of anything that had taken place during his illness, nor any real memory of the illness itself. It was as if he had awakened from a sound and lengthy sleep, from which he pronounced himself 'in charitee with all the world, and . . . wold all the Lords were'.[21] Such a wish may indicate that he had learned some things about the current situation – perhaps from Margaret – or that he simply remembered matters prior to his illness. Like someone who had been lost in a dream, he seems to have tried to pick things up where he thought he had left off, without clearly understanding how the situation might have altered.

---

[17] Inner Temple Library, Petyt MS 538.47, fol. 409x; published in *HMC, Eleventh Report*, App. VII, p. 282. The Catalogue of MSS in the Inner Temple Library, p. 877, tentatively dates it to c. 1460, which is certainly mistaken. I know of no other effort to date it.

[18] Griffiths, p. 304; *PPC*, VI, pp. 212–13, 232. Sever died in 1471 (Emden, *Oxford*, III, p. 1673).

[19] Gairdner, *PL*, II, pp. 320–1. For discussions of the situation and York's actions, see Pollard, *North-Eastern England*, pp. 259–60; Griffiths, 'Local Rivalries', pp. 342–53. Briefly, it appears that Exeter had determined to supplant York as protector and possibly even to replace Henry with himself. In later years, when her strength was greatest, Margaret showed little inclination to trust him (Storey, p. 147).

[20] Myers, 'Household of Queen Margaret', p. 90 and n. 4, where he reckons her household in 1452–53 to have consisted of 'not more than 130' persons. The 1454 measure allowed her 120 (*PPC*, VI, p. 233).

[21] Gairdner, *PL*, III, pp. 13–14.

This meant that Somerset would be released from the Tower and that York would be relieved of his protectorate. Somerset's official release on bail took place on 4 February at a great council meeting; the duke of Buckingham, the earl of Wiltshire, Lords Roos and FitzWarin stood surety for him.[22] It seems that he had already been spirited out of the Tower by Buckingham, Wiltshire and Roos on 26 January, perhaps in anticipation of York's opposition and to forestall possible trouble; this action may have prompted York's voluntary resignation.[23] York – no longer styled protector – was present at the council on the fourth, along with Salisbury and Warwick, though they could not have been happy with the outcome. Initially, however, matters did not all go Somerset's way either, for his bail was to last until the day after All Souls' (i.e. 3 November) when he would have to respond to charges, and he may have had to agree to have no more to do with governance and to keep a distance of twenty miles from the king.[24] Of Somerset's guarantors, only Wiltshire could be considered hostile towards York, and it seems likely that the majority of persons present at the meeting favored his release on the grounds that his continued imprisonment, without being formally charged or convicted, was illegal.[25] At the same time, he was neither widely liked nor trusted. For the moment, then, it appears that the treatment of the two rivals was actually relatively balanced.

A month later, this changed. On 4 March, Henry met with his lords at the queen's manor of Greenwich, where he declared Somerset 'his feithfull and true Liegeman and Subgitte' and discharged him from bail.[26] The king's statement of trust effectively repudiated the accusations of treason that York and Norfolk had made against him.[27] On the same day Henry took back the captaincy of Calais from York (which York had taken from Somerset during the protectorate) and returned it to Somerset two days later.[28] Nevertheless, both dukes were obliged to agree, to the tune of 20,000 marks each, to submit their remaining differences to arbitration and to abide by the arbiters' decisions.[29] On 7 March, Salisbury resigned the chancellorship and it was given to Archbishop Bourgchier of Canterbury.[30]

One would like to know what role, if any, Margaret played in all of this. At this point she seems a particularly shadowy figure. While it is likely that she favored Somerset's release, there is no evidence that she machinated to obtain it.

---

[22] *Foedera*, V, ii, p. 61; *CCR, 1454–61*, p. 44.

[23] Flenley ('Bale's Chron.'), p. 141: 'Wherfor . . . York yave up the kings swerd and noo longer wold occupie protector.' See also Griffiths, p. 739.

[24] *English Chron.*, p. 78. Here, the chronicle's account is somewhat muddled.

[25] Johnson, p. 152. This was precisely the argument that Somerset would soon make for his acquittal.

[26] *Foedera*, V, ii, p. 61; *CPR, 1452–61*, p. 226.

[27] Armstrong, 'Politics and the Battle of St Albans', p. 8.

[28] Ibid.; *Foedera*, V, ii, p. 62.

[29] Ibid., pp. 61–2; *CCR, 1454–61*, p. 49. Of the arbiters, Griffiths, p. 739, considers the earl of Worcester and Lord Cromwell likely to have favored York, while the earl of Wiltshire, Viscount Beaumont and Lord Stourton had close ties to the court. Though he doubts the neutrality of the remaining three, the duke of Buckingham – despite his role in Somerset's release – had not shown himself a committed partisan prior to this time; Thomas Bourgchier, archbishop of Canterbury and Buckingham's half-brother, had been elevated at the beginning of the protectorate and had further ties to York through his elder brother, who was York's brother-in-law; William Grey, bishop of Ely, would later be sympathetic towards York (ibid., pp. 727, 817, 860). The settlement was to be reached by 20 June.

[30] 'Benet's Chron.', p. 213; Giles, *Chronicon*, p. 47.

His return to power seems clearly to have followed Henry's own wishes, whatever the queen may have thought. Nor is there any sign that Margaret actively sought York's downfall. Just as Henry's recovery had ended the need for a protectorate, so had it undercut Margaret's erstwhile claim to represent the dynasty. Her importance naturally receded as Henry's returned. In any event, it appears that she had pulled back from the spotlight in the course of the protectorate – or that it had shifted away from her as York became established – and there in the background she remained for the time being, while older rivalries played out their course.

With Somerset's release and reinstatement, the fuse that had been left smoldering by his imprisonment at York's hands burst into flame. It was unthinkable that he should forgive or forget. The promise of a commission to arbitrate, however well intentioned in its inception, was like applying a band-aid to a broken leg. Henry's public declaration of his faith in Somerset had trivialized York's genuine concerns; the latter may have regarded arbitration as the approaching *coup de grâce*. At the same time, Somerset would not have felt himself secure. For each, the problem of political, if not physical, survival remained the same: to quickly and irrevocably neutralize the other.[31] Thanks to his renewed ascendancy, Somerset for the moment had the inside track.

Sometime between Salisbury's surrender of the chancellorship and mid-April, York and the Nevilles withdrew from the court – perhaps without permission – and began raising troops. In mid-April a council, from which they may have been deliberately excluded, met at Westminster. The chronology is uncertain; we do not know whether the April meeting was called in response to York's and the Nevilles' abrupt departure or whether they left in haste because of their intended exclusion from a council that they deemed to be hostile. There it was further determined to hold a great council at Leicester on 25 May. The ostensible purpose of the latter assembly was to take steps to assure Henry's safety. If we may assume that this was indeed one of the genuine reasons for meeting, it is possible to imagine Margaret's influence behind it. Surely the king's safety would have been among her greatest concerns at this point, and she held the castle, town and honor of Leicester, 'in the heart of the [presumably safe] Lancastrian homelands'.[32] Nevertheless, since there is no clear evidence of her involvement, the suggestion must remain speculative. Leicester may also have provided a venue in which to announce the arbitration results.[33] It is likewise possible that Somerset intended a formal settlement of the governance, to take effect if Henry suffered a relapse and which, naturally, would have excluded York.[34] Both of these suggestions make sense and go farther towards explaining York's decision to intercept the king's party and forestall the Leicester meeting. Be that as it may, it appears that what the king and court

[31] Johnson, pp. 154–5. For events surrounding the first battle of St Albans, the most comprehensive treatment remains Armstrong's 1960 article, 'Politics and the Battle of St Albans', upon which I have generally based the following account.

[32] Wolffe, p. 290. Armstrong, 'Politics and the Battle of St Albans', p. 14, thinks that the decision to hold the council at Leicester was Somerset's because of his unpopularity in London. Cf. Hicks, *Warwick*, pp. 113–14, who finds that Henry already had a predilection for the midlands.

[33] Griffiths, p. 742; Wolffe, p. 290.

[34] Johnson, p. 155.

envisioned was a political meeting, not a military confrontation. They seem not to have realized the seriousness and magnitude of the Yorkist military preparations until a few days before they were ready to ride to Leicester, at which point they had to take hasty steps to raise men.[35] Around this time it begins to make sense to speak of a genuine Yorkist faction; indeed, the three lords claimed to represent a party.[36]

When the king set out from Westminster for Leicester on 21 May, the queen stayed behind. Thus, she would only learn at secondhand, from Henry or others, what transpired. York had moved south more quickly than anyone had anticipated to confront Henry's company as it approached St Albans on the twenty-second. Although the king replaced Somerset with Buckingham as constable, and the latter attempted to negotiate – apparently in good faith[37] – these efforts ended in stalemate with York demanding that Somerset be handed over to him or else.[38] This was a demand to which Henry could not possibly accede, for it amounted to an assault on the king's authority.[39] Although Henry is not generally thought of as a 'strong' person, it may be correct to characterize his refusal to 'submit to [York's] dictation' as an act of courage and principle rather than of blind adherence to a favorite.[40] Fighting broke out in which Somerset, the earl of Northumberland, Lord Clifford and others were slain. Henry, who apparently stood by his standard, but took no other part in the fighting, was wounded slightly by an arrow in the neck, perhaps by accident.[41]

Though the Yorkists were at pains to submit themselves and to swear allegiance to Henry as soon as the fighting ended, there could have been little doubt as to who was actually in control. The next day, with great ceremony, they escorted the king back to London, where Margaret had taken refuge in the Tower with her son.[42] On Whitsunday the king wore his crown at St Paul's, placed on his head by York. After the week's festivities he retired with the queen and prince to Windsor, and then to Hertford. York and the Nevilles stationed themselves nearby, 'presumably to forestall any inclination by the king to raise forces'.[43] By the time parliament met in July, York had become constable again, Warwick had received Somerset's vacated post as captain of Calais, and

---

[35] Armstrong, 'Politics and the Battle of St Albans', pp. 11–12, 13–18.

[36] Ibid., p. 20.

[37] Griffiths, p. 744; Armstrong, 'Politics and the Battle of St Albans', p. 24, also observes that '[Henry] seems to have chosen Buckingham as a moderate, who could be counted on to concede but not to capitulate'. Indeed, unless one assumes Henry to have been entirely in Somerset's power – which, clearly, he was not – it appears that his own actions up to this point, insofar as they can be determined as what Somerset would likely *not* have done, were intended by his own lights to be moderate.

[38] Ibid., p. 29. Presumably Somerset was to be tried, though something more drastic is neither impossible nor unsupported (ibid., p. 32).

[39] See Watts's assessment of the constitutional issues involved in Kekewich, et al., *Politics of Fifteenth-Century England*, pp. 21–3.

[40] Armstrong, 'Politics and the Battle of St Albans', pp. 38–9.

[41] A number of more or less contemporary sources report this: Gairdner, *PL*, III, p. 30; 'Gregory's Chron.', p. 198; *English Chron.*, p. 72; 'Benet's Chron.', p. 214; Kekewich, et al., *Politics of Fifteenth-Century England*, p. 192.

[42] Watts, p. 317, n. 246, citing PRO, E159/232, comm., Mic., rot. 3, sees Margaret's presence in the Tower as evidence of widespread fears of York's intentions.

[43] Johnson, p. 158, n. 18. York was at Ware, adjacent to Hertford; Salisbury was at Rye on the Channel coast, and Warwick was at Hunsdon (Gairdner, *PL*, III, p. 32).

Viscount Bourgchier, York's brother-in-law, was treasurer in place of the earl of Wiltshire, who had escaped from St Albans alive and gone into hiding. During the summer parliament session a pardon was enacted that absolved the Yorkists and their supporters from all responsibility for anything that had happened at St Albans, while allocating blame to the duke of Somerset, Thomas Thorp and William Joseph, who were said to have kept the Yorkists' letters from the king during the negotiations preceding the battle. Though politically necessary from the Yorkist point of view – most importantly the pardon provided security against later private litigation – it obfuscated the real issue, which had been the inflexibility of their demands.[44] Parliament also provided the opportunity to have the Yorkists' loyalty to Henry recorded and asserted.

All of these actions can be considered prudent from the Yorkists' point of view; all are understandable. Yet to Margaret, looking on, they would have represented a very different reality. She could not have failed to see that Henry had become 'more or less a puppet in the hands of York and his associates'.[45] Although it was later glossed over, the fact that this situation had arisen through a military action, in which the king's own standard and person had been attacked, would have been to her a source of fear.

In a very real sense, St Albans marked a psychological turning point by leaving a residue of feeling and a model for action that would be invoked again. The battle also represented a real challenge to royal authority insofar as it was precipitated by the Yorkists' non-negotiable demands. Within this frame of reference, it made no difference whether their demands, their personal fears or their possible concerns for the realm were justified or not. Their elaborate protestations of loyalty and the official acceptance of their oaths in parliament did little to conceal the fact that the Yorkists had obtained their ascendancy through force.

As a result, tensions ran high. A letter from London of mid-July reports that although the king and his 'trwe Lordes' (i.e. the Yorkists) were all healed in body, 'not all [were] at hertes ees'. The earl of Warwick and Lord Cromwell had argued in the king's presence over who had actually started the fighting; each seems to have been trying to fob off responsibility on the other. Cromwell was sufficiently frightened by their encounter to ask the earl of Shrewsbury to lodge near him for his protection. But there were also signs of a more widespread unease. The official blaming of Somerset, Thorp and Joseph and the absolving of everyone else from all responsibility for what had occurred at St Albans, along with the requirement that the matter not be spoken of again, were grudged by 'mony a man . . . full sore'. Meanwhile, the Yorkists' men went about the city fully armed, while their lords' daily barges to Westminster were 'stuffed . . . full of wepon'. Perhaps as a result, a proclamation had just been issued in the king's name against the bearing of arms – to what effect the letter does not say. The writer's closing seems to offer little hope, for he asked that his letter be destroyed once it was read since he was 'loth to write any thing of any Lord'.[46]

[44] Armstrong, 'Politics and the Battle of St Albans', pp. 33, 60. On pp. 57–61 he discusses its conditions at length.
[45] Wolffe, p. 294.
[46] Gairdner, PL, III, pp. 43–5.

Such a situation offered little security. Although York clearly controlled the king, making any opposition to him dangerous, he could not speak with the king's authority. By the same token the king, whose legitimate authority had been reaffirmed by the Yorkists, could not freely act. As a consequence, no one ruled.[47] Widespread violence broke out in autumn, the worst involving a resurgence of the Courtenay/Bonville feud in the southwest. This was a direct result of the 'open season' alluded to earlier, which York's continuing public vendetta against Somerset had encouraged and which his own resort to violence at St Albans had in some sense legitimated.[48] Around this same time rumors also circulated that Henry had suffered a relapse.[49] Although he had required medical attention on a couple of occasions during June and July, perhaps in connection with his injury,[50] there is no other indication that he suffered health problems in autumn. Thus, violence provided a practical reason to establish authoritative government in the form of a protectorate, while fears for the king's health provided an excuse.[51] Under the circumstances, York was the only possible choice for the job.[52]

The process by which York obtained this second protectorate went through very quickly. Occurring as it did at the very beginning of the second parliamentary session and accomplished under great pressure, it has the look of advance planning and orchestration.[53] The whole thing took a week, from York's appointment by a great council on 10 November as king's lieutenant to open parliament in his absence (the session began on the twelfth), to his acceptance as protector on 17 November after assiduous and repeated lobbying of the lords by a delegation from the commons. His patent was issued on the nineteenth.[54] The leader of the commons' delegation was not the speaker, John Wenlock, but William Burley, an experienced MP who also happened to be one of York's councilors, adding perhaps to a sense that the commons' petitions were planned, but also suggesting that the commons were not unanimously behind them. The lords themselves were perhaps wary of anticipated events, for their attendance was thin compared to the previous summer session.[55]

The king, of course, officially mandated York's appointment, but York's own

---

[47] Johnson, pp. 167–8.

[48] Storey, p. 167, seems to make a similar claim. His chapter 13 describes developments in the southwest and the brutal murder of Bonville's advisor, Nicholas Radford, by the Courtenays.

[49] Gairdner, *PL*, III, p. 50: 'summe men ar a ferd that he is seek ageyn'. The writer further indicates that York, Warwick and Salisbury intended 'to conveye hym' somewhere, but the letter is damaged and one cannot know where they planned to take him, or for what purpose.

[50] *Foedera*, V, ii, p. 63, dated 5 June and requiring physicians' attendance on the twelfth, which does not seem to indicate an emergency situation; and PRO, E404/70/2/89, noted by Johnson, p. 167.

[51] *RP*, V, pp. 284–8. Violence in the west country is explicitly and repeatedly given as the rationale for choosing a protector; in comparison, the king's health and its likely effect on his ability to deal with the serious business of governance are presented more hypothetically.

[52] Lander, 'Henry VI and the Duke of York's Second Protectorate', pp. 77–9, has convincingly debunked the idea of a relapse. Griffiths, pp. 752–6; Johnson, pp. 168–70; and Watts, pp. 319–21, follow this part of his argument, although their views of the protectorate's purpose and York's intentions differ.

[53] Griffiths, pp. 752–3, and Lander, 'Henry VI and the Duke of York's Second Protectorate', pp. 82–4, discuss this in detail. As Lander succinctly puts it, 'someone was in a tremendous hurry to get things done' (p. 83).

[54] *PPC*, VI, pp. 261–2; *CPR, 1452–61*, p. 273; *RP*, V, pp. 284–8.

[55] Griffiths, p. 752; Lander, 'Henry VI and the Duke of York's Second Protectorate', pp. 82, 84.

articles accepting the position and suggesting its terms asserted the lords' role in 'takyng uppon [them] th'exercise of [the king's] auctorite, for such urgent, necessary and reasonable causes, as move [them] so to take uppon [them]'.[56] This formulation left any definition of what was 'urgent, necessary and reasonable' to the lords' discretion and may have marked a 'potentially revolutionary' shift in their understanding of the source of authority.[57] We should not assume, of course, that York intended to lead the march into unfamiliar philosophical territory. It is just as likely that in seeking to legitimate his own authority he hit upon this as an expedient and that it did in some sense reflect the reality of the current situation. As a potential policy statement, however, it allowed for circumstances in which the king's authority could legitimately be superseded and asserted that the decision as to when such circumstances existed lay with the lords. Wittingly or not, the lords present were quick to act upon it. York's conditions of tenure were altered from those of the first protectorate so that he could not be relieved of office simply at the king's pleasure, but only with the lords' advise and assent.[58]

Two possible – and opposite – reasons have been suggested for this clause. Either the lords feared that 'the free operation of [Henry's] "pleasure" could not be guaranteed' while he was in Yorkist hands, or they feared that York could be relieved of office by the machinations of his 'enemies in the household, rather as in . . . early 1455'.[59] A problem with the second suggestion is that it ignores the role of Henry's recovery in ending the first protectorate. With or without household intervention, once Henry was found to be well again, the rationale for the protectorate evaporated. More significantly, however, and undermining both suppositions, the act immediately following York's appointment, which provides that the prince might take over the protectorate when he came of age, includes the same clause regarding his tenure.[60] It appears, therefore, that it had little to do with York specifically, one way or the other, but a great deal to do with larger issues of authority and who ultimately possessed it. Whatever the initial impetus behind the second protectorate, it was not York who claimed an 'alternative authority',[61] but the lords themselves. It may be that the stalemate between a king too weak to assert his authority and an assertive duke seeking the key to legitimize his power pushed the lords into staking out a neutral high ground.

That there may have been a kind of balancing act going on is further suggested by the formal entrustment of government to the council at the same time as, or soon after, the protectorate was established. Naturally, it was done in Henry's name, but with the added requirement that the council 'shall

---

[56] RP, V, p. 286; cf. p. 242, where the king's illness provided the explicit reason for the lords' exercise of his authority in 1454. This point is made by Watts, p. 320, n. 258.

[57] Ibid., p. 320, sees it as the lords' willingness to transfer 'their allegiance and service to a man whose pre-eminence rested not on divine appointment, but on common approval'. I am less convinced of the solidity of the commons' support for York, and the apparent unanimity of the lords must be taken with a grain of salt, particularly in view of their low attendance.

[58] RP, V, pp. 287, 289.

[59] Watts, p. 320, n. 261.

[60] RP, V, pp. 288–9.

[61] Watts, p. 320.

late his highnes have knowelech what direccion they take . . . in all such matiers as touchen the honour, wurship and suertee of his moost noble persone'.[62] Whether this condition reflects Henry's own concern, that of persons around him or that of the lords as a group cannot be ascertained. The pervasive hold of traditional thinking, the possible unease with which the lords regarded both York and the authority they had claimed for themselves, and the drift that matters were taking can be seen in the manner in which they accepted the charge. After expressions of appropriate reluctance, the lords made a point of insisting that 'the high prerogative, pre-emynence and auctorite of his majeste Roiall, and also the soverauntee of thaym and all this lande, is and alwey mot reste and shall reste in [the king's] most excellent persone'.[63]

Professor Griffiths entitled a central chapter in his monumental biography of Henry VI 'The Political Education of Richard, Duke of York'. The years from 1453 to 1456 might likewise be looked upon as constituting the political education of Margaret of Anjou. During these years she would have learned to regard York as a threat. Perhaps she felt an added sense of betrayal, for she had been called upon to intercede in his behalf, and she had been at pains to give him signs that she was not his enemy. But she also would have learned that she could not rely on others to ensure the security of her husband or her son. Not on Henry himself, certainly, nor on his advisors, whose private interests did not necessarily coincide with her need, nor on well-intentioned lords whose efforts at crisis management further undercut the king's authority. Though we may doubt that either Henry's security or the succession was *actually* threatened quite so soon, from Margaret's vantage point there was ample reason for anxiety. Her earlier effort to be granted a formally recognized authority had failed. Now she would have to find ways to exercise power as she could, by means already available to her.

---

[62] *RP*, V, p. 290.
[63] Ibid.

Part IV

QUEEN'S RULE?

9

Conditions and Means

BY EARLY 1456 Margaret had determined to take action, in her own interest and in the interests of her husband and child, as she perceived them. The question was not whether to do it, but how. She had failed to obtain the authoritative power of a regency, but there were people who would follow her. As the king's wife, her position gave her potential influence over the king himself, while the contacts it afforded her allowed her to touch, and occasionally to pluck, the strings of power. At the same time, however, as king's wife she was denied any public acknowledgment or recognition of having a legitimate, direct political role. She was at all times both visible and invisible.

Margaret's approach to this conundrum was to continue to represent herself as subordinate and adjunct while asserting the king's authority, though in fact she wielded increased practical power herself. It is difficult to say to what extent this amounted to a deliberately thought-out policy on her part, but it was a natural one, for it built on understood relationships and, superficially at least, appeared not to violate the accepted order of things. Such an approach, however, necessarily limited the extent of the queen's power and hindered effective leadership.[1]

Anton Blok has observed that women tend to become leaders by establishing themselves as 'social males', with autonomy and independence from actual males; in particular, from husbands. Because of the 'mutual incompatibility between [the roles of] leader and wife', a woman who emphasized her female role of wife and mother would have difficulty in gaining recognition and acceptance as a leader.[2] Nevertheless, this was the course that Margaret generally chose because, for her as queen, it provided the only means to legitimately access political power. As a short-term solution involving specific situations or activities, it worked fairly well, but it offered no future. In the long run, the necessity of operating within this framework denied her a more lasting authority and made her vulnerable to charges of transgression when the extent and nature of her activities attracted notice.

The queen's new resolve, as well as the reactions it evoked, can be seen in the closing days of York's second protectorate. The protectorate's collapse has generally been blamed on disagreements over resumption, which cost York

---

[1] Watts, pp. 331, 350, 355, is more sanguine regarding the success of Margaret's efforts than I am.
[2] Blok, 'Female Rulers', pp. 12, 13.

the support of the lords.[3] Demands by the commons that the king take back grants made by the crown during his reign so that he might begin to 'live off his own' had been a recurring theme in the circumstances of the regime's perennial insolvency. Such calls for resumption tended to be regarded with suspicion by the lords, who potentially stood to lose the most unless they could obtain exemption. They came up again in the parliament of 1455–56, where the commons, with York's support, again vigorously promoted resumption.[4] While Margaret would have been concerned about its effects on her and would have been at pains to avoid any loss,[5] the resumption came on top of other developments that she already would have found disturbing. First among them would have been the Yorkists' challenge to royal authority – as well as to Henry's person – at St Albans, followed by their emphatic but increasingly tenuous assertions of loyalty to that same authority even as they continued, in effect, to undermine it. It is likely that the lords' opposition to a series of increasingly stringent proposals for resumption was triggered in part by similar concerns. By restricting the king's prerogative of making exemption, they threatened their own wealth and power.[6] For Margaret, the equation may have been a simple, but personal, one: if understood authority could be challenged, the holder of authority could be replaced.[7] Historical precedents existed for the king's replacement, the most recent within living memory.

By the winter of 1455–56, Margaret had gone into action, making it possible for John Bocking to describe her in a letter of 9 February as 'a grete and strong labourid woman [who] spareth noo peyne to sue hire thinges to an intent and conclusion to hir power'.[8] While some of her efforts probably involved resistance to the resumption,[9] it is even more likely that they were directed at the protectorate itself. Thomas Gascoigne blamed Margaret personally for ending York's tenure.[10] It can be no accident that the first rumors that the

---

[3] 'Benet's Chron.', p. 216, specifically cites opposition to the resumption as the cause of the lords' defection from York. Griffiths, p. 757; Wolffe, p. 300; Johnson, pp. 172–3; Watts, pp. 322–3, all consider the resumption to have been the central issue, though Watts gives it a more ideological spin.

[4] Johnson, pp. 172–3, provides a concise summary of the situation, acknowledging the difficulties in establishing a precise chronology of events.

[5] Hicks, 'Bastard Feudalism', p. 398, considers the resumption 'draconian . . . intended to dispossess the queen, the king's half brothers and their adherents'.

[6] Griffiths, p. 751; Watts, pp. 321–2, 332–3, who suggests that the queen's partisans – and by implication the queen herself – would have encouraged the lords' defection. The king and lords flatly rejected bills that would have affected liberties and franchises granted since 1422 and all grants of wardship and marriage (RP, V, pp. 328, 330).

[7] Watts, p. 323, suggests that York's failure to obtain 'adequate authority' in novel ways, through either the support of the lords or the commons, eventually led him to resort to other means, in his case a traditionally understood blood claim to the crown. Ironically, a kind of parallel process appears to have been going on with Margaret. Having found it impossible to gain adequate authority through the novel means of a regency, she resorted to the traditional and accepted, though largely informal and invisible, avenues to power afforded by queenship.

[8] Gairdner, PL, III, p. 75.

[9] Margaret was exempted in the king's response to the commons' petition (RP, V, p. 303).

[10] Gascoigne, Loci e Libro, p. 204: '[following St Albans] ipso duce Eboraci instituto protectore regni . . . regina Angliae, Margareta . . . laboravit sic per se et per caeteros dominos, qui putabantur mali domini in regno, quod ille dux dimisit auctoritatem suam'. ('When the duke of York was appointed protector of the realm, Queen Margaret labored so much herself and through other lords, who were considered the bad lords in the realm, that the duke gave up his authority.')

prince was a changeling appeared at this time.[11] They were joined by other allegations regarding Margaret's sexual conduct as her power increased. By the end of the reign and during the first uneasy years following Henry's deposition, they would become a regular part of Yorkist propaganda.[12]

When parliament resumed in mid-January, the political situation was in flux, its outcome uncertain. Bocking's letter reveals the extent of the destabilization in its report of York's efforts to hold onto power amid conflicting views of what was likely to happen. On 9 February he and Warwick arrived at parliament accompanied by 300 armed men, apparently in response to a rumor that he was about to be discharged. Some even believed that had he not appeared in arms, he 'shuld have been distrussid'. Meanwhile, another source had informed Bocking that Henry would keep York as his chief counselor, though with less power formally accorded him than he currently held as protector. York's saber-rattling display, which kept all the other lords away from parliament, casts doubt upon the likelihood of this outcome.[13] Whatever the reliability of any of these rumors and opinions at the time, Henry personally relieved York of his office in parliament on 25 February, with the advice and assent of the lords as required, and ordered him to have nothing further to do with it.[14]

Although it appears that the protectorate was terminated on a less-than-friendly note, York continued to be treated reasonably well. Efforts were made to see that he was paid money owed him for his service.[15] He seems to have attended several council meetings soon after his dismissal.[16] If, as seems likely, Margaret had actively sought York's ouster and an end to the protectorate, there is no evidence at this point that she pushed for further retribution. Indeed, if one takes Bocking's claim that she sought power for herself at face value, her next move might seem peculiar: she left town.[17]

Margaret's departure with her son for the midlands has been explained in various ways: as a sign of hostility towards York, who still enjoyed a measure of official favor after his removal from power, or of fear that he might attempt another coup; as an effort to avoid the unhealthful conditions of the London environs that were believed to prevail in summer; as a commitment to check up on her estates, the bulk of which were in this region; or as a move to consolidate strength in an area where her influence was greatest.[18] It is possible that she was moved to some degree by all of these considerations. There is a further

[11] 'Benet's Chron.', p. 216. It is worth recalling that John Helton's execution for bills alleging that the prince was not the queen's son took place on 23 February, two days before York was relieved of office. See above, p. 45.

[12] See below, pp. 176–8, 201, 203.

[13] Gairdner, PL, III, p. 75: 'But soome men thinken it wil ner can otherwise bee; and men speke and devyne moche matere of [York's] comyng this day in such array to Westminster.' In the next sentence Bocking mentions the sighting of a comet – long considered an omen of catastrophic change – but then links the likelihood of the protectorate's continuance to the passage of the resumption.

[14] RP, V, pp. 321–2; Foedera, V, ii, pp. 65–6.

[15] CPR, 1452–61, p. 278; Johnson, p. 175, for this and other examples of favorable treatment.

[16] Watts, p. 333, n. 301, who associates York's attendance with Henry's purported desire to retain his services as chief councilor. York's foray in arms on 9 February and the wording of his 'exoneration' seem to me to argue that this was no longer the case.

[17] Flenley (Rawlinson B. 355), p. 110, reports her departure after York's removal from office. By the early part of May she was at Tutbury (Gairdner, PL, III, p. 86).

[18] Griffiths, pp. 772–3; Wolffe, p. 303; Watts, pp. 334, 338, n. 326; Storey, p. 177.

observation that can be made, however: Margaret's withdrawal fits a pattern that can perhaps be seen as early as 1445–48 in the shifting tenor of her letters to Charles VII, that can certainly be seen in her behavior following the establishment of the first protectorate, and that would be repeated during the remaining years of the reign, even when her power reached its peak. In short, she stepped back.

The situation illustrates both the extent and limitations of the queen's influence. Margaret had encouraged, perhaps even led, the effort to remove York from power. Having accomplished this, however, her position allowed her nowhere else to go. She had reached a perceptible boundary; she could not simply replace York with herself, and she may not have known how or where to take the next step. Although her withdrawal may have marked a temporary return to 'normalcy' in one sense, it would have been unsettling in another, for she took the heir with her. By keeping him in her custody, she signaled to the realm at large that he might not be safe apart from her.[19]

It appears that some people followed her activities with both concern and an increased sense of her power. On 8 May, Bocking reported enigmatically that 'all is as it was with the Quene'; she and the prince were at Tutbury, while York was at Sandal in the north, Warwick was at Warwick castle, Buckingham had gone to Writell in a state of unease, and the king had just returned to Westminster after some days spent in London.[20] A week later, on the fifteenth, Bocking noted that Margaret was still at Tutbury and reported the false rumor of a battle in which Viscount Beaumont, the earl of Warwick and many others were said to have been slain.[21] Beaumont, of course, was the queen's man, whereas Warwick had been York's supporter during the protectorates. On 7 June the suspicion and hostility that had been building between the queen and the duke is more apparent in Bocking's report that they were eyeing each other from their respective positions at Chester and Sandal, each waiting for the other's next move.[22] By this time, Margaret would have had even more reason to regard York with anxiety. There had been disturbances in Kent that might have been assumed to have Yorkist connections; meanwhile, Sir William Herbert and Sir Walter Devereux – both York's men – had been causing trouble in the west midlands. By autumn their activities had spread into Wales.[23]

Over the course of the summer Margaret would have been given further cause for suspicion and further cause – if such were necessary – to seek a more meaningful and permanent diminution of York's power. In May, James II of

---

[19] Parsons, *Eleanor of Castile*, p. 38, notes that Eleanor's children typically stayed put with their households and did not travel with her during their early years.

[20] Ibid., p. 86. Buckingham's unease may have been caused by the riots that had recently occurred in London, directed against the Lombard merchants. Some of the perpetrators were punished and efforts were made to keep the peace, but the situation continued unstable. See Griffiths, pp. 790–2, for these incidents.

[21] Gairdner, *PL*, III, p. 87.

[22] Ibid., p. 92: '[he] wayteth on [her] and she up on hym'.

[23] Johnson, pp. 175–6. At the time of the Yorkists' attainders, it was alleged that there had been an attempt on Henry's life in June at Kenilworth (ibid., p. 176, citing PRO, KB9/35 m. 32). Since Henry remained in the south until August, it is hard to see this as anything more than the product of rumor or later Lancastrian propaganda.

Scotland, ever the opportunist, renounced the truce that had been in place with England since 1453 and began raiding across the border. Already the previous year he had importuned Charles VII to join him in military action to aid Henry VI against subjects who had seized him by force of arms and continued to hold him in captivity – and to regain Calais and Berwick for themselves by the by.[24] With the end of York's second protectorate, the excuse of aiding Henry no longer applied, but James apparently felt that the time was still ripe for action.[25] On 26 July a strongly worded rejoinder to James in Henry's name asserted that the Scottish king had always been a vassal of the English, condemned him for truce breaking and threatened retribution, although it nevertheless ended with the hope that Christ would lead James back to the way of truth and justice.[26] But it was York in the north who had the actual task of dealing with James's incursions. York's own letter a month later charging James with dishonorable and unkingly behavior in connection with his border raiding and challenging him to battle casts a somewhat different light upon the situation. While its explicit comparison is between York and James, its implicit comparison has to be between York and the absent Henry, as the duke's oft-repeated assertions of his own allegiance to his king make painfully obvious.[27] In a society that associated kingliness with martial prowess, York's military presence in the north and his bellicose posturing demonstrated nothing so much as his own fitness in contrast to the unprepossessing Henry.[28]

So long as Henry remained in the south, there was little of a practical nature that Margaret could do from the midlands to influence the course of events, unless it was to assure herself of support in the region where she was already strongest. All of this changed in late summer when Henry joined her. While it may be that his decision to retire to the midlands was prompted by the unrest in London and the disorders that had been cropping up elsewhere, it may also be that the queen herself persuaded him to this move.[29] Once Henry was with her, away from the more usual power setting of London and Westminster, it became possible to associate herself with and to manipulate his political authority toward ends that she believed would provide security for the dynasty. Over the next two years she worked to establish the links that would provide for her practical exercise of power and secure her dominance over York once and for all. Some of her efforts met with considerable success;

[24] Williams, *Official Correspondence of Thomas Bekynton*, II, pp. 139–41; Stevenson, I, pp. 319–22; Dunlop, *Life and Times of James Kennedy*, pp. 163–4, 166.

[25] He continued to seek French aid through autumn. Charles VII's eventual response in January 1457 is a study in diplomatic evasion (Stevenson, I, pp. 328–51).

[26] *Foedera*, V, ii, p. 69; Williams, *Official Correspondence of Thomas Bekynton*, II, pp. 141–2. Henry's role in the composition of 'his own' letter, which was initiated by privy seal, is not certain. If someone else wrote it for him, that someone could not have been York, who was in the north all summer. Cf. Griffiths, p. 773.

[27] Williams, *Official Correspondence of Thomas Bekynton*, II, pp. 142–4.

[28] Watts, p. 335, n. 312.

[29] Gascoigne, *Loci e Libro*, p. 204, says that she brought him to her manor along with the prince ('regina traxit ad locum mansionis suae . . . tam regem . . . quam principem'). It appears, however, that Margaret and Henry trusted each other: several years later they were reported to have a secret arrangement, known only to the two of them, to verify messages sent from one to the other ('Gregory's Chron.', p. 209).

others failed. Margaret's effort to extend her influence involved formal offices and institutions, the informal channels of patronage and mediation already available to her and the symbols of public image. I will discuss these matters in turn.

Institutional Influence

Margaret's experience since the crisis of Henry's illness and the establishment of York's first protectorate would surely have taught her that she could not gain more than a very temporary influence over events without access to the formal institutions of governance. Queenship provided no direct access, however; whatever was done had to be done through the king's authority. The first step for Margaret was to encourage the replacement of the government's chief officers by persons whose loyalty to the regime carried no Yorkist taint. The Bourgchier brothers, chancellor and treasurer, would clearly have to go. The latter had been appointed in the aftermath of St Albans, and though neither had done anything to suggest disloyalty to Henry, both had found it possible to cooperate with York. They, along with the Nevilles, had done very well during the second protectorate, and Viscount Bourgchier, of course, was married to York's sister.[30] The first change in personnel, however, may have come about through a bit of luck. On 24 September, Margaret's chancellor, Lawrence Booth, replaced Thomas Liseux, whose health was failing, as keeper of the privy seal.[31] Soon after, on 5 October, John Talbot, earl of Shrewsbury, replaced Viscount Bourgchier as treasurer. His appointment was repeated two days later when the great council convened at Coventry. Finally, on 11 October, William Waynflete, bishop of Winchester and Henry's confessor, replaced Archbishop Thomas Bourgchier as chancellor.[32] The presence of the council may have been necessary to lend credibility to the latter two appointments and to belay suspicion that they had been made at Margaret's bidding rather than the king's.[33] While there can be little doubt that she stood behind these changes and probably instigated them, it was particularly important for Henry to be visibly and willingly responsible for them. Thus, in the case of the chancellorship, Henry elaborately received

---

[30] Johnson, p. 159.

[31] Griffiths, p. 773. Liseux was dead by 13 October. Booth succeeded to Liseux's position as dean of St Paul's on 22 October (ibid., p. 830, n. 8). He had been the queen's chancellor since early 1452, following his brother William. In 1457 Margaret obtained his provision to the bishopric of Durham in preference to Henry's own candidate (ibid., p. 777; *Foedera*, V, ii, pp. 77–8), and he eventually became archbishop of York under Edward IV (Emden, *Cambridge*, pp. 78–9, for his career).

[32] Gairdner, *PL*, III, pp. 103, 108; *CPR, 1452–61*, p. 324; *Foedera*, V, ii, p. 69; *CCR, 1454–61*, pp. 211–12. Waynflete had baptized Prince Edward. For Henry's patronage and attachment to him, see Griffiths, p. 348. The reasons for Shrewsbury's appointment seem less clear. Allowing that such matters do not always have coldly rational explanations, we might remember that this Talbot's father, the warrior hero of France, had made a point of welcoming Margaret to England with the gift of a book as a token of his reverence and loyalty towards the new queen.

[33] Cf. Watts, p. 335, n. 315. It appears that people did associate the changes in officers with the queen's influence; Buckingham was reported to have been miffed at the dismissals of his Bourgchier half-brothers, leaving him in a position 'contrary' to Margaret (Gairdner, *PL*, III, p. 108).

the seals from Bourgchier and gave them to Waynflete in the presence of the council, including York.[34]

It is important to ask what Margaret did or did not gain from these appointments. While it is true that they would not have given her exclusive control of the government,[35] they would have provided her with a greater sense of security. Since it is unlikely that she could have obtained the appointments of three persons whose primary loyalty was believed to belong to her – and who might they have been in a world where authority was not perceived to be a female attribute? – it appears that the focus of Margaret's effort was to reconstitute a sense of the king's authority, through which she could exercise effective power. With Booth as keeper of the privy seal she had acquired a greater practical influence.[36] How far she could take it would depend both on specific circumstances and on her own inclination. Officially, of course, everything done by privy seal was done on the king's authority and according to his wishes, but it would be naive to think that Margaret had no interest in influencing its use.[37] It appears on balance, therefore, that she gained a set of officers in whom she placed more trust and whom she believed would be more responsive to her concerns. This is a more circumscribed view of her ambition than has frequently been posited, but it takes into account the very real limitations on what she could expect to achieve at that time. Her claim to authority had not been granted in 1454, nor would it have been reasonable to expect that it would suddenly be recognized in 1456. The change in officers did not deliver the government into her hands, but it provided her with greater access than she had had before.

The second area of institutional power to which Margaret turned her attention, and in which she made greater gains, involved the prince's council and control of his patrimony. On 28 January 1457 a formal council was appointed for Prince Edward's tutelage and guidance – which meant, in a practical sense, the management of his possessions and affairs until he was old enough to handle such matters himself.[38] All of the persons named to the council had solid and frequently lengthy associations with king, queen and court: William Booth, archbishop of York and Margaret's former chancellor; William Waynflete, bishop of Winchester and chancellor of England; Reginald Boulers, bishop of Coventry and Lichfield; John Stanbury, bishop of Hereford; Lawrence Booth, half-brother of William, keeper of the privy seal and Margaret's present chancellor; Humphrey Stafford, son and heir of the duke

---

[34] *Foedera*, V, ii, p. 69.

[35] Watts, p. 336 and n. 319, suggests that a conciliar authority of sorts still existed, to which Shrewsbury and Waynflete would have had some responsibility, and considers this a loss for Margaret.

[36] Storey, p. 181, calls this the 'key appointment', which gave Margaret control of 'the mainspring of all government action'.

[37] Watts, p. 336, n. 319, cites a single instance when Booth was at Kenilworth sealing letters – 'presumably with the queen' – while Henry was known to have been in London (PRO, E404/71/2/72). As he acknowledges, however, it is difficult to determine who exactly was authorizing policy. Though he attributes this to a government split between a still independently active council and the queen; he discounts any active role on Henry's part (ibid., p. 338, n. 328).

[38] *Foedera*, V, ii, p. 70; *CPR, 1452–61*, p. 359. The patent was by privy seal, but it also invoked the authority of parliament, which in the course of its 1455–56 sessions had granted the prince his possessions in Wales, Chester and Cornwall (*RP*, V, pp. 290–4; *CPR, 1452–61*, pp. 357–8).

of Buckingham; John Talbot, earl of Shrewsbury and treasurer; James Butler, earl of Wiltshire; John, Viscount Beaumont, Margaret's chief steward; John Sutton, Lord Dudley; and Thomas, Lord Stanley.[39]

The patent asserts the need to establish the 'most honorable, excellent, diligent and experienced *men*' as the prince's councilors,[40] a statement that is possibly formulaic and not particularly noteworthy in itself, but which becomes more evocative when, after a rehearsal of what the councilors are to do, it is announced that everything is to be done 'with the approval and agreement of our best-beloved consort the queen'. This presents an interesting mixture of social assumptions and hard-nosed reality. Naturally, the persons occupying official positions, the putative movers and doers, were to be men, yet they could not act without the queen's permission and authorization.[41]

To understand the function and importance of the gender construct, one has to imagine and ask whether the patent could have been written in a different way: first presenting the queen's right to approve and authorize any actions to be taken involving the prince's patrimony, which would then be carried out by a specially constituted group of men in response to her direction. The answer, simply, is no.

Lacking any institutional authority to which she could directly lay claim, the queen was thus able to establish her control by having her influence inserted into the institutional process by the king's authority. Superficially, the institution itself was not affected, but the queen had acquired a recognized role in its function.[42] This role was repeatedly noted in subsequent council warrants where grants were made in the prince's name with the advice of the council and the assent of his mother the queen.[43] The formula is significant: the prince's name provided authorization and legitimacy for whatever was done; these were *his* acts, although his actual participation was fictive. In practice, the council's deliberations together with the queen's assent produced the relevant decisions. Yet there is a second fictive layer, contained in the nature of the documents themselves. Only the queen's assent (to the council's 'advice') is stated; nowhere is it noted that the power to assent can become the power to deny, or that both together can amount to the power to initiate or to give direction. From a commonsensical point of view, the extent of the queen's power seems obvious; surely few who thought about it would have missed it. Nevertheless, in its formal representation it appears as if at one remove, its edges and its impact blurred by the more conventional phrases in which it is embedded.

Margaret also gained practical control over the prince's affairs – and his

[39] Griffiths, pp. 781–2. The appointment of Buckingham's son must have pleased, and may also have palliated, the father, who had been unhappy with the dismissal of the Bourgchiers.

[40] The word used is *viros* (emphasis added).

[41] Griffiths, pp. 781, 783.

[42] In contrast, Isabella of France, a powerful queen who played no small role in her husband's deposition, had no official place on her son's minority council (Baldwin, 'King's Council', p. 134).

[43] E.g., PRO, SC6/1217/3 m. 1–6, where the pattern 'princeps concessit ex deliberatione [or 'cum advisamento'] dominorum de consilio nostro unacum assensu precarissime matris sue Regine' ('the prince grants in accordance with the deliberation [with the advice] of the lords of our council together with the assent of our dear mother the queen') and similar variants can be seen.

resources – through the appointments of his officers. The earliest of these, on 26 September 1456, were the appointments of Robert Whittingham as his receiver-general and John Morton as his chancellor.[44] Whittingham was an usher of the king's chamber and husband of one of Margaret's ladies; by April 1458 he had become keeper of the queen's great wardrobe.[45] There is less indication as to why Morton was chosen unless it was a sense that he would prove capable and loyal. Although he was already a doctor of civil law, nearly all of his positions and advancements followed this appointment.[46] The next appointment, on 20 January 1457, was of Viscount Beaumont as the prince's chief steward.[47] On 25 January, Giles St Lo was appointed keeper of the prince's great wardrobe. St Lo had long been a servant of both Henry and Margaret; he was the queen's butler and usher of her chamber and, like Whittingham, was married to one of her ladies.[48] Rounding out these appointments on 20 February was Thomas Throckmorton as the prince's attorney general. He appears to have been chosen for his broad legal experience and for his familiarity with the west midlands.[49] All of these appointments were made by privy seal. While Margaret may not have been the sole force behind these selections, we can be sure that she would have been keenly interested in them. Whatever influence she wielded over their activities was given no formal expression. It remained informal, hidden in the interstices of overlapping service and personal contact.

On 24 February the prince's council was given control of his patrimony: all of the issues from Wales, the county of Chester and the duchy of Cornwall, save a portion reserved for his domestic expenses.[50] Besides making the prince's financial resources available to queen and court, control of the prince's interests in his name helped Margaret to consolidate and extend territorial power. Her own lands centered in the midlands, where she held the estates of Leicester, Tutbury and Kenilworth, and many of the regime's chief supporters were also powerful in the region. Through the prince's council judicial pressure could be

---

[44] *CPR, 1452–61*, p. 323.

[45] Myers, 'Household of Queen Margaret', p. 405, n. 2; Wedgwood, *Biographies*, pp. 943–4. He served on a number of commissions (*CPR, 1452–61*, pp. 403, 406, 559, 613, 614) and as a justice of the peace for Buckingham and Hertford (ibid., pp. 661, 667). Whatever his previous connections with Margaret, his loyalty proved to be absolute, for he followed her into exile in 1461 and was killed fighting for Lancaster at Tewkesbury in 1471.

[46] Emden, *Cambridge*, pp. 412–14, for his adventuresome career. As far as Margaret was concerned, he proved his loyalty beyond question. He was one of the persons who helped draft the attainder against the Yorkists in 1459 and was captured after Henry's deposition, but escaped from the Tower and joined the queen in exile. After the Lancastrian defeat at Tewkesbury, he made his peace with Edward IV and served on numerous diplomatic missions. When Edward died, he plotted against Richard III and became a supporter of Henry VII, whom he served for the rest of his life, ending up archbishop of Canterbury, cardinal and chancellor of England.

[47] *CPR, 1452–61*, p. 338.

[48] *CPR, 1452–61*, p. 334; Griffiths, p. 782; Myers, 'Household of Queen Margaret', pp. 405, 406. It will be remembered that he was the person who brought word of the prince's birth to the London common council.

[49] Griffiths, p. 782; Wedgwood, *Biographies*, pp. 852–3. Like Whittingham, he served on various commissions after his appointment and was a justice of the peace for Worcester (*CPR, 1452–61*, pp. 409, 443, 558, 565, 566, and 681).

[50] Ibid., pp. 357–8; Griffiths, p. 782.

brought to bear in areas such as south Wales, which had recently been disrupted by York's supporters.[51] Given the recurring problem of disorder, it was important to reestablish royal control and probably easier to do it one piece at a time. The appointment of Henry's half-brother, Jasper Tudor, on 21 April 1457 to the constableships of Carmarthen and Aberystwyth in place of York should be seen as a part of this effort.[52] The power Margaret possessed or was able to gain in the midlands, Wales and Cheshire through her own influence or in the prince's name provided a nucleus from which to expand. It appears, in fact, that the queen 'had begun to establish a "pale" of royal . . . authority in which lordship may have functioned more or less as it should have'.[53] It was not intended to be a new polity based on her son's authority. Although she was able to acquire power over the prince's council through the king's authorization and the use of 'veiling' language, her power over the officers of state could not be similarly designated. Nor would a minority rule have made the dynasty any safer, while it ran the risk of making her power more obvious – something that would have riled too many people. She had to 'rule' by indirect means, and so she needed Henry. Thus, the *English Chronicle*'s report that she was trying to get Henry to abdicate is likely to have been Yorkist propaganda.[54] Nor should her efforts be seen as an abandonment of national government. Instead, they attempted to build on existing strength, so that national government could be restored.

Informal Influence

Margaret pursued her consolidation of power through informal and more usual means as well. These were areas in which the queen was able to participate as intermediary in the course of business-as-usual or in which she could invoke her special position as intercessor to the king. While her actions might be resented or criticized, particularly by those who felt that others were given too much favor that they themselves were denied, there was nothing inherently illegitimate or improper about any of these actions.

Among the means that Margaret was able to use to advantage was marriage policy. Marriage, of course, was vitally important to family status and prosperity; it created links between families and, with any luck at all, bonds of indebtedness towards those who helped to forge such ties. During the course of 1457–58 a number of significant marriages were either accomplished or suggested. The queen's influence is most apparent in the 1457 marriage of her cousin Marie, bastard daughter of Margaret's uncle Charles, count of Maine, to Thomas Courtenay, the earl of Devon's son and heir. This marriage, which the earl seems actively to have sought, 'brought him into the royal circle and

---

[51] Ibid., p. 783; pp. 777–85, for a broader discussion of the geographical implications of the court's establishment at Coventry and how control of the prince's patrimony fit into this picture; PRO, SC6/1162/7,8, for the council's jailing of some negligent officers.

[52] Griffiths, p. 780.

[53] Watts, p. 340.

[54] *English Chron.*, p. 80; cf. Watts, p. 338 and n. 327.

decisively ended his association with York'.[55] A further set of marriages involved the duke of Buckingham's children. In 1457 his second son, Henry Stafford, was married to Margaret Beaufort, 'the wealthiest heiress in England', and in 1458, in what may have been a joint wedding, his daughter Katherine was married to the earl of Shrewsbury's son and heir, while his younger son John was married to the daughter of a rich midlands landowner.[56] Along with his eldest son's place on Prince Edward's council, these marriages would have served to reassure the duke of his own importance to the regime and to alleviate any lingering bitterness over the Bourgchiers' dismissals. Yet another marriage of 1457 between the earl of Shrewsbury's sister, Joan, and James, Lord Berkeley, temporarily resolved a family feud.[57] Although Margaret's role in the Buckingham and Shrewsbury marriages is less certain, they would have worked to her advantage in creating a new status quo. These were all important marriages in their creations of ties between families and of ties to the court.

Not all of the intended ties were domestic. In what may have been a 'bold initiative' on Margaret's part, marriages were proposed in 1457 between James II's two sisters and the duke of Somerset's brothers.[58] Not only would this have aimed at an alleviation of renewed border conflict, but it would also have undermined James's dalliance, real or imagined, with York. Although the marriages fell through, a truce with Scotland was agreed to in July that succeeded in limiting overt hostilities and kept James away from York until late 1459, when England descended into civil war.[59]

More ambiguous is the proposal of late 1458 for marriages between Prince Edward, a son of the duke of York and a son of the late duke of Somerset on the one hand and three French or Burgundian princesses on the other.[60] Sir John Wenlock, whose loyalties would later prove notoriously flexible, led the English embassy, but there is no firm evidence at this juncture that he was serving anyone but the Lancastrian regime.[61] He had been an usher of the queen's chamber from her arrival in England and her chamberlain from 1447/48 through 1453, and he had fought for Henry at St Albans.[62] Although he served as speaker for the 1455–56 parliament, his aloofness from the campaign to have York named protector suggests that he did not support it.[63] Wenlock was commissioned on Henry's authority,[64] and the inclusion of Somerset's son

---

[55] Griffiths, p. 802. In addition, Thomas Courtenay and his brother received comprehensive pardons that included their murder of Nicholas Radford (*CPR, 1452–61*, pp. 358, 393).

[56] Griffiths, pp. 802–3.

[57] Ibid., p. 803.

[58] Ibid., p. 812. The current duke would have been Henry Beaufort, son of York's rival Edmund, who received livery of his father's possessions on 1 March 1457 when he was 'nearly of age'. His two younger brothers were Edmund and John (GEC, XII, i, pp. 54, 57).

[59] Griffiths, p. 813.

[60] Stevenson, I, pp. 361–77. My interpretation of the domestic implications of this matter differs from what has heretofore been suggested. Cf. Wolffe, pp. 313–15; Griffiths, p. 816; Watts, p. 347 and n. 361.

[61] Roskell, 'John Lord Wenlock', p. 34, suggests that Wenlock's involvement in this embassy may indicate a drift in his leanings towards York, but, as he himself points out, Wenlock's new loyalty is only certain from autumn 1459. Cf. Griffiths' observation, p. 846, n. 270, that Wenlock could have been acting in the interests of the duke of Burgundy in early 1459.

[62] Roskell, 'John Lord Wenlock', pp. 26, 30.

[63] Ibid., pp. 31–2; Griffiths, p. 752.

[64] By sign manual: PRO, C81/1469/26.

in the proposal strongly suggests that York did not initiate it and that it did not primarily favor his interests. Indeed, the selection of grooms indicates that the proposal, on one level, was a part of the 'reconciliation' set in motion at the beginning of the year.[65] For now, it may be noted that the marriage project addressed diplomatic and domestic concerns that would have been of interest to the court and to Margaret. On the international front it might have defused tensions between England and France, who harbored mutual fears of invasion. It might also have derailed the Burgundians' growing disposition towards Warwick, at this time firmly in control of Calais and for the moment more of a thorn in the side of the regime than York.[66] Domestically, the equal opportunity offered to the sons of York and Somerset might have served as yet another patch to paper over their enmity. But it might also have appealed on its own merits to York, who had once eagerly pursued a French marriage for his son, and drawn him away from alliance with the Nevilles and back into a more stable relationship with the regime, but on the latter's terms. In any event, the project foundered.

The association of queenship and intercession offered another informal venue that was ripe for exploitation. By linking herself with the exercise of the king's justice as well as his mercy, Margaret was able to extend the court's reach and to expand her own practical influence. During the latter part of October 1456, immediately after the great council at Coventry ended, she was in the Welsh border country negotiating a pardon for the powerful but lawless Gruffydd ap Nicholas in return for his renewed loyalty.[67] This must be seen as a pragmatic, if somewhat cynical, move. Gruffydd's power had been established long before Margaret ever arrived in England and had grown as central authority weakened. His loyalty derived from the same equation: so long as he was given a free hand on his own turf, he was loyal.[68] Most recently, however, he may have been seeking an understanding with York's retainer Sir William Herbert, who, along with Sir Walter Devereux, had been causing trouble in south and west Wales and who was still at large. Margaret's efforts may have helped to change his mind.[69] In the long run, Gruffydd's activities might have worked against the regime's credibility, but Margaret's immediate concern was for increased security. In that context, his cultivation made sense.

The following spring Margaret was present as justice – and mercy – were visited on Herbert, Devereux and their men. In April a commission of oyer and terminer brought indictments against them. Some of the charges were retrospective and were popularly held to be overly harsh, but they may have provided the government with additional leverage against Herbert, who responded to an offer to submit in return for his life and goods and was subsequently pardoned

[65] Discussed below, pp. 240ff.
[66] Griffiths, pp. 814–16; pp. 809–10, for Warwick's piracies and their consequences for the government.
[67] Evans, *Wales and the Wars of the Roses*, p. 59; Griffiths, p. 780. See Griffiths, 'Gruffydd ap Nicholas', for his career. He and his sons received comprehensive pardons on 26 October (*CPR, 1452–61*, p. 326).
[68] Griffiths, 'Gruffydd ap Nicholas', pp. 202, 210, 219.
[69] Ibid., pp. 211–14, and Griffiths, pp. 779–80, for the background and context of this situation. At one point Herbert and Devereux had taken prisoner the king's half-brother Edmund Tudor, earl of Richmond, who had been sent to south Wales as a representative of legitimate authority and had run foul of Gruffydd in that capacity, before his presence proved awkward to York.

in June.[70] The immediate gain for the court was a shift in Herbert's allegiance, which lasted until 1460.[71] Devereux, who had already submitted at Coventry in autumn, fared less well, being imprisoned until February 1458. It may be that this disparity of treatment 'was intended to divide them'.[72] Though Margaret had no official role in these matters, her presence with Henry served as a reminder of her informal influence.

Symbolic Representation

Thus far, I have argued that Margaret could acquire and exercise political power by appealing to or manipulating the king's authority and by using it to tap into the fictive authority of their young son. In both cases her influence was distanced from whatever actions or decisions resulted through a kind of sleight of hand: either her influence was given no official expression or it was presented with verbiage that tended to obscure the full extent of her power. This is not to say that no one was aware of her activities; people did perceive that the queen's real power had grown mightily, and some of them were harshly critical. Gascoigne, for instance, was sufficiently upset to write that the queen ruled so that everything was done, for better or worse, according to her will.[73] Gascoigne favored the Yorkists and already bore a grudge against the queen for her arrival in England without a proper dowry and for the loss of Maine and Anjou. The point of his complaint, however, seems simply to be that she had taken an inappropriately active role.[74] Somewhat later both the *Brut* and the *English Chronicle* bemoaned an England in which 'the governance of the Reame stode moste by the Quene and her Counsell' while she and her affinity 'rewled . . . as her lyked'.[75] Still, not everyone complained. Others obviously were content – or found it personally beneficial – to follow Margaret's leadership. This demonstrates the gap that existed between what was theoretically perceived to be right order (and right relationships) and an objective reality of porous boundaries that could be accepted, to a point.

This kind of perceptual slippage can most easily be seen in certain public, ceremonial activities of the queen. They represent, on the one hand, a high

---

[70] Gairdner, *PL*, III, p. 118; *CPR, 1452–61*, pp. 360, 367.

[71] Evans, *Wales and the Wars of the Roses*, pp. 61, 64, 66, 71.

[72] Storey, p. 182. But cf. Griffiths, p. 780, who considers that leniency was intended 'to prise [both Herbert and Devereux] from York's side rather than turn them into outlaws'. In the case of Devereux, it is difficult to see how imprisonment was to accomplish this, and, indeed, he emerged from prison as Yorkist as he had gone in (Evans, *Wales and the Wars of the Roses*, p. 61).

[73] Gascoigne, *Loci e Libro*, p. 204: 'et tunc ipsa [regina] sic regnavit, anno Xti 1456, quod secundum voluntatem ipsius reginae quasi tota negocia regni facta fuerunt per fas vel per nephas'. ('And then in 1456 the [queen] so ruled that nearly all the realm's affairs were done according to her will, for better or worse.') Gascoigne probably wrote this in 1457, when Margaret's power had become more evident; he died in March 1458.

[74] Ibid., p. 205: 'Regina illa Margareta . . . plura fecit in regno Angliae, ut creditur, postquam maritus suus . . . incidit in manifestam stulticiam; et qualia sequentur ex reginae actibus, anno Domini 1457, Deus scit.' ('That Queen Margaret . . . did many things in England, as is believed, after her husband . . . fell into manifest foolishness; and what will follow from the queen's actions in 1457, God knows.')

[75] *Brut*, p. 526; *English Chron.*, p. 79.

degree of conventionality in their presentation of a queenly 'image' even as they stretch to emphasize her new importance. On those occasions when she pushed too far, she was quick to back off and to attempt to readjust her image to something more suitable. These situations reveal the dilemma of Margaret's power: while there was much that she could do, the constant need to dress her public persona in the expected trappings of conventional queenship and womanhood undercut effective leadership.

A prime example of this perceptual slippage and of how prevalent understandings of gender affected public representations of Margaret's persona may be seen in the reception given her by the city of Coventry on 14 September 1456, a few weeks before the great council convened.[76] Its context must be kept in mind: changes in the highest government offices were in the offing as the queen set out to reassert royal authority and to garner an appreciable share of practical influence for herself. Thus it makes sense to regard the reception in part as a power play. Nevertheless, it remains a highly gendered production. There is very little in it that associates Margaret with any of the qualities of leadership, and only at the very end does a dragon-slaying St Margaret appear in a ham-fisted turn as protectress and perhaps as symbolic stand-in for her namesake.

The first and most obvious image of Margaret to be presented by the pageants is that of Margaret-as-mother.[77] Seven of the eighteen 'speaking parts' (the first four plus three more) refer to the prince in glowing terms and, in essence, praise the queen for having borne him. Thus, in the first pageant Isaiah likens the joy accompanying the prince's birth to that surrounding the birth of Jesus, a comparison that makes Margaret a type of the Virgin Mary.[78] All of these passages represent motherhood as an end in itself, while the prince receives praise for his future character and accomplishments.[79] A second image involves Margaret-as-wife. Although this role receives less emphasis, it is by no means overlooked. The pageants refer to Henry three times, initially in a pathetically overblown description by the character of Alexander the Great as 'the nobilest prince that is born, whome fortune hath famyd . . . Unto whom meekly I wyll be obeying'. By referring to Henry as 'your sovereyn lorde' or 'your lege lord', these three pageants all spell out the queen's subordination.[80]

Somewhat less obvious are the overlapping themes of reputation and

[76] Harris, *Coventry Leet Book*, pp. 286–92. Ironically, more than a hundred years ago, Mary Ann Hookham, who found the pageants 'curious and quaint', noticed some of the passages in which the gender content is strongest, though she did not analyze them in these terms (Hookham, *Life and Times*, II, pp. 17–18). Cf. Wolffe, p. 306, who describes the reception as a 'triumphal entry' and uses the incident to illustrate Margaret's prominence in contrast to Henry's quietude. Both of them mistake the year of the reception.

[77] The council collected 100 marks for Margaret and her son, half of which was given to her upon her arrival, while the rest was kept for the prince's use when he should come to Coventry (Harris, *Coventry Leet Book*, pp. 285–6).

[78] Ibid., p. 287.

[79] E.g., Ibid., p. 291. Julius Caesar: 'The same blessyd blossom that spronge of your body, Shall succede me yn worship, I will it be so; All the landis olyve shall obey hym un-to.'

[80] Ibid., pp. 289–90. The last of these speeches declares that the king 'is present here' and makes an intriguing plea for his continued good health. Henry's presence in the background while Margaret was receiving the visible honors might suggest the kind of complicitous gender inversion that Blok discusses (Blok, 'Female Rulers', pp. 15–16), but the actual discursive content of the pageants undermines this assumption.

protection. Two speeches praise Margaret's 'virtuous life'.[81] Virtue, of course, had a different meaning for a woman than it had for a man, and we must remember that rumors regarding the prince's birth had begun to circulate. In addition, she was twice praised for the (primarily female) quality of meekness and once for being 'steadfast and true'.[82] Although the latter qualities were not generally regarded as female characteristics, they may have had a special meaning for Margaret in her situation. Surely they fit the image that she tried to convey through her actions.

The pageants also contain many references to the queen's need for protection. Though protection may be understood most easily in terms of countering a physical threat, it may also include the safeguarding of reputation and even the internal protections of conscience, as when Temperance promises to 'feythfully defende [Margaret] from all maner daunger'.[83] No less than six famous conquerors promise to obey or otherwise offer service to Margaret. This might seem to offer some acknowledgment of her leadership potential, except that in two cases the promise is clearly placed in the context of knightly service to a lady.[84] Thus, it seems that the primary image evoked is of the passive female surrounded and protected by male heroism. Finally, there is the dramatic appearance in the last pageant of St Margaret, who turns out to be more conventional than she initially seems. Having promised 'by [her] power' to protect Queen Margaret, she reveals the nature of that power:

> I shall pray to the prince that is endeles
>> To soccour you with solas of his high grace.
> He wyll here my peticion that is doutles,
>> For I Wrought all my lyff that his wyll wace;
>
> Therfore, lady, when ye be yn any dredefull cace
> Call on me boldly, therof I pray you,
> And trist to me feythefully, I woll do that may pay yow.[85]

The saint, much like the real queen, is depicted as intercessor and intermediary; right relationships are preserved, and anomaly is avoided.

It is nevertheless true that Margaret's self-representations were not always so circumspect, though her lapses seem incidental rather than matters of unswerving policy. Following the council meeting of February–March 1457, she was escorted from the city by the mayor and sheriffs in the same manner as the king at his departures. Thus, the mayor rode before her with his mace, following the sheriffs with their white 'yardes', just as they would have done for the king. The only thing missing was the king's sword, which was generally carried next to him. The city recorder was sufficiently shocked to note that such a thing had never occurred before, and that it had only been done because the queen's

---

[81] Harris, *Coventry Leet Book*, pp. 288, 290.
[82] Ibid., pp. 287, 291.
[83] Ibid., p. 288.
[84] Ibid., p. 290. Joshua: 'To the plesure of your persone, I wyll put me to pyne, As a knyght for his lady boldly to fight, Yf any man of curage wold bid you unright.' David: 'I . . . will obey to you, lady . . . And welcum you Curtesly as a kynd knyght, For the love of your lege lorde, Herry that hight.'
[85] Ibid., p. 292.

officers had insisted that she would be displeased if this recognition were not accorded her.[86] Although this can be seen as a symbolic claim to 'male' authority, it did not in any sense replace Henry with Margaret. The imagery was right, but the context was wrong, and, in any case, it appears that Margaret soon had to back-pedal.

Perhaps in response to the raised eyebrows and negative comment that her departure had occasioned, when Margaret came to Coventry on 15 June to see the Corpus Christi pageants the next day, she 'came prevely' and asked not to be met. There to enjoy the plays with her were the duke and duchess of Buckingham and 'all ther Childern', Lord Rivers and his wife, the dowager countess of Shrewsbury and her daughter-in-law and other lords and ladies, giving the impression of a domestic, familial gathering. During her visit the mayor and council regaled her with a gift of 300 loaves of white bread, a pipe of red wine, a dozen choice capons, a dozen pike, a large basket of peascods, another of pippins and oranges, comfits and a pot of green ginger. Upon her departure they accompanied her from the city 'with right a Good feliship of the said cite', whom she graciously thanked for their kindness – though we are not told with what ceremony they escorted her.[87] Unfortunately, although notices of other visits by the queen to Coventry exist, no other accounts provide descriptions of the manner of her comings and goings. When she and Henry participated in the Whitsunday processions a little earlier that year, the king went surrounded by his lords and officers and all the panoply of his estate, while the queen followed with her ladies.[88] Thus, it appears on balance that, although Margaret's visits naturally involved pomp and circumstance, such displays largely occurred within the gendered boundaries acceptable to her role.

[86] Ibid., pp. 298–9. Margaret had come 'suddenly' to Coventry on 12 February a few days before the council began, riding pillion behind a man and accompanied by her ladies in similar fashion. Perhaps because of the apparently unexpected nature of her arrival she asked that no one 'be laburd to mete her'. Her wishes were followed, but the style of her arrival suggests that it would not have been unnoticed (p. 297).

[87] Ibid., p. 300.

[88] Ibid., p. 299.

10

Control and Conciliation

SO FAR the discussion has centered on Margaret's efforts to gain and exercise practical power, a power that drew on and was used to reassert the king's authority rather than her own. The second part of her project attempted to find a way to nullify York and his Neville supporters so that they could never again pose a threat. Primarily in response to this part of Margaret's plan, she has been portrayed – and condemned – as a promoter of faction and division. Despite a diversity of interpretations of what went on in the later 1450s, historical assessment of Margaret has tended to support this view uncritically. Obviously, she and York did end up at each other's throats, giving no quarter, each certain that only complete victory could save him or her from otherwise assured destruction. This is the view from the end of the reign, from 1459 on, when conflict had spun out of control and there could be no turning back for either side. But was this the case from 1456? If we can agree that one of Margaret's goals was to nullify the Yorkists, what exactly did 'nullification' mean before 1459? Are we correct to characterize Margaret throughout this whole period as an implacable she-wolf bent on vengeance and the annihilation of her enemies?[1]

If the answer to that question is assumed to be yes, several corollaries must follow. First, it must be assumed that no evenhanded, much less favorable, treatment of York and the Nevilles could have had Margaret's support. Second, that being the case, any apparently moderate or conciliatory action must be seen as the work of others, contrary to Margaret's wishes. Third, it must likewise be assumed that any actions directed against York and the Nevilles must at least have had Margaret's tacit approval. This is largely the view that has prevailed, but all of these assumptions get in the way of analysis. What must be done is to put the first assumption – that Margaret from 1456 onward was an uncompromising she-wolf impelled by vendetta – on hold for the moment and to question its corollaries. We need to ask what 'nullification' meant.

Once the foregone conclusion has been set aside, it appears, in fact, that modest gestures toward evenhandedness were not necessarily inimical to Margaret's interests and that efforts at controlled conciliation could be made

---

[1] Cf. Griffiths, pp. 798ff, for a thoroughgoing exposition of the Yorkists' 'victimization' at the hands of Margaret and her associates; pp. 822–3, for his belief that Margaret intended to destroy them from 1456 on. There can be no doubt that York and the Nevilles later represented themselves as victims, probably with genuine conviction. As I shall argue in this and the next chapter, however, Margaret's actions were not of a single, unvarying piece.

to serve her needs. And, although it may be difficult to imagine that she would have grieved if something unpleasant had happened to York or the Nevilles, it is also difficult to see how the pursuit of personal vengeance by the heirs of St Albans would have strengthened the cause of royal authority. Thus, through much of 1457, nullification seems to have involved a process of intimidation and partial isolation, increasingly combined with careful efforts at amelioration. Its aim was not to destroy York, but to draw his teeth and eventually to bring him back into the polity on condition that he accept his place in a new status quo. In some ways naive, in others daring, it was dictated both by political necessity and by gendered realities. Ultimately, it failed.

The first signs of this approach are apparent at the Coventry council of October 1456, where James Gresham wrote that York had been with the king and had left him on good terms, though he was not on good terms with the queen. Moreover, some said that he would have been 'distressed' at his departure had not the duke of Buckingham intervened.[2] Although the queen's involvement in whatever actions were planned against York may be implied by the report, her role remains uncertain. Buckingham, despite his concern over the Bourgchiers' dismissals, appears as a peacekeeper rather than as a partisan, for Gresham says that he also intervened to save the young duke of Somerset from the town's wrath after the duke's men brawled with the watchmen, leaving several of the latter dead.[3] A less detailed but also less disjointed version of what may be the same event appears in 'Gough's Chronicle', which reports that at the Coventry council 'the toune sadly kept the pees for the yong duke of Somersett was purposed for to affrayed with the duke of Yorke but the kyng and the lordys made an end therof'.[4]

Altogether, York seems at this time and for the next couple of years to have lacked lordly support apart from the Nevilles. Though he may have had some sympathizers, none were willing to step forward to take his part.[5] There seem to be two possible reasons for this. Some may have been wary and fearful of the situation and felt it wiser to keep their heads down. Such may have been the case of Norfolk, who in late 1458 complained of having been warned away from his association with York.[6] Others may have questioned York's actions or those of his men and found them insupportable.

A second incident, alleged to have occurred at a Coventry great council – most probably the one of February–March 1457, may suggest the latter. The report of it comes from an obviously biased source, the preamble to the

[2] Gairdner, PL, III, p. 108. 'Benet's Chron.', p. 217, also notes Margaret's enmity towards York and Warwick at this time. London Chrons., p. 167, and Brut, p. 523, both report a threat to the Yorkists, but neither mentions the queen.

[3] Gairdner, PL, III, p. 108.

[4] Flenley (Gough), p. 159. The chronicle version is not without its own confusions. Although it is clear which council is meant, it is misdated to December, and the account partially conflates events at Coventry with a separate encounter in London between Somerset and Sir John Neville, one of Salisbury's younger sons.

[5] Griffiths, p. 798, who also notes the absence of neutrals in the sense of a 'middle party' that sought reconciliation. Certainly, loyalty to the king remained unshaken, and so whatever sympathy York had, it stopped well short of visualizing him as a legitimate alternative to Henry.

[6] Davis, PL, II, p. 176. Brut, p. 527, describing the situation in late 1459, says that people were afraid to disobey the queen.

Yorkists' attainder of 1459; nevertheless, recent historians have agreed that something of the sort took place, though they differ over when it happened.[7] The preamble states that at this council York was charged by the chancellor with unspecified matters involving 'jeopardy' to the king's person and the 'inquieting' of the realm, and that the duke of Buckingham 'and all other lords' knelt to beg the king that this should be his last warning. Thereafter, York and any others guilty of similar offenses should 'be punysshed after their deserte'. At that same time it was enacted that 'no Lord shuld attempt by wey of fayt ayenst other', but seek redress only according to the law. Both York and Warwick were said to have sworn oaths and signed the act as pledges for their future conduct.[8] Although the charges against York are frustratingly vague, a link may be posited between his rebuke and the upcoming prosecutions of Herbert and Devereux.[9] But they were not the only troublemakers; Somerset and others had also been causing problems.[10] It is possible that a number of lords were simply getting fed up. Though only York and Warwick were mentioned retrospectively in the preamble to the attainder, it seems likely that all lords present signed the enactment.[11] While Margaret may have welcomed York's humiliation, there is no evidence that she sought more drastic action against him.

An earlier incident that demonstrates intimidation and may also hint at York's impending isolation occurred in September 1456, when some dogs' heads 'with Scriptures in their mouthes balade wise' appeared one morning in Fleet Street, opposite the bishop of Salisbury's house where York was then staying.[12] The messages were threatening and alluded to York's faithlessness and opportunism, as portions of two verses demonstrate:

> My mayster ys cruell and can no curtesye,
> ffor whos offence here am y pyghte [exposed].
> hyt ys no reson that y schulde dye
> ffor hys trespace, & he go quyte.
>
> . . .
>
> Wat planet compellyd me, or what signe,
> To serve that man that all men hate?
> y wolde hys hede were here for myne,
> ffor he hathe caused all the debate.[13]

---

[7] Wolffe, pp. 309–10, and Johnson, p. 178, favor this dating, and I find their arguments compelling. The supposition that York's humiliation took place at this time also accords well with the image of Margaret being escorted from the city with kingly honors at the council's end. But cf. Storey, p. 180, and Griffiths, p. 800, who incline towards October 1456; and Hicks, *Warwick*, p. 157, who argues for June–July 1459.

[8] *RP*, V, p. 347.

[9] Johnson, p. 178; Storey, pp. 180–1 n. The commission of oyer and terminer was issued while the council met (*CPR, 1452–61*, pp. 348–9).

[10] See below, pp. 149–50.

[11] Although Warwick's presence at the 1457 council is not recorded (Harris, *Coventry Leet Book*, pp. 297–8), he did not depart for Calais until late April (Hicks, *Warwick*, p. 131). If the purpose of the enactment was to obtain widespread general agreement to forego self-help, he could have signed it before his departure.

[12] Flenley ('Bale's Chron.'), p. 144; 'Benet's Chron.', p. 217, blames the work on court officials ('curiales').

[13] Printed in Robbins, *Historical Poems*, pp. 189–90, and discussed on pp. xxxii–xxxiii, 355 (where he mistakenly identifies the duke of York as 'Edward').

Whether Margaret was personally behind them or whether she even knew about them until after the fact is impossible to say, but they almost certainly reflected sentiments that she would have endorsed. More importantly, it must be understood that, by its nature, all such propaganda aims for a wider audience than its immediate target. Unless there is some expectation that it will have a public resonance, it serves little purpose. Like the allegations concerning the prince's birth that were directed at Margaret, there had to be some public credibility – not to be confused with actual veracity – for the message to work. Obviously, it would not work on everyone, but there would have been an expectation that some who saw it would react with approval.

During this time royal patronage and perks were frequently bestowed upon the core of midland court supporters, household servants or the Yorkists' regional rivals.[14] The Yorkists may have felt that they were slighted. Nevertheless, they were not excluded from favor. On 6 March 1457 York was reappointed to the lieutenancy of Ireland for an additional ten years, effective from 8 December when his previous appointment was due to expire.[15] In July he received £446 0s. 11d.; the following March, license to ship 10,000 marks worth of wool free in payment for his lieutenancy. Although half of the wool allocation was later earmarked to cover compensation owed by York as part of the loveday settlement, he still stood to profit.[16] He also participated in the matrimonial politics of the period. In early 1458 the marriage of York's daughter Elizabeth and John de la Pole, the young duke of Suffolk, was settled.[17]

In other matters he also derived some benefit. The indictments of Herbert and Devereux in April 1457 carefully avoided casting blame on York for their activities, perhaps suggesting a bit of deal making at the 1457 Coventry council in return for his submission.[18] On 21 April 1457 he was allowed £40 annually in recompense for the constableship of the castles of Carmarthen, Aberystwyth and Carreg Cennen, to which he had helped himself after the death of Edmund, duke of Somerset, at St Albans and which had just been granted to the king's half-brother Jasper, earl of Pembroke.[19] In summer, he was given a charter for a weekly market at Fotheringhay, and in late September he was named, along with many others, to commissions of array in the southern counties, midlands and East Anglia. In mid-December he was further commissioned to raise

---

[14] Griffiths, pp. 803–4.

[15] *CPR, 1452–61*, p. 341. This occurred during the council meeting. Griffiths, p. 799, characterizes it as 'a serious, not to say fatal, error' for the Lancastrians, since York would later use Ireland as a refuge and a base from which to launch his attack on the crown.

[16] Johnson, pp. 179, 184, 197. The cash payment was authorized by privy seal. Johnson, p. 197, considers 'the Crown [to have] been marginally more conscientious in discharging its financial obligations [to York]' than he was in performing as lieutenant. During York's second term his only action was to replace the second engrosser of the exchequer in Ireland.

[17] Thomson, 'John de la Pole', p. 529.

[18] Johnson, pp. 178–9. That there was at least subjective reason to hold York responsible can hardly be doubted, even if it could not be explicitly proven (Griffiths, pp. 779–80; idem, 'Gruffyd ap Nicholas', p. 213). If York did 'get off', while allowing his retainers to dangle, that may in part explain Herbert's shift in loyalty.

[19] *CPR, 1452–61*, p. 340; *Foedera*, V, ii, p. 71. Johnson, p. 179, notes, however, that he never received payment.

archers.[20] This mobilization seems to have occurred primarily in response to a French attack on Sandwich in August and reflected perennial English fears of French intentions, though it may also have come in handy as a show of royal strength in connection with the council meetings that took place in November and again in late January at Westminster.[21] Looking ahead a bit, it may be possible to see the marriage proposal of late 1458 as part of a developing pattern of controlled inclusion for York.[22]

Nor were the Nevilles excluded. Salisbury had been appointed chief steward for life of the northern parts of the duchy of Lancaster on 15 February 1456, shortly before the end of the second protectorate, and he was allowed to keep this office until his attainder in 1459.[23] On 25 April 1457 his younger son, Sir John, was married to Isabel (or Elizabeth) Ingaldesthorpe, the daughter and heir of a Cambridgeshire knight, whose wardship and marriage had earlier been granted to Margaret.[24] Through her mother, who was sister and coheiress to the childless earl of Worcester, Isabel stood to come into a portion of the earldom.[25] Although Worcester himself was said to have 'brought about' the marriage, it must also have had Margaret's approval. At any rate, she intended to make some money from it.[26] In September 1457, at the same time as York was receiving commissions of array, the sheriffs of Nottingham, Derby, Cumberland, Westmorland and York were told to see to it that Salisbury received all necessary support to defend the west marches towards Scotland.[27] Along with York, he was commissioned to raise archers in December.[28] Perhaps more telling, although Lawrence Booth's appointment to the bishopric of Durham in August 1457 did lessen Neville influence in the area, it appears that the new bishop was willing to show the earl his continued favor.[29] It is unlikely that a man who owed most of his career to Margaret, in particular his most recent advancements, would have treated the earl and his affinity in a manner that was entirely contrary to her wishes.

---

[20] *CChR, 1427–1516*, p. 128; *CPR, 1452–61*, pp. 402–3, 406, 408. The earl of Salisbury was also named as a commissioner for York (ibid., p. 408). He may not have been included in the earlier commission since it did not apply to the north.

[21] Griffiths, pp. 804–5, 815–16; Johnson, p. 180.

[22] See above, pp. 137–8.

[23] Somerville, *Lancaster*, p. 421. Griffiths, p. 757, considers this 'a post which considerably enhanced his dominance in the north'.

[24] Gairdner, *PL*, III, p. 118, for the marriage; *CPR, 1452–61*, pp. 325 and 359, for grants of wardship by privy seal on 13 October 1456 and again on 26 January 1457. The girl's father, Sir Edmund, had served on commissions to obtain loans for the relief of Shrewsbury's army in France in 1453 and for the defense of Calais in 1454; he served as justice of the peace in 1455 and 1456 (ibid., pp. 52, 147–8, 661). Sir John Neville was the son who had been involved in the feud with the Percies.

[25] At that time, the earl had outlived two wives (the first had been one of Salisbury's daughters) and, though only thirty, had been a widower for five years. Only in 1467 would he eventually remarry (GEC, XII, ii, pp. 842–5). It may have seemed in 1457 that Isabel's prospects were reasonably good.

[26] Gairdner, *PL*, III, p. 118; *CCR, 1454–61*, pp. 300–1: a total of £1,000, payable in ten installments over six years.

[27] *CPR, 1452–61*, p. 400. He had been warden of the west marches since 1420, and had held the post jointly with his son, Warwick, since December 1453 (*CPR, 1446–52*, p. 184). The sheriff of Northumberland was similarly ordered to provide support to the earl of Northumberland as warden of the east marches.

[28] *CPR, 1452–61*, p. 408.

[29] Pollard, *North-Eastern England*, pp. 267–8, describes Booth's behavior as 'conciliatory' and demonstrates that the loss of Neville power was a relative thing: always partial and never complete.

The earl of Warwick's situation was more ticklish. He had obtained the captaincy of Calais by indenture with Henry in August 1455 when the king was under Yorkist control.[30] He had astutely taken possession in July 1456, by which time the impending rivalry between York and the queen was beginning to attract notice, and it may be that, initially, it was perceived to be easier to let him stay put than to try to dislodge him.[31] On 3 October 1457, as part of the military preparations then taking place, the king appointed him, with the council's advice and assent, 'to go on the sea with an armed force and to govern the same and war against the king's enemies'. Around the same time Lord Welles was sent to Calais with men-at-arms and archers to reinforce its defenses. Warwick's appointment appears to have been renewed on 26 November and confirmed a month later for a term of three years. His powers at this time included authorization 'to come to terms with any places [held by] the king's enemies', and also to arrest and punish pirates who were preying upon both English and foreign merchants.[32] The latter injunction is of particular interest since Warwick would soon be making a name for himself and causing the court great embarrassment by his own acts of piracy.[33]

Finally, it appears that the Yorkists were included in meetings of the great council, despite one chronicler's assertion a few years later that they had been excluded. Although the record of summons to the council is admittedly scanty, what there is suggests that their attendance was regularly requested and anticipated.[34] The statement in their attainder that they had been summoned 'dyvers tymes' to attend council meetings must also be taken at face value as it would make little sense to falsify, although the concurrent claim that they had failed to attend for frivolous – rather than valid – reasons must be regarded as suspect.[35]

At this point we must stop for a moment to ascertain where Margaret fit into this picture, meanwhile recognizing along with P.A. Johnson that 'the tone of English political life in 1457 is . . . peculiarly elusive'.[36] In the first place, as already noted, the queen's power, though real, was limited. Despite the complaints of her detractors, she could not simply rule as she liked;[37] the system would not allow it. Since she could not act upon her own authority, whatever she did had to be done through a certain amount of indirection and

---

[30] Griffiths, p. 843, n. 219. Its previous holder was the late duke of Somerset.

[31] See Harriss, 'Struggle for Calais', for the importance of Calais to the balance of power and development of conflict, and especially pp. 40–51 for Warwick's involvement and the Calais staple's support for the Yorkists in the late 1450s.

[32] CPR, 1452–61, pp. 390, 404, 413; CCR, 1454–61, p. 240. Along with the latest affirmation of his power, he was also granted subsidies of tonnage and poundage.

[33] Griffiths, pp. 808–10. As a single example, in May 1458, Warwick (along with Buckingham and others) were commissioned to investigate the complaint of a Spanish shipmaster whose cargo was said to have been taken by William Neville, Lord Fauconberg, who happened to be Warwick's uncle and was serving unofficially as his lieutenant at Calais (CPR, 1452–61, p. 438).

[34] PPC, VI, pp. 297, 298–9, 333–4; cf. Brut, p. 527. Kingsford suggests that this portion of the chronicle was written between 1464 and 1470 (EHL, p. 119).

[35] RP, V, p. 348.

[36] Johnson, p. 179.

[37] As claimed by the English Chron., p. 79. The chronicler seems to be talking about the situation around 1459; up to that point he has not once referred to Margaret as a participant in or controller of the government.

sleight of hand. As a second point, however, an effort to destroy the realm's highest ranking magnate would not have provided the optimum means for shoring up royal rule.[38] At best, it would have involved obtaining the at-least-passive acquiescence of the other lords, who as a matter of principle might be expected to resist the destruction of one of their own except in the most egregious of circumstances. Although it appears that the lords themselves had lost patience with York, agreeing to his severe punishment could have been another matter. The plea to make this York's last warning implies a belief that, having made him aware of the seriousness of his situation and of his lack of support, there would be no need to take further measures.[39] Moreover, by this time York appears to have become as suspicious of Margaret as she of him, and it was not to be expected that he should go quietly without a fight. Although what Margaret eventually got was a war, she did not need a war and its attendant risks to the dynasty. She did not need another St Albans. What she needed was York's capitulation as a loyal subject. To get it, a combination of the carrot and the stick, precisely balanced, offered the best hope. It is not necessary to portray Margaret as a gentle initiator of compromise, but it must be recognized that such palliative actions as did occur were not antithetical to her purposes and could likely be made to serve them.[40] That they, in fact, ultimately did not is another matter.

If a case can be made that Margaret herself would have found benefit in a less single-minded approach to the Yorkists during this period than has generally been thought, the same cannot be said of some others who numbered among her supporters. A number of incidents occurred in which certain of the Yorkists' enemies attempted to attack them. Each incident provided a potential excuse for retaliatory self-help; the possibility of a serious encounter raised the specter of a further Yorkist coup, with more serious consequences than in 1455.

At Coventry in 1456 the duke of Somerset apparently intended to attack York but was prevented through the efforts of the king, lords and townspeople.[41] Shortly thereafter, on 5 November, the dukes of Exeter and Somerset, the earl of Shrewsbury and Lord Roos 'rode ageinst [the earl of Warwick] to have distressed him' before he came to London. Warwick evaded them and made it into the city where, according to an admiring chronicler, his popularity kept him safe.[42] In December, a confrontation in London between Somerset and Sir John Neville began with hard looks and would have ended in an armed encounter when both went off for reinforcements had not the mayor set a

---

[38] As an example for comparison, the arrest of Humphrey, duke of Gloucester, followed by his probably natural death in 1447 had subsequently provided disgruntled parties with a martyr to use in attacking the regime, as Margaret and others would have been well aware.

[39] Cf. Watts, pp. 335–7. As a parallel example, although they had acquiesced to Somerset's imprisonment in 1453, they had been notably unwilling to participate in his further punishment.

[40] Cf. Griffiths, p. 804, who characterizes Margaret's attitude towards the Yorkists as one of 'unforgiving severity'. I differ less with him over his description of Margaret's posture vis-à-vis Henry's more apparent magnanimity than with the assumption it entails, that she could not have found conciliation useful and that she would have opposed it in all forms.

[41] See above, p. 144.

[42] Flenley ('Bale's Chron.'), p. 144: 'They durst not countre with him for he was named and taken in all places for the moost corageous and manliest knight lyvyng.'

special watch to keep the peace.[43] It may be that the Coventry council's
enactment against self-help also came about in response to incidents such as
these. As a matter of fact, and perhaps as a result of the enactment, there appear
to have been no further attempted ambushes or face-offs for about a year. The
hiatus ended in February 1458, when the lords gathered in London for the
council meeting that was supposed to resolve their differences. Somerset, Exeter,
and the Lords Egremont and Clifford apparently plotted to ambush York and
Salisbury on their way to Westminster, but again the efforts of the mayor and
the watch prevented violence.[44] As more lords arrived, tensions increased, and
on 9 March, Somerset and Northumberland attempted to 'meet' Warwick in
arms, but he was intercepted and escorted from the scene by other lords before
anything could happen. Undeterred, he promptly announced that he would go
to Westminster the next day in spite of them all.[45]

A last incident involving Warwick does not quite fit this pattern, but is worth
recounting since it sheds suggestive light on the other near-encounters thus far
noted. It appears that in November 1458, while the earl was attending a council
at Westminster, an altercation broke out between one or more of his men and
members of the king's household. Someone got hurt, most likely one of the
king's men. The battle spread as men from the household kitchen joined in,
wielding spits, pestles and whatever came to hand. Warwick's life was
threatened (if he was present), or believed to be in danger (if he was not). In
any event, the earl escaped harm as well as responsibility for the fracas and made
his way back to Calais.[46] He would later insinuate that there had been an
attempt to destroy him.[47] Nevertheless, while the threat to Warwick may have
become very real in the heat of the moment, the whole incident looks rather
more like a case of spontaneous combustion than a planned assassination
attempt. Looking back over the previous confrontations, it appears that
Warwick was a lightning rod for trouble; neither he nor his brother can
simply be accounted helpless victims.[48]

What this incident demonstrates above all is the extent to which petty
violence and the threat of worse persisted among the lords and the inability
of the crown to control it, even within the royal household. The grievances and
the fears that precipitated violence were real on both sides, but continuing

[43] Ibid. (Gough), p. 159; *London Chrons.*, p. 167; *Great Chron.*, p. 189.

[44] Flenley (Gough), p. 159. This is the only source that suggests a planned attack by named persons. Some
   chronicles simply report the extreme tension in the city due to the presence of what amounted to
   opposing armed camps and the mayor's efforts to maintain the peace (*London Chrons.*, p. 168; *Brut*,
   p. 525; *Great Chron.*, pp. 189–90; 'Benet's Chron.', p. 221). Others observe that those who saw
   themselves as out to avenge St Albans posed the greater threat (Flenley [Rawlinson B.355], p. 111;
   English Chron., p. 77; *Three Chrons.*, p. 71).

[45] Flenley (Gough), p. 160.

[46] Flenley (Rawlinson B.355 and 'Bale's Chron.'), pp. 113, 146; *English Chron.*, p. 78; *Brut*, p. 526. The
   date is confirmed by Hicks, *Warwick*, p. 152.

[47] *Reg. Whethamstede*, I, p. 340. He made this claim as the Yorkists faced the royalist forces at Ludlow in
   1459 (see below, p. 168, n. 56). Among all the sources, only the *Brut* suggests that a plot to assassinate
   Warwick preceded the fight. Flenley (Rawlinson B.355), p. 113, says that the whole thing started when
   someone from the king's household stepped on the foot of one of Warwick's men ('fuit magnum
   scisma . . . eo quod unus de domo regis suppeditavit pedem alterius de familiis comitis Warwici').

[48] Griffiths, p. 800, observes that Warwick was held to be particularly responsible for the killings at St
   Albans.

resort to self-help and to unilateral 'remedies' did not ultimately advance the cause of royal authority. If Margaret was able to see this in 1453–54 – and there is reason to believe that she did – she also would have been able to see it in 1456–57. The problem was that she needed support against persons whom she had come to regard as dangerous. The question to be asked is not whether Margaret would have promoted or even condoned the attempted violence, but whether she could have prevented it, and the answer would seem to be no. As long as the threat of such violence persisted, with attendant possibilities of escalation, royal authority remained a sham.

Thus, the need to resolve the threat posed by continuing vendetta had begun to coincide with the need to expand effective power from the base established by the Coventry regime. Although the consolidation of regional control had worked rather well, it could never be an end in itself or an alternative to ruling the realm. But that also meant bringing York and the Nevilles back into the fold as controlled participants. These matters came into sharper focus at the end of August 1457 with the French attack on Sandwich.[49] The perception of external danger and the fears that it evoked, coupled with the knowledge that domestic instability invited further trouble, precipitated a series of careful moves towards conciliation that culminated in the 'loveday' settlement.

The Loveday of 1458

The so-called 'loveday' reconciliation between the Yorkist lords and the heirs of their opponents slain at St Albans has often been viewed as a fairly silly exercise, likely to have been prompted by Henry VI himself and predestined to fail.[50] In retrospect, historians have observed that it neither resolved the feuds that it explicitly addressed, nor even addressed the more serious conflict between York and Margaret. In particular, they have viewed Margaret as a cynical participant, biding her time for the next opportunity to go on the attack.[51]

This view ignores what Margaret stood to gain from the loveday's intended success. Moreover, it ignores the constraints that gender placed upon her explicit role, even as the symbolism and imagery of the moment provided opportunity for gender roles to be blurred. If one looks closely at the known activities of king and queen around this time and at the theatrical enactment of the loveday itself, a kind of role reversal appears to have been going on. In short, Henry looks more like the 'queenly' intercessor for peace and harmony, while

---

[49] Storey, p. 184; Griffiths, p. 815. The attack apparently came in response to depredations on French commerce by ships out of Calais.

[50] Thus Storey, p. 185, and Wolffe, p. 312, dismiss it as 'empty', while Griffiths, pp. 805, 806, 807, characterizes it as naive and theatrical, 'an astonishing spectacle . . . hollow . . . and . . . shabby'. Cf. Hicks, *Warwick*, pp. 135–8. It is also discussed in Maurer, 'Margaret of Anjou and the Loveday of 1458'.

[51] Cf. Watts, pp. 341–6, who believes that the original initiatives towards reconciliation came from the council and whose subsequent analysis of the loveday differs substantially from others. Although he recognizes that a symbolic reconciliation was being enacted between queen and duke, he does not explore the possibilities of Margaret's role or its gendered implications.

Margaret comes closer to the 'kingly' role of stern, unbending justice brought to mercy. The reversal is not complete, however; it is mixed and messy. But it suggests that Margaret's stake in the performance was nothing less than York's acceptance of a new status quo, which involved recognition of her power and an acknowledgment of his place.

The move towards reconciliation began with the summoning of a great council to Westminster in November 1457. The meeting was accompanied by a muster of armed men about the city at the beginning of the month, on the king's orders. They may have been called up to overawe a frequently unruly London, or to keep the peace among the retinues of mutually hostile lords; in any case, their presence caused the city some anxiety.[52] The business of the great council is not precisely known. One suspects that it would have included defense measures following the French raid on Sandwich,[53] but it almost certainly involved or came to involve the initial mooting of a reconciliation among lords. On 29 November, noting that unfinished business still lay before the council that threatened the weal of land and people if it remained unresolved, the king called for a further session to meet on 27 January 1458.[54] Since the primary concern of the subsequent council – indeed, its explicit rationale – was the reconciliation, that must have been the unfinished business to which the summons referred.

A difficulty facing the autumn council that could have contributed to a decision to seek a general reconciliation may have been poor attendance. Although the duke of York seems to have been sufficiently reassured by the security measures to arrive for the council in early November,[55] this may not have been so with the earl of Salisbury, who was met at Doncaster by Viscount Beaumont and accompanied south by him.[56] Since Salisbury already would have been traveling south when Beaumont met him, it seems most likely that Doncaster was the point at which he perceived himself to be entering enemy territory and desired the reassurance that Beaumont's escort provided.[57] Besides

---

[52] Flenley ('Bale's Chron.'), p. 145. Griffiths, pp. 804–5; cf. Johnson, p. 180, for the rationale behind the muster. These troops appear to have come from the levies that had been called up in response to the perceived French threat.

[53] During the month of September a great many commissions of array were issued for the south and midlands; some call specifically for protection of the ports. Around the same time others were issued to guard against the Scots, and in October there were further commissions to arrest ships and mariners for defensive purposes (*CPR, 1452–61*, pp. 400–6). With preparations for defense so pervasively in the air, it is difficult to imagine that the council would not have discussed them.

[54] *PPC*, VI, pp. 290–1. The writ bears the sign manual. In it the king indicates that he took part in person in the discussion of certain important matters. The implication seems to be that these were the ones that still lacked resolution.

[55] Johnson, p. 180.

[56] *CPR, 1452–61*, p. 428. The order to Beaumont to meet Salisbury was issued on 16 November, under the privy seal. He was told to wait for Salisbury at Doncaster. A single source, Rawlinson B.355 (Flenley, p. 111), states that Beaumont came with Salisbury to the council session in 1458. It seems rather unlikely that Beaumont would have been given orders to meet him so far in advance, though it is not impossible. In either case, my suggestions regarding Margaret remain the same.

[57] Pollard, *North-Eastern England*, p. 268, is uncertain whether Beaumont was there to force Salisbury to attend the council or to assure his safe conduct. The circumstances of their meeting make the latter the more likely. Beaumont was married to Salisbury's sister. A letter of uncertain date written to him by the earl seems to indicate that they were, at least at one time, on terms of trust (Gairdner, *PL*, III, pp. 121–2).

being the king's man, Beaumont was, of course, the queen's man also, and it may be that the perception of her protection was the more important.[58] There appear to have been no specific threats or outbursts of violence at this council, but since we do not know exactly who attended, this situation may have owed more to absences than to the king's troops. The insistence on a full attendance when the council resumed in January seems to indicate that absences or reluctant attendees had been a problem. Oddly, however, although ninety-two were summoned, neither Salisbury's nor Warwick's name appears among them. The earl of Northumberland and Lord Egremont were also omitted.[59] Whatever the reasons for their omission, all four in fact attended the council and were key figures in the reconciliation.[60] Although we have no direct evidence of Margaret's attitude towards the autumn council or its business at this point, Beaumont's role in bringing Salisbury to London might be cautiously regarded as an indicator that she shared concerns over a full and representative attendance or, at least, that she was not vehemently opposed to the council's purposes.

A further piece of circumstantial evidence regarding Margaret's activities and position around this time, which must be regarded with at least equal caution but which is rather more intriguing, may be found in the gossipy – and treasonable – remarks of one Robert Burnet. In November 1457, Burnet was indicted for saying that the queen was waging men to go overseas, presumably to fight. More significantly, he blamed Henry for the loss of France and for sleeping too much and wished that the king had been killed at St Albans.[61] These remarks are interesting in their portrayal of the queen as an inappropriately active figure, even as they condemn the king for his lack of action. There seems to be no evidence to indicate that Margaret was raising troops at this time for any reason,[62] and one inevitably wonders where Burnet got his information about the king's sleeping habits. Whether these allegations were literally true or not, they illustrate a perceived imbalance in the activities of the king and queen, with the queen doing what the king should have done while the king failed to live up to the expectations of his role. It is difficult to know quite how to square this picture with the slightly later image of a Henry busily issuing commissions of array and ordering defensive measures. As usual, of course, the king's name

---

[58] Although involving a greater imaginative leap, it may not be amiss to wonder whether Lawrence Booth, who in his new capacity as bishop of Durham was demonstrating that he was not Salisbury's enemy, may have sent words of reassurance to the earl via Beaumont or some other in his capacity as keeper and queen's confidante.

[59] *PPC*, VI, pp. 292–3.

[60] Watts, p. 344 and n. 351, suggests that the Nevilles and the Percies were not summoned because the lords, perceiving their feud as the primary stumbling block to peace, intended to impose a settlement on them. A letter sent to the earl of Arundel on 14 February insisting that he stop foot-dragging and attend provides further evidence that full participation was expected (*PPC*, VI, pp. 293–4; Johnson, p. 181).

[61] PRO, KB9/287/53. He apparently said these things in August. In October a commission was appointed to investigate another case of treasonable speech concerning the king, queen and prince (see above, p. 46).

[62] Commissions to various lords in mid-July 'to resist and suppress . . . unlawful gatherings and combinations against the king's majesty' in the midland counties were authorized by king and council (*CPR, 1452–61*, pp. 370–1). Griffiths, p. 801, describes the recipients as 'courtier-magnates'.

and the king's authority justified policy, though we can never know for a certainty that such actions represented his private desires or initiatives.[63]

Although it appears that Margaret maintained her self-representation as intermediary and subordinate to Henry during this time, there are hints that a kind of informal and unplanned role reversal had been taking place. It was occasionally noted and criticized, but could never openly declare itself and, hence, could never be complete.[64] In this connection it may be helpful to recall the letters from king and queen in support of John Hals to the deanery of Exeter, written at this time.[65] Although both letters invoke the king's authority in recommending Hals, Margaret's is by far the stronger and more forceful of the two, and it is likely that Hals's promotion was her idea. Further indications of their partial role reversal appear after the council reassembled in 1458.

The assembling of bitter enemies in London in an effort to reach a rapprochement would prove a ticklish business. Before the November council ended, the mayor and aldermen were commissioned to provide 1,137 archers to patrol the city and its suburbs during Hilary term.[66] In January, in what may have been a move to make the seriousness of the crown's intentions clear, pardons were issued to York, Warwick and the earl of Wiltshire.[67] Nevertheless, as might have been expected, the various hostile parties brought substantial retinues to London. The earl of Salisbury and duke of York arrived first, on 25 and 26 January, and established themselves at their townhouses within the city. The duke of Somerset arrived at the end of the month, followed by the duke of Exeter, the earl of Northumberland, Lords Egremont and Clifford and Sir Ralph Percy. They all took up residence outside Temple Bar, perhaps in various bishops' houses. Last to arrive was the earl of Warwick on 14 February with a company decked out in his livery of red jackets embroidered with white ragged staffs. He moved into the Greyfriars within the city. Thus, two armed camps were established within and without, increasing the likelihood of confrontation.[68] In response the common council stepped up its peacekeeping measures by strengthening the watches, imposing curfews and making sure the gates were closed at night to keep the adversaries separated.[69] Despite a couple of near-incidents, these efforts succeeded in averting serious trouble.[70]

---

[63] Watts, pp. 106–7, discusses this issue.

[64] E.g., the contemporary Gascoigne's pronouncement that she 'did many things' following Henry's illness (*Loci e Libro*, p. 205).

[65] Discussed above, pp. 64–5.

[66] *CPR, 1452–61*, p. 410, dated 28 November. This preceded the widespread commissions of 17 December (ibid., pp. 406–10).

[67] Watts, p. 344, n. 351, who suggests that they were issued on conciliar authority.

[68] Estimates of the size of these retinues vary, although a general agreement that they were substantial prevails. Thus, Gairdner, *PL*, III, p. 125, gives York 140 horse; Salisbury, 400 horse and 80 knights and squires; Somerset, 200 horse; and Exeter, 'a grete felyshyp and strong'. The later *Brut*, p. 525, and *Great Chron.*, pp. 189–90, give York 400 men; Salisbury, 500 (a number close to the previous estimate); Warwick, 600; Somerset and Exeter, 800 between them; and the Northumberland contingent, 1,500 all told. Less specifically, Flenley (Rawlinson B.355), p. 111, and the *English Chron.*, p. 77, assert respectively that the Yorkists (or their opponents) arrived in force.

[69] CLRO, Journal VI, fols 191b, 192, 193b, 194 (Binder 2, photo pp. 170, 171, 174, 175). Barron, 'London and the Crown', pp. 95–7, finds that there was very little pro-Yorkist sentiment in London at this time. She concludes that the City's eventual decision to support the Yorkists was made for pragmatic reasons, rather than for any particular love or aversion for either side.

[70] Flenley (Gough), pp. 159–60. See above, p. 150.

Soon after everyone had assembled, Henry addressed the council on the dangers of internal division, particularly in making the realm more vulnerable to external threat, and exhorted the lords to make peace according to God's will.[71] He then retired to Berkhamsted, perhaps to emphasize his own impartiality or to allow the arbitration discussions to proceed in a more normal fashion.[72] These were kingly acts; at the same time, however, it is also possible to view Henry's address as a kind of mediation.

While the king was at Berkhamsted, probably on 23 February, Somerset, Exeter, Clifford and Egremont all rode out to call upon him. Not long thereafter Northumberland also paid a visit.[73] The purpose of their visits is not known, although it may reasonably be thought that they called upon the king (and possibly the queen, though she is not mentioned) to argue for their own positions and their own concerns. Whatever was said and whatever its effect, the negotiations in London soon produced apparent progress in an agreement among the parties to recognizances 'in great sums' to keep the peace till Michaelmas.[74] Nevertheless, the attempted attack on Warwick by Somerset and Northumberland on 9 March and Warwick's resulting bluster led to increased tensions and a stalemate, so that on 15 March, John Bocking reported that the king would come 'this weke' to bring things 'to a good conclusion'. Margaret was also expected to arrive, accompanied by the duke of Buckingham, his eldest son the earl of Stafford and many other people. At this point the council, under the aegis of Thomas Bourgchier, archbishop of Canterbury, had been meeting at the Blackfriars in the mornings to accommodate the Yorkists within the town, and at the Whitefriars in Fleet Street in the afternoons for the lords without. The archbishop had been at great pains to arrive at a settlement, which thus far proved elusive.[75] On the morning after Henry's arrival, he led 'a generall procession to praie for the pees'; that afternoon, Margaret arrived.[76]

The juxtaposition of the king's and queen's activities presents an interesting and possibly curious picture. Henry's prayers, made to a Higher Authority, cast him in the role of intercessor. Assuming Bocking's information was correct, Margaret's arrival seems more evocative of royal power.[77] The duke of Buckingham belonged to neither camp in the current negotiations. His instincts were unerringly loyal to the crown, and he was the highest-ranking secular lord whose record was untainted by any whiff of wavering or of unwonted rashness.[78]

---

[71] *Reg. Whethamstede*, I, pp. 296–7. Sixty French ships had been sighted off the Sussex coast around this time, and people feared a new attack (Gairdner, *PL*, III, p. 126).

[72] Johnson, p. 182. J.W. Bennett, 'Mediaeval Loveday', discusses its origins and practice. By requiring the lords to attend and to submit to arbitration, the king had already departed from a tradition of voluntary participation.

[73] Gairdner, *PL*, III, p. 126. The date has been lost, but the letter appears to have been written fairly soon after Henry left Westminster.

[74] Ibid.; *CCR, 1454–61*, pp. 292–3, 306, for the amounts established and formalized on 23 March, which bound all parties to abide by the terms of the eventual settlement.

[75] Gairdner, *PL*, III, p. 127.

[76] Flenley (Gough), p. 160, which gives the date of Henry's arrival as 16 March. *Brut*, p. 525, opts for the seventeenth. These are the likelier dates. Cf. *London Chrons.*, p. 168; *Great Chron.*, p. 190; 'Benet's Chron.', p. 221.

[77] Watts, p. 344, n. 350.

[78] York's loyalty, of course, was suspect. Exeter had shown himself to be an uncertain quantity during the first protectorate, and he was, in any case, highly combustible. Somerset, though loyal, was another

Comparison is difficult. We don't know how Henry's arrival looked or with what ceremony it or Margaret's was accompanied. We have only the fragments of images, which go unsupported by any hint of an overt claim to authority, and there were limits to what could be done or represented. It seems unlikely that Margaret could have appeared in procession praying for peace between the lords as Henry had, which may suggest that some forms of intercession could only be performed by the king. If there was something going on that can be called a role reversal, it is to be found in a co-optation by each of the images that in different circumstances might be more appropriate to the other.

Agreement to a settlement was reached on 23 March, and Henry himself announced its terms the next day. It formally addressed only those matters that had officially been on the table: recompense and memorials for the lords slain at St Albans, with a nod to prior grudges in the case of the Nevilles and the Percies, and recognition of all the lords of St Albans, living and dead alike, as the king's faithful liegemen.[79] Superficially at least, it did not deal with the more important power relationship between York and the queen. But how could it have? As Johnson observes, 'it would have been difficult to incorporate the queen into any written public agreement, as she enjoyed no obvious political role within the constitution of the realm as then understood'.[80] Just so. And, thus, to understand Margaret's place in the reconciliation it is necessary to turn from written agreement to enacted symbol.

The final act of reconciliation, the loveday itself, took place on 25 March, Lady Day. Although the date of the loveday may have come about coincidentally, the queen would have been aware of the psychological capital to be gained by associating herself with and exploiting the intercessory image of the Virgin.[81] Margaret's part in the loveday performance tapped into this image, even as it partially subverted it. King, queen and all of the parties to the settlement went in public procession at St Paul's, thanking God for their having reached accord. First came Somerset, Salisbury, Exeter and Warwick, hand in hand, 'and so one of the one faction, and another of the other'.[82] Next came the king alone, wearing his crown and royal robes. Behind him came the duke of York and Queen Margaret, hands joined and behaving towards each other 'with great familiaritie to all men's sights'.[83] The image played upon notions of queenly intercession, but the act also neatly symbolized for onlookers the all-important

---

loose cannon. Norfolk's vehement support of York in 1453–54 had left him compromised and subject to warnings regarding his associations. The first three were also subjects of the reconciliation.

[79] *Reg. Whethamstede*, I, pp. 298–308. Hicks, *Warwick*, p. 134, finds the settlement to have been a reasonable compromise. Cf. Griffiths, pp. 806–7, and Watts, pp. 343–4, who consider it punitive towards the Yorkists; and Johnson, p. 184, who argues that York made out very well.

[80] Ibid., p. 183.

[81] See Parsons, 'Ritual and Symbol', p. 66.

[82] The absence of the Percies is evocative and possibly significant. Their feud with the Nevilles, in any event, was far from over.

[83] Stow, *Annales*, p. 660. Hall, *Chronicle*, p. 238, gives a similar description of the hand holding. It is difficult to say whether Hall was Stow's source for the loveday or whether both got it elsewhere. Although Stow evinces doubt about the sincerity of the reconciliation in view of the denouement, Hall assumes dissimulation and condemns it in a heavily-embroidered – and anti-Margaret – diatribe. Kingsford dismissed Hall's work as 'Tudor fiction based on Yorkist misrepresentation', while characterizing Stow, who indefatigably searched the records, as 'an original authority of importance' (*EHL*, pp. 265, 266, 269).

reconciliation between queen and duke. On a deeper level, however, it constituted 'a move in the queen's struggle for hegemony'.[84]

By taking York's hand – and, considering respective status, this is how we must imagine the transaction – Margaret agreed to a concession, but she did so from a position of strength. Like a stern king moved to mercy by the intercessory pleadings of his queen, she granted York conditional forgiveness and acceptance. That is, conditional in the sense that it required him to submit to and accept an order in which his own power and influence were more circumscribed. Henry's mediations had permitted her to modify her position vis-à-vis York: in essence, to be seen publicly to change her mind in a way that reflected magnanimity and wisdom. The role reversal is never complete, however; it remains mixed and murky. Henry had not become the exact equivalent of an intercessory queen, pleading from a marginal position 'outside the . . . authority of male office'.[85] Nor had Margaret replaced him with herself. Henry remained to all intents and purposes the image and focus of regnal authority.

This public perception in fact reinforced Margaret's power. Since she was not – nor could be – a party to the formal agreement, her actual, though informal, power went unrestrained. In publicly agreeing to the settlement and accepting the king's award, York had in fact recognized the queen's power through the language of symbolic gesture.

Ironically, the text of the settlement as given in Whethamstede's *Register*, which may have been a copy or translation of the original document,[86] casts Margaret in the traditional role of intercessor. It is the only text to accord her any form of active influence. Along with the labors and advice of the council, it attributes the settlement to 'the great request, cordial desire and entreaties made [to Henry] by [his] dearest and most beloved wife, the queen, who was, and is, so desiring of . . . unity, charity and harmony as is to her possible'.[87] Although it seems likely that Margaret regarded the reconciliation as a necessary and potentially useful, albeit risky, step, there is no reason to think that she lobbied for it in quite such a fashion. This formulation, however, reflected a contemporary understanding of the way things were supposed to happen, in which the queen's role was already prescribed. The actual performance of the loveday was another matter, in which accepted images were both maintained and briefly co-opted to support a non-traditional reality.

---

[84] Watts, p. 344, who does not consider how hegemony was contained within the enactment or how it played on and partially undermined gender roles.

[85] Strohm, *Hochon's Arrow*, p. 104.

[86] Hicks, *Warwick*, p. 133.

[87] *Reg. Whethamstede*, I, p. 301: 'ad magnam instantiam, cordiale desiderium, et preces, nobis facta per nostram carissimam et amantissimam uxorem, Reginam, quae fuit, et est, ita desiderabilis . . . unitatis, dilectionis, et concordiae, prout sibi est possible'.

11

The Road to War

ALTHOUGH the loveday failed and, failing, appeared in retrospect as farce, for a time the public atmosphere conveyed a sense of relative normality. While some of this likely involved pretense and the dissimulation of still-festering anxieties and grudges for the sake of appearance, it does not necessarily follow that a gulf existed between the desires of the queen and of the lords.[1] Peace, however contrived, served everybody's interests, at least for the time being.

And so the king and queen went to St Albans over Easter as further proof of reconciliation, where three visiting monks of Cluny called upon the queen and were well-entertained by the abbot at her direction.[2] After returning to London, the royal couple presided over celebratory jousts at the Tower and Greenwich, in which the duke of Somerset played a prominent role.[3] Meanwhile, government proceeded in a more or less evenhanded fashion. Arrangements were made to pay York pension arrears, and he was named to commissions of the peace.[4] Whatever his thoughts of the future – and one need not imagine him either entirely pleased or blindly trusting – he gave no overt indication of being unable to live with the situation.[5]

Warwick also continued to be favored, though his position was more complicated. On the one hand, he had already been commissioned to go on the sea before the loveday, and he continued to receive commissions that indicate apparent trust.[6] On 9 May the earl rode through London by the king's command 'with a goodly felauship', perhaps to keep order.[7] On the other hand,

---

[1] Cf. Watts, pp. 345–7.

[2] 'Benet's Chron.', p. 221; *Reg. Whethamstede*, I, pp. 318–19.

[3] Flenley (Gough), p. 160; *London Chrons.*, p. 168; *Great Chron.*, p. 190. It may not be too great a stretch to observe that, while Somerset was bashing other gentlemen for the sake of entertainment, he was too busy to think of bashing anyone else for more serious reasons.

[4] Johnson, p. 185, whose observation that York's commissions involved no new positions is consistent with the notion that the duke's 'readmission' into the polity was to be carefully controlled: he was to receive his due, but no more.

[5] Wolffe, p. 314; Beaucourt, *Histoire de Charles VII*, p. 260, for a French report that York had approached Charles VII in the spring of 1458 for support against Henry and had been rebuffed. Since York's later attainder did not charge him with conducting private – and hostile – diplomacy, it may be doubted that such alleged, patently treasonable negotiations took place.

[6] Watts, p. 346, n. 357, for this and for favorable matters involving other Nevilles. In particular, Warwick's commission to investigate the activities of his own uncle and lieutenant, Lord Fauconberg, may be noted (*CPR, 1452–61*, p. 438).

[7] Flenley ('Bale's Chron.'), p. 146. Griffiths, p. 796, suggests that this followed an outbreak of violence in Fleet Street in which one of Margaret's attorneys was killed. The date of that event is not certain,

the unwillingness or inability of the exchequer to pay the Calais garrison's wages during his tenure as captain left him in an awkward spot and provided him with both the need and opportunity to indulge in piracy.[8] These acts became more blatant after the loveday. Apart from partially addressing Warwick's financial difficulties, they supported his carefully cultivated image and brought him a measure of approving notoriety, even as they discomfited the Lancastrian government that ultimately had to answer to his victims.[9] As a part, then, of this sequence of events, an official effort may have been made towards the end of 1458 to remove Warwick from office. Or it may not. The only identifiable source for its occurrence appears to have been Warwick himself. A newsletter to Charles VII from an informant at the court of Burgundy, probably written in early 1459, reports Warwick's understanding that a 'great parliament' would have removed him from office had matters gone as planned and his public declaration that he would not give up Calais, whatever the cost to his English holdings.[10] If such an effort was made, Margaret's role is nowhere explicitly indicated, although one might reasonably suspect that she supported it.[11]

In fact, the problem of possible motivations and likely intentions of all parties to the impending struggle becomes particularly murky at this point. This is frustrating to the historian, who knows the outcome and would like to see the pieces fit, especially since the months from later 1458 through early 1459 seem to mark the period during which matters progressed beyond recall, leaving battle and direct confrontation the only remaining option. In sorting through the evidence, it may be helpful to remember that the persons who were involved could not predict the future, although undoubtedly they both hoped and feared. When outcomes are uncertain, one ought not to be surprised by the appearance of confusion and contradiction.

The great council that was summoned to meet in October 1458 was obviously called for a purpose; unfortunately, we cannot be entirely sure of what it was.

---

however, and none of the chronicle accounts make any reference to Warwick as a subsequent peacekeeper (*Brut*, p. 525; *London Chrons.*, p. 169; *Great Chron.*, p. 190).

[8] Harriss, 'Struggle for Calais', p. 49. The task of weighing willful intention against perennial insolvency is difficult. While it is easy to blame the court and Margaret for wanting to get Warwick out of Calais, it must also be noted that when the previous captain, Edmund Beaufort, duke of Somerset, was killed at St Albans, arrears due to the garrison exceeded £65,000 (ibid., p. 46). Warwick could only take possession after a complex deal had been worked out with the company of the staple to pay off these arrears, so that he entered with a clean slate (ibid., pp. 44–7).

[9] Ibid., p. 48; Griffiths, p. 809. For an attack on Spanish ships see Gairdner, *PL*, III, p. 130; *London Chrons.*, pp. 168–9; Flenley (Gough), p. 160. For a later attack on ships from Lübeck that occasioned an investigation in early August, see *Foedera*, V, ii, p. 82; *CPR*, 1452–61, p. 443; *Three Chrons.*, p. 71. Flenley (Rawlinson), p. 112, conflates the two episodes.

[10] Stevenson, I, pp. 368–9: 'Est renommee que se le grant parliament du roy se fut tenu ainsi quil avoit este propose, le conte de Warwic eust este despointie du gouvernement de Calais, et est ce tout notoire; et ainsi il lentend. Et au contre, il a declare publiquement que pour abandonner toutes ses terres, et ce quil a en Angleterre, il ne rendera Calais devant le temps a lui ordonne.' See Wolffe, p. 315 and n. 10, for the dating. By 'parliament', the great council summoned to meet in autumn could be meant (*PPC*, VI, p. 297). *English Chron.*, pp. 78–9, more vaguely reports an attempt to discharge Warwick by a letter of privy seal. The chronology is very muddled: his attempted removal appears to coincide with the appointment of Somerset as captain, actually occurring in October 1459 (see *Foedera*, V, ii, p. 90) around the time of the Yorkists' attainders, but both are said to follow 'soon after' the brawl at Westminster between Warwick's men and the household servants.

[11] See, e.g., Harriss, 'Struggle for Calais', p. 48; Jacob, *The Fifteenth Century*, p. 515.

Henry's formal request of 26 August for 'youre sadde advys in . . . suche matiers as concerne specially oure honeure and worship, the welfare of this our land and subgittes' potentially covers a lot of territory.[12] If Chancellor Waynflete's letter of 7 September to Hugh Pakenham can be considered a window on matters that were to be set before the council, its business would have included preparations against rumors of an impending French attack and the resolution of difficulties created by Warwick's piracies.[13] What sort of resolution was envisioned remains less certain. The council's intended makeup has been described as 'moderate' in that most of the persons summoned had been members of the protectorate councils, whereas the more resolutely anti-Yorkist Exeter, Somerset, Devon, Northumberland, Clifford and Pembroke were excluded.[14] Nevertheless, among those invited were persons such as William Booth, Lyhert, Boulers, Stanbury, Beaumont, Shrewsbury, Wiltshire, Dudley and Stanley, who were on the prince's council or otherwise associated with the queen and who could scarcely have been indifferent to her concerns.[15] Although York, Salisbury and Warwick were all summoned, it appears that only Warwick attended belatedly after receiving an additional summons.[16] If the council did intend to do something about Warwick, whatever it may have been, it seems likely that he had departed again before it could take action.

The confrontation at Westminster between Warwick's men – and possibly the earl himself – and men of the royal household, which occurred while Warwick was attending the council meeting, provides an explanation of what happened.[17] A year later, when greater violence had broken out, the earl would refer to the incident as an assassination attempt.[18] However the fracas started and whoever was genuinely responsible, Warwick left England to return to Calais posthaste. From there, though it is not clear how soon thereafter, he issued bellicose pronouncements to the effect that he would not give up his office under any circumstances.[19]

Around this same time and possibly in reaction to his son's misadventure at Westminster, Salisbury took action. Sometime after All Hallows he called a meeting of his council at his castle of Middleham, where it was determined that they 'sholde take ful parte with the ful noble prince the duke of Yorke'. It was understood by at least one person present that the result could be war. Sir

[12] *PPC*, VI, p. 297.
[13] As suggested by Hicks, *Warwick*, pp. 151–2; see Anderson, *Letters . . . of Southampton*, pp. 12–13.
[14] Watts, p. 347 and n. 363, who identifies the latter as 'the queen's more partisan supporters'. The problem with this construction lies in its assumption that Margaret's interests were principally upheld by the 'extremists' and would have had little in common with the interests of a 'moderate' council. As I have shown, the reality of Margaret's interests and influence was more complex.
[15] Chancellor Waynflete and Lawrence Booth may also be presumed to have attended, though neither received a formal summons (ibid.). The latter, certainly, would have looked out for Margaret's interests.
[16] Hicks, *Warwick*, p. 152.
[17] See above, p. 150. Storey, p. 186, suggests that this 'vulgár brawl' marked the point of no return.
[18] *Reg. Whethamstede*, I, p. 340. Warwick claimed to have been summoned to the council by a letter of privy seal, and, indeed, he was so summoned when he failed to appear when the council met, although he was in England at the time (Hicks, *Warwick*, p. 152). It is possible, though speculative, that a connection exists between his summons and the *English Chronicle*'s account of an effort to dismiss him from office by means of a similar letter (pp. 78–9).
[19] Stevenson, I, p. 369.

Thomas Harrington, who attended the meeting, decided to enfeoff his lands to William Booth, the earl of Shrewsbury and Lord Clifford – all men of the 'contrarie partie' – as a precautionary measure in case the anticipated war went against the Yorkists.[20] Although the date of this meeting has been questioned,[21] it is difficult to imagine another year in which it could have occurred. Since military preparations did not immediately result, the agreement may best be understood as a contingency plan. Soon after, either because Lancastrian intentions were already moving in this direction or because recent events had provided new cause to mistrust the Nevilles, a number of Neville associates were removed from office. In early December an agreement was also reached with the staple merchants, by which they would loan the household substantial sums in return for tax-free shipping. This may have been intended to separate their interests from Warwick's.[22] Though it is difficult to sort out cause and effect, it is possible to understand Warwick's declaration from Calais as a response to the agreement and a move to retain the merchants' sympathy.

The marriage proposals sent to France and Burgundy in the later autumn of 1458 must be considered in the context of these developments.[23] Although the English embassy received royal authorization at the end of August to enter into peace negotiations, it seems not to have arrived on the continent until the end of October.[24] At that time it may have been thought well to take some action that would drive a wedge between York and the Nevilles. This would be especially true if Warwick's dismissal from Calais were about to be attempted or had already run aground. York had shown himself desirous of a French marriage for his son years before; it would have been a tempting lure. And the inclusion of young Somerset in the proposal also makes it unlikely to have originated with York or his supporters as part of a plan to undermine Henry.

There are some puzzling things about the proposal, however. Why was it made to both France and Burgundy? This fact alone occasioned uncertainty and suspicion in both courts.[25] The possibility that Sir John Wenlock, who led the embassy, was acting as a double agent for both the English court and the Yorkists must also be considered, although the matter cannot be resolved

---

[20] Whitaker, *History of Richmondshire*, II, pp. 261–2; discussed by Pollard, *North-Eastern England*, p. 270. Though writing much later, Stow, *Annales*, p. 661, offers a provocative explanation of events that may be worth considering: After the 'attack' on Warwick, York and Salisbury consulted, and resolved that Salisbury should march on the king in force to complain about the attack. If he prevailed in his suit, 'he should not . . . let passe the occasion given for revenge of displeasures to him done, both by the Queene, and hir Counsell'. Salisbury raised men, whereupon the queen 'imagined that the earl of Warwick had kindeled this fier, to the intent, to set the crowne on . . . Yorkes head', and took action accordingly.

[21] By Hicks, *Warwick*, p. 155. Although this story appeared in the later 1480s in connection with an inheritance dispute, the only part of it that has any direct bearing on that conflict is the enfeoffment itself. The rationale behind it would have been irrelevant, and its blithely self-serving nature is such as to make it seem entirely credible. The use of a special day as a memory aid in recalling approximately when something happened is, of course, common.

[22] Watts, p. 349, n. 371, for this point and for various measures taken against Neville supporters from the end of November into early December; *CPR, 1452–61*, pp. 500–1, for the agreement with the staple.

[23] Stevenson, I, pp. 361–9; discussed above, pp. 137–8.

[24] Wolffe, p. 313; Stevenson, I, pp. 358–9. The warrant is by sign manual (PRO, C81/1469/26).

[25] Stevenson, I, pp. 361–77.

conclusively.[26] Warwick had established friendly personal relations with the duke of Burgundy.[27] Considering that most of the negotiations would have taken place at the end of 1458 and the beginning of 1459, it is at least possible, if not likely, that he would have tried to influence their outcome to serve his own ends. Whatever the reason, both France and Burgundy were suspicious of the circumstances and motives behind the proposal and would not commit to any substantive agreement.

While it may be suspected that a plan had been set in motion to separate York's interests from the Nevilles', it is more certain that other preparations were simultaneously being made to protect the crown against all eventualities. Besides the strengthening of coastal defenses, a supply of pikes and leaden clubs was ordered on 2 December for the royal household, along with three serpentines, to guard against a threat posed by 'certain misruled and seditious persons'.[28] In mid-February 1459, commissions of array were issued for the southern and eastern counties; neither York nor any Neville associate was named to any of them.[29] At the same time, other commissions continued to provide the earl of Warwick with seamen through the month of March.[30] In April and June repairs were ordered at Westminster palace, the Tower of London and others of the king's castles and manors along the Thames valley. On 7 May 3,000 bow staves and 3,000 sheaves of arrows were ordered to be purchased to supply the Tower in consideration of 'thennemies on every side aprochyng upone us, as well upone the see as on lande'.[31] Nevertheless, the three men who presumably would have been considered prime enemies continued to appear on commissions of the peace well into summer, with little or no sign of ostracism. From November 1458 through August 1459, York was named to forty-two commissions in twenty-five counties plus the three ridings of Yorkshire; the latest was on 29 August for Wiltshire. So far as the extant records indicate, he was not dropped from any commission on which he had customarily served. In the same period, Salisbury was named to thirteen commissions spread over eight counties and the three ridings, the latest being of 28 August for Essex. In two instances he was named to commissions in Nottingham and Wiltshire in November, but was not named to later commis-

[26] He had been Margaret's chamberlain at least through 1453, had fought for Henry at St Albans, and while speaker in 1455 had stayed aloof from the push to make York protector, but he was attainted as a Yorkist supporter in 1459 (Roskell, 'John Lord Wenlock', pp. 30, 32; RP, V, p. 349). Griffiths, p. 846, n. 270, notes that Wenlock seems to have falsely reported French hostility on his return to England, perhaps indicating that he had cast his lot with Burgundy. In reality, the French were amenable to peace overtures, though highly suspicious of the circumstances in which they were offered, as were the Burgundians.

[27] Ibid., pp. 816–17.

[28] Wolffe, p. 315, citing PRO, E404/71/3/43. See Stevenson, II, ii, p. 510, for an earlier privy seal letter of 1 September 1458, authorizing payment for various artillery pieces, including the transport of four serpentines from Kenilworth to London and 'ij chambers for a gret gonne of brasse at oure towne of Calais'.

[29] York was omitted from the commissions for Essex and Suffolk, while Edward Neville, Lord Bergavenny, was omitted for Kent (Watts, p. 348, n. 370; CPR, 1452–61, pp. 494–5).

[30] Ibid., pp. 494, 495, 496, for the arrest of masters and mariners to serve under Warwick.

[31] Ibid., pp. 496, 487; Stevenson, II, ii, p. 511. Griffiths, p. 816, considers that by this time the threat to the crown was known to come 'from Calais and the Burgundian allies whom the Yorkist lords had acquired'.

sions in February and August respectively. Warwick was named to sixteen commissions in nine counties and the three ridings; the latest was of 22 July in Warwickshire. He appears on two commissions for Nottingham in February, although he had not been named to the previous one in November.[32] Moreover, in June, Salisbury received £1,578 as warden of the west march.[33] One has to wonder about these things. Even at this late date it is not clear what course the Lancastrians were pursuing. If Margaret and her allies were bent on Yorkist destruction, the least that can be said is that they were playing a very strange game. It may be that as they prepared for the eventuality of war, whoever the enemy might be, they also aimed to give the Yorkists no legitimate complaint of overt harassment with which to support rebellion.

The assumption that Margaret was actively hostile to the Yorkists at this point rests in large part upon a single piece of evidence, which, if true, may be damning, but which, like so many other pieces of the puzzle, is peculiar if not suspect. According to 'Benet's Chronicle', the king held a great council at Coventry in summer, at which certain persons – all absent – including the archbishop of Canterbury, the duke of York, the earls of Salisbury and Warwick, the bishops of Ely and Exeter, the earl of Arundel and Viscount Bourgchier were subsequently indicted on the queen's advice. Upon hearing of their indictments, the three Yorkists determined to go to the king, but Henry gathered many men together and moved on to Nottingham.[34]

Several things may be observed. Foremost is the lack of corroborating evidence of any overt action taken against any of the Yorkists in connection with these alleged indictments. Between 29 June and 29 August, York alone was named to nine commissions of the peace as if nothing had happened.[35] Salisbury and Warwick were each named to three within the same period.[36] Had an indictment been pushed forward, it is difficult to see how they could have continued on these commissions; in fact, distinctly political changes in the commissions seem only to have followed the Yorkists' attainders in November.[37] Second, none of the other persons allegedly indicted seems to have been particularly alarmed or punished in any way. A third, more subjective point involves the queen's presence and the chronicler's representation of her role.

---

[32] *CPR, 1452–61*, pp. 660–83. A few counties show no record of any commissions of the peace during these months, and York was not named to any of the known commissions for Bedford, Cumberland or Sussex during the entire decade.

[33] Griffiths, p. 813 (citing PRO, E403/819 m. 4).

[34] 'Benet's Chron.', p. 223: 'Rex tenuit magnum consilium apud Coventriam presentibus regina et principe, ad quod consilium non fuerunt [those named] et alii. Et propter hoc per consilium regine indictati sunt omnes Predicti domini . . . Quo audito [York, Warwick and Salisbury] intenderunt pergere ad regem quare rex congregavit sibi multos iuxta Coventriam et intransivit rex Notingam.'

[35] *CPR, 1452–61*, pp. 661, 665, 667, 673, 675, 680, 681.

[36] Ibid., pp. 661, 665, 673, 680.

[37] C. Arnold, 'The Commission of the Peace', pp. 121–2, notes that although the number of persons serving on the West Riding commission was reduced in November 1458, its composition still included known Yorkist supporters. She suggests that this may have involved 'a calculated attempt' by the Lancastrian government to reassure persons 'associated with its opponents'. Once the opponents' status had been formally declared by means of an indictment, however, the renewal of their own appointments would seem a pointless subterfuge. As it happens, York, Salisbury and Warwick themselves were only removed from the West Riding commission on 8 December 1459 (*CPR, 1452–61*, p. 683).

The impression given by 'Benet' is that Margaret was somehow presiding over the council.[38] This seems quite out of character when compared with her known activities. Moreover, there is the problem of authority. That Margaret would have had the authority, even with her not-yet-six-year-old son on her lap, to call for and obtain the serious indictment of no less a person than the archbishop of Canterbury is a bit difficult to swallow. Thus it appears that the indictments, if they occurred, could not have been so serious as many have believed: perhaps amounting to no more than a slap on the wrist for non-attendance.[39]

There is a further possibility, and that is that the chronicle's account of the indictments was intended to justify the Yorkist's later actions.[40] In that case, it need not have been entirely true, but simply believable within the context of events. Unfortunately, it does not seem possible either to prove or to disprove the story on the basis of independent evidence. Such evidence as there is may be sufficient to cast doubt upon it, but no more.

By autumn of 1459 there were more concrete indications of trouble. Salisbury was raising a substantial army in the north; York was gathering more men at Ludlow, and Warwick had arrived from Calais with several hundred men with the intention of joining forces to confront the king, who was at Coventry.[41] It seems likely that their plans had been in place since summer. In the Yorkists' attainders, Alice, countess of Salisbury, Sir William Oldhall and Thomas Vaughan were accused of imagining and compassing the king's death and also of stirring and provoking the duke of York and the earls of Salisbury and Warwick to the 'rerying of werre' against the king. The countess's activities were said to have taken place on 1 August at Middleham in Yorkshire; Oldhall's and Vaughan's, on 1 July at Garlickhithe in London.[42] Whatever transpired at Coventry, Margaret had also been busy recruiting the men of Cheshire in her son's name. They were given the prince's swan badge.[43] Thus, through word and

---

[38] Henry may have been at Westminster as late as 29 June, when three letters were written in his name to excuse the prior of St John from attending a chapter on Rhodes (*PPC*, VI, pp. 299–301), though he was most likely at Coventry by 6 July (*CPR, 1452–61*, pp. 507–8).

[39] But cf. Hicks, *Warwick*, pp. 156–8. Warwick, at least, seems to have been otherwise occupied at the beginning of July, committing acts of piracy against the Genoese and the Spaniards (Flenley ['Bale's Chron.'], p. 147).

[40] As suggested by Watts, p. 350, n. 375, who does not go so far as to declare it spurious. Johnson, p. 186, expresses puzzlement over the queen's actions at this time and suggests that the number of persons charged may have been exaggerated, but accepts the story's general veracity. The chronicle, which seems to have been transcribed between 1462 and 1468, is Yorkist in sympathy and hostile to Margaret ('Benet's Chron.', pp. 157, 163, 169).

[41] The size of Salisbury's force is variously reported from 3,000 to 7,000 men (Flenley ['Bale's Chron.'], p. 148; 'Benet's Chron.', p. 224; *Reg. Whethamstede*, I, p. 348; *Three Chrons.*, p. 72; *English Chron.*, p. 80). Warwick was said to have 300 or 500 men (Flenley, p. 148; 'Benet's Chron.', p. 223).

[42] *RP*, V, p. 349. Johnson, p. 186, finds some support for the charges against the countess in the accusation that the bailiff of Bawtry in the West Riding had incited acts of treason in mid-August (see also *CPR, 1452–61*, p. 518). Bawtry was one of Warwick's lordships (C. Arnold, 'The Commission of the Peace', p. 122). Nevertheless, he was allowed to continue in office after the attainders (*CPR, 1452–61*, p. 527). Griffiths, pp. 817 and 847, n. 274, considers that Oldhall and Vaughan, both York's councilors, may have provided Warwick with information about the Coventry council's indictments, thus setting in train the events that led to armed conflict. This assumes, of course, that 'Benet's' report of the council is entirely reliable. Since it may be best to withhold judgment in this matter, the most that can be said is that it seems probable that Oldhall and Vaughan were in contact with Warwick, although the content of their communications cannot definitely be ascertained.

[43] *English Chron.*, p. 79.

visual symbol Margaret again masked her power by invoking male authority while representing herself as its intermediary.

This force, under the leadership of James Tuchet, lord Audley, attempted to head off Salisbury; the two armies met at Blore Heath southwest of Newcastle-on-Lyme on 23 September, and Salisbury, though outnumbered, won a stunning victory.[44] Chronicle accounts of the battle, all written after the event and from a Yorkist point of view, are unanimous in describing Audley's force as the queen's army, sometimes as 'the queen's gallants'.[45] Mocking Audley's men as 'gallants' insinuated that they were fops whose pretensions exceeded their substance.[46] Although Margaret had played an instrumental role in raising these men, there was a further reason to explicitly label them as hers. Up until York openly claimed the throne in 1460, the Yorkists continued to maintain that they were the king's true liegemen. To suggest that Audley's force served the king and acted at his genuine volition would have amounted to a denial of the Yorkists' own position and contradicted their 'official' reason for deposing him. More-over, in the years following the deposition, while Margaret's activities seemed to pose a continuing threat to Yorkist dominance, it was important to portray her as a disorderly woman whose actions disordered the workings of regnal authority.[47] Thus began a period of fierce though sporadic warfare that lasted a year and a half and ended in the deposition of Henry VI by York's son.

To understand Margaret's actions at this time and in the months that followed, it is also necessary to ask just what the Yorkists were up to. One need not accept the official and undoubtedly exaggerated charge in their later attainder that they intended the immediate destruction of the king, the queen and the Lancastrian succession.[48] Nevertheless, their own claim, made from Ludlow on 10 October in a letter to the king, that they meant only to plead their case as the innocent victims of others' malice and covetousness is surely disingenuous. Since this letter followed at least two other communications, it may reasonably be suggested that it represented the latest stage in some strategic backpedaling.[49]

Initially, however, the Yorkists' posture would have seemed genuinely threatening. Their assembly of three forces to approach the king from different directions had to be interpreted as a military offensive.[50] Moreover, a bill

---

[44] See Griffiths, pp. 819–22, for a more detailed account of the battle and its sequel. For an alternative account, more focused on the specific movements of the contending parties, see Goodman, *Wars of the Roses*, pp. 26–31.

[45] 'Benet's Chron.', p. 224; 'Gregory's Chron.', p. 204, refer to them as 'gallants'. See also Flenley ('Bale's Chron.'), p. 148; *Three Chronicles*, p. 72; *English Chron.*, p. 80.

[46] Scattergood, *Politics and Poetry*, pp. 342–4, for associations with 'gallant'; Gillespie, 'Cheshiremen at Blore Heath', describes the Cheshire participants and their fate. Few of those with gentleman's status possessed significant military experience; moreover, it appears that most of them fled.

[47] For Yorkist charges that Henry had violated his oath, see below, p. 202; for a discussion of the nexus between the queen's alleged disorderly conduct and disorder in the realm, see pp. 177–8.

[48] *RP*, V, p. 348.

[49] *English Chron.*, pp. 81–2. The letter refers to an indenture made by the three at Worcester, a copy of which was conveyed to the king – perhaps together with another letter – by the prior and other clergymen, and to later messages sent in writing and orally via garter herald to both the king and the 'worthy lordes' about him.

[50] Johnson, p. 187, makes this point, though he still believes that the Yorkists' intention was 'to lobby . . . rather than attack'.

produced by Warwick en route from Calais would have done little to allay fear.[51] Calling for the restoration of good governance and the removal and punishment of evil and covetous counsel, the document identifies the Yorkists and 'lordis of like disposicon' as the king's true liegemen and those who oppose them as the evildoers. Its suggestion that other lords stood with them seems to have been wishful thinking, but since the bill would have been intended for some form of public consumption, it made political sense to hint at broader support.[52] Although it avers that the Yorkists' intent was not 'to take upon us eny private reule or entre into any mater for our owne profite or to call to mynde eny olde debate . . . bitwene ene estate of this lande and ene of us', it can hardly be imagined that they would have gone in peace if the king refused their offer 'tobe assistente yif it be his pleasir' in carrying out their desires. Thus, while they may have hoped for Henry's acquiescence and enough support to press for it, it seems likely that they were prepared to take possession of Henry's person through military intervention, as they had at St Albans, and to restore their own preeminence as his 'legitimate' advisors by force if necessary. The accusation in their attainder that they had sought to take the king by surprise at Kenilworth supports this view, if stripped of its more sinister trappings.[53] This does not preclude the notion that they also acted out of fear for their own security. Whether or not a Coventry council had indicted the Yorkists, the continuing tenuousness of their situation – particularly Warwick's – and the long-term prospect of diminished political influence and the increasing marginalization of their interests would not have offered much assurance.

Matters did not go according to plan, however. The king, perhaps under the influence of those around him, proved to be more prepared and less cooperative than had been expected. Despite Salisbury's victory at Blore Heath, his younger sons Thomas and John were taken prisoner in the aftermath and held at Chester castle by the queen's men, while signs of support from other lords were remarkably thin on the ground.[54] When the Yorkists met up at Worcester, they undertook a solemn indenture with each other that was likely to have involved a military pact of mutual aid.[55] At this point they sent messages to the king along with copies of the indenture to underline their seriousness. But the royal power could not be swayed or intimidated and, with a swelling host, pursued the Yorkists back to Ludlow.

It would appear that somewhere along the way, though probably about a

---

[51] Printed by Kekewich, et al., *Politics of Fifteenth-Century England*, pp. 208–10. Quotations are taken from its last paragraph. See ibid., pp. 27–9, for John Watts's analysis of Warwick's manifesto; cf. Hicks, *Warwick*, pp. 160–2, for a much harsher judgment.

[52] Ibid., p. 162, considers it an 'exercise in publicity', whose imagined audience may have been 'specifically mercantile and London-based'.

[53] *RP*, V, p. 348. Goodman, *Wars of the Roses*, p. 236, n. 35, suggests that Warwick may have intended a 'solitary stroke against the king' from Coleshill, where both 'Gregory's Chron.', p. 205, and the *English Chron.*, p. 80, place him. The latter says that Warwick 'wolde haue ryde to the kyng [there]'.

[54] *Brut*, p. 526; *London Chrons.*, p. 169; *Great Chron.*, p. 191; Richmond, 'Nobility and Wars of the Roses', pp. 74–5, for a tabulation of lordly presence in the opposing forces from Blore Heath (October 1459) through Towton (March 1461). Griffiths, pp. 821–2, notes the paucity of support for the Yorkists in 1459, as does Watts, p. 351, whose observation that 'they represented little more than themselves' neatly sums up the situation.

[55] Griffiths, p. 818, characterizes it as a 'brotherhood-in-arms'.

week into October, further messages were exchanged: an offer of pardon to York, Warwick and any with them who submitted within six days. Salisbury, who had already taken up arms, was excluded.[56] The Yorkists refused. On 9 October summonses were issued to a parliament to meet at Coventry the following month, from which the Yorkists were excluded, and that same day the duke of Somerset was given the captaincy of Calais.[57] With the writing clearly on the wall, the Yorkists sent their letter of 10 October from Ludlow, protesting that they had been 'proclamed and defamed . . . vnryghtefully [and] vnlawfully', insisting that this surely could not represent the king's own will and declaring – perhaps in anticipation of impending forfeiture – that their enemies were motivated by desire for their lands, offices and goods. To this they added the equally strategic assertion that they would not resort to arms unless 'provoked by necessyte'.[58] The one thing they did not offer to do was to submit to the king.

Two days later, their letter having availed them nothing, the Yorkists drew up their battle lines at Ludford, south of the town, to confront the much larger royal force. In a brash ploy to allay the misgivings of men who found themselves opposing the king's banners, rumors were circulated that the king was dead. A personal appearance by Henry and a further offer of pardon to those who returned to their allegiance sufficed to undermine these tales, but by then it was too late in the day to fight.[59] That night the Yorkists were plagued by desertions. Andrew Trollope and the experienced men from the Calais garrison who had come over with Warwick slipped away to the royalist camp. Trollope subsequently became a commander in the Lancastrian army and fought for them at Wakefield, Second St Albans and Towton, where he was killed.[60] Around the middle of the night the Yorkists themselves decamped and fled westward into Wales, leaving the remnants of their army to surrender in the morning. Warwick, Salisbury and York's eldest son, Edward, earl of March, found their way back to Calais; York and his second son, Edmund, earl of Rutland, fled to Ireland.

When parliament met on 20 November, the business of the Yorkists' attainders stood at the top of the agenda. Already, steps had been taken to

[56] *RP*, V, p. 348, states that heralds made the offer, with a writ signed by Henry himself as authentication. This may correspond to the communications via garter king-of-arms mentioned in the Yorkists' letter of 10 October. *Reg. Whethamstede*, I, pp. 339–41, provides an alternative account, in which Richard Beauchamp, bishop of Salisbury, conveys the offer of pardon and receives the Yorkists' refusal from Warwick, who blames Henry's regime for an attempt on his own life. My placement of the exchange depends in part on the six-day grace period offered. The Yorkists drew up their lines at Ludford Bridge on 12 October, and the desertions that took place at this time or shortly before may indicate that the offer of pardon was running out.

[57] *CCR, 1454–61*, pp. 420–2; *Foedera*, VI, ii, p. 90. Somerset's appointment was authorized by king and council, during pleasure. On 31 January he was reappointed for a twelve-year term by the king with the authority of parliament.

[58] *English Chron.*, p. 82.

[59] *RP*, V, p. 348; *Reg. Whethamstede*, I, pp. 342–3. The official attainder claims that the rebels fired guns.

[60] 'Gregory's Chron.', p. 205, says that Trollope deserted upon learning that Warwick was going to the aid of York instead of the king, as he had previously thought. This account puts his defection earlier, around the time that Warwick was at Coleshill. Cf. *London Chrons.*, p. 169; *Great Chron.*, p. 191; Waurin, *Croniques*, p. 276, which say that he deserted from Ludlow. On balance, that seems the more likely. *Croyland Chron.*, p. 454, claims that Warwick had deliberately misled Trollope into believing that they were going to aid the king.

confiscate all their possessions, and a commission of oyer and terminer had been issued to deal with 'treasons, insurrections, rebellions' and a long list of other crimes in the west midland counties.[61] Nevertheless, it would be wrong to consider the attainders a *fait accompli*, rubber-stamped by a packed and compliant parliament.[62] Although it may have had the highest attendance of lords of any Lancastrian parliament, elections to the commons appear to have been properly conducted.[63] John Bocking's newsletter of 7 December indicates that discussion was still ongoing at that time, with the particulars of the attainders and forfeitures still to be worked out.[64] In general terms, the final document was built around two points: that York's treason, which was of long standing and consisted of his intent to take the throne from Henry, could not be pardoned and must be severely punished, and that Henry was and ever had been a just and 'fit' king. Their juxtaposition might seem a little strange in that the validity of the charge against York would not seem to require an assertion of Henry's fitness. But both claims involved smoke and mirrors; taken together, both had a bearing on Margaret's continued exercise of political power.

The first point – the matter of York's crimes – was originally broached in a different form involving a different claim in a tract known as the *Somnium Vigilantis* that was probably circulated shortly before or during the parliamentary session to convince persons of moderate persuasion to support the attainders.[65] In essence, the *Somnium* consists of six articles supposed to represent the Yorkists' justification and defense, followed by six articles of rebuttal. Although 'the fynall destruccion of this gracyous kynge' is alleged as the Yorkists' real purpose in the response to 'their' first article,[66] at no point in the tract are they directly accused of wishing to replace Henry with York. Even allowing that 'destruction' can cover a wide range of intentions, it appears in the *Somnium* that the Yorkists' real crime lay in 'thaire odible and contamynable usurpinge of the kynges power apon thaim' in claiming for themselves a special right to counsel the king and to determine the common weal.[67] The real issue, then, was the control of the king or whether the king should be openly

---

[61] *CPR, 1452–61*, pp. 561, 557, for commissions dated 14 and 30 October. See also Gairdner, *PL*, III, p. 196, for a reference to commissions to arrest and execute the Yorkists' associates, in a letter of uncertain date.

[62] As alleged by the virulently Yorkist *English Chron.*, p. 83, which also condemns the proceedings for not allowing the Yorkists to answer charges made against them – a rather difficult requirement in view of their flight. Cf. *Reg. Whethamstede*, I, p. 537, which considers them 'proper and lawful'.

[63] Roskell, 'Problem of Attendance of the Lords', p. 195; Payling, 'Coventry Parliament of 1459', pp. 349–52; Watts, p. 352. Johnson, pp. 189–90, finds the results of any manipulation of the commons' elections unimpressive.

[64] Gairdner, *PL*, III, p. 198.

[65] Gilson, 'A Defence of . . . the Yorkists', pp. 512–25, for the text; Kekewich, 'Attainder of the Yorkists', pp. 25–34, for a discussion of its genre, date and purpose. Kekewich believes that one of the persons to be persuaded was Henry himself (p. 26). The *Somnium* and its relationship to the attainder are also discussed by Johnson, pp. 190–1; by Watts, pp. 43–6, as a statement of Lancastrian political philosophy.

[66] Gilson, 'A Defence of . . . the Yorkists', p. 517. Further on, an attempt on Henry's life at St Albans is intimated via a rhetorical question that addresses a 'Yorkist claim' to have meant no harm to any save persons who deserved it: 'Was it no harme to kyle that mercifull and most gracyous kynge that now is? And how be it that the blyssed grace of God saved him . . . thay dyd neverthelesse thaire utterly devoure to undo him, and proceded as farre tharin as thay might' (p. 520).

[67] Ibid.; Johnson, p. 191.

controlled; the danger was that a renewal of pardon and leniency would amount to 'a wylfull submyssioun and exposynge of the kynge to [the Yorkists'] wylle'.[68] Linked to this was a philosophical position: that there could be no common weal without obedience to the king's authority; the one flowed from the other.[69]

The problem with the *Somnium*'s discussion, even if it was framed in a manner to make hash of the 'Yorkist' position, was that it openly raised a very real concern that was not so readily dismissed. It was no secret that Henry had not been a model of kingly competency. On two occasions in the last six years a protectorate had governed in his name, and at least on the first occasion there could be no doubt that something of the sort had been necessary. Most awkwardly, in both these instances the competent protector had been the duke of York, about to be charged with some form of attempted usurpation of the king's authority. It would not have been in Margaret's interest to look closely at the question of Henry's fitness. Whatever power she wielded owed its existence to her assertion of his competent authority. If the matter were to be seriously addressed, as a question, and if it were to be acknowledged, however reluctantly, that the weal of the realm required the king's continued tutelage, the only person or persons who could have filled such an office would have been male.

This is not to say that the persons having regular dealings with Henry would have been unaware of his limitations, or that they would have been blind to the queen's increasing influence. It is scarcely to be imagined that a William Waynflete, a Lawrence Booth or a Buckingham would not have understood perfectly well what was going on. Booth, certainly, owed his advancements and his present position in the government to Margaret. At the same time, however, it would be unwise – and unnecessary – to insist that understanding went hand in hand with enthusiastic approval. For some, perhaps, it did. For others, it may have been enough to grudgingly admit that the situation somehow worked. For work it did, not perfectly, but somehow. Despite the Yorkists' complaints, the realm was not falling apart. Inertia can sometimes be a motivating force. The system did not provide a ready, easy means for acknowledging, much less dealing with, the ongoing incompetence of an adult king: witness the reluctance and awkwardness with which the crisis of Henry's illness had been handled. Nor did the system provide any official place for a power-wielding queen. Thus, it may have seemed simpler and better to let matters run on as they were, without insisting upon closer inspection. If the assertion of Henry's authority involved a pretense that directly served Margaret's interests, it was a pretense in which a great many other persons willingly colluded.

---

[68] Gilson, 'A Defence of . . . the Yorkists', p. 517. This is, in fact, the charge that is best supported by both the Yorkists' pronouncements and behavior in 1459.

[69] This is the point that Watts makes, esp. pp. 43–4. If I understand his argument correctly, he places this philosophical stance in a causal relationship to the practical matter of control. If obedience becomes 'the fundamental basis of the state' (p. 44), then disobedience becomes treason and control of the king cannot be contemplated. My own inclination is to reverse the linkage: if, as a practical matter, one wished or needed to argue that the king (i.e. *this* king) should not be controlled, it would make a great deal of sense to give primacy to obedience rather than to discussions of the common weal. The person whose interest had the most to gain from such an argument was Margaret.

Thus, the attainder, as recorded in parliament, made much of Henry's fitness, both moral and physical, as a king. It commended his generosity and magnanimity towards York and the Nevilles in times past; it rehearsed in loving detail his most recent hardiness in the field. At no point were the protectorates mentioned or even alluded to; it was as if they had never occurred. But in the same breath the Yorkists' crimes were simplified: York had desired the crown itself, being motivated by envy and greed rather than by any concern for the common weal, and the Nevilles had willingly joined him in a despicable plot to destroy king, queen, prince and any lords who stood by them. In support, much was made of the Yorkists' 'rearing of war' against the king's banners, a point that could not be denied. When the king was present with his banner displayed, the treason of rebels who stood against him under their own banners did not have to be proved, but could be assumed. Their possessions could be forfeit without legal process. Hence the detailed description in the attainder of the confrontation at Ludford Bridge to demonstrate that these conditions had been met.[70] All in all, it made a plausible story, whether every detail was absolutely true or not,[71] and it officially evaded the long-term issues of whether Henry could actually manage and, if not, who might have to manage for him.

In practical terms attainder involved the forfeiture of all the Yorkists' possessions, bringing lands 'of unprecedented extent' into the crown's hands.[72] Following a formula that had been used against Cade in 1450 and in a posthumous petition against Suffolk in 1451, they were declared corrupt of blood and their heirs disabled from inheritance.[73] Their estates were not dismembered; very few pieces of property, in fact, were granted to crown supporters, even as leases. This meant that restoration remained a possibility, although it may be considered more likely that the estates, largely intact, were seen as a source of revenue for the financially ailing regime.[74] In addition to the forfeitures, a bill of resumption was passed affecting all who opposed the king at St Albans, Blore Heath or Ludford Bridge.[75] Despite the fact that there was no wholesale land giveaway, the forfeiture of entailed property may have brought

---

[70] Bellamy, *Law of Treason*, pp. 197–204, for a discussion of the 1459 attainders and the significance of this charge.

[71] Johnson, p. 191: 'The case against York was a good one, and was never satisfactorily refuted by his supporters, and it remains a plausible basis for interpreting his actions, even when all due allowance has been made for the partiality of the compilers.'

[72] Griffiths, p. 825. Twenty-three men and one woman (Alice, countess of Salisbury) were subjected to attainder and forfeiture. An additional three men – Richard Grey, Lord Powys, Walter Devereux and Sir Henry Radford – were pardoned of their lives for seeking the king's mercy at Ludford, although their possessions remained forfeit (*RP*, V, p. 349). Grey subsequently received full pardon (*CPR, 1452–61*, p. 536).

[73] Bellamy, *Law of Treason*, pp. 187–8. This act set a standard that was followed for the rest of the Wars of the Roses (ibid., pp. 178–9, 192).

[74] Johnson, pp. 192–3; Griffiths, pp. 825–6, who agree on the facts of distribution but differ somewhat over what it all meant. Johnson notes that in a number of cases administrative structure and personnel were retained to cause the least disruption (although these appointments were made during pleasure); Griffiths sees a permanent Lancastrian grip in the appointment of other court-aligned stewards, receivers and bailiffs for life. The evidence of the patent rolls supports both views (e.g. *CPR, 1452–61*, pp. 526, 530–1, 533, 536, 539, 569).

[75] *RP*, V, p. 366.

the Yorkists some sympathy.[76] Together with such redistribution as there was, it may have prompted the Yorkist charge, made retrospectively in the *English Chronicle*, that 'the quene with such as were of her affynyte rewled the reame as her lyked, gaderyng ryches innumerable' by various means, including the disinheriting of rightful heirs.[77]

To balance this severity, property that the attaindees held to the use of others was protected, as were their wives' jointures.[78] In addition, at some point during these proceedings a further offer of pardon was made, which may have been connected with the arrival of the duchess of York on 6 December.[79] A separate account of her mission opens up intriguing possibilities:

> The Duchyes of Yorke com unto Kyng Harry and submyttyd hyr unto hys grace, and she prayde for hyr husbonde that he myght come to hys answere to be ressayvyd unto hys grace; and the kynge fulle humbely grauntyde hyr grace, and to alle hyrs that wolde come with hyr, and to alle othyr that wolde com yn with yn viij dayes. And after viij days to done the execusyon of the lawe as hit requyryd. And many men . . . come whythe Syr Water Deverose . . . and alle hadde grace and marcy bothe of lyffe and lym.[80]

Given a past history of pleading on her husband's behalf, it does not seem at all unlikely that the duchess would have come to lay her case before the king, and perhaps before Margaret as well. Although the duchess may have come in response to an offer of pardon already made,[81] 'Gregory's Chronicle' seems to suggest that the offer was made in response to her entreaties. A number of pardons for 'treasons, rebellions, insurrections, [etc.]' were granted through December, with the bulk of them issued between the eighth and the twentieth while parliament remained in session; further pardons continued to be issued well into March.[82] The duchess herself was provided with 1,000 marks annually for life from some of her husband's forfeited lands 'for the relief of her and her infants', and she was sent to live with her sister the duchess of Buckingham.[83] In a final affirmation of royal mercy the last clause of the attainder reserved the king's right 'to shewe such mercy and grace as shall please his Highnes . . . to eny persone or persones whos names be expressed in this Acte, or to eny other that myght be hurt be the same'.[84] There is no particular reason to believe that Henry specifically intended to deal mercifully with York, Warwick and Salisbury

---

[76] Storey, p. 187; Wolffe, p. 324.

[77] *English Chron.*, p. 79.

[78] *RP*, V, p. 350. Alice, countess of Salisbury, was excepted, being attainted herself.

[79] Bocking's letter of 7 December dates her arrival (Gairdner, *PL*, III, p. 198).

[80] 'Gregory's Chron.', p. 206.

[81] Johnson, p. 192, n. 116, believes that it would have been made around the end of November.

[82] *CPR, 1452–61*, p. 531, for the earliest on 2 December; pp. 526, 527, 529, 530, 532, 535, 536, 537, 538, 539, 548, 568, 570, for pardons issued 8–20 December; 541, 545, 549, 552, 554, 568, 569, 573, 577, 581, 587, for those issued January–March. Storey, pp. 213 and 216, citing PRO, C67/43, notes that a general pardon was granted in January, which had 342 takers.

[83] *CPR, 1452–61*, pp. 542–3; *Brut*, p. 528; 'Gregory's Chron.', p. 207. The latter reports that 'she was kept fulle strayte and many a grete rebuke'. If the preamble to the attainder may be trusted in its assertion that the duke of Buckingham was fed up with York's activities some years earlier (*RP*, V, p. 347), it is not to be wondered that York's duchess became the target of her sister's and brother-in-law's wrath.

[84] *RP*, V, p. 350. *Reg. Whethamstede*, I, p. 356, says that this clause was added at the king's insistence, so that he might show mercy to any who humbly sought it without having to call another parliament.

against the wishes of a 'court faction' led by Margaret; in any event, the three did not appeal for pardon, though a number of lesser persons subsequently did. It seems more likely that this offer of leniency was intended to draw support away from any Yorkist cause that might be brewing;[85] its assertion of the king's authority was itself in keeping with the queen's own necessary mode of influence.

On 11 December sixty-six peers swore an oath of allegiance to the king.[86] While pledging their lifelong fidelity to Henry, they were required to provide an unprecedented endorsement of his title.[87] Although the oath may indeed have opened the door to the possibility of future choice in this matter, it seems more likely to have been viewed at the time as a necessary corollary to the Yorkists' attainder. By accusing York of designs on the throne – which avoided direct confrontation with the genuinely thorny issue of whether the king needed a keeper – the attainder required a refutation of any claim that York or any future challenger might be imagined to have. The simplest way to accomplish this was by asserting Henry's right and title. This connection is borne out by the oath's requirement that its signers 'resiste, withstond, and subdue' anyone who would oppose its premises.

In addition, in an equally noteworthy departure from custom the signers pledged 'to doo all that may be unto . . . the wele, suerte, and preservyng of the persone of the moost high and benigne Princesse Margaret the Quene . . . she being [the king's] wife'.[88] The wording of this oblique acknowledgment of her importance is unremarkable but instructive: nowhere is any sort of queenly authority alluded to, as none was presumed to exist, and the queen's claim to loyalty is explicitly based on her identity as the king's wife. Her power, undefined, remained embedded in and justified by the king's authority. Finally, the signers also asserted their loyalty to Prince Edward, twice identified as Henry's first-begotten son, and promised to accept his succession and that of his lawful heirs of the body. Thus, any current allegations about the prince's legitimacy were officially scotched; on paper, at least, the regime had done what it could to assure its long-term security.

Meanwhile, a series of practical measures were set in train to prepare for the likely occurrence of further fighting while providing the government with broad-based support. On 21 December commissions of array were issued throughout England; at the end of April 1460, with invasion becoming more imminent, a second flurry of commissions primarily involving the southern and midland counties authorized their recipients 'to call together and lead all persons . . . able to labour . . . to resist the . . . rebels' as soon as they entered

[85] On 3 March, Prince Edward was authorized to admit persons to pardon who submitted voluntarily in Wales and the marches; on 5 June similar authorization was given to the duke of Somerset to grant pardon to persons in Calais (*Foedera*, V, ii, pp. 93, 97; *CPR, 1452–61*, p. 578). In both cases, persons who had been attainted were specifically excluded, and it is clear that the aim was to draw real or potential support away from the Yorkists.

[86] *RP*, V, pp. 351–2.

[87] Watts, p. 353, n. 388, calls attention to what he sees as the constitutional implications of this endorsement.

[88] In 1455 following St Albans an oath was taken to the king alone, and the validity of his title was assumed (*RP*, V, pp. 282–3).

the realm.[89] Between these dates individual commissions were issued to take muster, to move ordnance or in other ways to raise the level of military preparedness.[90]

A number of these measures were aimed specifically at countering the earl of Warwick, who was proving to be indefatigable in thumbing his nose at the royalists. By the time Somerset reached Calais with the men and materiel that were to assure his takeover as captain, Warwick was already there, well ensconced and impossible to winkle out. Efforts to cut off supplies to the garrison raised the stakes and invited retaliation. In mid-January, Warwick sent a 'task force' to raid Sandwich; it succeeded not only in bringing back ships and sailors, but also in kidnapping Lord Rivers and his son, who had been commissioned to relieve Somerset.[91] Margaret's fear of Warwick and her personal interest in getting rid of him is attested by a secret appeal that she made to Pierre de Brezé, seneschal of Normandy, in February. Brezé duly reported to Charles VII that Margaret had asked him to take ('gagner') Warwick's ship and asked permission to proceed. He warned that the queen could not be implicated; if she were found out, even her supporters would turn against her and kill her.[92] Whatever came of this, Warwick remained at large, and his ability to hold Calais and to make all who went against him look like fools weighed heavily for the Yorkists when invasion did occur.

Meanwhile, policy towards the loyal, or the hoped-to-be-loyal, at home was avowedly inclusionary as commissions of various kinds were spread throughout the nobility.[93] In short, it appears that a genuine effort was mounted to provide the sort of 'good governance' that would offset Yorkist charges of favoritism and corruption. The next move would be theirs.

---

[89] *CPR, 1452–61*, pp. 557–61, 602–4.

[90] Ibid., pp. 527, 563–6, 604–6.

[91] Stevenson, II, ii, p. 512; *CPR, 1452–61*, pp. 555, 556; *Brut*, p. 528; *English Chron.*, pp. 84–5; *Three Chrons.*, pp. 72–3; Gairdner, *PL*, III, pp. 204–5. A second raid followed in June, despite the appointment of the duke of Exeter to keep the sea against him with 3,500 men (*Brut*, 529; *English Chron.*, pp. 85–6; Scofield, *Life and Reign of Edward IV*, I, p. 60).

[92] Brezé's letter of 24 February is printed in Basin, *Histoire*, IV, ed. Quicherat, pp. 358–60. See also Beaucourt, *Histoire de Charles VII*, VI, pp. 287–8; Bernus, 'Le rôle politique de Pierre de Brezé', pp. 333–4. It seems likely that Margaret's appeal came in response to Warwick's attack on Sandwich.

[93] Watts, p. 354 and n. 390. Griffiths, p. 829, also notes the government's willingness 'to temper its ruthlessness with conciliation' at this time in order to retain support.

12

Words and Deeds

ON 26 JUNE the earls of Warwick, Salisbury and March crossed from Calais to Sandwich. Warwick had been in Ireland conferring with York from mid-March until late May, and it is difficult to imagine that some agreement on a course of action had not been reached.[1] Whatever their conclusions had been, it was politic for the Calais lords to represent themselves as Henry's loyal, if misunderstood, liegemen.[2] There is every indication that the lords as a whole took their oath to Henry seriously; the fear of oath breaking along with a more generalized reluctance to contemplate the deposition of an anointed king – moreover, one who had been accepted as king since infancy – made them resist York's claim when it was made a few months later. Nevertheless, the propaganda that accompanied the Yorkist invasion was mixed, combining protestations of loyalty to Henry with darker hints about the future of the Lancastrian dynasty.

To this end, the invasion was preceded by a letter sent to the archbishop of Canterbury and the commons generally, asserting the dreadful state of affairs in England, the Yorkists' own victimization, their loyalty to Henry and their determination to set matters straight.[3] Among their complaints, they specifically blamed the earls of Wiltshire and Shrewsbury and Viscount Beaumont for 'stirring' the king to hold a parliament at Coventry that would attaint them and for keeping them from the king's presence and likely mercy, asserting that this was done against his will. To this they added the charge that these evil counselors were also tyrannizing other true men without the king's knowledge.[4] Such claims of malfeasance obliquely raised the question of Henry's fitness as a king, for how could he be deemed competent if such things happened without his knowledge and against his wishes? They also tied in to rumors circulating somewhat earlier in the southern counties and likely to have originated in Calais

[1] Jones, 'Edward IV, the earl of Warwick and the Yorkist Claim', makes a strong case for an early agreement that York would claim the throne.

[2] Griffiths, pp. 856–7; Watts, pp. 357–9; Johnson, pp. 205–6, 212; but cf. Storey, p. 188, and Wolffe, p. 323, who believe that the earls were ignorant of York's plans.

[3] Its text is given in the *English Chron.*, pp. 86–90. Johnson, pp. 201–3, 204, discusses the Yorkists' charges in detail and their public resonance, concluding that the letter made credible propaganda.

[4] It can be no accident that Shrewsbury and Wiltshire were named, for many of the Yorkists' complaints concerned taxation, extortion, the king's poverty and other financial matters, and they were Henry's past and present treasurers. Wiltshire had just been involved in June in an ugly situation in Newbury, Berks., involving hangings and imprisonments for tax resistance, to which the letter may have alluded (ibid., p. 203).

that Henry was really 'good and gracious Lord to the [Yorkists]' since, it was alleged, he had not known of or assented to their attainders. On 11 June the king was compelled to issue a proclamation stating that they were indeed traitors and that assertions to the contrary were to be ignored.[5]

Although neither Margaret nor the prince were mentioned in the Yorkists' letter,[6] they were dealt with through rumor and innuendo. Shortly before the Yorkists' landing, around the same time that the letter was circulated, a ballad appeared tacked to the gates of Canterbury that was surely written by a Yorkist sympathizer if not by someone privy to their less guarded words and thoughts. Its second verse likened England in its current circumstances to the 'realm of Satan' since

> filii scelerati have broughte it in dystresse.
> This prevethe fals wedlock and periury expresse,
> Fals heryres fostred, as knowethe experyence,
> Unryghtewys dysherytyng with false oppresse.[7]

The allusion to 'false heirs' seems to target Prince Edward, with an added dig at the validity of his parents' marriage.[8] It will be remembered that Henry had considered marriage with an Armagnac princess before the negotiations over Margaret's hand took place; the *Brut* blames England's later troubles on Henry's allegedly broken promises to the Armagnacs.[9] In this context 'unrighteous disheriting' takes on a double meaning by calling to mind those persons attainted at Coventry, one of whom was York, who, in the larger picture, would soon explicitly claim to have been disinherited from the crown that should have been his by blood right. These necessarily veiled allegations appear to echo blunter sentiments expressed by Warwick in Calais and duly reported to Pius II by the papal legate, Francesco Coppini. According to Coppini, Warwick called Henry 'a dolt and a fool', whose power lay 'in the hands of his wife and those who defile the king's chamber', and further asserted that 'the Duke of York . . . would now be on the throne if there were any regard for justice'. Coppini's report goes on to have the earl qualify this openly treasonous notion with the prediction that 'we shall drive our foes from the King's side and ourselves govern the kingdom. The King will retain only the bare name of sovereign.'[10] One may, of course, question whether Warwick actually said what

---

[5] *Foedera*, V, ii, p. 97; *CCR, 1454–61*, pp. 415–16. Commissioners were named to deal with rebels. Between 4 and 22 June various commissions of oyer and terminer were issued over a slightly wider area, as well as commissions to arrest and imprison the Yorkists' adherents; Wiltshire was named to nearly all of them (*CPR, 1452–61*, pp. 613–14).

[6] Johnson, p. 204, finds this deliberately evasive.

[7] *English Chron.*, pp. 91–2. The entire ballad goes to p. 94. It is also printed and discussed in Robbins, *Historical Poems*, pp. 207–10, 369–71.

[8] Ibid., p. 369; *EHL*, p. 246. Since the verse appears to have more than one heir in mind, one may wonder whether this interpretation should be broadened to include the Lancastrian dynasty as a whole. Surely that was the point of York's later claim to the throne.

[9] *Brut*, p. 512.

[10] Pius II, *Commentaries*, pp. 269–70. In March, Coppini wrote enigmatically to Francesco Sforza about matters in England and claimed that 'although we have no actual certitude, it is believed, nevertheless, that *the one newly chosen* together with Warwick will perform marvels' (*CSP, Milan*, I, p. 21; emphasis added). He subsequently connects their hope of success with his own desire for advancement.

the legate passed on. Comparing this with other things that the earl was supposed to have said at different times, the bluster, at least, seems to be of a piece. And in early May rumors were circulating at the papal court that Warwick had already invaded England and would depose Henry.[11]

Rumors concerning the prince's legitimacy – and by extension Margaret's morality – were not new, but they appear to have been given fresh impetus around this time. The *English Chronicle*, which reported the rumor that the prince was 'a bastard goten in avoutry', also alleged that Margaret, fearing that her son would not succeed, was 'makyng pryue menys to some of the lordes of Englond for to styre the kyng that he shulde resygne the croune to hyre sone'.[12] The combination of these two rumors would have been unsettling; given any credence, they would have prepared the ground for consideration of an alternative succession. There is no independent evidence that Margaret contemplated Henry's abdication, though rumors that she had continued to surface.[13]

Some reason for their appearance may be found in the flurry of commissions that the prince had received in February and March 1460.[14] On 23 March his ageing nurse was allowed to retire, with a note that the prince was 'now so grown as to be committed to the rules and teachings of men wise and strenuous . . . rather than to stay further under the keeping and governance of women'.[15] At the age of seven, the prince's 'duties' still would have been carried out by others in his name, but this inevitable milestone in his life may have been intended as a timely and prudent reassurance to the realm that he was growing up and that his education was proceeding as it should. Nevertheless, these changes in the prince's status would have lent credibility to suggestions that Henry's abdication was in the offing. Whether the Yorkists were responsible for such rumors at this time and whether they believed them or not may be open to question. Encouraging rumors of the prince's illegitimacy would address all eventualities, while also serving to criticize Margaret's activities by the by.

In this connection, the rumors deserve further consideration. Notions regarding female sexuality underlay most contemporary assessments of what constituted 'good' and 'bad' women. It was the single area in which a woman's reputation was most vulnerable. Christine de Pisan recognized this reality in the emphasis she placed upon the value of chastity for women of all social levels.[16] At the same time, she observed that 'the greater a lady is, the more is her honour

---

[11] *CSP, Milan*, I, p. 22.

[12] *English Chron.*, pp. 79–80. Its description of the situation in England, including the bastardy rumor, is written as if it pertains to the period before Blore Heath. Nevertheless, its complaints of bad governance, presented as factual description, very closely parallel the charges made in the Yorkists' letter from Calais of 1460 in both substance and language, suggesting that the later chronicle may have been based upon Yorkist propaganda and probably reflects views that they actively propagated after their failure at Ludlow.

[13] *CSP, Milan*, I, pp. 55, 58.

[14] *CPR, 1452–61*, pp. 562, 564, 565, 605, 606.

[15] Ibid., p. 567.

[16] Christine, *Treasure*, pp. 56, 74–6, 86–7, 89–105, 115–17, 150–2, 171–5. She even made a point of extending her advice – and exhortations to reform – to prostitutes, though she considered there to be 'nothing more abominable' than the lives they led (p. 171).

or dishonour celebrated through the country than that of another ordinary woman'.[17] Thus, allegations of adultery were potentially damning to Margaret; insinuations of disorderly sexuality suggested that other aspects of her conduct and activities were disorderly as well. The label of sexual transgression effectively defined her as a woman out of place.[18]

Even more importantly, allegations of disorder in the royal family could be linked to charges of disorder in the realm.[19] This connection underlies Warwick's insinuation of Margaret's promiscuity: the king was betrayed by his wife; she and her lovers held power that should have been his. Private transgression had subverted public order. Thus, rumors of the queen's adultery were an integral part of the larger charge of misrule, while labeling Prince Edward a bastard paved the way for drastic change. This purpose became clearer immediately after the battle of Northampton when an Italian newsletter reported that 'it is thought that [Warwick and his companions] will make a son of the Duke of York king, and that they will pass over the king's son, as they are beginning already to say that he is not the king's son'.[20]

Besides alluding to the prince's bastardy and, hence, his incapacity to reign in his turn, the Canterbury ballad also hints at Henry's likely fate. In the fifth stanza, after complaining that the king has banished his own true blood, it asks rhetorically:

> What prynce by thys rewle may have long enduryng,
> That also in moste povert hath be long whyle?

The answer is provided in stanzas seven and eight:

> Tempus ys come falshede to dystroy,
> Tempus eradicandi the wedes fro the corne,
> Tempus cremandi the breres that trees noye,
> Tempus evellendi the fals hunter with his horne.

> Send hom, most gracious Lord Jhesu most benygne,
> Sende hoom thy trew blode un to his propre veyne,
> Richard duk of York, Job thy servaunt insygne . . .
> Set hym ut sedeat in principibus, as he dyd before.[21]

R.H. Robbins has suggested that, failing alternative identification, the 'hunter' in the ballad may represent the earl of Wiltshire.[22] Since he identifies the 'hunt' (for huntsman) in a later poem, appearing shortly after Northampton and

[17] Ibid., p. 125.
[18] Howell, *Eleanor of Provence*, pp. 149–50, for personal slander used to discredit an earlier English queen; Gibbons, 'Isabeau of Bavaria', pp. 57, 67–8, for the linkage of sexual charges and politics; Macdougall, *James III*, pp. 54–6, for rumors of sexual promiscuity used against Margaret's contemporary, Mary of Guelders, queen regent of Scotland; Levin, 'Power, Politics and Sexuality', pp. 97, 101–2, for similar criticism of Elizabeth I.
[19] Bührer-Thierry, 'La reine adultère', pp. 299, 301, 302–4, 311–12, discusses popular perception of this linkage.
[20] *CSP, Milan*, I, p. 27.
[21] *English Chron.*, pp. 92–3.
[22] Robbins, *Historical Poems*, p. 370, line 52.

containing borrowings from the ballad, as the king,[23] it may not require too great a speculative stretch to suggest that the 'hunter' in the ballad may also refer to Henry. The juxtaposition of these lines to the reference to false heirs does not appear to bode well for the Lancastrian succession. In contrast, the later poem, written when Henry was captive but his son was still at large, avoids this issue by expressing loyalty to Henry alone, without any reference to the prince.

After their landing at Sandwich, the earls wasted no time. They entered London on 2 July after initial resistance. Although some Londoners were great admirers of Warwick,[24] the City's decision to open its gates seems to have been prompted as much by fear of the Kentish following the earls had collected en route as by anything else.[25] Nevertheless, cooperation may have come at a price, for on the next day the earls swore publicly at St Paul's in the presence of Archbishop Bourgchier that they would do nothing against their allegiance to Henry.[26] Accompanying the earls, and perhaps instrumental in reassuring the City that pragmatism also served a higher good, was Francesco Coppini, the papal legate.[27] Coppini had attached himself to them in Calais after initially having been sent to England the year before to drum up support for a crusade against the Turks. When that effort was hampered by England's domestic troubles, he was next given the task of reconciling disputes. But that was to prove inimical to Coppini's temperament. Yearning after a cardinal's hat and already busily scheming with the duke of Milan, Coppini took to the Yorkists' enterprise like a duck to water and may have found a kindred spirit in the earl of Warwick.[28] According to one chronicler, while the Yorkists still remained in London, they announced that they had papal bulls supporting their cause and ordering the excommunication of all who opposed them.[29]

On 4 July, Coppini wrote a lengthy letter to Henry that was also made public in London, while a copy appears to have been sent to the queen.[30] It was a remarkable letter; despite its assertions of sincerity and concern, it can only be characterized as psychologically threatening. In essence, it warned Henry of the bloodshed sure to come and for which he would be accountable before God if he did not follow the legate's counsel. To avoid such an outcome, Coppini asserted, Henry must put from him all 'suspect' persons, ignore any who said he had cause to fight and permit the lords of Calais to come to him strongly armed

[23] Ibid., pp. 369 and 372, line 42; see pp. 210–15, for the poem.

[24] E.g., Flenley ('Bale's Chron.'), p. 144: 'the moost corageous and manliest knight lyvyng'.

[25] Barron, 'London and the Crown', pp. 96–7; Griffiths, p. 860; Johnson, p. 205; cf. Watts, pp. 355–6.

[26] Stevenson, II, ii, p. 773; English Chron., p. 95. Flenley ('Bale's Chron.'), p. 150, indicates that 'the worship and weel of the King' was a matter of explicit concern. The earls had previously paused in Canterbury to visit Becket's tomb, where they probably gave thanks for the capitulation and subsequent backing of the men who had been ordered to hold the city against them, and possibly affirmed their loyalty to the king (Searle, Chronicle of John Stone, p. 79; Reg. Whethamstede, I, pp. 371–2). Johnson, p. 205, notes their need to make such repeated pledges.

[27] Watts, p. 355, for his likely influence.

[28] Scofield, Life and Reign of Edward IV, I, pp. 71ff. Coppini's primary motivation, as she points out (p. 74), was likely to have been self-aggrandizement. CSP, Milan, I, p. 21, indicates that he had left England on Warwick's advice.

[29] Baskerville, 'London Chron. of 1460', p. 125.

[30] Ibid., pp. 23–6, for the letter; p. 38, for an allusion to Margaret's copy.

(for their own safety) to state their cause.[31] Together with this letter, Coppini seems to have included a further document, written by the earls at Calais the day before they all sailed for England and addressed to him, though no doubt with the knowledge that he would pass it on in due course to the king.[32] In it they asserted their own good intentions; nevertheless, they also stated that if they could not obtain the settlement they desired, they were prepared to fight, trusting in the Lord since justice was on their side.[33] One can imagine that such messages would not have been received with much trust or optimism. Margaret, at least, appears to have regarded Coppini thereafter with hatred and contempt.

As the Yorkists marched from London to confront the king, leaving Salisbury behind to hold the city and to deal with a group of Lancastrian supporters who had holed up in the Tower, rumors circulated that royal troops from Lancashire and Cheshire had been told that they might pillage the southeast.[34] These were areas in which Margaret had actively recruited support, and a substantial portion of the men who had fought under Lord Audley at Blore Heath had been from Cheshire.[35] It seems most unlikely that such license would have been given, since it stood to increase sympathy in the 'target area' and perhaps elsewhere for the Yorkists. That suggests a partisan origin for the rumors.[36] The further allusion they provided to female-caused disorder in the wider realm would have served the Yorkist cause. Meanwhile, other rumors circulated that the duke of York would soon 'descend upon the country with a large number of troops' supported by a separate invasion by the king of Scotland.[37] Although it is difficult to imagine how a Scottish invasion would have increased York's popularity in England, there may have been some truth to the rumor. In a letter that M.K. Jones has convincingly redated to 28 June 1460, James II again tried to persuade Charles VII that the time was ripe to attack England, suggesting that it would be in their mutual interest to give York the aid James said he had requested in support of his claim to the crown.[38] Whether James seriously intended an invasion or not became moot when he was accidentally killed in a cannon explosion on 3 August while he was besieging Roxburgh castle.[39]

The armies met at Northampton on 10 July, and the Yorkists sent one or more of the bishops who had accompanied them from London to the king's

---

[31] Cf. Ellis, *Original Letters*, I, pp. 88–97, for a longer Latin version; towards the end it includes the hope that God may open Henry's eyes (a recurring theme) and a final reminder of the Judgement in which all would stand.

[32] Such an intention is implied in Coppini's letter to Henry (*CSP, Milan*, I, p. 24).

[33] Ellis, *Original Letters*, pp. 85–8, but p. 86: 'Alias si ista non concedentur nobis, vel non fiat honesta concordia . . . nos sumus parati, et habemus favores, et necessitas nos impellit experiri arma et fortunam nostram, et speramus in Domino quia habemus justitiam.' ('Otherwise, if these things are not granted to us, or [if] an honorable agreement is not reached . . . we are ready and we have supporters, and necessity impels us to put our arms and fortune to the test, and we place our hope in God because we have justice.')

[34] *English Chron.*, p. 98.

[35] Gillespie, 'Cheshiremen at Blore Heath', p. 79.

[36] Griffiths, p. 858.

[37] *CSP, Milan*, I, p. 27. James II was also said to have married one of his daughters to one of York's sons.

[38] Jones, 'Edward IV, the Earl of Warwick and the Yorkist Claim', pp. 349–50; Stevenson, I, pp. 323–6, dated it to 1456.

[39] His actions prior to his death appear to have been limited to continued harassment of the borders.

camp to parlay.[40] The gist of the delegation's message, as reported, involved an appeal to avoid the spilling of blood. It may not be entirely coincidental that this appeal, particularly as Whethamstede describes it, seems to echo parts of Coppini's letter to Henry. In the *English Chronicle* version it is Buckingham who, in Henry's presence, sends the bishops packing with the contemptuous observation that they are not men of peace but men of arms.[41] If Buckingham had seen Coppini's letter, his response to a clerical delegation bearing similar messages becomes more understandable and less unreasonable. As at St Albans, the Yorkist temper does not seem to have been conciliatory or compromising, as evidenced by Warwick's ultimatum that he would either speak with Henry at two hours past noon 'or elles dye in the feeld'.[42] Thus at 2:00 p. m. the armies engaged and the royal forces, badly outnumbered, were defeated.[43] It was later charged – and widely believed – that the legate Coppini had excommunicated the royalist army or certain of its leaders prior to the battle.[44] Buckingham, Shrewsbury, Beaumont and Egremont were killed; Henry was found inside his tent. As they had done after St Albans, the Yorkists formally submitted to the king and swore that they desired his welfare and prosperity and that of his realm above all else.

There could be little doubt, however, that despite their pledges of loyalty, the king was in the Yorkists' hands and subject to their control.[45] Upon their return to London six days later, Henry was lodged in the bishop of London's palace. Meanwhile, rumor spread that the prince was not his son, and people began to speculate that Warwick, who was expected to maintain his control of the government, would make a son of the duke of York king in the prince's stead.[46] At the end of the month the officers of state were replaced by Yorkists: George Neville, Warwick's brother and bishop of Exeter, became chancellor of England; Viscount Bourgchier was once more treasurer, and Robert Stillington, arch-deacon of Wells, became keeper of the privy seal. Replacements went on at the lower levels as well and throughout Henry's household until it became 'a Yorkist institution controlling a monarch who was completely in its power'.[47] Yet the government, as it was being reconstituted, had only limited support among the

---

[40] The only detailed accounts of what ensued are in the *English Chron.*, pp. 96–8; *Reg. Whethamstede*, I, pp. 372–5; and Waurin, *Croniques*, pp. 296–301. See Griffiths, p. 862; Goodman, *Wars of the Roses*, pp. 37–9, for modern reconstructions of the battle.

[41] *Reg. Whethamstede*, I, pp. 372–3; *English Chron.*, p. 96.

[42] Ibid., p. 97.

[43] Some of the royal levies had not yet arrived, but the outcome was determined by Lord Grey of Ruthin's defection to the Yorkists (Goodman, *Wars of the Roses*, p. 38).

[44] Pius II, *Commentaries*, p. 270; 'Benet's Chron.', p. 225; *Three Chrons.*, p. 153; Baskerville, 'A London Chronicle of 1460', p. 125; cf. *English Chron.*, p. 94, for the more obscure observation that Coppini had been authorized to treat for peace, but 'toke oponne hym more power thanne he had'. In early January 1461, Coppini wrote to a subordinate who was with the queen, frantically denying that he had excommunicated anyone (*CSP, Milan*, I, p. 38). By that time London was anticipating the advance of Margaret's army from the north; the legate's fear is palpable. See below, pp. 311–12.

[45] Flenley ('Bale's Chron.'), p. 151, observes that he was kept 'in his magestie Roiall' at their pleasure.

[46] *English Chron.*, p. 98; 'Benet's Chron.', p. 226; *CSP, Milan*, I, p. 27, which makes clear that the Yorkists were encouraging the bastardy rumors. Watts, p. 357, n. 410, finds it suggestive that Henry was taken to the bishop's palace instead of to Westminster and that he did not go crowned during a pilgrimage to Canterbury taken in company with the Yorkists in August (citing Searle, *Chronicle of John Stone*, p. 81).

[47] Griffiths, p. 864, for all these changes and their effect.

peerage; hence it was necessary to move matters towards a more official conclusion by summoning a parliament to meet in October.[48]

Henry was moved to Westminster palace and was present when parliament opened on 7 October. One of its first acts necessarily was to repeal the attainders passed at Coventry against 'certayne of the grete, noble and faithfull true Lordes . . . [who] ever hadde grete and feithfull love, to the preferrying and suertee of the welfare of [the king's] most Roiall persoon'. In keeping with the Yorkists' charges before Ludford and in their pre-invasion letter, the attainders were blamed on the malice and covetousness of evildoers out to lay hands on their property.[49] It is difficult to imagine, however, that all this loyal posturing was not accompanied by a certain unease and apprehension. Such feelings would have been well-justified, for on the tenth York arrived at Westminster with an impressive company, marched into the parliament chamber with his sword borne upright before him and claimed the throne by lineal right.[50]

Although everyone present appears to have been discomfited by the manner of York's appearance, it is unlikely that anyone could have been very much surprised. Upon the duke's return from Ireland in early September, he omitted reference to the regnal year as well as the usual 'saving allegiance to the king' clause from his indentures and began a measured, if circuitous, march from Chester to London that increasingly took on the trappings of a royal progress.[51] It would have been clear to observers that he had more in mind than a renewal of his protectorate. Since persons attending parliament would have had a practical need to know just what was going on, it is likely that some had informants posted to notify them of York's activities.[52] Warwick, who had met with him at Shrewsbury en route, surely knew his plans. In light of the rumors of the prince's bastardy that the Yorkist earls had put about or otherwise encouraged over the past months, it appears that a change in dynasty had been part of a long-term agenda. The earls may have envisioned difficulties in deposing Henry outright – as they indeed encountered – but it is difficult to square the allegations about Prince Edward with any intention that he should succeed.[53]

But a second propaganda theme, which had gotten the earls from Calais to Northampton and beyond, had consisted of repeated assertions, both oral and written, of their loyalty to Henry. These, together with the oath that so many

[48] Johnson, pp. 206–10, for the lack of support and for efforts to restore order and obtain acceptance; *PPC*, VI, pp. 304–6, for privy council attendees in August.

[49] *RP*, V, p. 374. No one was named specifically in the act of repeal, but Beaumont, Shrewsbury and especially Wiltshire had been singled out for blame in the letter from Calais. Wiltshire, having fled before the fighting at Northampton, was in Holland (*English Chron.*, p. 90). Such claims regarding covetous seizure had a public resonance (Gairdner, *PL*, III, pp. 242–3).

[50] Johnson, p. 214, for a contemporary letter sent to the earl of Worcester, who was then in Venice, describing the scene (taken from BN, MS Fr. 20136, fol. 65). See also 'Gregory's Chron.', p. 208; Stevenson, II, ii, p. 774; *Reg. Whethamstede*, I, pp. 376–7.

[51] Griffiths, pp. 867 and 879, n. 65.

[52] Ibid., p. 376, for the rumors that followed York's arrival. Waurin, *Croniques*, pp. 310–12, says that York was encouraged to take the throne by people along his route. If such a thing occurred, either spontaneously or by stage management, and he hoped to be swept in on a wave of public sentiment, matters did not go as he might have imagined. For the details of York's return and the subsequent debate over his claim, see Johnson, pp. 210–18.

[53] Hicks, *Warwick*, p. 211, reaches the same conclusion.

had sworn at Coventry the year before, made it very difficult to support his deposition. The importance of these oaths is confirmed by the primacy they were given in a list of objections to York's claim and by the nature of the claim itself.[54] York's argument of prior lineal right to the throne based on inheritance through females, if accepted, meant that oaths upholding Henry's right automatically became invalid.[55] But it appears that the lords did not readily buy his argument. A letter to the earl of Worcester reported that the discussions caused 'many a slep to be broken', and the official parliament record indicates that repeated prodding by the new chancellor, George Neville, by York's council and by the duke himself was required to overcome unanimous reluctance to weigh the merits of his claim.[56] The formal agreement, which allowed Henry to keep the crown for life with the succession to York and his heirs, observed with what may have been a virtual sigh of relief that 'othes that the . . . Lordes had made unto the Kynges Highnes at Coventre, and other places [were] saved, and their consciences therin clered'.[57]

Although the disinheritance of Prince Edward would be expected to arouse resistance, it does not appear to have been so worrisome a matter as might be thought. Though it clearly involved some oath breaking, the lords did not quibble, as far as the record shows. Rumors of the prince's bastardy may have softened incipient support for him, and the formal acceptance of the legitimacy of York's claim would have removed any need to consider their truth or falsehood more carefully. He was, in any event, a mere child compared with York's two eldest sons, recognized as his likely heirs, who were eighteen and seventeen respectively. And the settlement delicately allowed that it might please Henry 'to ley from hym' the crown before his natural lifespan reached its end.[58] Although York was ten years older than Henry, the odds that he or his nearly mature sons could consolidate power before Prince Edward became a threat in his own right may not have seemed overly daunting. Such a view would have underestimated Margaret's tenacity in upholding her son's right and the degree of support she would initially command. The ineptitude of Yorkist efforts to lure her out of hiding and the carelessness of York's expedition to put down the Lancastrian threat in the north suggest that this was indeed the case.[59] For the moment, the focus of their attention was on Henry.

While parliament deliberated York's title, Henry remained at Westminster. Since his capture at Northampton, he seems for the most part to have been a pliant and spiritless captive, treated with honor but offering no real resistance to his captors' bidding.[60] It does not follow, however, that he was not cognizant of

<hr />

[54] See also *Reg. Whethamstede*, I, pp. 378–80, for repeated references to perjury among the public protests that York's claim was said to have engendered.

[55] *RP*, V, pp. 376, 377; Storey, pp. 188–9. The female links were Anne Mortimer, York's mother, and Anne's grandmother Philippa, who was the only child of Lionel, duke of Clarence, the second surviving son of Edward III.

[56] Johnson, p. 213; *RP*, V, pp. 375–7.

[57] Ibid., pp. 377–8.

[58] Ibid., p. 379.

[59] Discussed in the next chapter. Cf. Griffiths, p. 856, who considers the settlement 'the least happy of [possible] outcomes' for the Yorkists. I suspect they did not realize how unhappy it was going to be.

[60] In April 1461, following the Yorkist victory at Towton, George Neville, bishop of Exeter and chancellor, referred to Henry in a letter as 'that puppet of a king' (*CSP, Milan*, I, p. 61). While it is

what was happening or that he was mindlessly cooperative.[61] On 17 October, after York had presented the document containing his claim to parliament, the lords went en masse to the king, whom the chancellor asked what should be done. Henry replied that *they* should discover all possible objections to York's claim, perhaps his only option under the circumstances, but one that left the onus of dealing with the situation squarely on their shoulders. Evidently, this was not the answer they had desired, for they urged him yet again to think of reasonable objections, but to this no reply was recorded.[62]

Further insecurity as to the extent of the king's cooperation was demonstrated more clearly on the twenty-fifth when the lords returned to Henry with the results of their deliberations. The chancellor, who was to do the talking, cautiously assured himself that the others 'wuld abyde by hym howe so ever that the Kyng toke the mater'. In the event, the record only shows that Henry agreed to the settlement after 'good and sad deliberation and avyce had with all his Lordes' and to avoid 'the effusion of Cristen blode'.[63] It may be that some strategic pressure had been necessary to obtain his willing assent, though, realistically, it is difficult to imagine how he could have refused. While the reference to bloodshed may be a kind of boilerplate, it was also the threat that Coppini had dangled over Henry before Northampton: that blood would be shed if he continued uncooperative and that he would be held accountable. Blood had been spilled at Northampton, in particular that of persons who had been his close advisors, perhaps even his friends. As a speculation, then, if this weighed heavily upon him, it would have provided an effective means to pressure him further.[64] Formal oaths were taken on the last day of the month. York and his sons swore to uphold Henry's royal dignity and to do nothing 'to the abriggement of [his] naturall lyf', with the proviso – which they insisted should be recorded – that their oaths were valid only so long as the king's oath to them remained unbroken. Then Henry swore that he accepted 'of his free will and libertee' that the succession should go to York and his heirs and that any attempt on the duke's life should be adjudged treason.[65] That night, Henry was removed from Westminster against his will and sent back to London to lodge in the bishop's palace.[66]

With these oaths, Henry was caught in a cleft stick. By accepting York's claim, he disinherited his son, but to disavow his actions was to free York from his oath. No matter what he did, there would be blood. In the days he spent at

---

possible that the remark was meant as a general characterization, it must be remembered that Neville had become chancellor after Northampton and that it is to the period of Henry's 'Yorkist captivity' that the letter immediately refers.

[61] Much ink has been spent in efforts to extrapolate Henry's frame of mind and mental capacity, particularly during the years following his illness. My discussion here refers only to the period after Northampton, while Henry was in Yorkist hands and subject to overt Yorkist control, and should not be taken as a more broadly applicable description.

[62] *RP*, V, p. 376.

[63] Ibid., p. 378.

[64] Pius II later stated that the settlement was reached 'by the wisdom of the Legate' (Pius II, *Commentaries*, p. 271). Whatever Coppini's actual role may have been, it does not seem out of character for him to have taken credit for the settlement.

[65] *RP*, V, pp. 378–80.

[66] 'Gregory's Chron.', p. 208.

Westminster, aware of what was happening, he would have come face to face with his own failure as a king. It is likely that he also went in fear. When York arrived on 10 October to claim the throne, he forced his way into the royal lodgings in Westminster Palace and set himself up there in regal style.[67] York's presence with a retinue of armed men would have been intimidating, and one chronicler reported that the duke 'kepte [Henry] there by fors and strengythe, tylle at the laste the kynge for fere of dethe grauntyd hym the crowne'.[68] In these circumstances it is not so difficult to imagine the visits that Henry was later reported to have made to the adjacent abbey to pace out the spot where he intended to be buried.[69]

[67] *English Chron.*, p. 99; and *Reg. Whethamstede*, I, p. 377, say that he broke the doors or their bars, and both agree that York took over the king's apartments. Cf. *Croyland Chron.*, p. 455; Johnson, p. 214 (the letter to Worcester); Baskerville, 'A London Chronicle of 1460', p. 126.

[68] 'Gregory's Chron.', p. 208, who also believed that on the night that Henry was moved back to London, York visited him by torchlight and pressed his claim again. His intention may have been to see if he could force an abdication. Waurin, *Croniques*, V, p. 313, says that York put six of his men to guard the king; cf. 'Benet's Chron.', pp. 227–8, who says that York would not see or speak to Henry for three weeks. Whether York saw Henry personally or not, with his men in attendance his presence would have been felt.

[69] Stanley, *Historical Memorials of Westminster Abbey*, pp. 152–3, 506–14. In 1498 twelve 'witnesses' were deposed in support of the abbey's effort to obtain Henry's remains for reburial. Of the ten deponents who tried to provide a date for his visit(s), seven opted for the last several years of the reign, and three associated it with All Hallows. Rather than attributing the visit(s) to a habitually morbid nature, it may make more sense to ascribe them to a time when Henry had particular reason to contemplate his death.

13

Revenge and Reversals

WHILE these matters transpired, Margaret's public role and public importance entered a new phase. With Henry's captivity she emerged as the acknowledged and avowed leader of a genuine Lancastrian party. Momentarily stripped of pretense, it became possible, for the first time in her career, to obtain a symbolically separate identity that might have permitted her to exercise genuine authority. It was a separation that she had not sought, however, and that she likely would have regarded as temporary if she even recognized it. Since her failed bid for a regency, her efforts had been directed towards upholding the king's authority or the potential authority of her son, and this she continued to do. Ultimately, this posture placed her in an untenable situation as the representative and intermediary of a king whose authority had been revealed as a sham.

Margaret had not accompanied the king to Northampton. Given the uncertainties attending any situation involving armed confrontation, it was prudent for the prince and his mother to remain apart until the outcome was known. With Yorkist victory, the prince's freedom became a guarantee of his father's life. Although the prospect of a child-king in itself could not strengthen the Lancastrian cause, Henry's outright deposition or death could have created a backlash against its Yorkist perpetrators and driven increased support to his heir.[1]

Upon learning of the royalist defeat at Northampton, Margaret fled with her son and a small escort into Wales.[2] Although they were ambushed and robbed en route, they finally made their way safely to Harlech castle. From Wales they took ship to Scotland, arriving there by early December.[3] Long before they reached this relative haven, however, Margaret had begun to take action and to encourage any rumors and sentiment that might hinder the Yorkists and

---

[1] It can be no accident that Edward IV kept Henry alive for so long, or that he was killed so shortly after his son's death at Tewkesbury in 1471. Ironically, York's death at Wakefield, in an encounter that owed much of its brutality to vendetta, could be used to foster support for his son.

[2] The Italian newsletter reporting the rumor that the prince would be denied succession states that 'the queen also runs great danger', though its nature is not specified (*CSP, Milan*, I, p. 27).

[3] Griffiths, p. 866. 'Gregory's Chron.', pp. 208–9, provides the most circumstantial account of her flight, but believes that she did not go to Wales until after the parliamentary settlement – clearly impossible in view of York's landing and slow progress through the marches. Cf. *English Chron.*, pp. 98–9; Stevenson, II, ii, pp. 773, 774. Davis, *PL*, II, pp. 216–17, has her in Wales around 12 September, when the letter actually appears to have been written (see below, n. 13).

help her cause. From mid-August onwards the Yorkist government issued a
spate of commissions to arrest and imprison persons guilty of spreading 'false
news', accusing others of treason, uttering 'falsehoods' that could lead to
discord and the like.[4] Some of this rumor-mongering likely originated in
predictable uncertainty regarding the Yorkists' real intentions following
Northampton and would not have required Lancastrian initiative to get it
going, though the latter would surely have encouraged it. The commissions
continued into January – the last is from the twelfth – by which time it is clear
that letters from the queen, the prince and their immediate supporters were
implicated.

The parliament that met in 1460, apart from its discomfiture and dithering
over York's claim, was not particularly well attended.[5] Though absenteeism was
likely to have reflected old animosities as well as disavowal of any Yorkist
project, there were also currents of sentiment that specifically favored the queen
and prince. Friar John Brackley, one of the Paston correspondents and an avid
supporter of Warwick, wrote that the bishop of Norwich, the duchess of Suffolk
and others, with all their men, were very well disposed towards Margaret and
the prince and urged that strong measures should be taken against the Yorkists'
enemies.[6] Some of these enemies were already causing trouble in the north even
as parliament met. Seditious talk had been rife in York since summer, and the
earl of Northumberland and his associates were raising an army 'to rescue the
king', though in the meantime they were happy to raid the Yorkists' estates.[7] A
series of commissions had already been issued in an effort to gain control, and
more would follow. All would be disregarded.[8]

Whether Margaret was directly responsible for Northumberland's activities or
not is unclear, but she was quick to build on the opportunity they afforded. She
was soon in contact with Somerset, who had given up the attack on Calais and
returned to England, as well as with the earl of Devon and Alexander Hody.[9] She
instructed them to raise men and meet her at Hull, where a force under the duke
of Exeter was being formed. This would be no mean feat, since the three were
then in the south – Somerset at Corfe castle.[10] Margaret also sent word to her
chief officers to summon 'alle tho servantys that lovyd hyr or purposyd to kepe

---

[4] *CPR, 1452–61*, pp. 609, 611, 612, 614, 650, 651, 652, 654, 658, 659.
[5] Stevenson, II, ii, p. 774, says that nearly all the clergy were there, but that many of the secular lords,
     particularly northerners, stayed away. Watts, p. 359, n. 417, discusses likely attendees.
[6] Gairdner, *PL*, III, p. 228. The bishop of Norwich was, of course, Margaret's confessor, and the duchess
     of Suffolk was an old friend who had accompanied and perhaps mothered her on her way to England.
     Although Bishop Lyhert's restoration to the list of duchy feoffees and other reappointments of
     Margaret's overt supporters have been interpreted as a sign of parliamentary conciliation (Watts, p. 359
     and n. 417), it seems more likely that the Yorkists saw them as a means to split the opposition, a tactic
     that Margaret apparently used on previous occasions.
[7] Johnson, p. 219; Stevenson, II, ii, pp. 774–5. The reversal of the Yorkists' attainders in parliament,
     restoring their property rights, was a foregone conclusion with them once more in power.
[8] Pollard, *North-Eastern England*, pp. 279–80, discusses these matters. As an illustration of the situation,
     on 8 October the mayor, aldermen and sheriffs of York were told to see to it that the city's inhabitants
     were 'ready to obey the king's mandates and no other' (*CPR, 1452–61*, p. 650).
[9] The latter had served on various commissions in the southwest, many of a military nature (*CPR, 1452–
     61*, pp. 148, 221, 405, 409, 443, 489, 558, 613).
[10] 'Gregory's Chron.', pp. 209–10. Lords Roos, Clifford, Greystoke, Neville, and Latimer were said to be
     'waytyng a-pon' Exeter. Goodman, *Wars of the Roses*, p. 241, n. 3, suggests that Hull's accessibility by
     sea and river made it a good victualling depot.

and rejoyse hyr offysce' and likewise proceed to the rendezvous.[11] The Lancastrians were at pains to keep their movements secret, and by this time the Yorkists were so preoccupied with parliament that they did not fully realize what was happening until the gathering had taken place.[12] Although the exact chronology is difficult to pin down, it seems likely that the muster began before the settlement was reached. York's intentions could have been guessed from soon after his arrival in England and were publicly declared on 10 October. It is also reasonable to assume that Margaret would have taken steps to provide for a Lancastrian counteroffensive as soon as she was able, without waiting for the full implications of the Yorkist victory to emerge.[13] This assembly of an army from different points and outside the normal campaigning season was a 'striking achievement'.[14]

Although the Yorkists were unaware of the extent of Lancastrian military preparations, they knew that Margaret's and the prince's escape were dangerous to them and to their plans. Certainly, the prince's continued freedom posed a long-term threat to any Yorkist hope of a dynastic change. Accordingly, they attempted to lure the queen to London with messages and counterfeit tokens purportedly from the king. This may have been the effort that Coppini later referred to, made while parliament was sitting, in which he tried to induce Margaret to come to terms. The ruse did not work, for Henry and Margaret had already agreed at their parting in Coventry that she would not join him unless she received a special token that only the two of them knew. Despite 'Gregory's' assertion that the Yorkists considered Margaret 'more wyttyer then the kynge', there is an element of naiveté and underestimation in their assumption that she would fall for such a ploy and more than a little misogyny in Coppini's characterization of her communication to him as displaying 'too great passion'.[15] In all probability, these efforts by the Yorkists only strengthened her resolve to mount an effective resistance.

Underestimation is more plainly evident in the Yorkist response to the threat that was forming in the north.[16] When York and Salisbury set out from London in early December to suppress rebellions, they were poorly accompanied. They may have thought that they could recruit as they went, as 'Bale's Chronicle' implies and as is suggested by the writs *de intendendo* to the sheriffs of Cambridge and Huntingdon, Nottingham and Derby, Lincoln, York, Cumberland, Westmorland and Northumberland that were appended to Salisbury's commission of 10 December to aid York's endeavor.[17] These counties all lay

---

[11] An undated circular letter from the queen may suggest the tenor of her demand, although it cannot be ascribed with certainty to this situation: 'We wol and charge you that all excusacions cessing and other occupacions y left, ye shape yow for to be with us in all haste possible for certeine causes that moven us, which shalbe declared unto yowe at yor coming' (BL, Add. MS 46,846, fol. 33).

[12] 'Gregory's Chron.', p. 210.

[13] The redating of one of the Paston letters supports an earlier starting point for Margaret's communications than is generally assumed (Davis, *PL*, II, pp. 216–17 and n. 12).

[14] Goodman, *Wars of the Roses*, p. 42, who accepts 'Gregory's' view that Lancastrian actions followed the settlement.

[15] 'Gregory's Chron.', p. 209; *CSP, Milan*, I, p. 38.

[16] Goodman, *Wars of the Roses*, pp. 42–3; Johnson, pp. 222–3; Griffiths, p. 870.

[17] Flenley ('Bale's Chron.'), p. 152; *CPR, 1452–61*, pp. 653–4. *Brut*, p. 530, and *English Chron.*, p. 106, say that York was named protector again; cf. *London Chrons.*, p. 106, *Great Chron.*, p. 193, and Stevenson,

along a possible route north or were in the 'target area'. If this was the case, their recruiting was not very successful.[18] Though the date of their departure is uncertain, it may have been linked to letters that the common council received from Margaret, Prince Edward and Jasper Tudor on the second.[19] The content of a pair of extant letters from the queen and prince to the City indicates that they were written between the settlement and York's death at Wakefield. Although their positive identification as two of the letters received by the council is not certain, it may be considered likely. The prince's letter begins with an assertion of York's malice, as demonstrated by his feigned loyalty and subsequent oathbreaking.[20] In pursuit of 'the destruccion of my lord and of my lady and the disheritying of us', York is charged with sowing rumors that the Lancastrians would assemble a 'grete numbre of straungeres' to despoil and rob the city and the king's true liegemen. The prince's shocked denial that he, 'rightfully and lynialy borne bidiscent of the blood roiall tenherite the premynence of this realme', could intend such a thing answers a further rumor that is left unacknowledged: the bastardy charge. The Lancastrians' purpose is 'thenlarging' (i.e. the freeing) of the king, and the city and all true subjects will be expected to help when the time comes. Again the prince promises that 'noone of you shalbe robbed, dispoiled nor wrongid by any persone that shall . . . come with us', under pain of the most severe punishment, and ends the letter with an appeal to protect the king from harm.[21]

Margaret's letter echoes the prince's themes of York's evil intentions and again promises that the city will not be harmed, but there are telling differences.[22] If these two letters are compared with the pair of letters written by Margaret and Henry in 1457 in support of John Hals,[23] similar observations apply. The seven-year-old prince's letter presents him as the active party capable of raising a military force and of coming to free the king. Margaret is only mentioned as a potential victim of the Yorkists' malice. In her letter, she and the prince together are the actors. By this time there can be no doubt that she was the person giving direction and that others were following her willingly. Yet she could only claim authority through association with her son. What the letter

II, ii, p. 774, which say that he was regent. Nothing in the parliament record supports either claim, though the sweeping powers he was given may have left such an impression.

[18] Johnson, p. 222.

[19] *London Chrons.*, p. 193, and *Great Chron.*, p. 193, say they left on the second; 'Benet's Chron.', p. 228, says it was the fifth; Flenley ('Bale's Chron.'), p. 151, and 'Gregory's Chron.', p. 210, the ninth. On 8 December York, Warwick, Salisbury and others received commissions to investigate treasons in the midlands and the northern counties (*CPR, 1452–61*, pp. 652–3). CLRO, Journal VI, fol. 279 (because of damage, accessible to the reader in Binder 4, photopage 425), for the letters.

[20] BL, MS Add. 48031A, fol. 31–31b; copied by Stow (BL, MS Harl. 543, fols 147b–148); published by Kekewich, et al., *Politics of Fifteenth-Century England*, pp. 142–3, and discussed by Watts in the same work, pp. 36–7.

[21] Some of these themes were probably repeated in a letter from the earl of Northumberland to the city in mid-December (CLRO, Journal VI, fol. 284). Flenley ('Bale's Chron.'), p. 152, and *English Chron.*, p. 108, also note the Lancastrians' claim that their intention was to free the king.

[22] BL, MS Add. 48031A, fol. 30b; Stow's copy in BL, MS Harl. 543, fol. 147; pub. in Kekewich, et al., *Politics of Fifteenth-Century England*, p. 142. I concur with Cron, 'Margaret of Anjou and the Lancastrian March on London', p. 593, in considering it to have been written before York's death.

[23] See above, pp. 64–5.

hints at would be graphically represented by the Lancastrian army itself, in which every man bore the prince's livery.[24]

At stake was the claim to legitimate authority. By insisting that Henry was a prisoner who needed rescuing, the Lancastrians could claim that the settlement was illicitly obtained and should not be obeyed. And, although Henry may not have been imprisoned in the strictest sense, certain aspects of his situation did lend themselves to this interpretation. On the other hand, parliament had given York the king's full power to put down insurrection, charging all to support him in his endeavors and making any who opposed him traitors.[25] To make good on this claim, he had to act quickly. The letters received in London may have encouraged York to resolve matters in the north before the queen was able to solicit real support from the Scots or the French. It may also be that the Yorkists simply did not believe that people would really throw in their lot with a fugitive queen and a small child on behalf of a puppet king; perhaps they expected some of the Lancastrian loyalty to evaporate as soon as they appeared on the scene.

In the event, matters took their own course. York and Salisbury found themselves confronted with a greater problem and a larger force than they had anticipated, faced by men who were prepared to use deceit and trickery and who likely believed themselves to be doing no worse than the Yorkists had done before. At Wakefield on 30 December, York's second son fell in battle; according to one source the duke was captured and mocked with a paper crown for his pretensions before he was killed. That night Salisbury was captured and killed, and the heads of all three were placed atop the gates of York.[26] A month later the Milanese ambassador to the French court remarked that York 'seem[ed] rather to have been slain out of hatred for having claimed the kingdom than anything else'.[27]

While the battle of Wakefield was being fought, Margaret was at Lincluden in Scotland seeking aid from Mary of Guelders, the widow of James II. The two women had some things in common: both were the mothers of young sons, and both found themselves in temporary positions of authority – Mary through the death of her husband and the establishment of a formal regency, and Margaret by default through her husband's captivity.[28] Of the two, Mary was in a better bargaining position, but Margaret's strength lay in the growing military power of her supporters in the north and in the knowledge that the disposition of the English crown would not be finally resolved without a further military confrontation.[29] She had already applied to Charles VII for safe conducts for herself and her son, but the French king's response was equivocal. Although he

---

[24] 'Gregory's Chron.', p. 212.

[25] RP, V, pp. 382–3.

[26] Reg. Whethamstede, I, p. 382; but cf. Stevenson, II, ii, p. 775; Brut, p. 531; 'Greory's Chron.', p. 210; Three Chrons., p. 76; 'Benet's Chron.', p. 228, whose tamer versions of York's demise seem more likely.

[27] CSP, Milan, I, p. 48.

[28] James III was born in May 1452. His custody and the government during his minority were given to his mother and the lords of her council upon his father's death (Macdougall, James III, pp. 51–2). Bishop James Kennedy, with whom Mary fell out over foreign policy, complained that she promoted faction – never admitting his own contribution to division – and may also have attempted to discredit her with rumors of sexual promiscuity (pp. 53, 54, 56).

[29] Ibid., pp. 57–9, argues that such realistic assessments of Lancastrian and Yorkist strength and a willingness to play one side against the other formed the basis for Mary's policy.

eventually did provide the safe conducts, he initially indicated that he would prefer Margaret not to use them. Fearing domestic repercussions that might lead to a civil war of his own, Charles would not commit himself to Margaret's cause, though he urged the Scots to give her all possible support.[30] The negotiations between Margaret and Mary of Guelders apparently included a proposal of marriage between Prince Edward and a sister of James III, though the surrender of Berwick does not appear to have been on the table at this time.[31] Their discussions were hurried to a conclusion by news of Wakefield.

Word of the Lancastrian victory at Wakefield probably took Margaret by surprise. Although she surely would have approved the outcome, she cannot take credit or blame for it. The Lancastrian decision to attack was made by commanders in the field – Somerset, Exeter, Northumberland and Andrew Trollope – who saw an opportunity and took it. Their victory strengthened Margaret's credibility and enabled her to reach an agreement of some sort with Mary of Guelders on 5 January. It also meant that she would have to act immediately to take advantage of the opportunity that it afforded. By 20 January she was at York, where her supporters promised to labor Henry to uphold the Lincluden agreement.[32] A proclamation was also issued in the names of the king, queen and prince to the county of York: since the queen and prince had been kept 'unrichtfully and unnaturally' from the king's presence, they were going to his relief, and they called on every loyal man to 'be redy in his best araye to avance uppon thaim to the same entente'.[33] Soon the Lancastrians were marching southward with a substantial army to confront their enemies and to effect Henry's rescue.[34] Margaret probably brought some Scottish soldiers with her from Lincluden,[35] but the need for haste suggests that they may have been fewer in number than later reports of her invading alien army made out. It may also be doubted that she would have desired a large Scottish presence at this time; her appeal to Brezé some months earlier reveals a keen awareness of the danger in associating herself with a foreign military intervention.[36] The *ad hoc* nature of the resulting campaign hurt Margaret's cause more than the actions of her enemies.

Moving in the dead of winter, it is likely that the army had difficulty finding

---

[30] Scofield, *Life and Reign of Edward IV*, I, pp. 114–16; Beaucourt, *Histoire de Charles VII*, VI, pp. 296–7, 311. Charles's son, Louis, with whom he was at odds, was a 'guest' at the court of Burgundy, whose duke hated Charles and had shown signs of favor towards the Yorkists. The Yorkists nonetheless took defensive measures against a possible French attack on the Isle of Wight (*CPR, 1452–61*, pp. 637, 638).

[31] Craigie, *Asloan Manuscript*, p. 230, for the marriage. Dunlop, *Life and Times of James Kennedy*, p. 216, for Berwick. Both Macdougall, *James III*, p. 58, and Nicholson, *Scotland*, p. 400, suggest that its cession became necessary when Henry and Margaret arrived in Scotland as refugees following the Lancastrian defeat at Towton.

[32] Basin, *Histoire*, IV, pp. 357–8. Its terms are not stated. Twelve lords, including two bishops, signed. The document has recently been discussed and reprinted from the original (BN, MS fr. 20488, fol. 23) by Hicks, 'A Minute of the Lancastrian Council'.

[33] BN, MS latin 11892, fol. 187.

[34] 'Gregory's Chron.', pp. 210, 212, says that 15,000 assembled at Hull before Wakefield, but that only 5,000 were with the queen at Second St Albans; 'Benet's Chron.', p. 228, says that 20,000 were at Wakefield. Stevenson, II, ii, p. 776, in an excess of enthusiasm gives the Lancastrians 80,000. *Brut*, p. 531; *English Chron.*, p. 107, simply remark its size.

[35] *Three Chrons.*, p. 155.

[36] Basin, *Histoire*, IV, ed. by Quicherat, pp. 358–60; see above, p. 174.

provisions, and the Yorkists made efforts to cut off any supplies that it might receive from the south.[37] Food shortage may explain some of the pillaging that took place. The contemporary Auchinleck Chronicle indicates that Margaret had sought provisioning from the Scots,[38] but the need to strike quickly may have sent her army forward before these arrangements were effectively in place. Significantly, on the day following the battle at St Albans the queen sent to London to obtain victuals.[39] It is clear, moreover, that the Yorkists were also troubled by provisioning difficulties that winter. An Italian source reported that they suffered defeat at Wakefield because they had 'allowed a large part of [their] force to go pillaging and searching for victuals', while another wrote that Warwick's army suffered desertions before the encounter at St Albans because of lack of food.[40] Pillage was a fact of life and a perennial fear when armies were on the move, but in conditions of civil war such behavior only alienated potential support. It was in each side's interest to try to control its troops or to minimize their damage, while at the same time painting its opponent's activities in the blackest shade possible.[41] There can be little doubt that Margaret's army behaved badly and that she and her commanders were unwilling or unable to enforce discipline. The pillaging began as early as 12 January, at Beverley in Yorkshire,[42] and it continued all the way south to St Albans.[43] Such behavior played upon natural fears and confirmed the Yorkists' dire predictions;[44] certainly, tales of Lancastrian atrocities lost nothing in the telling.

At this time, another element appeared in the rumor mix: not only was an army running amuck and bearing down on London, but it was an army made up specifically of northerners – of strangers and barbarians. Thus, on 23 January, Clement Paston wrote: 'the pepill in the northe robbe and styll, and ben apoyntyd to pill all thys cwntre, and gyffe a way menys goods and lufflods in all the sowthe cwntre'.[45] This theme reached its apogee in Whethamstede's *Register*, where the entire conflict from Wakefield to the Lancastrian withdrawal after Second St Albans was depicted as a monumental confrontation between north and south in which the northerners represented the forces of evil and impiety.[46] Warwick and the Yorkist government deliberately stoked such fears of

[37] Goodman, *Wars of the Roses*, p. 156. Both Norfolk and Cambridgeshire were suspected of shipping food to the 'rebels' (*CPR, 1452–61*, pp. 658, 659).
[38] Craigie, *Asloan Manuscript*, I, p. 230: 'help and suple'.
[39] *Brut*, p. 531.
[40] *CSP, Milan*, I, pp. 42, 54.
[41] Goodman, *Wars of the Roses*, pp. 214–15, discusses this phenomenon and its particular embodiment in 1460–61.
[42] Ibid., p. 45. This may suggest yet another reason to march south as soon as possible: if the assembled force was becoming unruly, its leaders may have thought better to give it something to do than to allow it to disintegrate.
[43] 'Benet's Chron.', p. 229; *English Chron.*, 107; *Three Chrons.*, pp. 76, 155.
[44] Flenley ('Bale's Chron.'), pp. 152–3, retrospectively dismissed Lancastrian assertions that they intended to rescue the king in the light of these depredations.
[45] Gairdner, *PL*, III, p. 250. See also *Croyland Chron.*, pp. 421–2: 'the northmen . . . in the impulse of their fury attempted to overrun the whole of England'; and *Three Chrons.*, p. 155, which describes a Lancastrian army made up of Scots, Welsh, 'et aliorum alienigenarum et Northenmen' ('and of other foreign-born and northerners').
[46] *Reg. Whethamstede*, I, pp. 386, 388–401: e.g. p. 400 – 'Gens Boreae, gens nequitiae, gens abs[que] pietate' ('People of the north, people of wickedness, people without piety'). Pollard, *North-Eastern*

'mysruled and outerageous people in the north parties . . . comyng toward thees parties to the destruccion therof . . . and subversion of alle our lande' at the end of January to aid in raising a defensive force.[47] The references to misrule, malice and wanton destruction, though usually understood as regional bias, can also be read within a gendered context. The reversal of right order implicit in female leadership, the ill will and anger believed to characterize the transgressive woman: all are supported by the same complaints that were directed against northern barbarians. Combined by rhetoric, gender and regional bias made a natural-seeming and very potent mixture.

Although it may be reasonable to assume that the bulk of Margaret's army was composed of northerners, characterizing it as a 'northern army' is misleading insofar as it imposes a false geographical limitation on her support. In the first place, it must be recalled that Somerset and Devon had been told to raise and bring men north, and one writer at least believed that they arrived at the rendezvous with many men from the western parts.[48] And then there were Margaret's chief officers, who were also to raise support.[49] Whatever numbers they raised could not all have been northerners, for most of Margaret's holdings were in the midlands. Unless these people all evaporated into thin air, they were likely to have still been with the army that marched south. The evidence of East Anglian support for Margaret around the time parliament met suggests that she may have picked up some people along her route, though the total number of her force probably decreased.[50] The 'Short English Chronicle' reports that after Wakefield 'the quene reysed all the northe *and all other pepull by the wey*, compelled, dispoyled, rubbed, and destroyed all maner of cattell, vetayll, and riches to Seint Albones'.[51] Indeed, there is considerable evidence of sympathy for the queen in the midlands and the south. From mid-January the patent rolls show substantial Yorkist concern about unlawful gatherings, impeding the 'king's lieges' from assembling and the like.[52] Though some troublemaking was probably opportunistic, the overall impression is of insecurity regarding people's loyalties.

This impression is strengthened by Warwick's eagerness to see the legate Coppini receive promotion to the rank of cardinal – and validation of his legatine authority. The campaign for Coppini's elevation had begun by early August. Soon after Wakefield, if not before, the Lancastrians 'had put about the report that he was not a legate and [that] the pope had recalled him and was displeased about the things which had happened through his efforts'.[53] On 11 January the earl dispatched letters to Pope Pius II and the duke of Milan

England, p. 25, considers that northeasterners acquired a 'fearful reputation' in the later fifteenth century because of the depredations of Margaret's army.

[47] PPC, VI, pp. 307–10.
[48] Stevenson, II, ii, pp. 774–5; cf. *English Chron.*, p. 106, which says they raised 800 men. Waurin, *Croniques*, p. 325, has her raising all the west and Cornwall.
[49] 'Gregory's Chron.', p. 210, implies that these people, along with Somerset's and Devon's troops, contributed substantially to the 15,000 said to be at Hull.
[50] Goodman, *Wars of the Roses*, p. 47, suggests that the army's strength diminished as it moved south.
[51] *Three Chrons.*, p. 76, emphasis added. The allusion to Margaret's support is often overlooked amid the more interesting details of pillage.
[52] Goodman, *Wars of the Roses*, pp. 44–5; CPR, *1452–61*, pp. 655–9.
[53] CSP, Milan, I, p. 42.

pressing the importance of Coppini's advancement to the Yorkist cause, for 'the people will then see that our adversaries, who daily spread lying reports, are false and not true men'.[54] This was, of course, the essence of the debate: Margaret's propaganda, together with the Lancastrian victory at Wakefield, had renewed the question of who the king's true men really were. The pope's promotion of Coppini, had it occurred, would have provided timely reassurance that he approved the legate's doings and, by extension, that it was the Yorkists who stood on the side of righteousness, while the queen and her people were traitors and rebels.[55]

Coppini himself was genuinely terrified of what might befall him if the Lancastrian offensive proved successful, though he was still not above double-dealing. On 9 January he wrote to Lorenzo de Florencia, his friar and subordinate, who was then with the queen. Having first directed the friar to declare that he had excommunicated no one (though he as much as admitted that there had been some little problem with burials following Northampton because people believed the dead to be excommunicate), he insisted on his love and reverence for the queen, for whose 'wellbeing [he was] ready to suffer anything in this world'. Coppini then offered 'an honourable peace' to the queen and the lords about her, though it appears that he expected his man to speak with the lords only and to appeal specifically to their interests. They were to know that 'the pope [had] sent [him] authority and power to raise up and defend the cross after the manner of a true legate *de latere*' and that they should 'see to it that they are not criminals and rebels, for the retribution of Justice is made ready against them'. Although Coppini may have been alluding to his hoped-for cardinalship, it seems more likely that he was insinuating his ability in the present circumstances to excommunicate, for he emphasized that if they disregarded the pope's – and, by extension, *his* – authority, they would not be 'true Christians'. He insisted, further, that Henry favored the Yorkists, that it was the king's wish to see peace made and that the lords should heed his offer since it would be 'to their honor and advantage'. Unfortunately, Coppini dared not commit his conditions to writing – nor, apparently, to the bearer of his letter – for he indicated that Lorenzo de Florencia should come to him to see them.[56] On the same day he also wrote to Francesco Sforza, duke of Milan, to say that letters and commissions had been drawn up to obtain a settlement with the Lancastrians, but that his need for papal support was desperate if the project was to succeed.[57] Neither the Lancastrians nor the pope responded to Coppini, and he escaped to Holland on 10 February.[58]

---

[54] Letter to Pius II, *CSP, Venice*, I, p. 96; cf. *CSP, Milan*, I, p. 44. In this instance the former translation is preferable since the latter appears to drop part of this sentence. In all other respects they are nearly identical. The letter to Francesco Sforza is on p. 97 (in English translation) and pp. 43–4 (in Latin) of these calendars respectively.

[55] According to the terms of the parliamentary settlement, the men who attacked York at Wakefield were guilty of treason.

[56] *CSP, Milan*, I, pp. 37–41.

[57] Ibid., pp. 41–2.

[58] Ibid., p. 53. Somewhat later, Camulio heard that he had promised Warwick to excommunicate the Lancastrians and bless the Yorkists, but that 'seeing the bad weather, and the queen's power, and not feeling well, he did not go' (ibid., p. 60). As there seems to have been no falling out between Coppini and the Yorkists, the story may be doubted, though it may well describe the legate's frame of mind.

On 17 February two armies met for the second time at St Albans. On this occasion a combination of surprise, clever strategy and plain tenacity gave the victory to the Lancastrians. Warwick's army collapsed and fled.[59] Margaret's whereabouts during the battle are uncertain. Since she was present at no other pitched battle during the Wars of the Roses, it is reasonable to assume that she and her son were in some safe place a few miles from the field. Nevertheless, a single source gives her a more prominent role. If Prospero di Camulio's second or third hand account can be believed, she was at one point in the thick of things in the middle of town.[60] Since no English source accords her any active part in the battle itself, her presence seems doubtful.

In contrast, Henry is unanimously represented as a passive bystander. The significance of his passivity merits further consideration rather than dismissal as a symptom of inanity. The linkage of Henry's lack of spirit and failure to encourage 'his' troops with sympathy for his wife's side permits of a subversive interpretation.[61] It is difficult to see how he could have put up an active resistance without inviting his own death.

The reunion of king and queen brought an end to Margaret's quasi-independence. With the 'freeing' of the king, she had accomplished her declared objective. The question was: what next? As had happened in 1456 with the end of York's second protectorate, Margaret found herself without an acknowledged position to step into. Although she had openly assumed leadership during the last months, it had always been exercised in the king's behalf or in the interest of her son. Now that Henry had been restored to his rightful authority – to use the terms in which Margaret's campaign had been presented – it was incongruous for her to lead. So again she stepped back.

Shortly thereafter, the king knighted his son, and the prince in turn conferred knighthoods on thirty men.[62] These ceremonial acts, grounded in notions of masculinity and male power, serve to illustrate and in some sense symbolize the return to a masculine order based on male authority. Such an order is also exemplified in the judgments passed by Prince Edward on Lord Bonville and Sir Thomas Kyriell, who had been taken prisoner during the battle.[63] Here again we see the performance of a male ritual involving the reassertion of order in the wake of male combat. Whether Margaret desired these deaths or not, she could not authorize them.[64]

---

[59] See Goodman, *Wars of the Roses*, pp. 45–8, for an account of the battle. York's eldest son, Edward, was not with Warwick but in the Welsh marches where his own army had defeated a Lancastrian force led by the earls of Pembroke and Wiltshire at Mortimer's Cross on 2 or 3 February.

[60] *CSP, Milan*, I, p. 54: 'The Duke of Somerset after midday came with 30,000 horse to scent out the Earl of Warwick and the king's forces and wore them down with his attack, and the Earl of Warwick decided to quit the field, and to break through against them. Accordingly . . . he pushed through right into Albano, where the queen was with 30,000 men. The earl, seeing himself alone and the day far spent, returned to camp, closely pressed by . . . Somerset.' The numbers, if nothing more, must be regarded as suspect.

[61] *Reg. Whethamstede*, I, p. 392. Goodman, *Wars of the Roses*, pp. 119–20, notes the subversive potential in the situation.

[62] 'Gregory's Chron.', p. 214; Stevenson, II, ii, p. 776; *London Chrons.*, p. 173; *Great Chron.*, p. 194.

[63] *Brut*, p. 602; 'Gregory's Chron.', p. 212.

[64] *English Chron.*, p. 108, reports that the queen, the duke of Exeter and the earl of Devon called for their executions. The chancellor, George Neville – certainly an interested party – later merely wrote that they

Yet her own leadership could not be cleanly set aside. The 'restoration' of a king who had never been a very satisfactory leader and who had most recently been a puppet was not easily accomplished. The result was a certain confusion over who was actually in charge, which worked against both Henry and Margaret. Such confusion can best be seen in the apppointment of a women's delegation to negotiate for London. The incident also serves to highlight some of the difficulties facing the Lancastrians, which help to account for their disastrous withdrawal.

In the aftermath of battle, it was strategically important for the Lancastrians to obtain London's submission. At the same time, as a practical matter, they needed food. On the day after the battle they sent to London for victuals.[65] The common council discussed this request on the nineteenth and agreed to send food at their cost. The council also decided to send the duchess of Bedford, the duchess of Buckingham and Lady Scales, along with other representatives, to the king, queen and prince to explain the City's position and to negotiate.[66] It is significant that women – moreover, these women – were sent as negotiators. Both Jacquetta, the dowager duchess of Bedford, and Ismania, Lady Scales, had been among the women who had escorted Margaret from France, and Lady Scales had remained in her household as a personal attendant.[67] All three ladies had been recipients of New Year's gifts at various times,[68] and Anne, duchess of Buckingham, had stood godmother to Prince Edward. Though the personal relationships that existed between Margaret and these women are difficult to assess, it is apparent that the mayor and aldermen believed that they would be received with trust and favor. Their presence in the delegation and, it seems, their selection to be in it ahead of anyone else demonstrate the City's regard for Margaret's present power. Although the king was still the king, and the Lancastrians' – and Margaret's – position was that he had been 'rescued and restored', she was the person with whom the City ultimately had to deal.

A letter from London of the same date reports that the mayor sent to the king and queen 'it is supposed to offer obedience, provided they were assured that they would not be plundered or suffer violence'. The writer also observed that the gates were well guarded and that people were staying close to home. Since

---

had been taken and beheaded (*CSP, Milan*, I, p. 61). Since he disparagingly referred to Margaret in the same letter, it seems strange that he would let pass an opportunity to cast blame on her. Sir John Neville, Lord Berners and Sir Thomas Charlton were also taken prisoner, but were conveyed to York by the Lancastrians and placed in the mayor's custody (ibid.; *Brut*, p. 602; *English Chron.*, p. 108). Why they should have been treated differently is not clear, but their survival argues against using the Bonville/Kyriell executions as evidence of Margaret's bloodthirstiness (cf. Wolffe, p. 329).

[65] *Brut*, p. 531, says that this occurred on Ash Wednesday, which would have been 18 February. 'Gregory's Chron.', p. 214; *London Chrons.*, p. 173; *Great Chron.*, p. 194; Stevenson, II, ii, p. 777, also note their attempt to obtain food. 'Benet's Chron.', p. 229, says that they sent to the city for money – which could also be used to obtain provisions. The Journal entries for the next week and several contemporary letters provide a clearer sense of chronology than do most of the chronicles. In reconstructing a timeline, I have relied on them and fitted in material from the chronicles where it appears to correspond.

[66] CLRO, Journal VI, fol. 10 (photopage 454).

[67] Myers, 'Household of Queen Margaret', p. 404. The duchess of Bedford had married Richard Woodville, Lord Rivers. Their eldest daughter Elizabeth joined Margaret's household and would later marry Edward IV.

[68] Myers, 'Jewels', pp. 124, n. 6; 125.

'the queen and prince [had] not descended in fury with their troops . . . we are all hoping that . . . the gates may be opened to them upon a good composition'. Less optimistically, however, the writer believed that 'the least lack of control would ruin everything'.[69]

That, in fact, appears to be what happened. A letter of 22 February recounts the sequel.[70] The delegation returned on Friday the twentieth with word that 'the king and queen had no mind to pillage the chief city . . . and so they promised; but at the same time they did not mean that they would not punish the evildoers'. A proclamation was then issued to keep the peace, 'so that the king and his forces might enter'. Within the hour, however, confusion erupted in response to wild rumors that 'York [sic] with 60,000 Irish and March [York's son Edward] with 40,000 Welsh' were on their way. Since the city already went in terror of northerners, it is not clear how the approach of these other 'strangers' was supposed to help; it does not seem reasonable. But perhaps one ought not to expect reason and rationality when panic sets in. A bit farther on the letter indicates that people were also disturbed by the beheadings of Bonville and Kyriell.[71] The mob set up a brewer as their leader and tried to get the gate keys from the mayor. 'That day this place was in an uproar', the writer declared, 'so that I was never more afraid than then that everything would be at hazard.' Separate confirmation and elaboration of the disturbances are to be found in the *Annales* of pseudo-Worcester, which reports that early on Friday the commons destroyed carts with food bound for the queen's embassy at Barnet and also attacked Sir Baldwin Fulford and Sir Alexander Hody of her party, who were at Westminster with many armed men.[72]

Once the mayor and council managed to regain control, they tried a different strategy. On the twenty-first they agreed to send a delegation to Barnet to meet with Sir Edmund Hampden, Sir John Heron and Sir Robert Whittingham to arrange for their entry with 400 men into the city 'without the disturbance or slander of anyone'.[73] The next day they again agreed to the entry of the three knights as before and issued a proclamation throughout the city in that regard.[74] The letter of the twenty-second elaborates upon this picture by noting that the same ladies were to be included in the delegation and that four [sic] knights 'in whom the king and queen had perfect trust' were to be brought back to reach an

[69] *CSP, Milan*, I, p. 49.
[70] Ibid., p. 50. Because it provides such a feel for what was happening, I have quoted it at length.
[71] Ibid., p. 51.
[72] Stevenson, II, ii, p. 777. See also 'Gregory's Chron.', pp. 214–15, for an idiosyncratic account of these same events that is less clear about the time frame. *London Chrons.*, p. 173, and *Great Chron.*, p. 194, describe what appear to be two separate events. One following the 'ladies' embassy', which began when Lancastrian foreriders were denied entry to the city, involved some robberies at Westminster, and ended with several of them killed by the citizens at Cripplegate; and a second occurred apparently some days later, when food-laden carts were stopped at Cripplegate. By comparison, the letters report no incidence of violence prior to Friday.
[73] CLRO, Journal VI, fol. 10b (photopage 455). Hampden and Whittingham had ties to the queen. The former was Prince Edward's chamberlain; the latter was the prince's receiver-general and Margaret's keeper of her great wardrobe (Wedgwood, *Biographies*, pp. 413–14; *CPR, 1452–61*, pp. 323, 429). Both would become members of her court-in-exile. Heron was constable of Bamburgh Castle (ibid., p. 512). All three had been named to various commissions of June 1460 to investigate treasons and to arrest Yorkist supporters in the midlands and southern counties (ibid., pp. 613–14).
[74] CLRO, Journal VI, fol. 10b (photopage 455).

accord whereby 'the king, queen, prince and all the nobles with their leaders [might enter the city] without the body of the army'. The writer reports that the delegation set out 'this morning' (i.e. Sunday, the twenty-second) and that everything was quiet, the mayor and sheriffs and their men – who were the only ones armed – keeping good order. In closing, he notes that some of the Lancastrians' prisoners had been spared for one reason or another, the most immediately relevant being 'to remove misgivings' caused by the previous executions, and that 'the queen has withdrawn a part of her army to Dunstable'.[75] The movement of troops was probably dictated by logistics: it was difficult in the best of circumstances to keep and feed a large number of people in one place. Continued pillage was not in Margaret's interest as it would only antagonize more people and make access to London more difficult. Its continuation suggests that it was prompted by food shortage rather than by Margaret's vengefulness, though the latter made good propaganda.[76] The move to Dunstable may have been taken to mitigate its effects and to decrease the threat to London, which she had promised not to harm.[77]

The council's proclamation seems to have been framed in part to reassure the City of the queen's good will as well as to keep the peace, but its assertion that Margaret was acting as an intercessor only muddied the water as to who was in charge. It begins with an explanation: the knights Hampden, Heron and Whittingham and the 400 with them were sent by the king and queen on the advice of the king's council to learn the City's disposition. The citizens are next assured that the queen's mediation and the advice of the council will move the king to preserve the city and its inhabitants, rich and poor alike. They are therefore ordered not to cause any trouble for the knights, their servants and fellowships, on pain of death and forfeiture.[78] In this document the formal representation of Margaret as mediator sits uneasily with the understanding that *both* king and queen are sending the delegation and that it will be reporting back to *both* of them. The council's power, too, is hazy. To whom is it really answerable?

A final letter of 23 February provides a cryptic ending to what went wrong. The night before, a certain number of 'king's men' came to Aldgate and were denied entry. They remained outside all night (one suspects that a curfew was in place) since the mayor would 'never consent to their coming in'. The writer adds ominously that 'it seems that they were of the opposite party'. That day, when the knights coming from the queen were supposed to enter, they heard about the others and 'drew back towards the king and queen', only sending two esquires in to fetch the embassy, probably those persons whom they had dealt with before. The letter closes on a grim note, which may help to sort out what was going on:

---

[75] *CSP, Milan*, I, pp. 50–1.

[76] *Three Chrons.*, p. 172; 'Benet's Chron.', p. 229; *Reg. Whethamstede*, I, p. 394.

[77] Stevenson, II, ii, p. 776; 'Gregory's Chron.', p. 214.

[78] CLRO, Journal VI, fol. 35b (photopage 457). Although the proclamation is recorded under the date of 25 February, its content links it to the arrangements discussed in council on the twenty-first and twenty-second, while the conditions in the city on the twenty-second suggest that it had been publicized and was being enforced. The original folio appears to have been damaged along the right side, and the text ends in the middle of a sentence with the rest cut off.

I do not like this; God grant that both sides may so control themselves that men may not be inflamed more than they are already. On the other hand they say that Warwick and the Duke of Norfolk have been taken and are in the hands of the king and queen . . . I do not know what to believe.[79]

Three questions must be asked. Who were these 'king's men', and what is meant by 'opposite party'? And what was the alternative to the rumor that Warwick was captured? Since the writer freely refers to the king and queen and their people on other occasions, there would seem to be no need to hedge. Nor does it make sense to speak of the king and queen as 'opposites' after their reunion. As a suggestion, then, which seems inescapable: these men were Yorkists or Yorkist sympathizers, who probably knew that Warwick and March were only a couple of days away from London. They would have been few, and they were allowed inside to share their news once the gates were unlocked in the morning.

Margaret's failure to capitalize on her victory at St Albans can be explained in a number of ways. The resistance of London, the approach of a new Yorkist force, her alliance with a northern regional interest, the debilitating influence of Henry's personality – all can be used to shed light on Margaret's dilemma.[80] Opinion in London was undeniably divided between a council that was ready to deal with whoever currently held sway in an effort to save the city's skin and a populace who feared that their individual skins might still be on the line if the deal fell through. Their fear of northerners and other barbarians was genuine, and it was genuinely encouraged; the pillage done by Margaret's army was real, and behind it lay the accounts of what had happened at Wakefield. Persons like Coppini, who saw a personal threat in the queen's advance, fled.[81]

Nevertheless, one plain fact emerges in all the accounts of what happened between the second battle of St Albans and Margaret's withdrawal to the north: she never got the money and supplies that she had requested. Without provision and not knowing how many she would have to face, she could not fight another battle. It was as simple as that. Although it is possible that Margaret's army could have 'taken' London in the immediate aftermath of St Albans or that she could have forced its capitulation through fear, she had promised the City its safety. To 'take' it would have been to lose it utterly. Each time she made that promise, it became harder to renege on it.[82] So, in the end, she was forced to withdraw to await another day. Although this was a setback, she probably did not regard it as the end. Henry was at her side; he still was king. Perhaps she thought ahead to obtaining reinforcements. Perhaps she thought that London would remember how she had stayed her hand. Meanwhile, her army moved north. Perhaps because it was still hungry, it continued to pillage as it went.[83]

---

[79] CSP, Milan, I, p. 51.

[80] See, e.g., Bagley, Margaret of Anjou, p. 115; Griffiths, p. 874; Goodman, Wars of the Roses, p. 48; Watts, pp. 360–2; Wolffe, p. 329, for various emphases and combinations of these factors.

[81] For others who fled, including the younger sons of York, who were sent to Utrecht by their mother, see London Chrons., p. 174; Great Chron., p. 195; English Chron., p. 109.

[82] Goodman, Wars of the Roses, p. 48, notes that the Lancastrians, for whatever reason, were more interested in obtaining food than in occupying the city.

[83] English Chron., p. 109, says that the areas the army passed through had almost no beasts left for spring plowing; some of them may have been eaten.

The Yorkists entered London on 26 or 27 February.[84] With Lancaster in retreat, a past record of having given aid and succor and no possibility of further battle for the moment, there was no reason for the City to keep them out. Relief was genuine. In contrast to Henry, York's heir, Edward, was 'kingly': a warrior tested in battle, a victor. It could be argued, too, that Henry had broken faith with the oaths sworn in parliament, thus freeing the Yorkists from their oaths.[85] More practically, the Yorkists had just lost a king, and without a king to call their own their lives could not be guaranteed.[86] The convergence of these three points led to an obvious conclusion. On 1 March, Edward's title was recognized by well-orchestrated acclamation, and on the fourth his accession was formally celebrated.[87]

But gaining a crown is one thing, and holding it another, especially when the new king has been installed by a minority faction.[88] Edward moved quickly and decisively. Obtaining funds from London and gathering more men, he set out north on Margaret's trail.[89] As the Lancastrians moved northward and allegations of their pillage and rapine began to seem less threatening, charges regarding the queen's disorderly conduct once more came to the forefront.[90] First, it was reported that she and the duke of Somerset had persuaded Henry to abdicate in favor of the prince and then had left him behind. Soon after, it was added that Margaret had poisoned Henry and that she would 'unite with' Somerset.[91] A little later came the rumor that Henry had believed the prince to be the son of the Holy Spirit.[92] Taken together, all of these tales labeled Margaret as a malicious woman, while implying that the remaining Lancastrian enterprise was illicit and contrary to divinely established order and denying the possibility of a legitimate dynastic succession.

Edward's army caught the Lancastrians at Towton, a little southwest of York. On 29 March, in a battle that would be remembered for its ferocity, Margaret's army was shattered.[93] If a later report can be believed, it had carried the queen's

---

[84] The latter seems the more likely. The common council received letters on Thursday the twenty-sixth concerning the Yorkists' arrival (CLRO, Journal VI, fol. 13 [photopage 458]), and a letter from London of 4 March describes their entry on Friday (CSP, Milan, I, p. 54). Cf. Armstrong, 'Inauguration Ceremonies', p. 55, n. 2. It is possible that they arrived on the twenty-sixth, but made a formal entry on the twenty-seventh.

[85] This was the formal charge made in Edward IV's first parliament as justification for Henry's attainder (RP, V, pp. 465–7).

[86] Scofield, Life and Reign of Edward IV, I, p. 149; Ross, Edward IV, pp. 32–3.

[87] Armstrong, 'Inauguration Ceremonies', pp. 55–63.

[88] Ibid., p. 56; Storey, p. 193; Wolffe, p. 330.

[89] Barron, 'London and the Crown', p. 97, argues that London's loans to the Yorkists were motivated more by self-interest and survival than by partisanship. Her Table 2 (pp. 103–4) and nn. 66–7 (p. 107) show two major clusters of loans: between 4 and 13 July and a longer period from shortly after Wakefield through Edward's victory at Towton. These were times of great uncertainty and anxiety, when the very immediate dynamics of power and fear determined London's choices.

[90] The Lancastrians had in the meantime begun to spread rumors of the Yorkists' intended depredations (Scofield, Life and Reign of Edward IV, I, p. 160).

[91] CSP, Milan, I, pp. 55, 58. English Chron., p. 75, would later revive the notion of Margaret as a poisoner with its report of the earl of Devon's death at Abingdon Abbey in February 1458, 'poisoned, as men said, and being there at that time with queen Margaret'. There is no reason to believe this slander.

[92] CSP, Milan, I, p. 58.

[93] Wolffe, p. 331, observes that 'three-quarters of the surviving peerage . . . were engaged, most of them on the Lancastrian side'. See also Richmond, 'Nobility and Wars of the Roses', pp. 76–7, for charts showing individual noble involvement on both sides in the battles of 1459–61.

banners bearing the inscription: 'Judica me deus discerne causam meam de gente non sancta.'[94] If it did, the appeal would undoubtedly have held great meaning for Margaret going into the battle, but, true or false, allusions to God's judgment were more useful to the Yorkists in its aftermath. Margaret, Henry and their son were in York when Towton was fought. Upon learning of its outcome, they managed to escape to Scotland.[95]

Thus, Henry's deposition was ultimately guaranteed by force of arms. Nevertheless, it is difficult to see how Margaret would have managed politically if he had continued as king. Possession of his person brought an end to her *de facto* independence as a political actor. Once more she was obliged to wear the mask and to claim power only through association with his authority. It was a mask that she seems to have worn comfortably and that she never entirely shed. In Henry's case, however, the reverse was true. He had not been an able king, but it had been in the nature of things to believe in his authority as king, even when his own meaningful exercise of it had been sadly lacking. The Yorkist settlement of 1460, forced upon a captive king, tore off the mask. Restored to Margaret, but revealed as a pawn, he could no longer support the arrangement that had been built up prior to Northampton. As the king's wife, without any claim of her own to political authority, her political fate was bound to his. When the king fell, the queen, his wife, fell with him.

Margaret's subsequent treatment and attainder by the Yorkist's first parliament differed from Henry's. As its very first item of business, it commended Edward IV for proceeding against 'Margarete late called Quene of England, *hir* sone Edward' and others, who had intended the destruction of the realm with the aid of northerners, along with enemy Scots and French.[96] Next came Henry's attainder. He was charged with dissimulation in accepting the settlement and with deliberately breaking his oath to the Yorkists, in particular in his adherence to Margaret and in his assenting to her activities.[97] Margaret was then convicted of the 'transgressions and offences aforespecified, committed ayenst her feith and Liegeaunce to . . . oure Soverayne and Liege Lord Kyng Edward' and attainted.[98] In this way, while acknowledging her status as the Yorkists' leading adversary, the language of the charges depicted Margaret, who had taken no oaths, as a 'contrary' woman, guilty of sexual transgression and of faithless – female? – mutability.

---

[94] Goodman, *Wars of the Roses*, pp. 50–2; *CSP, Milan*, I, p. 73: 'Judge me, God, [and] distinguish my cause from [that of] unholy people.'

[95] 'Benet's Chron.', p. 230; 'Gregory's Chron.', p. 217; *London Chrons.*, p. 175.

[96] *RP*, V, p. 462, emphasis added.

[97] Ibid., pp. 463–7, 476–8.

[98] Ibid., p. 479.

Conclusion: Endings

Aftermath

IN RETROSPECT, the battle of Towton brought an end to Henry VI's reign and marked the beginning of a new dynasty. Beaten, but not yet broken, Margaret would continue her efforts to win back the crown for another ten years. Although at first the Lancastrians seemed to pose a credible threat to Edward IV's new reign, it is evident that without tenure of the crown they had become bargaining counters in the greater game of international politics. Margaret's efforts gained limited practical support and only short-lived success. Henry's capture in 1465 brought a hiatus to the game. Only domestic troubles in England marked by the falling out between Edward IV and his erstwhile mentor, Warwick, made it possible for Margaret to try again. Henry's brief 'readeption' ended in two Yorkist military victories, his son's death and his own.

Not long after Towton it was predicted that 'fresh disturbances [would] arise' and that the people would support Henry and Margaret if they were not captured.[1] It may be for that very reason that rumors circulated during the weeks following the battle that they *had* been captured.[2] Because Yorkist rule remained insecure it was necessary to keep reminding people of why it was a good thing. To this end a series of propaganda poems continued to publicize Edward IV's virtues while condemning Lancastrian faults. Thus, within a year of Henry's deposition, one verse again rehearsed northern intentions 'to stroy the sowthe cuntre' had Edward not prevented it, while another proclaimed that he was 'conseived in wedlock, and comyn of blode ryall', inviting comparison with the allegations of Prince Edward of Lancaster's bastardy.[3] In 1462 a second poem recalled that Richard II's deposition by 'unrightful heyres' had started all the troubles. Although it also condemned Henry for his foolishness, its real venom was reserved for Margaret, whose efforts at that time to obtain continental support helped to feed the invasion rumors.

> Moreovyr it ys Right a gret abusion,
> A woman of a land to be a Regent –
> Qwene margrete I mene, that ever hath ment
> To gouerne all engeland with might and poure,
> And to destroye the Ryght lyne was here entent . . .

---

[1] *CSP, Milan*, I, p. 74. Camulio believed that the English would not be disinclined towards further bloodshed since they saw it as a means of getting rid of more of the nobility! Incipient 'class' consciousness aside, he also seems to imply that the Lancastrians were not yet bereft of domestic support.

[2] Ibid., pp. 66, 72, 73, 76, 89.

[3] Robbins, *Historical Poems*, pp. 216, 219 and 380, n. 35.

And now sche ne rought, so that sche myght attayne,
Though all engeland were brought to confusion;
Sche and here wykked affynite certayne
Entende uttyrly to destroy thys regioun;
ffor with theym ys but Deth and distruccioun,
Robbberye and vengeaunce with all Rygour.[4]

In 1464, by which time the Yorkist victory had begun to seem more secure, she
was again blamed for Lancaster's failure as Henry supposedly lamented:

I weddyd a wyf at my devyse,
That was the cause of all my mon.

Thyll her intente seyd I euer naye;
Ther-for I morne and no thynge am mery.[5]

The image of Margaret that these poems projected was the familiar one of
stereotype: of an angry woman driven by malice, spreading sorrow, disorder and
confusion in her wake.

After Towton, when the Lancastrian refugees arrived in Scotland in April
1461, their bargaining position was much diminished. In order to obtain aid
and safe haven Henry ceded Berwick to the Scots on 25 April and agreed to
surrender Carlisle if it could be taken.[6] Berwick had long been contested
territory, its possession a matter of pride and 'face' to both parties. Its cession
bought a limited Scottish cooperation,[7] but further damaged Henry's reputation in England. Meanwhile, Margaret's appeal for French aid was left in limbo
by the death of Charles VII on 22 July. His successor, Louis XI, was reluctant to
commit to any adventure whose benefits to him were uncertain. On 30 August
two of her emissaries to the French court, Robert, Lord Hungerford, and
Robert Whittingham, wrote to her in Scotland from Dieppe, reporting that
they were presently in custody but expected to be taken to the new king shortly.
They warned the queen that neither she, nor the prince nor King Henry should
attempt to cross the sea, which was patrolled by Yorkist ships, except as a last
resort. Their promise to come to her as soon as they had regained their
freedom

without deth take us by the wey, the which we trust he woll not, till we see the
Kyng and you peissible ayene in your Reame; the which we besech God soon to
see, and to send you that your Highnes desireth,[8]

---

[4] Ibid., p. 224.
[5] Ibid., p. 197.
[6] Griffiths, p. 886; Macdougall, *James III*, p. 58, suggests that Berwick may already have been under Scottish attack and indefensible when it was ceded. An attempt on Carlisle in May failed (Gairdner, *PL*, III, p. 276).
[7] Reports reached Bruges by June that negotiations were moving ahead for a marriage alliance between Prince Edward and James III's sister (*CSP, Milan*, I, pp. 93, 98).
[8] Gairdner, *PL*, III, pp. 306–7. Their letter appears to have been intercepted at sea (ibid., p. 312). Whittingham was, of course, the prince's receiver-general. Hungerford had been one of the Lancastrian lords who held out in the Tower of London against the Yorkists in 1460 and was among the few who escaped. He was captured and executed after the battle of Hexham (GEC, VI, pp. 619–20).

suggests the depth of their loyalty. In April 1462, with Henry's authorization, Margaret became her husband's envoy to France, eventually obtaining a truce and a secret agreement with Louis whereby Calais was made security for a French loan of 20,000 *livres tournois*.[9]

Long before Margaret's negotiations with Louis even began, however, talk of impending invasion by both Scots and French ran rife in England.[10] By early 1462 the rumored size and scope of the anticipated Lancastrian invasion had grown to stupendous proportions, involving hundreds of thousands of men and most of the crowned heads of western Europe.[11] In February the earl of Oxford, his son and others were executed for their alleged involvement in a Lancastrian plot. Different versions of what they had been up to had them plotting Edward IV's assassination or preparing the ground for a Lancastrian invasion.[12] Apparently around the same time the abbot and monks of Bury St Edmunds were arrested and fined for having posted a bill saying that the pope, who disapproved of Coppini's doings, had granted plenary absolution to the Lancastrians and excommunicated the Yorkists instead.[13] In March, King Edward approached Thomas Cook and his fellow aldermen of London to raise money from their wards to resist the invasion plans of his 'adversary Henry', who was 'moved therto by the malicious and subtill suggestion and enticing of the seide malicious wymman Margarete his wife' with the view that her uncle, Charles of Anjou, and other Frenchmen should be given 'the domynacion, ruel and gouvernaunce' of England.[14] Although such rumors would have played on existing fears and uncertainties, it is also clear that they were deliberately used to discourage lingering Lancastrian sympathy while bolstering support for the Yorkists.

In contrast, Margaret's actual 'invasion', which landed her near Bamburgh in late October 1462 with 800 French soldiers and some Scots, was less than a shadow of what common talk had made it.[15] Although the Lancastrians were able to take and hold the castles of Alnwick, Dunstanburgh and Bamburgh for a time as bases from which to raid the north country, they were never able to push real control much beyond the Northumbrian littoral. In July 1463, Margaret again sailed with her son to the continent, leaving Henry at Bamburgh while she set up a modest court-in-exile at St Mihiel-en-Bar and tried to head off Edward IV's diplomatic efforts to reach a favorable understanding with France. In this she was unsuccessful: an Anglo-French truce was reached in October containing an agreement not to aid each other's

---

[9] Scofield, *Life and Reign of Edward IV*, I, p. 246, n. 3, for Henry's authorization; Waurin, *Anchiennes cronicques*, III, pp. 176–7, for the agreement signed by Margaret.

[10] *CSP, Milan*, I, pp. 90, 93–4, 98; Gairdner, *PL*, III, p. 283, for rumors of June 1461.

[11] Ibid., IV, p. 32, for word of a three-pronged attack plan involving 120,000 men; *Three Chrons.* p. 158, for an even more elaborate design, in which combined Lancastrian/Breton/Burgundian/Scottish/Spanish attacking armies would be joined and supported by the kings of France, Denmark, Aragon, Navarre, Sicily (the latter being Margaret's father, René of Anjou) and Portugal, with 225,000 more men!

[12] Scofield, *Life and Reign of Edward IV*, I, pp. 231–4.

[13] Ibid., p. 233; *Three Chrons.*, p. 162; *CSP, Milan*, I, p. 107.

[14] Kekewich, et al., *Politics of Fifteenth-Century England*, pp. 135–7, for the letter to Cook. A similar appeal was made to the prior of Worcester and, no doubt, to others (*HMC*, XIV, p. 179).

[15] Wolffe, p. 334.

enemies. A similar agreement between England and Scotland followed in December.[16]

These developments brought imminent danger to Henry, who by then had returned to Edinburgh. Edward had already sought his extradition, and the truce with Scotland increased the likelihood that he would get it.[17] Soon Henry was back in Bamburgh, sending messages to Margaret, to Louis XI, to René of Anjou and to the duke of Brittany in an effort to elicit aid. Margaret had already informed her husband that Francis II, duke of Brittany, and Charles, count of Charolais, were offering him their support. His instructions to her of 22 February demonstrate that she was expected to coordinate continental support in his behalf through a series of mediations with all the other parties.[18] It was a role for which Margaret, as queen and woman, was particularly suited.

Despite continuing uncertainties and the difficulties of the previous year, the Lancastrians may actually have felt that things were at last coming together in a way that offered them hope of success. Serious disturbances in England provided credible evidence that Henry still retained some backing there, though what it might have amounted to if its extent had been seriously tested is difficult to say, and it may not have amounted to much. Meanwhile, the Lancastrians did not expect a major Yorkist offensive in the north before summer, and they had recently extended the area under their control.[19] Had they been given the time in which to coordinate continental support with lingering domestic loyalty, the story might have been different. Instead, thanks to a chance encounter and its aftermath, their cause was lost. On 25 April 1464, Warwick's brother John Neville, now Lord Montagu, while on a mission to escort some Scottish ambassadors to York met and defeated a band of Lancastrians at Hedgeley Moor. In mid-May, following up on his earlier success, Montagu fell upon a much smaller Lancastrian force encamped near Hexham; virtually all of the Lancastrian leaders were captured and executed. Soon after, the Northumbrian strongholds fell, bringing an end to Lancaster's foothold in the north. Only Henry himself escaped the debacle. He had been staying at Bywell castle at the time of Hexham, a few miles from the field, but when the Yorkist victors arrived to take him prisoner, he had vanished, seemingly into thin air. Although Henry had been a miserable failure as king, he proved to be a tenacious fugitive, eluding capture for more than a year, though captured he eventually was in July 1465.[20]

During the next five years, while Henry endured a relatively genteel captivity in the Tower of London, his cause understandably languished, though not for

[16] Griffiths, pp. 887–8.

[17] See Kekewich, et al., *Politics of Fifteenth-Century England*, p. 145, for an undated letter from Edward IV to James III castigating him for succoring 'our . . . traitours and rebellis' and demanding that he 'delyver [them] unto us withoute delay . . . yif they be comen not your lieges and subgettes'.

[18] Scofield, *Life and Reign of Edward IV*, I, pp. 315–18; II, pp. 463–6; Waurin, *Anchiennes cronicques*, III, pp. 178–81.

[19] Ross, *Edward IV*, pp. 57–9; Scofield, *Life and Reign of Edward IV*, pp. 314–15, 318–20. Some of the disturbances were probably orchestrated by the duke of Somerset, who had returned to his Lancastrian affiliation – if, indeed, he had ever sincerely left it – after a brief reconciliation with Edward.

[20] Wolffe, pp. 336–7, provides the most detailed account of these events. Ross, *Edward IV*, pp. 60–1, provides a tally of some thirty-one or two persons executed after Hexham.

Margaret's lack of effort. Already, in December 1464 while he remained a fugitive, she had tried to enlist the support of the king of Portugal in behalf of his cause, assuring the latter that she had been in communication with Henry, who remained 'in gude hele, out of the handes of his rebelles, and in sewerte of his persone'. Through Alphonso V's shared Lancastrian descent and present familial ties, she hoped also to obtain backing from the German emperor and a possible alliance with Spain.[21] Despite Lancastrian disillusionment with Louis XI, who by this time was clearly playing both sides off against each other, she appealed to him again for aid in February 1465, when it appeared that the earl of Warwick and Edward IV were at odds. At the least, she hoped that Louis would 'allow her to receive assistance from [his] lords who [were] willing', perhaps a reference to the duke of Brittany and count of Charolais, though she also put him on notice that if he refused all help, she would still 'take the best course that she [could]'. Louis derided and dismissed her request.[22]

In 1470 an opportunity to revive the Lancastrian cause presented itself when the earl of Warwick, having turned against Edward IV, fled to France seeking support.[23] The possibility of a Lancastrian alliance with Warwick had been bruited, apparently by the French, as early as May 1467, though how seriously it was considered by any of the parties at that time is uncertain.[24] Sometime after May 1469, Margaret's chancellor, Sir John Fortescue, proposed a marriage between Prince Edward and Warwick's daughter Anne.[25] In 1470 Margaret would have recognized that a bargain with Warwick provided the best and possibly the last chance to achieve her goals. That does not mean that she had to like it. She had ample reason to hate and mistrust the earl and therefore took her time in coming to terms with her old enemy.[26] The formal rapprochement took place on 22 July at Angers, where Margaret required Warwick to beg her forgiveness on his knees.[27] Three days later Prince Edward and Anne Neville were betrothed in symbolic testimony to the agreement. It appears that they were married in December at Amboise.[28]

Since time was of the essence if their plans were to succeed, Warwick returned to England before the marriage took place. Because Margaret still mistrusted

---

[21] Clermont, *Works of Sir John Fortescue*, pp. 25–8, for Margaret's instructions to John Butler, earl of Ormond, at the court of the king of Portugal. Alphonso was the great-grandson of John of Gaunt; his sisters were married to the emperor and to the king of Spain.

[22] Hicks, *Warwick*, p. 262; Scofield, *Life and Reign of Edward IV*, I, p. 379, notes that Margaret's brother, John of Calabria, and Edmund, the new nominal duke of Somerset, were with Francis II and Charles later in the year; *CSP, Milan*, I, p. 116: 'Look how proudly she writes.'

[23] During the intervening years Margaret continued to be implicated in uprisings and plots against Edward IV (ibid., pp. 121, 125, 126, 128 and n.; Ross, *Edward IV*, p. 113 and n. 4).

[24] *CSP, Milan*, I, p. 120. An earlier exchange between John of Calabria, Margaret's brother, and Louis XI (ibid., p. 117) cannot be regarded as evidence of Lancastrian intentions. John had been speaking abusively of Warwick over dinner, and when Louis praised him for favoring peace with France, the duke retorted that 'as he was so fond of him he ought to try and restore [Margaret] in that kingdom', to provide better assurance of peace. The writer described the men's continued twitting of each other as 'half joking'. They both may have been a little tipsy!

[25] Calmette and Périnelle, *Louis XI et l'Angleterre*, p. 304, who mistakenly identify the daughter as Isabel. See Hicks, *Warwick*, p. 292, n. 36, for the *terminus a quo* for the proposal.

[26] Ibid., pp. 292–4, provides the most recent discussion of the agreement.

[27] *CSP, Milan*, I, p. 141.

[28] Calmette and Périnelle, *Louis XI et l'Angleterre*, pp. 133, 319–20.

him she refused to let her son return to England with him or join him without her. Warwick's ouster of Edward proved temporary and Henry's 'readeption' brief, lasting only from October 1470 into April 1471. Margaret and her son returned to England on 14 April, only to learn that a crucial battle had been fought at Barnet hours before they had landed. Edward IV was victorious; Warwick was dead, and Henry was once more a prisoner. On 4 May 1471 the battle of Tewkesbury ended Margaret's hopes. Prince Edward was killed in the course of the battle; she was found a few days later hiding in a religious house. According to the official account of the Yorkist restoration, she was brought before Edward IV at Coventry, the town that had once provided the base for her own power.[29] On 21 May the victorious king returned to London with Margaret displayed in his entry procession like the spoils of war.[30] That night, Henry VI was murdered in the Tower, probably on Edward IV's orders.

Margaret survived for another eleven years. After some months' confinement, she was sent to live in the custody of the duchess of Suffolk, whose husband had arranged her marriage and who had accompanied her to England and perhaps become her friend. In 1476, Louis XI ransomed her for 50,000 crowns as part of a deal struck with King Edward, but she was obliged to renounce all her English claims before being handed over. Once in French hands, she was required to sign over to Louis all her rights of inheritance to both her parents' lands.[31] Thereafter, Margaret continued as Louis's pensioner until her death at the Château de Dampierre near Saumur on 25 August 1482 at the age of fifty-two.

Queenship, Gender and Political Power in Fifteenth-Century England

Margaret of Anjou is remembered for the anomalous circumstances of her queenship. These conditions permitted and, indeed, forced her to act in unexpected ways. In doing this she pushed at boundaries that were ill defined and porous to begin with and, in pushing, may have made them somewhat more visible and concrete. This, of course, would not have been her intent. As she became increasingly caught in the struggle for political survival, it is more likely that her thought was drawn to whatever means and methods looked like they would get her through. Yet, as a woman of her world, she could not dispense with ingrained notions of queenship or of what constituted her gendered place. It is her adherence to these standards, rather than a mythic disregard for them, that is striking. The tension between Margaret's representations of herself alongside her growing power reveals the possibilities and pitfalls of queenship in late medieval England.

Although heightened expectations accompanied Margaret to England, the extraordinary nature of her queenship could not have been predicted. In many

---

[29] Ross, *Edward IV*, ch. 7, for the details of Edward's return; Griffiths, pp. 891–2; Wolffe, p. 346; Bruce, *Historie of the Arrivall*, pp. 31–2.

[30] *EHL*, p. 375, from BL, MS Arundel 28, fol. 25v: 'in curru precedente exercitu' ('in a carriage preceding the army'); *Croyland Chron.*, p. 466.

[31] Gairdner, *PL*, V, p. 131; Calmette and Périnelle, *Louis XI et l'Angleterre*, pp. 210–12.

ways she made a normal beginning. When she arrived in England, it was anticipated that she would fill a familiar role. Like other queens before her, her marriage was supposed to bring political advantage to king and realm. Domestically she was to exercise good ladyship, to respond to appeal and to use her influence to obtain benefit for her appellants. As intercessor she was to 'soften' kingship, to help provide for mercy and reconciliation along with justice. It was assumed, too, that she would present the kingdom with an heir in timely fashion. There is every reason to believe that Margaret knew what was expected of her and that she came to England expecting to fill her appointed role.

That she ended up doing something rather different is a matter of record. Her marriage did not provide the hoped-for ending to the Hundred Years War nor even a favorable interlude, while the years it took to produce an heir encouraged rivalry and fostered insecurity. Both of these matters cast further doubt upon an already less-than-vigorous kingship and provided ammunition for the disgruntled and the disaffected, some of it directed at Margaret herself. In 1453, Henry's catastrophic illness precipitated a political crisis that brought about Margaret's emergence in stages as a political actor and eventual leader of a Lancastrian party.

Up to that point, Margaret's activities had been, for the most part, conventional and non-controversial even when they were decidedly political. A careful reading of her letters to Charles VII shows her playing the accepted role of intermediary, offering goodwill and encouragement while deferring at all times to her husband's authority. Likewise, though her actual influence on the pardons of Cade's rebels remains shadowy, her acknowledged role paints her as an intercessor. In both these situations the queen's participation can be regarded as an enabling device that was supposed to help programs go forward that were deemed necessary, while minimizing loss to the theoretical image of kingly strength.

Prior to Henry's illness Margaret does not appear to have been anyone's avowed enemy. She was certainly not the enemy of Richard, duke of York, but was regarded by him and his wife as a potential intercessor in his behalf. Whatever her private feelings may have been, she appears to have purposely cultivated an image of accessibility, in part through her gifts. Indeed, it appears that her first publicly political response to the crisis should be seen as an attempt to bridge differences rather than as partisan support of a particular faction. Moreover, the notion of faction itself must be questioned, for it grew out of circumstantial cooperation and temporary convenience and could at times be altered by changes in the wind. 'York' – identified as a firm alliance between the duke of York, the Neville earls of Salisbury and Warwick and their associates – appeared as a distinct faction around the time of the first battle of St Albans, while 'Lancaster' remained more amorphous, composed of persons who for one reason or another remained actively loyal to Henry, though only some of them bore specific grudges against York or the Nevilles. Without 'York' there was, in fact, no 'Lancaster'.

Though Margaret may well have regarded the duke of York with wariness from 1453 if not before, she acquiesced to his first protectorate, instead of the regency she had desired, without overt hostility. The first battle of St Albans in 1455 and York's second protectorate changed that. Having pushed for his ouster, she soon sought expanded public power for herself again, though this time through the more traditional and informal avenues of influence to which she already had access as queen. Nevertheless, through the next couple of years it appears that she was content to pursue a policy that combined control with limited conciliation and that stopped well short of seeking anyone's destruction. Though the picture becomes very murky as the situation deteriorated to the outbreak of civil war, by which time Margaret had become an uncompromising partisan, it is clear that she came to this posture rather late. Nor does she appear as the vengeful she-wolf until nearly the end of the reign, when the circumstances of a Yorkist military victory and settlement of the crown had made her one.

Margaret's surviving letters, written for the most part before 1455, shed some light upon her personality and her concerns, borne out in her later actions. They reveal a woman who could be both determined and indefatigable once she set her mind on something – and impatient when her wishes were not met. At times she was peremptory or overbearing, but she also made an effort to be seen as fair-minded and just. Above all, though willing to take advantage of the influence her position afforded, she was generally sensitive to the formulas through which her power had to be perceived. Thus, with few exceptions, she represented herself throughout the reign in terms and images that conveyed acceptable notions of queenship. She was an intercessor, a supporter of the king's intentions, a mother. On those occasions when she pushed or blundered past a boundary and found herself on tenuous ground, it appears that she backed off. We see this in her acceptance of York's first protectorate and in her withdrawal to the midlands when his second protectorate came to an end. She may have backtracked again when her ceremonial escort out of Coventry occasioned negative comment, and this pattern certainly appears in her retreat from London. In each of these instances, when Margaret found herself with no real place to stand, it may have been easier to step back into her gendered place than to pursue a claim to more overt leadership. This phenomenon, whatever it may say about Margaret's character, really had more to do with her situation as a woman in what was understood to be a man's political world. Even in exile she acted as Henry's agent only after receiving his initial authorization, and in all her directives and appeals she made sure to represent herself as acting in his behalf.

Throughout her career as queen, gender dictated the terms on which Margaret could aspire to and exercise power. In a world that largely denied female authority and assumed female subordination, she had to rely upon informal channels of influence. Some of this had always occurred openly in the normal course of intermediation, of request and referral that informed the process of 'business as usual' in a face-to-face society. In the expressly political arena, when her effort to gain formally recognized authority came to naught, she fell back upon the traditionally accepted postures of queenship, cloaking her influence in the authority of her husband or her son and presenting herself as their representative or intermediary. It was a strategy that had its parallels in the discrepancies between theory and practice in the real lives of more ordinary women, and for a time it worked.

But the queen was more visible than other women, and it was more difficult for the discrepancies to be overlooked. Yorkist propaganda, attempting to discredit the regime, did not attack Margaret so much as the political queen, but as the transgressive woman 'out of place' whose sexuality was suspect.[32] In suggesting that Margaret was disorderly, a deeper disorder in the kingdom was implied. Thus, the queen's alleged transgression became the stand-in for all that was wrong. This propaganda neatly dovetailed with York's lineal claim to the throne, which also assumed that 'right order' had been subverted. By encouraging public fears that Margaret would use 'strangers and aliens' to fight for her, a charge made more credible by her own French origin, the Yorkists were able to strengthen the image of female disorder while linking it to disorder threatening the realm.

Margaret's exercise of power required the appearance of the king's authority, and the more passive, the more a puppet, Henry was perceived to be, the less it appeared that he had any authority that the queen could invoke or represent. The hollowness of the construct was revealed in her 'rescue' of the king at the second battle of St Albans and its aftermath. The striking thing about Margaret's quest for power is not the extent to which she offended gender expectations, but the effort she made to at least appear to live up to them.

---

[32] Rosaldo, 'Woman, Culture, and Society', p. 34, observes: 'Societies that define women as lacking legitimate authority have no way of acknowledging the reality of female power. This difference between rule and reality is reflected in our own society when we speak of powerful women as "bitches".'

Appendix I

'Mahometan Manifesto' or
Angevin Parody?

The 'Satirical Proclamation' published by F.J. Furnivall in 1866,[1] though unusual, is not unique. Thus far, it appears to be one of three similar documents, which I here try to correlate.

Furnivall evidently found it puzzling as well as intriguing, for he consulted James Gairdner and G.E. Cokayne in the course of attempting to determine its date and identify its subject. The satirical 'proclamation', itself a copy, carries the internal date of 'mccccxvj'. Both Gairdner and Cokayne agreed that 'the frensh woman son' could only refer to Henry VI, who had been born in 1421, and that the document's subject was René of Anjou. This meant that the date of 1416 had to be the copier's mistake. Furnivall printed their comments, tentatively ascribed the piece to 1436, as suggested by Cokayne, and left it at that. More recently, Ralph Griffiths has accepted the identification of René, but has argued that the mistranscribed date was most probably 'mccccxlvj'. This would place the satire a year or so after Margaret's marriage, by which time the difficulties in obtaining a more substantive peace and the conditions under discussion were likely to have been attracting comment.

Furnivall was apparently unaware that a similar, though not identical, 'manifesto' had already been discovered and published by Cecil Monro in 1863, along with a number of Margaret of Anjou's letters.[2] 'For want of a better name' Monro called it 'a Mahometan Manifesto', though he recognized it as a parody. In this version the alleged writer sends 'gretyng to yor kyng of Englond and of Fraunce, and to Edward Prince of Wales'. Like Furnivall's 'proclamation', it also contains a marriage offer, which is similar in tenor while differing in its details:

> And, yf he [the king or the prince?] will wed my doghter, I will become cristen man, and all my regions and my reames; and they that will not converte with me shalbe brent. And I will giffe with my doghter viii myllions of gold, and paye within v Sondays. And I shall delyver hym the holye crosse that yor Lord died upon, and the spere that stroke hym to the herte, and mony other relikes that I have in my kepyng; and shall make hym Emperour of xviii. Kings londs.[3]

---

[1] Furnivall, *Political . . . Poems*, pp. 12–14; its source is BL, Cotton Vespasian B. XVI, fol. 5.
[2] Monro, pp. 166–7; all come from BL, Add. MS 46, 846, and all are copies.
[3] See above, p. 28, for Furnivall's version.

This version has no date, but if we are still safe in associating it with Henry VI and René of Anjou – and I believe we are – it would have to have been written after 1453 when Prince Edward of Lancaster was born, but before the middle of 1460 when Henry was captured by the Yorkists at Northampton.

The parallels and similarities between the two texts suggest that they had a common prototype unless one was derived from the other. If Griffiths' surmise regarding the date of Furnivall's version is correct, then it is possible that Monro's version, which is somewhat less detailed, is based upon it. But there is a further possibility in dating the 'earlier' text, and that is that the date should have been written 'mcccclvi' by substituting one numeral for another. A date of 1456 would perhaps suggest more strongly that both derived from the same source and are representative of a 'thread' of criticism current at the time. Although there seems to be no specific evidence to corroborate this idea, 1456 would be a likely year for such criticism and satire to occur, for it brought an end to York's second protectorate and saw the rise of Margaret's power. Our analysis of René as its subject would remain the same, but for those contemporaries who saw the texts or heard them read the connection would involve a process of harking back to past troubles and losses that would still resonate with perceived difficulties in their present.

A question still remains, however: where did the idea for such a document come from in the first place? As Monro noted, the French chronicler Enguerrand de Monstrelet reported a 'letter' in a similar vein. Shorter than the other two and purporting to be written by the sultan of Babylon to the kings of Germany, France, England and others, it threatens them with destruction if they do not pay tribute for their lands and renounce their Christian faith.[4] But it also appears to be a parody (and Monstrelet's editor, J.A. Buchon, characterized it as a fake) for it begins with an overblown list of the 'sultan's' titles, including such things as 'crumpler of helms, splitter of shields . . . flower of chivalry . . . terror of enemies', and so on and on. At the same time, there is nothing in it to suggest a link to René or to Henry VI. Its dating clause claims that it was written 'in the tenth year from our coronation, the second year after our . . . victory [over] Cyprus', and it is editorially ascribed to the year 1427. Something around that time seems likely since a large Muslim force attacked Cyprus in 1426, captured its king, and plundered Nicosia. Assuming, however, that the letter is indeed a fake, I suggest that it originated and was circulated in something resembling this form to ridicule the Islamic threat and to lampoon the practice of Muslim rulers of attaching elaborate titles and epithets to their names. See, e.g., a letter of 1456 from Al-Malec-al-Aschraf-Aboul-Nasr-Inal, the sultan of Egypt,[5] which Monro also noted and took to be 'not wholly unlike [his] manifesto'.[6] In fact, the letter is not at all like any of the parodies, but simply a letter. It appears, then, that later references to René and Henry may have been grafted onto an existing anti-Muslim prototype to use as a vehicle of criticism. Whether Monstrelet's 'letter' is the source in question must remain uncertain,

[4] Monstrelet, *Chroniques*, V, pp. 175–6.
[5] Published in Mas Latrie, *Histoire de l'Ile de Chypre*, III, pp. 73–5.
[6] Monro, p. 166.

although its naming of the 'writer' as 'Baldadoch' allows comparison with the 'Balthasar' of Monro's text.

Nevertheless, if the 'writer' of the later parodies is supposed to be understood as René, his representation as a Muslim in both Furnivall's and Monro's texts and 'his' offer to stand against Christian kings in the former are odd, to say the least. Both versions present him as Christian-born (in England!), fallen into Lollardy and a Muslim convert. If my suggestions regarding the origins and alteration of the text are correct, the awkwardness of fitting René into what seems initially to have been an anti-Muslim parody may account for the bizarre religious allusions in the result.

It seems likely that the English were hoping for Angevin support in extracting a better deal from the French during their further negotiations or even for cooperation against the French crown.[7] Something of the sort is perhaps alluded to, albeit very strangely, in these texts. The very extravagance of the 'writer's' offers suggests that they cannot possibly be genuine. The audience should then suspect that the acceptance of such an agreement could only be seen as extremely foolish policy.

---

[7] Watts, pp. 222–3.

Appendix II

Letter from the Earl of Salisbury to
the Prior of Erdebury, 7 March

Although the earl of Salisbury's letter has been known for some time, it has not received much attention until recently. C.L. Kingsford provided a brief notice of it in 1913, in which he attributed it to 1455 and identified 'Erdebury' as Arbury. His description of its content is scanty, noting only that Salisbury 'with many protestations of loyalty' sought the mediation of the prior of Erdebury with Queen Margaret 'in the matter of the accusations against himself, the Earl of Warwick, and the Duke of York'.[1] Jessie H. Flemming, who accepted Kingsford's dating and repeated the gist of his commentary, subsequently published a transcript of the letter in 1921.[2] Although Kingsford correctly identified Arbury,[3] his dating of the letter is surely incorrect, and his outline of its content misses some of its intriguing references.

The letter in fact touches on several matters. It begins by thanking the prior for his efforts to obtain the queen's good ladyship towards the earl. Her favor, however, is conditional: it depends upon a certain promise that Salisbury has made to her via the prior, regarding which the latter has become uneasy. Salisbury assures him that he will 'at al tymes kepe yow or eny other that labour for me to that entent undishonored and nat to varie fro my said promisse' and asks that he continue his efforts with Margaret. It appears that the prior's labors have already borne fruit, for Salisbury next refers gratefully to the queen's recent letters to the council in the service of 'rest and unitee'. He insists that the lords and 'also al thoo whome the matiers of the . . . lettres touchen [should] yeve laud and thanke to hire said highnesse therefore, as that I doo in my moost humble wise'. These matters take up the bulk of the letter.

Only at this point does the earl have a complaint to air. The prior has written to him that he has heard 'language of accusacions of right hie estates to bie made by my lord of Yorke, my son of Warrwice, and me, in matters that have nat bee disclosed herebifore to their grete rebuke'. Salisbury launches into an aggrieved denial that he ever 'ymagined, thought, ne saied eny such matter . . . in my dayes'. Nor can he imagine York or his son ever saying such things, as he

---

[1] *EHL*, p. 213.

[2] Flemming, *England under the Lancastrians*, pp. 129–9.

[3] It was a house of Augustinian canons a little north of Kenilworth in the heart of Margaret's midland holdings (Knowles and Hadcock, *Medieval Religious Houses*, pp. 137, 145). The prior would have been either William Woodcock, who resigned sometime in 1456, or John Bromley, his successor (Page, *VCH, Warwick*, II, pp. 89–91).

is sure they will attest for themselves. The letter closes with a further appeal to the prior to speak for him in this 'or in eny othere [matter] concernnyng my trouth' and the standard offer to do him favor in return.

With its allusions to promises, deal making and slander, the letter hints at intriguing possibilities. The problem is deciding where to place it in the chronology of events. The letter bears only a date of 7 March and the statement that it was written in London. These must be considered along with content to determine where it fits. As rough boundaries we may claim a *terminus a quo* for the letter of 1454, since the political alliance of York, Warwick and Salisbury had only begun that winter (i.e. 1453/4). Likewise, 1459 must be the *terminus ad quem* because of the Yorkists' flight and attainder in the autumn of that year.

Kingsford's suggested date of 1455 can be dismissed on two grounds. First, Salisbury's statement that he had heard of Margaret's letters to the council indicates (at the least) that he was not present when they were received and read, no doubt with due elaboration by her messenger. Salisbury was still chancellor until 7 March, and his presence with the council is attested on the fourth. It does not seem likely that he would have missed many meetings during office, particularly at a time when the political situation had grown delicate with York's resignation of his protectorate and Somerset's release from the Tower. Second, and more subjectively, can we believe that the earl would have written *this* letter on the day that he relinquished office? Though I suppose it is possible, it seems to me unlikely.

A different date and a challenging analysis of the letter have recently been offered by Michael Hicks. He has attributed the letter to 1459 on the grounds that it is the only year that satisfies certain conditions: that Salisbury was in London where the council was then meeting, but not a council member; that the queen was in the midlands near Arbury, at a distance from which she had to communicate with the council by letter; and that 'York and Warwick were not immediately to hand.'[4] Although they seem reasonable, these conditions may, in fact, be questioned. First, although Salisbury's reference to 'my lordes of the counseill' does support the inference that he was not a member, it must be noted that he was writing to the prior as a private person with personal matters at stake, not as a council member. It is possible that the council received Margaret's letters while he was simply not in attendance. Second, since it would have been irregular for the queen to attend council meetings, any formal communication that she had with them would necessarily have been by letter, typically supported by the bearer's words in her behalf. While it may seem likely that she was in the midlands, the point of Salisbury's writing to the prior was to offer reassurance so that the skittish prior would continue his mediations. As Hicks points out, Arbury was a small house. If proximity was the only factor, it should have been possible to find a more important person in the neighborhood to act as go-between. Hence, we may conclude that the queen held the prior in some regard as one whom she could trust and that this was the deciding factor in his choice as intermediary. Finally, whether York and Warwick were in the next county or the next room, Salisbury could credibly speak only for himself.

---

[4] Hicks, *Warwick*, p. 155. His analysis of the letter is found on this and the following page.

Although he indicated his own belief in the others' innocence, he knew that they would have to answer for themselves, as he makes clear in his letter. Whether they ever communicated with Margaret by any means in this regard is not known; we have no evidence.

This brings us to the nature of the charge. Just who was it that was being accused of transgression, and by whom? A careful reading of this part of the letter suggests that the Yorkists were said to be accusing other persons 'of right hie estates' of matters previously undisclosed, which, if true, would be to the 'great rebuke' of the accused. In other words, the Yorkists were believed to have charged others with serious offences.[5] Who might the accused have been, these persons of 'right hie estates'? Several points argue against them having been the king, queen or prince. Despite the vehemence of Salisbury's own personal denial, 'as ferre as ever I herd or in eny wise knowe' seems a mild defense of his son and brother-in-law in such hypothetical circumstances. Moreover, if Henry were believed to be the target of Yorkist accusations, might we not expect to find some protestations of loyalty to him? There are none. But finally, can we reasonably believe that the queen would have just written to the council in a manner that seemed favorable to Salisbury if she thought he stood behind allegations of her son's bastardy or any other charges directly affecting her honor?[6]

If these arguments seem to go against 1459, an alternative date to consider is 1454. In this year, as in 1455, Salisbury is known to have attended council meetings that bracket the critical time, on 13 February and 12 March.[7] Although it is risky to assume his absence during the intervening period,[8] this may afford a more likely window in which her letters could have been received than 1455. In this case, a possible target of Yorkist accusation could have been Cardinal Kemp. He had apparently come under fire from the duke of Norfolk, who had supported York in the autumn, and clearly felt himself to be in some danger from that or other quarters. The duke of Somerset can be ruled out. Since York had already accused him openly of treason, Salisbury's denial in this instance would have been laughable.

Comparison of the letter's content with the situation in 1454 suggests a possible fit. In early March, although York had been authorized to hold parliament, the governance remained unsettled. The one significant concession that would have gratified nearly everyone (and could have prompted Salisbury's effusions) would have been Margaret's decision to bow out of the running, still leaving unresolved the question of a governing council or a protector and council. She would have done so with conditions: the formal recognition of her son's inheritance and perhaps all the clauses guaranteeing that he could take

---

[5] Cf. Hicks, who understands it to mean that persons of 'right hie estates' were accusing the Yorkists of something that, if true, would have been to their (i.e. the Yorkists') 'grete rebuke' and probably treasonable. Although the language is not as clear as one might wish, I believe he has misread this passage. For one thing, would Salisbury have used the pronoun 'their' ('to their grete rebuke') to refer to York, Warwick and himself?

[6] Cf. Hicks, *Warwick*, p. 156.

[7] PRO, C81/1546/73, 75, 76, 78.

[8] He must have been attending parliament on 28 February, when fines were imposed upon unexcused absentees (*RP*, V, p. 248).

over when he came of age. The charter of 15 March creating Edward of Lancaster prince of Wales comes at about the right time to fit into such a scenario. As a further precaution she may have required some personal reassurance of responsibility from Salisbury, who was by that time associated with the duke of York.

She may have felt that he could provide a moderating influence upon York. Salisbury's loyalty had never been questioned; he had stood reliably with Henry at Dartford in 1452 when York had demanded Somerset's arrest.[9] And there is some reason to believe that he had formerly been on comfortable terms with Margaret. In happier times she had gone hunting in his park of Ware.[10] Salisbury's letter to the prior of Erdebury may reflect some memory of an easier relationship between them, though it also seems to acknowledge a sense, new perhaps, of her own power. It is noteworthy that it does not seek her intercession or intermediation with the king, but is most concerned with making assurances of Salisbury's own faithfulness *to her*.

What we know of Margaret's letters to the council supports this analysis. She appears to have addressed it as if it held authority. If the king were well and at least theoretically in charge, would she not have associated her proposals regarding 'rest and unitee' with his will and presented them in his support? This seems a strong point in favor of 1454, when the king was unquestionably incapacitated. In addition, the reference to rest and unity itself sorts well with what seem to have been Margaret's concerns at this time, just as it echoes the council's expressed intent when it summoned York's attendance the previous autumn.[11]

Margaret does appear to have accepted the eventual protectorate without protest. Assuming that a bargain had been struck, it may be that she initially hoped for a government by council, which might later change its mind about her role. Kemp's death, of course, brought matters to a more abrupt denouement. Her hopes for Henry's recovery – and requests for holy water – as well as the reluctance of just about everyone to take responsibility or to serve on a protectorate council accord with such a picture. In short, although a date of 1454 is not without its problems, it seems that Salisbury's letter can be made to fit quite well into its circumstances.

In summation, then, although at this point 1454 seems to me to be the more likely date, since it cannot be proven, it must be considered provisional.

[9] Johnson, pp. 111–12.
[10] Monro, pp. 90–1, for her letter advising the earl's parker that Salisbury will be 'right well content and pleased' for her to hunt there and asking him to spare the game for her. At risk of sounding like Hookham, I am bound to observe that the tenor of the letter seems more 'charming' than peremptory, as if written with nothing more in mind than the anticipation of good sport.
[11] *PPC*, VI, p. 164.

BL, Cotton Vespasian F xiii (i), art. 64

[Addressed on dorse: To the reverent father in god and my right especiall and tendre frende the priour of Erdebury][12]

Reverent father in god and my right especial and tendre frende I recomaunde me to yow, and in my right hertie and feithfull wise thanke yow of al your true and grete diligences and undelaied devoire that ye have many tymes put yow in at my special request and prayer to that that myght serve to theobteignyng of my right fervent desire to knowe and fele the good ladyship of the Quene oure soverein lady to me hir humble true servaunt, and in especial of your grete labour in that bihalve sith my last speche with yow, as by your lettres brought me by the berer of thies. I conceive at large wherin among othre thing is contenede your desire and exhortacion me nat to varye from that I have promitted hertofore right largely by yow opennede to hire said highnesse and that (*yet*) I see ye be nat dishonorede of your reportes in that bihalve, wherunto will ye wit that of eny promysse that I have made unto yow at eny tyme for my declaracon unto the said highnesse, and to have and stand in the favoure (*favours*) of hire good grace for the whiche oon of my moost erthly desires I pray yow as tendrely as I can to contynue therin your good will and devoir for my singular consolacon, I shal at al tymes kepe yow or eny other that labour for me to that entent.undishonored and nat to varie fro my said promisse (*promisses*) with godes mercie. And as toward the blessed disposicon of the said good grace [et?][13] (*yet*) unto that that myght serve to rest and unitee comprised in hire gracioux lettres late directed to my lordes of the counseill wherof to my grete joy I have herd and god shal I doubt nat bie pleased therwith and prospre hire hie estate and the said lordes nat oonly, bot also al thoo whome the matiers (*matiere*) of the said blessed lettres touchen owe humbly and lowly to yeve laude and thanke to hire said highnesse therfore, as that I doo in my moost humble wise as soo on my bihalve as hire true servaunt with al myn hert and service, in that that mowe bee to hir hie pleasure I pray yow to declare me unto hire said grace.[14] And where in your said lettres it is expressed that ye have herd language of accusacions of right hie estates to bie made by my lord of Yorke, my son of Warrwice and me in materes that have nat bee disclosed herebifore to their grete rebuke and etc., truely it is to my grete mervail by whate coloure reason or grounde eny such language by eny personne erthly myght bie utred or saied, for as for myn own partie as I wol aunswere to our lord I nevere ymagined, thought ne (*or*) saied eny suche matter or eny thing like therunto in my dayes. And in like wise I dare well say for my said lord and son as ferre as ever I herd or in eny wise knowe (*knewe*) unto their honire (*this houre*) as I doubt nat thai wol at al tymes right largely declaire theim silf. And therfore therin or in eny othere concernyng my trouth I pray yow alway to

---

[12] Where Flemming and I have come up with different words in our transcriptions, I have put her version in parentheses and italics following mine. My own comments are in square brackets.

[13] There is a small hole and a smudge at this word.

[14] Flemming ends this sentence after 'pleasure' and makes the following clause ('I pray yow to declare me . . .' part of the next sentence. These differences in placement affect the overall sense of the passage.

aunswere largely for me. And if there bee thing that I may doo fo (*to*) your wele certifieth me, and ye shal to the performing therof fynde me right hertly disposed as our lord knoweth, which have yow ever in his blessed keping. Writen at London the vij day of Marche.

Your good frende Richard
Erl of Salisbury

Bibliography

Unprinted Primary Sources

London

British Library:
  Additional MSS 46,846; 48031A
  Cotton Vespasian F xiii (i)
  Harley MS 543
  Royal MS 15 E. VI

Corporation of London Record Office:
  Journals IV–VI

Inner Temple Library, London:
  Petyt MS 538.47

Public Record Office, London:
  Chancery: C66/471 (patent rolls); C81/1469, 1546 (warrants for the great seal)
  Exchequer: E28/84 (council and privy seal records), E404/70 (warrants for issues)
  King's Bench: KB9/256, 287 (ancient indictments)
  Special Collections: SC6/1162, 1287 (ministers' and receivers' accounts)

Paris

Bibliothèque Nationale:
  MSS français 4054, 20488
  MS latin 11892

Printed Primary Sources

Anderson, R.C., ed. *Letters of the Fifteenth and Sixteenth Centuries from the Archives of Southampton* (Southampton, 1921)
Arnold, T., ed. *Memorials of St Edmund's Abbey*, III, Rolls Series (London, 1896)
Basin, T. *Histoire de Charles VII*, 2 vols, ed. and tr. C. Samaran, 2nd edn (Paris, 1964–65)
Basin, T. *Histoire des règnes de Charles VII et de Louis XI*, 4 vols, ed. J. Quicherat (Paris, 1855–59)
Baskerville, G. 'A London Chronicle of 1460', *EHR* 28 (1913), pp. 124–7
Blackstone, W. *Commentaries on the Laws of England*, I, intro. by S. Katz, facsimile edn (Chicago, 1979)
Bouvier, Gilles le, dit le Héraut Berry. *Les chroniques du roi Charles VII*, ed. H. Courteault and Léonce Celier (Paris, 1979)

Brie, F.W.D., ed. *The Brut, or the Chronicles of England*, 2 vols, EETS, original series 131, 136 (London, 1906–08)

Bruce, J., ed. *Historie of the Arrivall of Edward IV in England*, Camden Society, old series 1 (London, 1838)

Bruneau, C., ed. *Charles d'Orléans et la poésie aristocratique* (Lyon, 1924)

Calendar of the Charter Rolls Preserved in the Public Record Office, VI, *1427–1517* (London, 1927)

Calendar of the Close Rolls Preserved in the Public Record Office: Henry VI, 5 vols (London, 1933–71)

Calendar of Entries in the Papal Registers relating to Great Britain and Ireland, Papal Letters XII A.D. 1458–1471, ed. J.A. Twemlow (London, 1933)

Calendar of the Patent Rolls Preserved in the Public Record Office: Henry IV, 4 vols (London, 1903–09)

Calendar of the Patent Rolls Preserved in the Public Record Office: Henry VI, 6 vols (London, 1901–10)

Calendar of the Patent Rolls Preserved in the Public Record Office: Richard II, 6 vols (London, 1895–1909)

Calendar of State Papers and Manuscripts relating to English Affairs existing in the Archives and Collections of Milan, I, ed. A.B. Hinds (London, 1912)

Calendar of State Papers and Manuscripts relating to English Affairs existing in the Archives and Collections of Venice, I, ed. R. Brown (London, 1864)

Capgrave, J. *Liber de Illustribus Henricis*, ed. F.C. Hingeston, Rolls Series (London, 1858)

Chambers, R. *A Course of Lectures on the English Law Delivered at the University of Oxford, 1767–1773*, ed. T.M. Curley (Madison, 1986)

Christine de Pisan. *The Treasure of the City of Ladies*, tr. with intro. by S. Lawson (New York, 1985)

Clermont, Lord, ed. *The Works of Sir John Fortescue*, I (London, 1869)

Commynes, P. de. *Memoirs: The Reign of Louis XI, 1461–83*, tr. with intro. by M. Jones, Penguin edn (Harmondsworth, 1972)

Craigie, W.A., ed. *The Asloan Manuscript: A Miscellany in Prose and Verse*, I, Scottish Text Society 14 (Edinburgh, 1923)

Davies, J.S., ed. *An English Chronicle of the Reigns of Richard II, Henry IV, Henry V, and Henry VI*, Camden Society, old series 64 (London, 1856)

Davis, N., ed. *Paston Letters and Papers of the Fifteenth Century*, 2 vols (Oxford, 1971–76)

Devon, F. *Issues of the Exchequer* (London, 1837)

Ellis, H., ed. *Original Letters Illustrative of English History*, first series, I (London, 1824)

Escouchy, M. d'. *Chronique de Mathieu d'Escouchy*, 3 vols, ed. G. du Fresne de Beaucourt (Paris, 1863–64)

Flemming, J.H., *England under the Lancastrians* (London, 1921)

Flenley, R., ed. *Six Town Chronicles of England* (Oxford, 1911)

Foxe, John, *Acts and Monuments*, 8 vols, ed. Stephen Cattley (London, 1837)

Furnivall, F.J., ed. *Political, Religious and Love Poems*, EETS, original series 15 (London, 1866)

Gairdner, J., ed. *Historical Collections of a Citizen of London in the Fifteenth Century*, Camden Society, new series 17 (London, 1876)

Gairdner, J., ed. *The Paston Letters*, 6 vols (London, 1904)

Gairdner, J., ed. *Three Fifteenth-Century Chronicles*, Camden Society, new series 28 (London, 1880)

Gascoigne, T. *Loci e Libro Veritatum*, ed. J.E.T. Rogers (Oxford, 1881)

Giles, J.A., ed. *Incerti Scriptoris Chronicon Angliae de Regnis . . . Henrici IV, Henrici V et Henrici VI* (London, 1848)

Gilson, J.P. 'A Defence of the Proscription of the Yorkists in 1459', *EHR* 26 (1911), pp. 512–25.

Gower, John. *Mirour de l'Omme*, tr. W.B. Wilson, rev. N.W. Van Baak, with foreword by R.F. Yeager (East Lansing, 1992)

Hall, E. *Hall's Chronicle*, ed. H. Ellis (London, 1809)

Harris, M.D., ed. *The Coventry Leet Book*, EETS, original series 134, 135, 138, 146 in one vol. (London, 1907–13)

Harriss, G.L., and M.A. Harriss, eds. 'John Benet's Chronicle for the Years 1400 to 1462', *Camden Miscellany* 24, Camden Society, fourth series IX (London, 1972), pp. 151–233

Historical Manuscripts Commission: Fifth Report (London, 1876), *Eleventh Report* (London, 1888); *Various Collections*, I (London, 1901), IV (Dublin, 1907)

Hoccleve, T. *The Regiment of Princes*, ed. C.R. Blyth (Kalamazoo, 1999)

Hugh of St Victor. *On the Sacraments of the Christian Faith*, tr. R.J. Deferrari, Medieval Academy of America, no. 58 (Cambridge, Mass., 1951)

Hunter, J., ed. *Three Catalogues, describing the Contents of the Red Book of the Exchequer, of the Dodsworth Manuscripts in the Bodleian Library, and of the Manuscripts in the Library of the Honourable Society of Lincoln's Inn* (London, 1838)

Institoris, H. and J. Sprenger. *Malleus maleficarum*, tr. with intro. by M. Summers (London, 1969)

Jacobus de Cessolis. *Caxton's Game and Playe of the Chesse, 1474*, with intro. by W.E.A. Axon (London, 1883)

Kekewich, M.L., C. Richmond, A.F. Sutton, L. Visser-Fuchs and J.L. Watts. *The Politics of Fifteenth-Century England: John Vale's Book* (Stroud, 1995)

Kingsford, C.L., ed. *The Chronicles of London* (Oxford, 1905)

Kingsford, C.L. 'An Historical Collection of the Fifteenth Century', *EHR* 29 (1914), pp. 505–15

Kipling, G. 'The London Pageants for Margaret of Anjou', *Medieval English Theatre* 4, no. 1 (1982), pp. 19–23

Kipling, G., ed. *The Receyt of the Ladie Kateryne*, EETS 296 (Oxford, 1990)

Monro, C., ed. *Letters of Queen Margaret of Anjou and Bishop Bekington and Others*, Camden Society, old series 86 (London, 1863)

Monstrelet, E. de. *Chroniques d'Enguerrand de Monstrelet*, V, ed. J.A. Buchon (Paris, 1826)

Myers, A.R., ed. *English Historical Documents*, IV, *1327–1485* (New York, 1969)

Myers, A.R., ed. 'The Household of Queen Elizabeth Woodville, 1466–7', *BJRL* 50 (1967–68), pp. 207–35, 443–81

Myers, A.R., ed. 'The Household of Queen Margaret of Anjou, 1452–3', *BJRL* 40 (1957–58), pp. 79–113, 391–431

Myers, A.R., ed. 'The Jewels of Queen Margaret of Anjou', *BJRL* 42 (1959–60), pp. 113–31

Nicolas, N.H., ed. *Proceedings and Ordinances of the Privy Council of England*, VI, *22 Henry VI 1443 to 39 Henry VI 1461* (London, 1837)

Pius II, Pope. *The Commentaries of Pius II: Books II and III*, tr. F.A. Gragg with intro. and notes by L.C. Gabel, Smith College Studies in History 25 (Northampton, Mass., 1939–40)

Rawcliffe, C. 'Richard, Duke of York, the King's "Obeisant Liegeman": A New Source for the Protectorates of 1454 and 1455', *Historical Research* 60 (1987), pp. 232–9

Riley, H.T., ed. *Ingulph's Chronicle of the Abbey of Croyland* (London, 1854)

Riley, H.T., ed. *Registrum Abbatiae Johannis Whethamstede*, 2 vols, Rolls Series (London, 1872–73)

Robbins, R.H., ed. *Historical Poems of the XIVth and XVth Centuries* (New York, 1959)

Robbins, R.H., ed. *Secular Lyrics of the XIVth and XVth Centuries*, 2nd edn (Oxford, 1955)

Rotuli Parliamentorum, V, *1439–1468* (London, 1832)

Rymer, T., ed. *Foedera, conventiones, literae . . .*, V (The Hague, 1741)

Searle, W.G., ed. *The Chronicle of John Stone, Monk of Christ Church, 1415–1471*, Cambridge Antiquarian Society 34 (Cambridge, 1902)

Sharpe, R.R., ed. *Calendar of Letter-Books . . . of the City of London: Letter-Book K* (London, 1911)

Sheppard, J.B., ed. *Christ Church Letters*, Camden Society, new series 19 (London, 1877)

Sheppard, J.B., ed. *Literae Cantuarienses*, III, Rolls Series (London, 1889)

Stevenson, J., ed. *Letters and Papers Illustrative of the Wars of the English in France during the Reign of Henry VI*, 2 vols in 3, Rolls Series (London, 1861–64)

Stow, J. *The Annales of England* (London, 1592)

Thomas, A.H., and I.D. Thornley, eds. *The Great Chronicle of London* (London, 1938)

Virgoe, R. 'Some Ancient Indictments in the King's Bench Referring to Kent, 1450–1452', in *Documents Illustrative of Medieval Kentish Society*, ed. F.R.H. Du Boulay, Kent Archaeological Society Monograph Series 17 (Ashford, 1964)

Waurin, J. de. *Anchiennes cronicques d'Engleterre*, 3 vols, ed. E. Dupont (Paris, 1858–63)

Waurin, J. de. *Recueil des croniques et anchiennes istories de la Grant Bretaigne*, V, ed. W. Hardy and E.C.L.P. Hardy, Rolls Series (London, 1891)

Williams, G., ed. *Official Correspondence of Thomas Bekynton*, II, Rolls Series (London, 1872)

Worcestre, W. *Itineraries of William Worcestre*, ed. J.H. Harvey (Oxford, 1969)

Wright, T., ed. *Political Poems and Songs Relating to English History*, II, Rolls Series (London, 1861)

Secondary Sources

Archer, R.E. '"How ladies . . . who live on their manors ought to manage their households and estates": Women as Landholders and Administrators in the Later Middle Ages', in *Woman is a Worthy Wight: Women in English Society c. 1200–1500*, ed. P.J.P. Goldberg (Stroud, 1992), pp. 149–81

Armstrong, C.A.J. 'The Inauguration Ceremonies of the Yorkist Kings and their Title to the Throne', *TRHS*, fourth series 30 (1948), pp. 51–73

Armstrong, C.A.J. 'Politics and the Battle of St Albans, 1455', *BIHR* 33 (1960), pp. 1–72

Arnold, C. 'The Commission of the Peace for the West Riding of Yorkshire, 1437–1509', in *Property and Politics*, ed. A.J. Pollard, pp. 116–38

Bagley, J.J. *Margaret of Anjou, Queen of England* (London, 1948)

Baldwin, J.F. 'The King's Council', in *The English Government at Work, 1327–1336*, I, ed. J.F. Willard and W.A. Morris (Cambridge, Mass., 1940), pp. 129–61

Barron, C.M. 'London and the Crown 1451–61', in *The Crown and Local Communities in England and France in the Fifteenth Century*, ed. J.R.L. Highfield and R. Jeffs (Gloucester, 1981), pp. 88–109

Beaucourt, G. du Fresne de. *Histoire de Charles VII*, 6 vols (Paris, 1881–91)

Bellamy, J.G. *The Law of Treason in the Later Middle Ages* (Cambridge, 1970)

Bennett, J.M. 'Public Power and Authority in the Medieval English Countryside', in *Women and Power*, ed. M. Erler and M. Kowaleski, pp. 18–36

Bennett, J.W. 'The Mediaeval Loveday', *Speculum* 33 (1958), pp. 351–70

Bernus, P. 'Le rôle politique de Pierre de Brezé au cours des dix dernières années du règne de Charles VII, 1451–1461', *Bibliothèque de l'École de Chartes* 69 (1908), pp. 303–47

Blok, A. 'Female Rulers and their Affinities', in *Transactions: Essays in Honor of Jeremy F. Boissevain*, ed. J. Verrips (Amsterdam, 1994), pp. 5–33

Brooke, C.N.L., and V. Ortenberg. 'The Birth of Margaret of Anjou', *Historical Research* 61 (1988), pp. 357–8

Bührer-Thierry, G. 'La reine adultère', *Cahiers de civilisation médiévale* 35 (1992), pp. 299–312

Bullough, V.L., B. Shelton and S. Slavin. *The Subordinated Sex: A History of Attitudes toward Women*, rev. edn (Athens, Georgia, 1988)

Cadden, J. *Meanings of Sex Difference in the Middle Ages* (Cambridge, 1993)

Calmette, J. and G. Périnelle. *Louis XI et l'Angleterre, 1461–1483* (Paris, 1930)

Carpenter, J., and S.-B. MacLean, eds. *Power of the Weak: Studies on Medieval Women* (Urbana, 1995)

Chamberlayne, J.L. 'Crowns and Virgins: Queenmaking during the Wars of the Roses', in *Young Medieval Women*, ed. K.J. Lewis, N.J. Menuge and K.M. Phillips (Stroud, 1999), pp. 47–68

Chibnall, M. *The Empress Matilda: Queen Consort, Queen Mother and Lady of the English* (Oxford, 1991)

Cokayne, G.E. *The Complete Peerage of England, Scotland, Ireland, Great Britain and the United Kingdom . . .*, 12 vols in 13, ed. V. Gibbs et al. (London, 1910–59)

Crawford, A., ed. *Letters of the Queens of England 1100–1547* (Stroud, 1994)

Cron, B.M. 'The "Champchevrier Portrait": A Cautionary Tale', *The Ricardian* 12, no. 154 (2001), pp. 321–7

Cron, B.M. 'The Duke of Suffolk, the Angevin Marriage, and the Ceding of Maine, 1445', *Journal of Medieval History* 20 (1994), pp. 77–99

Cron, B.M. 'Margaret of Anjou and the Lancastrian March on London, 1461', *The Ricardian* 12, no. 147 (1999), pp. 590–615

Davis, W.G. *The Ancestry of Mary Isaac* (Portland, Maine, 1995)

Duggan, A.J., ed. *Queens and Queenship in Medieval Europe* (Woodbridge, 1997)

Dunlop, A.I. *The Life and Times of James Kennedy, Bishop of St Andrews*, St Andrews University Publications 46 (Edinburgh, 1950)

Dunn, D. 'Margaret of Anjou, Queen Consort of Henry VI: A Reassessment of her Role, 1445–53', in *Crown, Government and People in the Fifteenth Century*, ed. R.E. Archer (New York, 1995), pp. 107–43

Eckhardt, C.D. 'Woman as Mediator in the Middle English Romances', *Journal of Popular Culture* 14 (1980), pp. 94–107

Emden, A.B. *A Biographical Register of the University of Cambridge to A.D. 1500* (Cambridge, 1963)

Emden, A.B. *A Biographical Register of the University of Oxford to A.D. 1500*, 3 vols (Oxford, 1957–59)

Enright, M.J. *Lady with a Mead Cup: Ritual, Prophecy and Lordship in the European Warband from La Tène to the Viking Age* (Blackrock, 1996)

Erlanger, P. *Margaret of Anjou: Queen of England*, tr. E. Hyams (London, 1970)

Erler, M., and M. Kowaleski, eds. *Women and Power in the Middle Ages* (Athens, Georgia, 1988)

Evans, H.T. *Wales and the Wars of the Roses*, repr. of 1915 edn with intro. by R.A. Griffiths (Stroud, 1995)

Facinger, M.F. 'A Study of Medieval Queenship: Capetian France, 987–1237', in *Studies in Medieval and Renaissance History* 5, ed. W.M. Bowsky (Lincoln, Nebraska, 1968), pp. 1–48

Farmer, S. 'Persuasive Voices: Clerical Images of Medieval Wives', *Speculum* 61 (1986), pp. 517–43

Ferrante, J. 'Public Postures and Private Maneuvers: Roles Medieval Women Play', in *Women and Power*, ed. M. Erler and M. Kowaleski, pp. 213–29

Finucane, R.C. *Miracles and Pilgrims: Popular Beliefs in Medieval England* (London, 1977)

Fisher, N.R.R. 'The Queenes Courte in her Councell Chamber at Westminster', *EHR* 108 (1993), pp. 314–37

Fradenburg, L.O., ed. *Women and Sovereignty*, Cosmos 7 (Edinburgh, 1992)

Fries, M. 'Feminae Populi: Popular Images of Women in Medieval Literature', *Journal of Popular Culture* 14 (1980), pp. 79–86

Fryde, N. *The Tyranny and Fall of Edward II, 1321–1326* (Cambridge, 1979)

Gibbons, R. 'Isabeau of Bavaria, Queen of France (1385–1422): The Creation of an Historical Villainess', *TRHS*, sixth series 6 (1996), pp. 51–73

Gillespie, J.L. 'Cheshiremen at Blore Heath: A Swan Dive', in *People, Politics and Community*, ed. J.T. Rosenthal and C. Richmond, pp. 77–89

Gillingham, J. *The Wars of the Roses* (Baton Rouge, 1981)

Given-Wilson, C. *The Royal Household and the King's Affinity* (New Haven, 1986)

Goodman, A. *The Wars of the Roses: Military Activity and English Society 1452–97* (London, 1981)

Gransden, A. *Historical Writing in England*, II, *c. 1307 to the Early Sixteenth Century* (London, 1982)

Green, V. *The Madness of Kings: Personal Trauma and the Fate of Nations* (Stroud, 1993)

Griffiths, R.A. 'Duke Richard of York's Intentions in 1450 and the Origins of the Wars of the Roses', in idem, *King and Country*, pp. 277–304

Griffiths, R.A. 'Gruffydd ap Nicholas and the Fall of the House of Lancaster', in idem, *King and Country*, pp. 201–19

Griffiths, R.A. *King and Country: England and Wales in the Fifteenth Century* (London, 1991)

Griffiths, R.A. 'The King's Council and the First Protectorate of the Duke of York, 1453–1454', in idem, *King and Country*, pp. 305–20

Griffiths, R.A. 'Local Rivalries and National Politics: The Percies, the Nevilles, and the Duke of Exeter, 1452–55', in idem, *King and Country*, 321–64

Griffiths, R.A. *The Reign of King Henry VI: The Exercise of Royal Authority, 1422–1461* (Berkeley, 1981)

Griffiths, R.A. 'The Sense of Dynasty in the Reign of Henry VI', in idem, *King and Country*, pp. 83–102

Gross, A. *The Dissolution of the Lancastrian Kingship: Sir John Fortescue and the Crisis of Monarchy in Fifteenth-Century England* (Stamford, 1996)

Hall, D.J. *English Medieval Pilgrimage* (London, 1965)

Harriss, G.L. 'The Struggle for Calais: An Aspect of the Rivalry between Lancaster and York', *EHR* 75 (1960), pp. 30–53

Harvey, I.M.W. *Jack Cade's Rebellion of 1450* (Oxford, 1991)

Haswell, J. *The Ardent Queen: Margaret of Anjou and the Lancastrian Heritage* (London, 1976)

Head, C. 'Pope Pius II and the Wars of the Roses', *Archivium Historiae Pontificae* 8 (1970), pp. 139–78

Hicks, M. 'Bastard Feudalism, Overmighty Subjects and Idols of the Multitude during the Wars of the Roses', *History* 85 (2000), pp. 386–403

Hicks, M. 'From Megaphone to Microscope: The Correspondence of Richard Duke of York with Henry VI in 1450 Revisited', *Journal of Medieval History* 25 (1999), pp. 243–56

Hicks, M. 'A Minute of the Lancastrian Council at York, 20 January 1461', *Northern History* 35 (1999), pp. 214–21

Hicks, M. *Warwick the Kingmaker* (Oxford, 1998)

Hookham, M.A. *The Life and Times of Margaret of Anjou, Queen of England and France*, 2 vols (London, 1872)

Horrox, R., ed. *Fifteenth-Century Attitudes: Perceptions of Society in Late Medieval England* (Cambridge, 1994)

Horrox, R. 'Service', in *Fifteenth-Century Attitudes*, ed. R. Horrox, pp. 61–78

Howell, M. *Eleanor of Provence* (Oxford, 1998)

Howell, M.C. 'Citizenship and Gender: Women's Political Status in Northern Medieval Cities', in *Women and Power*, ed. M. Erler and M. Kowaleski, pp. 37–60

Huneycutt, L.L. 'Intercession and the High-Medieval Queen: The Esther Topos', in *Power of the Weak*, ed. J. Carpenter and S.-B. MacLean, pp. 126–46

Jacob, E.F. *The Fifteenth Century* (Oxford, 1961)

Johnson, P.A. *Duke Richard of York 1411–1460* (Oxford, 1988)

Jones, M.K. 'Edward IV, the Earl of Warwick and the Yorkist Claim to the Throne', *Historical Research* 70 (1997), pp. 342–52

Jones, M.K. 'Somerset, York and the Wars of the Roses', *EHR* 104 (1989), pp. 285–307

Jones, M.K., and M.G. Underwood. *The King's Mother: Lady Margaret Beaufort, Countess of Richmond and Derby* (Cambridge, 1992)

Jordan, C. *Renaissance Feminism: Literary Texts and Political Models* (Ithaca, 1990)

Joubert, A. 'Le mariage de Henry VI et de Marguerite d'Anjou d'après les documents publiés en Angleterre (1444–5)', *Revue historique et archéologique du Maine* 13 (1883), pp. 312–32

Karras, R.M. 'The Regulation of Brothels in Late Medieval England', *Signs* 14, no. 2 (1989), pp. 399–433

Keen, M. 'The End of the Hundred Years War: Lancastrian France and Lancastrian England', in *England and her Neighbours, 1066–1453*, ed. M. Jones and M. Vale (London, 1989), pp. 297–311

Keen, M. *England in the Later Middle Ages* (London, 1973)

Kekewich, M. 'The Attainder of the Yorkists in 1459: Two Contemporary Accounts', *BIHR* 55 (1982), pp. 24–34

Kelly-Gadol, J. 'Did Women have a Renaissance?' in *Becoming Visible: Women in European History*, 2nd edn, ed. R. Bridenthal, C. Koonz and S. Stuard (Boston, 1987), pp. 175–201

Kingsford, C.L. *English Historical Literature in the Fifteenth Century* (Oxford, 1913)

Kipling, G. '"Grace in this Lyf and Aftirwarde Glorie": Margaret of Anjou's Royal Entry into London', *Research Opportunities in Renaissance Drama* 29 (1986–87), pp. 77–84

Knowles, D., and R.N. Hadcock. *Medieval Religious Houses* (London, 1971)

Lamphere, L. 'Strategies, Cooperation, and Conflict among Women in Domestic Groups', in *Woman, Culture, and Society*, ed. M.Z. Rosaldo and L. Lamphere, pp. 97–112

Lander, J.R. *Conflict and Stability in Fifteenth-Century England* (London, 1969)

Lander, J.R. *Crown and Nobility 1450–1509* (Montreal, 1976)

Lander, J.R. 'Henry VI and the Duke of York's Second Protectorate, 1455–6', in idem, *Crown and Nobility*, pp. 74–93.

Lander, J.R. 'The Hundred Years' War and Edward IV's 1475 Campaign in France', in idem, *Crown and Nobility*, pp. 220–41

Lander, J.R. *The Wars of the Roses* (New York, 1965)

Lecoy de la Marche, A. *Le roi René, sa vie, son administration, ses traveaux artistiques et littéraires d'après les documents inédits des archives de France et d'Italie*, 2 vols (Paris, 1875)

Lee, P.-A. 'Reflections of Power: Margaret of Anjou and the Dark Side of Queenship', *Renaissance Quarterly* 39 (1986), pp. 183–217

Levin, C. 'John Foxe and the Responsibilities of Queenship', in *Women in the Middle Ages and the Renaissance: Literary and Historical Perspectives*, ed. M.B. Rose (Syracuse, 1986), pp. 113–33

Levin, C. 'Power, Politics, and Sexuality: Images of Elizabeth I', in *The Politics of Gender in Early Modern Europe*, ed. J.R. Brink, A.P. Coudert and M.C. Horowitz, Sixteenth Century Essays and Studies XII (Kirkville, 1989), pp. 95–110

Levin, C. and P.A. Sullivan, eds. *Political Rhetoric, Power, and Renaissance Women* (Albany, 1995)

Little, A.G. *Studies in English Franciscan History*, University of Manchester Publications, Historical Series, no. 29 (Manchester, 1917)

Lovatt, R. 'A Collector of Apocryphal Anecdotes: John Blacman Revisited', in *Property and Politics*, ed. A.J. Pollard, pp. 172–97

McCulloch, D., and E.D. Jones. 'Lancastrian Politics, the French War, and the Rise of the Popular Element', *Speculum* 58 (1983), pp. 95–138

Macdougall, N. *James III: A Political Study* (Edinburgh, 1982)

McFarlane, K.B. *England in the Fifteenth Century* (London, 1981)

McLeod, E. *Charles of Orleans: Prince and Poet* (London, 1969)

McNamara, J.A., and S. Wemple. 'The Power of Women through the Family in Medieval Europe: 500–1100', in *Women and Power*, ed. M. Erler and M. Kowaleski, pp. 83–101

Marchalonis, S. 'Above Rubies: Popular Views of Medieval Women', *Journal of Popular Culture* 14 (1980), pp. 87–93

Mas Latrie, M.L. de. *Histoire de l'ile de Chypre*, III (Paris, 1855)

Mathew, G. *The Court of Richard II* (London, 1968)

Maurer, H. 'Delegitimizing Lancaster: The Yorkist Use of Gendered Propaganda during the Wars of the Roses', in *Reputation and Representation in Fifteenth-Century Europe*, ed. D. Biggs, A.C. Reeves and S.D. Michalove (Leiden, forthcoming)

Maurer, H. 'Margaret of Anjou and the Loveday of 1458: A Reconsideration', in *Traditions and Transformations in Late Medieval England*, ed. D. Biggs, S.D. Michalove and A.C. Reeves (Leiden, 2002), pp. 109–24

Mauss, M. *The Gift: The Form and Reason for Exchange in Archaic Societies*, tr. W.D. Halls, foreword by M. Douglas (London, 1990)

Mendelson, S., and P. Crawford. *Women in Early Modern England 1550–1720* (Oxford, 1998)

Meneley, A. *Tournaments of Value: Sociability and Hierarchy in a Yemeni Town* (Toronto, 1996)

Mertes, K. 'Aristocracy', in *Fifteenth-Century Attitudes*, ed. R. Horrox, pp. 42–60

Morrison, S.S. *Women Pilgrims in Late Medieval England* (London, 2000)

Murray, H.J.R. *A History of Chess* (Oxford, 1913)

Murray, J. 'Thinking about Gender: The Diversity of Medieval Perspectives', in *Power of the Weak*, ed. J. Carpenter and S.-B. MacLean, pp. 1–26.

Nicholson, R. *Scotland: The Later Middle Ages* (Edinburgh, 1974)

Orlin, L.C. *Private Matters and Public Culture in Post-Reformation England* (Ithaca, 1994)

Ortner, S.B., and H. Whitehead, eds. *Sexual Meanings: The Cultural Construction of Gender and Sexuality* (Cambridge, 1981)

Otway-Ruthven, A.J. *The King's Secretary and the Signet Office in the XV Century* (Cambridge, 1939)

Owst, G.R. *Literature and Pulpit in Medieval England*, 2nd rev. edn (Oxford, 1961)

Page, W., ed. *The Victoria History of the County of Warwick*, II (London, 1908)

Parsons, J.C. *Eleanor of Castile: Queen and Society in Thirteenth-Century England* (New York, 1995)

Parsons, J.C. 'Family, Sex, and Power: The Rhythms of Medieval Queenship', in *Medieval Queenship*, ed. J.C. Parsons, pp. 1–11

Parsons, J.C. 'The Intercessionary Patronage of Queens Margaret and Isabella of France', *Thirteenth Century England*, VI (Woodbridge, 1997), pp. 145–56

Parsons, J.C., ed. *Medieval Queenship* (Stroud, 1994)

Parsons, J.C. 'Mothers, Daughters, Marriage, Power: Some Plantagenet Evidence, 1150–1500', in *Medieval Queenship*, ed. J.C. Parsons, pp. 63–78

Parsons, J.C. 'The Queen's Intercession in Thirteenth-Century England', in *Power of the Weak*, ed. J. Carpenter and S.-B. MacLean, pp. 147–77

Parsons, J.C. 'Ritual and Symbol in the English Medieval Queenship to 1500', in *Women and Sovereignty*, ed. L.O. Fradenburg, pp. 60–77

Payling, S.J. 'The Coventry Parliament of 1459: A Privy Seal Writ concerning the Election of Knights of the Shire', *Historical Research* 60 (1987), pp. 349–52

Pollard, A.J. *North-Eastern England during the Wars of the Roses: Lay Society, War, and Politics, 1450–1500* (Oxford, 1990)

Pollard, A.J., ed. *Property and Politics: Essays in Later Medieval English History* (Gloucester, 1984)

Pronger, W. 'Thomas Gascoigne', *EHR* 53 (1938), pp. 606–26; 54 (1939), pp. 20–37

Pugh, T.B. 'Richard Plantagenet (1411–60), Duke of York, as King's Lieutenant in France and Ireland', in *Aspects of Late Medieval Government and Society*, ed. A.G. Rowe (Toronto, 1986), pp. 107–41

Reiter, R.R. 'Men and Women in the South of France: Public and Private Domains', in *Toward an Anthropology of Women*, ed. R.R. Reiter (New York, 1975), pp. 252–82

Reynolds, C. 'The Shrewsbury Book, British Library, Royal MS 15 E.VI', in *Medieval Art, Architecture and Archaeology at Rouen*, ed. J. Stratford (London, 1993), pp. 109–116

Richmond, C. 'The Nobility and the Wars of the Roses, 1459–61', *Nottingham Medieval Studies* 21 (1977), pp. 71–85

Rosaldo, M.Z. 'The Use and Abuse of Anthropology: Reflections on Feminism and Cross-Cultural Understanding', *Signs* 5 (1980), pp. 389–417

Rosaldo, M.Z. 'Woman, Culture, and Society: A Theoretical Overview', in *Woman, Culture and Society*, ed. M.Z. Rosaldo and L. Lamphere, pp. 17–42

Rosaldo, M.Z., and L. Lamphere, *Woman, Culture and Society* (Stanford, 1974)

Rosenthal, J.T. 'Kings, Continuity and Ecclesiastical Benefaction in Fifteenth-Century England', in *People, Politics and Community*, ed. J.T. Rosenthal and C. Richmond, pp. 161–175.

Rosenthal, J.T., ed. *Kings and Kingship*, Acta 11 (Binghamton, NY, 1986)

Rosenthal, J.T. *Patriarchy and Families of Privilege in Fifteenth-Century England* (Philadelphia, 1991)

Rosenthal, J.T. *The Purchase of Paradise: Gift Giving and the Aristocracy, 1307–1485* (London, 1972)

Rosenthal, J.T., and C. Richmond, eds. *People, Politics and Community in the Later Middle Ages* (Gloucester, 1987)

Roskell, J.S. 'John Lord Wenlock of Someries', *Bedfordshire Historical Record Society* 38 (1958), pp. 12–48

Roskell, J.S. *Parliament and Politics in Late Medieval England*, 3 vols (London, 1981–83)

Roskell, J.S. 'The Problem of the Attendance of the Lords in Medieval Parliaments', *BIHR* 29 (1956), pp. 153–204

Ross, C. *Edward IV* (London, 1974)

Scattergood, V.J. *Politics and Poetry in the Fifteenth Century* (New York, 1971)

Schofield, A.N.E.D. 'England and the Council of Basel', *Annuarium Historiae Conciliorum*, V, no. 1 (1973), pp. 1–117

Schulenberg, J.T. 'Female Sanctity: Public and Private Roles, ca. 500–1100', in *Women and Power*, ed. M. Erler and M. Kowaleski, pp. 102–25

Schwoerer, L.G. *Lady Rachel Russell 'One of the Best of Women'* (Baltimore, 1988)

Scofield, C.L. *The Life and Reign of Edward IV*, 2 vols (London, 1923)

Searle, W.G. *The History of the Queen's College of St Margaret and St Bernard in the University of Cambridge, 1446–1560* (Cambridge, 1867)

Somerville, R. *History of the Duchy of Lancaster*, I (London, 1953)

Stanley, A.P. *Historical Memorials of Westminster Abbey* (London, 1868)

Storey, R.L. *The End of the House of Lancaster* (New York, 1967)

Strickland, A. *Lives of the Queens of England from the Norman Conquest*, II, rev. edn (London, 1885)

Strohm, P. *Hochon's Arrow: The Social Imagination of Fourteenth-Century Texts* (Princeton, 1992)

Thomson, J.A.F. 'John de la Pole, Duke of Suffolk', *Speculum* 54 (1979), pp. 528–42

Vann, T.M., ed. *Queens, Regents and Potentates* (Cambridge, 1993)

Virgoe, R. 'The Death of William de la Pole, Duke of Suffolk', *BJRL* 47 (1964–65), pp. 489–502

Warnicke, R.M. 'Henry VIII's Greeting of Anne of Cleves and Early Modern Court Protocol', *Albion* 28 (1996), pp. 565–85

Warnicke, R.M. *The Marrying of Anne of Cleves* (Cambridge, 2000)

Watts, J. *Henry VI and the Politics of Kingship* (Cambridge, 1996)

Waugh, S.L. *The Lordship of England: Royal Wardships and Marriages in English Society and Politics 1217–1327* (Princeton, 1988)

Wedgwood, J.C. *History of Parliament: Biographies of the Members of the Commons House, 1439–1509* (London, 1936)

Whitaker, T.D. *An History of Richmondshire*, II (London, 1823)

Wolffe, B.P. *Henry VI* (London, 1981)

Index

Aldgate (London) 199
Aberystwyth 136, 146
Abingdon 201n.
Agincourt, battle of (1415) 17, 81
Aiscough, William, bishop of Salisbury 42
Alany, Guille 63n.
Al-Malec-al-Aschraf-Aboul-Nasr-Inal, sultan of
	Egypt 214
Alnwick 205, 206
Alphonso V, king of Portugal 205n., 207
Amboise 207
Angers 207
Anjou 23, 26–8, 30, 34, 139
	duke of, *see* René
Annales of pseudo-Worcester 198
Anne of Bohemia, queen of Richard II 17n., 71n.
Aragon, king of 92, 205n.
Arbury 216, 217
	prior of 216–17, 219; *see also* Bromley, John;
		Woodcock, William
Armagnac, count of 28, 40
	daughters of 40, 176
Arnold, Alice 84–5
Arundel, earl of (William FitzAlan) 153n., 164
Asheby, George 61, 62n.
Auchinleck Chronicle 193
Audley, James Tuchet, lord (d. 1459) 166, 180

Bagley, J.J. 3, 23, 53, 54, 70, 107–8
'Bale's Chronicle' 45, 78, 189
Bamburgh 48n., 198n., 205, 206
Barnet 198
	battle of (1471) 208
battles, *see* Barnet, Blore Heath, Hedgeley Moor,
		Hexham, Mortimer's Cross, St Albans,
		Tewkesbury, Towton, Wakefield
Bawtry 165n.
Beauchamp, Eleanor, countess of Somerset 60–1,
		62, 88, 89–90, 92n., 93
Beauchamp, Richard, bishop of Salisbury 96,
		104n., 168n.
Beauchamp, Richard, earl of Warwick (d. 1439)
		89
Beaufort, Edmund, duke of Somerset (d. 1455)
		37, 41, 45, 47n., 62, 64, 79n., 82n., 84, 85,
		87, 89, 92n., 96, 101–2, 103–4, 113, 115,
		117–20, 217, 218, 219
	blamed for French losses 83, 90, 95, 97–8
	as captain of Calais 117, 119, 160n.

character of 61 *and* n., 92 *and* n.
dominance at court 90–1 *and* n., 92–3, 117–18
and Maine 36n., 61, 87n.
rivalry with duke of York 42, 44n., 83, 85, 90,
		95, 96, 100, 118; *see also* Richard
sons of, *see* Beaufort, Edmund, Henry *and* John
wife of, *see* Beauchamp, Eleanor
Beaufort, Edmund, duke of Somerset (d. 1471)
		137 and n., 207n.
Beaufort, Henry, cardinal 56
Beaufort, Henry, duke of Somerset (d. 1464) 47
		and n., 137 *and* n., 154–6, 159, 161, 162,
		173n., 188, 192, 194, 196n., 201, 206n.
	as captain of Calais 160n., 168, 174
	seeks vengeance 83, 144, 149–50, 155
Beaufort, John (d. 1471) 137 and n.
Beaufort, Margaret 137
Beaumont, John viscount (d. 1460) 61, 69, 92n.,
		93, 101–2, 107, 114, 115, 117n., 130, 134,
		135, 152–3, 161, 175, 181, 182n.
	wife of (Katherine Neville) 152n.
Beauvau, Bertrand de 32n.
Bedale, Robert 56
Bedford, county of 164
Bedford, duchess of, *see* Jacquetta
Bedford, John, duke of (d. 1435) 17
'Benet's Chronicle' 103, 164–5
Bergavenny, lord (Edward Neville) 163n.
Berkeley, James, lord (d. 1463) 137
Berkhamsted 155
Berners, lord (John Bourgchier) 197n.
Berwick 131, 192, 204
Beverley 193
Blackfriars (London) 155
Blackheath 19, 68, 69, 70, 71, 72, 73n.
Blok, Anton 127
Blore Heath, battle of (1459) 166, 167, 171, 177n.,
		180
Bocking, John 128, 129, 130, 155, 169
Bonville, William, lord (d. 1461) 101–2, 196, 198
Booth, Lawrence, bishop of Durham 132–3, 147,
		153, 161n., 170
Booth, William, archbishop of York 56n., 96, 115,
		132n., 133, 161, 162
Boston 63n.
Botill, Robert, prior of St John's 80n., 107, 114,
		165n.
Boulers, Reginald, bishop of Coventry and
		Lichfield 107, 114n., 133, 161